POPOL VUH

THE SACRED BOOK
OF THE MAYA

at Classic of

n Spirituality,

n the

xt

Ph.D.

University of Oklahoma Press   Norman

Library of Congress Cataloging-in-Publication Data

Popol vuh. English.
    Popol vuh : the sacred book of the Maya / Allen J. Christenson. —
Oklahoma ed.
        p. cm.
    "The great classic of Central American spirituality, translated from the
original Maya Text."
    Originally published: Winchester, U.K. ; New York : O Books, 2003.
    Includes bibliographical references and index.
    ISBN-13: 978-0-8061-3839-8 (pbk. : alk. Paper) 1. Popol vuh. 2. Quiché
Indians—Religion. 3. Quiché mythology. I. Christenson, Allen J., 1957– II.
Title.
    F1465.P8P68 2007
    299.7'8423082—dc22   2006028164

Design: Jim Weaver Design

The paper in this book meets the guidelines for permanence and
durability of the Committee on Production Guidelines for Book
Longevity of the Council on Library Resources, Inc. ∞

Originally published by O Books, Alresford, Hants, U.K., copyright © 2003
by Allen Christenson. Oklahoma edition published 2007 by the University
of Oklahoma Press, Norman, Publishing Division of the University, by
arrangement with O Books. All rights reserved. Manufactured in the U.S.A.

5   6   7   8   9   10

To my wife, Janet
Xa at nu saqil, at nu k'aslemal
chib'e q'ij saq

CONTENTS

LIST OF ILLUSTRATIONS

(All drawings and photographs are by the author unless otherwise noted)

MAPS

ACKNOWLEDGEMENTS

This volume is the culmination of nearly twenty-five years of collaboration with friends and colleagues who have been more than generous with their time, expertise, encouragement, and at times, sympathy. It has become a somewhat clichéd and expected thing to claim that a work would not be possible without such support. It is nonetheless true, at least from my experience, and I am indebted to all those who helped move the process along.

First and foremost, I would like to express my sincerest gratitude to my Maya teachers, colleagues, and friends who have selflessly devoted their time and knowledge to help carry out this project. Without their efforts, none of it would have ever gotten off the ground. I would like to particularly recognize in this regard don Vicente de León Abac, who, with patience and kindness, guided me through the complexity and poetry of K'iche' theology and ceremonialism. Without his wisdom, I would have missed much of the beauty of ancestral vision that is woven into the very fabric of the *Popol Vuh*. I dearly miss him. I would also like to acknowledge the profound influence that Antonio Ajtujal Vásquez had on this work. It was his kind and gentle voice that I often heard when I struggled at times to understand the ancient words of this text. Others who have aided this work include Diego Chávez Petzey, Nicolás Chávez Sojuel, Felix Choy, Gregorio Chuc, Juan Mendoza, Francisco Mendoza, and Juan Zárate.

I am deeply indebted to Jim Mondloch for his extraordinary generosity in offering to read through the translation. His depth of knowledge with regard to K'iche' grammar, syntax, and modern usage were invaluable. I purchased a copy of his "Basic Quiché Grammar" in 1976 to help in my quest to learn the language at a time when such aids were very rare. The book was a steadfast friend and companion during the next few years. Not only was it a brilliant work but it proved to be just the size and weight to dispatch mosquitos on the wall of my adobe shack. I thus owe to him, not only much of my initial knowledge of the K'iche' language, but my red blood cell count in those days as well.

I am also grateful to John Robertson for his guidance, particularly with regard to the orthography of the text. He was a patient educator to me when

I began work with the K'iche' language nearly twenty-five years ago, helping to prepare a dictionary and grammar. He was an ideal boss and a wise teacher. It is a great honor for me to occupy the office next door to his at the university.

I am sincerely indebted to my friend and colleague Ruud van Akkeren who went to extraordinary lengths to share with me his profound understanding of highland Maya ethnohistory. I value his knowledge, experience, and generosity in reading through various versions of this volume and offering his insights.

As in much of what I do that is of worth in the academic world, I acknowledge the influence of my mentor, Linda Schele. As a graduate student, Linda encouraged me to complete the translation of the *Popol Vuh* at a time when I was content to throw up my hands after I had worked through the mythic sections. It was her love for the Maya people and passion for their language that reminded me why we take on overwhelming tasks such as this, and why it's worth the price in life and heart that we put into them.

Among the many who have contributed in invaluable ways to this project, I would like to recognize with my sincerest thanks the following individuals: Claude Baudez, Karen Bassie, James Brady, Linda Brown, Margaret Bruchez, Michael Carrasco, Garrett Cook, Doris Dant, John Early, Sam Edgerton, Enrique Florescano, John Fox, David Freidel, Stephen Houston, Kerry Hull, Julia G. Kappelman, Peter Keeler, Justin Kerr, Bob Laughlin, Bruce Love, John Monaghan, Dorie Reents-Budet, Julia Sanchez, Joel Skidmore, Carolyn Tate, Mark Van Stone, Bob Walch, Andrew Weeks, Jack Welch, and Diane Wirth.

I would also like to thank my graduate students who keep me constantly on my toes and challenged with their curiosity and energy. Among these students, Spencer Jardine helped with the initial transcription of the text used in this volume, and Scott Brian created the beautiful maps. I am indebted to them for their efforts.

TRANSLATOR'S PREFACE

A little over twenty years ago I was helping to compile a dictionary in the Quiché-Maya language in the mountains of northwestern Guatemala near a small village called Chihul. At the time, Quiché was almost completely an orally-communicated language, with very few native speakers who could read or write it. One summer evening, after a long day of work with one of my best sources, I realized that I had lost track of time and needed to hurry down to the valley where I had a small home before it got dark. The region had no electricity and hiking steep mountain trails at night was dangerous, particularly because of the numerous packs of wild (and often rabid) dogs that roamed freely about. I therefore started down a small footpath that appeared to be a more direct route than the usual winding road taken by buses.

About a third the way down the mountainside, I passed an isolated adobe and thatch house built in a clearing surrounded by pine forest. A small group of men were seated on a low wooden bench in front of the house conversing. When they saw me, they called out a greeting and beckoned me

Figure 1. Adobe and thatch house near Chihul with plank and thatch cooking house on the right.

to join them. After introductions were properly exchanged, a requirement in formal Quiché conversation, I was offered a warm cup of toasted corn coffee and a space on the bench was opened up for me to sit down.

One of the men had heard that there was a fair-skinned young man that people called *raqän us* (mosquito legs) who was visiting in Chihul, and he asked if that would be me. My name is difficult to pronounce in Quiché, so I had been given that rather unfortunate nickname, derived no doubt from my lanky physique in those days. I told him that I was the one they had heard about. They asked what I was doing, and I explained that I was interested in collecting the words of his people so that I could carry them with me back to my own town beyond the mountains to the north. Another of the men was curious as to how I could "collect" words and carry them away, since he assumed that his language could only be spoken, not written.

Quichés in that area had, of course, seen documents and books like the Bible written in Spanish but had little conception at the time that it was possible to use phonetic letters to record their own language. This is a great tragedy, because until about five hundred years ago the Maya were the most literate people in the Americas, preserving their history and culture with a sophisticated hieroglyphic script in hundreds of folded screen books. The Spanish conquest in the early sixteenth century was a devastating blow to Maya literacy in Mexico and Guatemala. Christian missionaries burned great numbers of hieroglyphic texts in an attempt to eradicate indigenous religious practices. Native scribes were singled out for persecution to such an extent that within one hundred years, the art of hieroglyphic writing had virtually disappeared from among the Maya people.

My new friends were therefore very interested in the notes I had written that day in their language. Excited by the possibility of preserving their own thoughts in written form, they asked me to demonstrate how to write a number of words and phrases. After writing a few phrases for them in Quiché, I asked the oldest of them if he would like me to write something for him. He said that he did and I waited a long time for the words he wished me to write. Finally he asked me to record a few brief words of counsel for his son. I didn't know it at the time but his five year old boy was the last of twelve children, all of whom had died in childhood, mostly to tuberculosis. That week his last surviving child had begun to cough up blood and he knew that his hope for posterity would inevitably die with him.

By this time I knew I would never make it down to the valley before dark so my elderly friend invited me to stay in his corn loft. Before the others left for the night, I asked if they would like to hear the words of their fathers. This was greeted with indulgent smiles of disbelief, since few of their parents were alive and they were sure that I couldn't have known them. But I told them that it wasn't their fathers' words that I carried with me, but rather those of their fathers' fathers' (repeated many times) fathers, dating back nearly five hundred years. I happened to have with me a copy of the *Popol Vuh* manuscript, a book that was compiled in the mid-sixteenth century at a town that still exists less than thirty miles from where we sat. I began to read from the first page of the book:

> THIS IS THE ACCOUNT of when all is still silent and placid. All is silent and calm. Hushed and empty is the womb of the sky.
>
> THESE, then, are the first words, the first speech. There is not yet one person, one animal, bird, fish, crab, tree, rock, hollow, canyon, meadow, or forest. All alone the sky exists. The face of the earth has not yet appeared. Alone lies the expanse of the sea, along with the womb of all the sky. There is not yet anything gathered together. All is at rest. Nothing stirs. All is languid, at rest in the sky. There is not yet anything standing erect. Only the expanse of the water, only the tranquil sea lies alone. There is not yet anything that might exist. All lies placid and silent in the darkness, in the night.
>
> All alone are the Framer and the Shaper, Sovereign and Quetzal Serpent, They Who Have Borne Children and They Who Have Begotten Sons. Luminous they are in the water, wrapped in quetzal feathers and cotinga feathers (*Popol Vuh*, pp. 67–69).

After I had read a page or two from the account of the creation of the earth, I stopped and waited for their reaction. No one spoke for some time. Finally, the elderly man with the sick boy asked if he might hold the unbound pages of the manuscript copy for a moment. He gently took it from my hands and with great care turned its pages.

"These are the words of my ancient fathers?" he asked.

"Yes."

"Do you know what you have done for them?" I wasn't quite sure what he meant, so I didn't answer at first. "You make them live again by speaking their words."

The word he used was *k'astajisaj*, meaning "to cause to have life," or "to resurrect." The written word has the power to survive the death of its author, to preserve the most precious souvenirs of human existence—thoughts, hopes, ideals, and acquaintance with the sacred. We tend to take writing for granted. The Maya do not. The ability to write words and have them preserved long after the death of the author is a miracle.

Many of the larger highland Maya communities possess wooden chests containing books and clothing owned by their ancestors which they revere as precious relics. These objects are said to bear the *k'ux*, or "heart" of the ancestors. On special occasions, the contents are removed ceremonially to "feed" them with offerings of incense and prayers. Many of these books are of great antiquity. I attended the opening of one of these old chests in the town of Santiago Atitlán which contained a

Figure 2. Contents of the chest of Santiago Atitlán removed to receive offerings.

number of loose manuscript pages, birth and death registries, and several bound leather books, one of which I could see was a seventeenth century missal.

When brought out into the open, such books are reverently offered incense and prayers, but no attempt is made to open them or read them. Partly this is because few contemporary Maya know how to read the early script of the colonial period, and partly out of respect for the words themselves. When the words of the ancestors are read, or spoken aloud, it is as if that person had returned from death to speak again. Reading ancient texts is therefore a very delicate matter, filled with peril if the words are not treated with sufficient respect.

While working as an ethnographer and translator in the Guatemalan highlands, I collaborated with a number of Maya shaman-priests called *aj q'ijab'* (they of days, or daykeepers). Prior to reading the words of ancient Maya manuscripts like the *Popol Vuh*, it was customary for one of them, don Vicente de León Abac of Momostenango, to first purify my xeroxed copy of the text by waving copal incense smoke over it and asking forgiveness of the ancestors who had written the original for disturbing them. When I asked why he did this, he replied that to read the thoughts of ancient ancestors is to make their spirits present in the room and give them a living voice. Such power must be approached with great seriousness, and all care taken to be faithful to their original ideas in any transcription or translation. At the end of our work sessions, he politely dismissed the gods and ancestors involved in that day's reading with his thanks and asked pardon for any offense we might have given.

Most of the people who lived on the American continents prior to the arrival of Europeans lacked a written script. Even in Mesoamerica, where there was a long tradition of hieroglyphic writing among some of the ancient cultures of the region, such as the Maya and Zapotecs, other neighboring cultures preserved their history and theology principally through the spoken word, passed from generation to generation. This was true even of highly sophisticated cultures such as the Aztecs, whose painted texts relied primarily on a rebus or picture form of writing incapable of recording abstract ideas phonetically. Yet the concept of oral poetry held by the Aztecs is exemplary of the view of such discourse throughout Mesoamerica, including the Maya.

For the ancient Aztecs the highest form of sacred communication was poetry, what they called *xochicuicatl* ("flower-song"). These were delicately beautiful hymns meant to be recited orally, often to musical accompaniment. In paintings, Aztec poets are depicted with speech scrolls issuing from their mouths. These scrolls are often colored a rich blue or green, symbolic of the precious nature of the poets' words as if they were composed of jade or sacred quetzal feathers. Aztecs looked upon poetry as the actualization of a creative act inspired by divinites who were called upon to be present at the performance. Thus the poet Ayocuan Cuetzpaltzin of Tecamachalco believed that his songs came from heaven, but lamented that his own words could not express them as they came undefiled from the gods:

> From within the heavens they come,
> The beautiful flowers, the beautiful songs.
> Our longing spoils them,
> Our inventiveness makes them lose their fragrance
> (León-Portilla 1980, 257).

Such songs exist only at the moment of their performance, their sound hanging briefly in the air, then fading to silence. It is only when they are spoken that they reveal their divine origin, transforming the poet into a messenger of deity:

> Now I am going to forge songs,
> Make a stem flowering with songs,
> Oh my friends!
> God has sent me as a messenger.
> I am transformed into a poem   (León-Portilla 1969, 80).

Most poems were learned by heart and were lost forever if forgotten. Thus Aztec poetry had no permanent reality of its own, no more than a dream. It is only by an accident of history that we know of them at all. Soon after the Spanish conquest of the Aztec empire in 1521, a few Spanish missionaries such as Fr. Andrés de Olmos and Fr. Bernardino de Sahagún attempted to preserve long transcriptions of ancient Aztec history, theology, and poetry utilizing the Latin script. Olmos and Sahagún relied for these accounts on elderly members of the Aztec nobility who had memorized them in their youth. Unfortunately these invaluable books were vigorously suppressed soon after their completion for fear that the Indians would learn of them and use them as an excuse to revert to their former paganism. Sahagún himself faced censure in 1577 for his work during the reign of King Philip II, who ordered his representative in Mexico to gather all copies of Sahagún's transcriptions of Aztec texts and secrete them away:

> It seems that it is not proper that this book be published or disseminated in those places.... We thus command that, upon receiving this Cedula, you obtain these books with great care and diligence; that you make sure that no original or copy of them is left there; and that you have them sent in good hands at the first opportunity to our Council of Indies in order that they may be examined there. And you are warned absolutely not to allow any person to write concerning the superstitions and ways of life of these Indians in any language, for this is not proper to God's service and to ours   (León-Portilla 1980, 38).

The Spanish authorities realized that preserving a record of the literary heritage of the Aztecs constituted an intolerable danger to their own political and religious domination of the region. By suppressing cultural memory, missionaries could more effectively extirpate it from the life of the people they sought to convert to Christianity.

The suppression of indigenous culture was far more difficult among the Maya who did not have to rely on the spoken word to preserve their literary heritage. More than fifteen hundred years prior to the Spanish conquest, the Maya developed a sophisticated hieroglyphic script capable of recording complex literary compositions, both on folded screen codices made of bark paper as well as texts incised on more durable stone or wood. The importance of preserving written records was a hallmark of Maya culture as witnessed by the thousands of known hieroglyphic inscriptions, many more of which are still being discovered in the jungles of southern Mexico and northern Central America.

Being a phonetic script rather than a pictorial form of writing, Maya hieroglyphs were capable of recording any idea that could be spoken. Ancient Maya scribes were among the most honored members of creative society. They were often important representatives of the royal family, and as such were believed to carry the seeds of divinity within their blood. Among the titles given to artists and scribes in Classic period Maya inscriptions were *itz'aat* ("sage") and *miyaatz* ("wise one"). In an important royal tomb at Tikal (Burial 116), an incised bone depicts a deified scribe's hand emerging from the gullet of an open-mouthed creature. In Classic Maya art, the open jaws represent a portal that leads from this world to the world of the gods. In his or her hand is a calligraphic paintbrush used to both write and illustrate the ancient Maya codex books. The message of this incised bone is that the activities of the scribe come closest to those of the gods themselves, who paint the realities of this world as divine artists.

The Spanish conquest of the Maya region in the sixteenth century resulted in the abrupt destruction of indigenous political power as well as many of its cultural institutions. Christianity was formally established in Guatemala in 1534 under Bishop Francisco Marroquín, who sent out priests with portable altars to the various highland Maya towns and villages in an effort to baptize the indigenous population and to destroy any remnants of "idolatry" that they might find. Ancient temples, as well as the carved and painted images which they contained, were systematically destroyed, their stones used to build Christian churches. Missionaries singled out hieroglyphic codices for destruction in an effort to protect the Indians from their former religious beliefs. Alonso de Zorita wrote that in 1540 he saw numerous such books in the Guatemalan highlands which "recorded their history for more than eight hundred years back, and which were interpreted for me by very ancient Indians" (Zorita 1963, 271–2). Fr. Bartolomé de las Casas lamented that when found, such books were destroyed:

> These books were seen by our clergy, and even I saw part of those which were burned by the monks, apparently because they thought [they] might harm the Indians in matters concerning religion, since at that time they were at the beginning of their conversion   (Las Casas 1958, 346).

One of the most zealous of these early missionaries was Fr. Diego de Landa who burned hundreds of ancient Maya books while serving as the bishop at Maní in northern Yucatán:

> We found a large number of books of these characters, and as they contained nothing in which there were not to be seen superstition and lies of the devil, we burned them all, which they regretted to an amazing degree and which caused them much affliction   (Landa 1941, 78).

Of the numerous hieroglyphic books that once existed in the Maya lowlands, all that escaped the Spanish purges of the sixteenth century are four incomplete codices. Of those written in the highlands of Guatemala, not a single Precolumbian codex is known to have survived.

But these tragic acts of destruction did not mean that Maya literacy ended with the arrival of the Europeans. Soon after the Spanish conquest, literate members of the highland Maya nobility made a number of transcriptions of their Precolumbian books utilizing a modified Latin script in an effort to preserve what they could of their recorded history and culture before they could be destroyed or lost. By far the most important extant example of such a transcription is the *Popol Vuh*, a lengthy document composed by anonymous members of the Quiché-Maya aristocracy in Guatemala soon after the fall of their capital city to the Spanish conquerors. The authors of the manuscript described the text as an *ilb'al* (instrument of sight) by which the reader may "envision" the thoughts and actions of the gods and sacred ancestors from the beginning of time and into the future. The opening chapters of the *Popol Vuh* describe the creation of all things as if it were occuring in the immediate present, time folding back upon itself to transport the reader into the primordial waters of chaos at the very moment the first land emerged:

THIS IS THE ACCOUNT of when all is still silent and placid. All is silent and calm. Hushed and empty is the womb of the sky.... The face of the earth has not yet appeared. Alone lies the expanse of the sea, along with the womb of all the sky. There is not yet anything gathered together. All is at rest. Nothing stirs (*Popol Vuh*, p. 67).

This passage is written in present progressive tense, suggesting that the narrator *sees* it before him as he writes. This is consistent with the way stories are told in contemporary Quiché households. The story-teller invites the listener to imagine the setting of his tale, and nearly always tells the story as if it were happening right then, even if it happened in the distant or mythic past.

The text of the *Popol Vuh* was kept hidden by indigenous elders for centuries in the town of Chichicastenango in Guatemala. So successful were these efforts to preserve early Colonial texts that two hundred years after the Conquest, a Spanish priest living in Chichicastenango named Francisco Ximénez wrote that the people of that town possessed many ancient books, including the manuscript of the *Popol Vuh*. Ximénez wrote that these books were kept in secret so that local Christian authorities would not learn of them. Far from being forgotten tales, he found that these texts were "the doctrine which they first imbibed with their mother's milk, and that all of them knew it almost by heart" (Ximénez 1929–31, I.i.5). Ximénez was able to convince the elders who kept the *Popol Vuh* manuscript to allow him to borrow it for the purpose of making a copy.

Figure 3. The *convento* of the church at Chichicastenango. It was here that Fr. Francisco Ximénez transcribed the contents of the sixteenth century *Popol Vuh* manuscript.

After Ximénez made his copy, the original text was presumably given back to the Maya although it has not been seen since the early 1700s. Today we, in the Western world, know of this great book only through Ximénez's transcription, which has become one of the principal resources used by European and American scholars who study Maya history and theology. It is unfortunate, however, that the great majority of Maya people have not had access to it for centuries in their own language. Literacy has slowly eroded away among the contemporary Maya such that few are literate in their native tongue.

The sacred records of the Maya were forcibly taken from them and destroyed in the fires of the Spanish conquest. It is only in the past hundred years or so that fragments of what they have lost are beginning to be redis-covered and read widely. For the Maya each ancient word, whether read or spoken aloud, is life-giving in its power to reach across the centuries. The Maya people can understand the preciousness of such documents in ways that we who have never been denied literacy can hardly imagine.

In preparing this translation of the *Popol Vuh*, I often remembered that evening near Chihul when I had the opportunity to read passages from this great book to its authors' descendents. The words were meant for them, not me. In translating the text, I have tried to bear in mind that this process gives voice to the ancients so that their words may be heard again. It is my sincerest hope that I have been faithful to their voices.

This work is published in two volumes. The first consists of an English translation of the *Popol Vuh* with commentary aimed at elucidating the meaning of the text in light of contemporary highland Maya speech and practices, as well as current scholarship in Maya linguistics, archaeology, ethnography, and art historical iconography. No text can be translated from one language into another without losing a certain amount of the beauty and nuance of the original. The poet Stéphane Mallarmé felt that his poetry should never be translated because the symbolism, flow, and sound of the words were so closely bound to the French language. To convey even a por-tion of the associated meaning that colored his poems would require exten-sive explanatory notes, and for Mallarmé "to *name* an object is to suppress three-quarters of the enjoyment to be found in the poem, which consists in the pleasure of discovering things little by little: *suggestion*, that is the dream" (Lucie-Smith 1972, 54).

To a great extent, this is also true of the language found in the *Popol Vuh*, which is replete with esoteric language, plays on words, and phrases chosen for their sound and rhythm as much as for their meaning. I've tried to adhere as closely as possible to the tone and syntax of the Quiché text, however, certain liberties are unavoidable in order to make the narrative understandable in the English language. For example, the Quiché language stresses passive verb constructions, which when translated into European languages are difficult to follow. The authors of the *Popol Vuh* also routinely used passive forms to create gerunds that are hopelessly awkward in English. Thus, the words "manifestation, declaration, and expression" in lines 11–13 are actually written, "its being manifested, its being declared, its being expressed."

To partially compensate for the inadequacy of a grammatic English version to adhere precisely to the wording of the original, the second volume of this work contains a "literal" word for word translation of the text. I have chosen to use this arrangement because I believe that language is reflective of the flavor of the culture that utilizes it. When the original phraseology and grammatical construction of the ancient text is preserved, subtle nuances of meaning become evident. The first line of the *Popol Vuh* declares the book to be *u xe' ojer tzij*, which may be translated literally as "its root ancient word." The phrase indicates that this is the beginning of the ancient history of the Quiché people. The remainder of the book is thus seen as growing like a plant from this "root." The imagery is a beautiful expression of the Quiché world view as an agricultural society.

One of my hopes for this project was to make the original Quiché text of the *Popol Vuh* available to the Quiché people themselves in a form that is consistent with the modern script taught in the Guatemalan school system. I have therefore utilized in the literal translation an entirely new transcription of the original Quiché text using modern orthography. I have also included a transcription of the Latin orthographic version of the *Popol Vuh* as it was written by its Quiché authors in the sixteenth century for comparative purposes.

The *Popol Vuh* is the most important example of Precolumbian Maya literature to have survived the Spanish conquest. Its significance may be seen in the numerous versions of the text that have been published. In the past three hundred years, the *Popol Vuh* has been translated approximately thirty times into seven languages. Unfortunately most of these translations were not based on the original Quiché-Maya text, but rather on various Spanish versions derived from it. The translation contained in this book is entirely new, based primarily on my own knowledge of the language, as well as dictionaries and grammars compiled in the last century by García Elgueta (1892, ca. 1900, ca. 1910), Sáenz de Santa María (1940), León (1954), Edmonson (1965), Alvarado López (1975), Mondloch and Hruska (1975), Siméon (1977), García Hernández and Yac Sam (1980), Ajpacaja Tum, Chox Tum, Tepaz Raxuleu and Guarchaj Ajtzalam (1996), López Ixcoy (1997), Pérez Mendoza and Hernández Mendoza (2000), and Par Sapón and Can Pixabaj (2000). I have also relied on consultations with native Quiché speakers in the highland Guatemalan towns of Momostenango (and the surrounding aldeas of Santa Ana, Canquixaja, Nimsitu, and Panca), Totonicapán (and its aldeas of Nimasak, Chuxchimal, and Cerro de Oro), Nahuala, Cunen (and its aldeas of Los Trigales, Xesacmalha, Xetzak, Las Grutas, Chitu, and Xepom), and Chihul.

It is fortunate in this regard that the Quiché language has changed surprisingly little in the centuries since the *Popol Vuh* was composed. With important exceptions, most of the vocabulary is still understandable to modern Quichés. For terms and phrases associated with Maya religion and ritual, I have also worked with a number of Quiché *aj q'ijab'*, who continue to conduct traditional calendric and divinatory rites in a manner little different from that practiced at the time the *Popol Vuh* was compiled. I am particularly indebted to don Vicente de León Abac of Momostenango for his wisdom and patience with me in this regard.

For archaic and non-Maya loan words which are no longer used by modern Quichés, I have relied on dictionaries, grammars, and theological treatises prepared by Spanish priests in the early Colonial period, principally those compiled by Fr. Domingo de Vico (ca. 1555), Bishop Francisco Marroquín (ca. 1560), Fr. Alonso de Molina (1571), Fr. Marcos Martínez (ca. 1575), Fr. Antonio de Ciudad Real (ca. 1590), Fr. Thomás de Coto (ca. 1656), Fr. Bartolomé de Anléo (ca. 1660), Fr. Tomás de Santo Domingo (ca. 1690), Fr. Benito de Villacañas (1692), Fr. Domingo de Basseta (ca. 1698), Fr. Francisco de Vare[l]a (1699), Fr. Francisco Ximénez (ca. 1701–4), Fr. Pantaleón de Guzmán (1704), Fr. Damián Delgado (1725), Fr. Francisco Herrera (1745), and Fr. Angel (ca. 1775).

Translation is an art whose cloth is woven from a variety of threads. Any defects are solely the fault of the weaver. Its beauty is solely dependent on the threads themselves.

Allen J. Christenson
Provo, December 27, 2002

INTRODUCTION

QUICHÉ HISTORY

The *Popol Vuh* was written by anonymous members of the Quiché-Maya nobility, a branch of the Maya that dominated the highlands of western Guatemala prior to the arrival of Spanish conquerors in 1524. Their present population is something over half a million, spread thinly through a series of market towns and smaller agricultural villages in the modern Guatemalan states of Quiché, Totonicapán, and Quetzaltenango. Their homeland is some of the most beautiful country in the world, dominated by a range of high mountains, volcanoes, and steep-walled plateaus, wrapped in green pine forest, and watered by numerous rivers and waterfalls. Its high elevation keeps the climate comfortably cool in the summer, while its location in the tropics prevents the extreme cold temperatures usually associated with mountainous environments. Guatemala's boast of being the "Land of Eternal Spring" is no exaggeration.

Although the highland Maya have lived in this area for more than two thousand years, the *Popol Vuh* suggests that they came to be dominated

Figure 4. The Guatemalan highlands above Cunen.

by a militaristic group of relative newcom-
ers, led by the Cavec-Quiché lineage, who
claimed to have come from somewhere in
the East where the sun rises (*Popol Vuh*,
pp. 204–205), likely the Maya lowlands
during the early Postclassic phase (ca. AD
900–1200). During this period of history,
many of the most important Maya ruling lineages throughout the region were
multilingual and heavily influenced by
ideas from beyond their borders, particularly from Nahua speakers, the language
of central Mexico. According to Bernardino
de Sahagún, a Spanish priest who worked
among the Aztecs soon after the Spanish
conquest, the lowland Maya area was
known as Nonoualcat (land of the dumb)
because it was occupied by non-Nahua

Figure 5. Chichen Itza. View of the Castillo from the Temple of the Warriors.

speakers, although he asserted that many could speak Nahua as a second
language (Sahagún 1959–63, Book X, 170; cf. Carmack 1981, 46). Nahua,
the language of the Toltecs and later Aztecs, had become a kind of *lingua
franca* among elite groups throughout Mesoamerica by the last centuries
prior to the Spanish conquest. The highland Maya in particular remembered the legendary Toltecs, the ruling class of central Mexico in the early
Postclassic period, as the greatest of artists and sages (*Popol Vuh*, p. 80
n.102) and adopted many Nahua words that reflect political as well as esoteric ceremonial concepts.

In the Terminal Classic (AD 800–900) and Early Postclassic (AD 900–
1200) phases, central Mexican influence spread rapidly through much of
Mesoamerica (Thompson 1970, 18–21; Fox 1978, 274). The most impressive
center of Mexican influence in the Maya world during this time was Chichen
Itza, located in the northern region of the Yucatán Peninsula. Diego de
Landa, one of the first Spanish priests to work among the Maya of Yucatán,
was told that the city was visited by a non-Maya priest-ruler who came from
across the Gulf of Mexico named Kukulcan (Yucatec: "Feathered Serpent").
This legend dovetails well with similar myths recorded in Aztec sources concerning the Toltec priest-ruler Topiltzin Quetzalcoatl who sailed across the
Gulf of Mexico toward Yucatán at approximately the same time (ca. AD 978

according to Aztec chronicles) (Landa 1941, 20–23; Coe 1987, 132). Yet central Mexican influences at Chichen Itza are much older than this legendary visit by Kukulcan. The supposedly Toltec-inspired Great Ballcourt at Chichen was dedicated on a date corresponding to November 18, 864, and current archaeological evidence indicates that all of the principal buildings of the city were completed well-before AD 1000 (Schele and Mathews 1998, 200).

Rather than the result of a single event, such as the arrival of Kukulcan, central Mexican influence in the Maya world should be seen as a long continuum of mutual interaction extending back to at least the third or fourth century with the arrival of merchants and perhaps military invaders from the great central Mexican city of Teotihuacan. There is clear evidence of the presence of armed warriors from Teotihuacan who arrived at the largest of lowland Maya centers, Tikal, in AD 378. There the foreigners oversaw the establishment of a new dynasty of heavily Mexican-influenced rulers, if not Teotihuacanos themselves (Martin and Grube 2000, 29–36). That this was no isolated event is attested by the presence at about the same time of Teotihuacan architectural, ceramic, and artistic influences throughout the Maya world, particularly in the Guatemalan highlands centered at the major site of Kaminaljuyu (Kidder, Jennings, and Shook 1946; Sanders 1977; Michels 1979; Hatch 1997) and in the Tiquisate area (Hellmuth 1975, 1987; Bove 1989).

Despite these influences from central Mexico, Tikal and its neighbors maintained their fundamentally Maya character and within a brief time reestablished their own native dynasties. Chichen Itza as well, notwithstanding its taste for central Mexican motifs and concepts, was also likely ruled by native Maya lineages. Their claims to "Toltec" ancestry were part of the political climate of the age where such legendary Mexican connections were essential to establishing legitimacy based on ancient precedent. Schele and Mathews suggest that the Itza-Maya rulers of Chichen Itza used central Mexican imagery as a means of proclaiming themselves the legitimate inheritors of Toltec power in the same way that kings throughout Europe declared themselves to be successors to the Holy Roman Empire, regardless of their familial and social histories (Schele and Mathews 1998, 201). Indeed the Cavec Quiché lineage that produced the Popol Vuh likely had Itza-Maya connections (Akkeren 2000). Chichen Itza dominated the Yucatán peninsula and southern Gulf Coast regions, establishing a tradition of Toltec-inspired power and spiritual mystique that persisted long after Toltec rule, centered at Tula Hidalgo, collapsed in approximately the twelfth century. By the time of the Spanish conquest nearly all Maya rulers prided themselves on their Nahua/Toltec heritage (Morley, Brainerd and Sharer 1983, 166).

The ruling lineages of highland Guatemala were no exception. The *Popol Vuh* claims that the divine creators who formed the first ancestors of the Quichés were *Aj Toltecat* (Toltecs) (p. 80 n.102; line 568). The text also emphasizes that the Quichés were "brothers" with the Yaqui (a general term for Nahua speakers) of Mexico and that the Quichés' principal god, Tohil, was in fact equivalent to the Mexican god Quetzalcoatl (Nahua: "Feathered Serpent") (p. 231. This affinity for foreign Mexican culture helps to explain the many Nahua loan words in the *Popol Vuh* (Campbell 1970, 8; Carmack 1983, 17–18).

According to the *Popol Vuh*, the founders of the various Quichean lineages traveled a great distance eastward "across the sea" to an epi-Toltec city called Tulan Zuyva where they received their titular gods and tokens of kingship (pp. 209–212, 256–259). Tulan is a Nahua word meaning "place of reeds," or more broadly "city," in the sense that it is filled with a great multitude of people as reeds crowd the shores of a lake or river. Many major Toltec-influenced ceremonial and administrative centers were therefore called Tulan. As a result, it is difficult to identify precisely which Tulan the Quiché progenitors saw as the origin of their power, although it was likely located somewhere on the Yucatán Peninsula (Carmack 1981, 48; Akkeren 2003). Chichen Itza, or its successor Mayapan, are good possibilities for this Tulan.

Carmack suggests that the founders of the Quiché ruling lineages arrived in Guatemala about the time of Chichen Itza's collapse, which Yucatec Maya histories date around AD 1221. More recent archaeological evidence suggests that this date should be pushed back significantly in time, and that, in any case, the ultimate downfall of the city was preceded by a long period of decline after the tenth century (Morley, Brainerd, and Sharer 1983, 167; Schele and Mathews 1998, 197–255; Akkeren 2000, 314–315). Chichen Itza had been the dominant force in the lowland Maya world. Its collapse disrupted the traditional politics and interregional trade of the region, resulting in the displacement of numerous groups of people seeking new power bases and economic opportunities (Fox 1978, 2). Many of these groups claimed authority based on the old Mexican-influenced symbols of power and prestige (Roys 1967, 88–98; Schele and Mathews 1998). It is possible that elements of what would become the ruling Cavec-Quiché lineage and related highland Maya progenitors were part of this human wave.

Thus, at Tulan, the founding lineages of the various highland Maya kingdoms were given their titular gods, as well as tokens of "Toltec" rule (many of which bore Nahua language names) and commissioned to leave in search of places to conquer (pp. 213, 257–260). Numerous highland Maya documents speak of this pilgrimage to Tulan as a means of securing tokens of power and legitimacy. This account is from the *Annals of the Cakchiquels*:

> Then we arrived at Tulan in the darkness and in the night. Then we gave the tribute, when the seven tribes and the warriors carried the tribute. We took our places in order at the left part of Tulan.... And after the seven tribes had arrived, we the warriors came. So they said. And commanding us to come, they said to us, our mothers, and our fathers: "Go, my daughters, my sons. I will give you your wealth, your domain; I will give you your power and your majesty, your canopy and your throne. Thus shall they pay tribute to you.... Truly, your glory shall be great. You shall not be disparaged. You shall become great with the wealth of the wooden shields. Do not sleep and you shall conquer, my daughters, my sons! I will give your domain to you, the thirteen chiefs, to all of you equally: your bows, your shields, your domain, your majesty, your greatness, your canopy, and your throne. These are your first treasures." Thus they spoke to the Quichés when the thirteen groups of warriors arrived at Tulan (Recinos and Goetz 1953, 50).

The authors of the *Popol Vuh* wrote that their brethren scattered in many different directions after departing from Tulan (pp. 230–232). Indeed, the Quichés described their ancestors more as refugees than as well-prepared and organized military colonists:

> This is what preoccupied their hearts as they passed through their great afflictions. They did not have food or sustenance. They would only sniff the bottoms of their staffs to feel as if they were eating. But they did not eat when they came (p. 221).

As outlined in the text, the Quiché forefathers were gradually able to dominate most of western Guatemala and set up their own militaristic kingdom which ultimately extended from the Pacific Coast in the west to the borders of the Petén rain forest in the east. The Quichés soon adopted the language and traditions of the more numerous highland Maya inhabitants of the places they conquered, retaining only a few lowland Maya and Nahua words which had no local equivalent, particularly those related to military, political, and theological concepts.

The *Popol Vuh* account of a simultaneous mass migration of all the major Quichean lineage groups into the Guatemalan highlands should not be taken literally. Rather, this was more likely a slow process carried out over a period of several centuries involving a complex series of historical and social interactions (Carmack 1981, 43–74). Indeed, many of these lineages had always lived in the highlands, although their authority to exercise military or political authority may have been obtained from outside centers of power. The confederation of people known as the Quiché was more likely a complex and linguistically diverse group of lineages composed of native highland Maya, Mexicanized clans from nearby Pacific Coastal areas, and immigrants (particularly the Cavec) from the Maya lowlands (Akkeren 2000). The interrelationship between these groups was dynamic and changed significantly over time. The *Popol Vuh* does not contain what we would call "objective history." It is instead a collection of traditions, partly based in historical fact and partly based on mythic interpretation, to describe the rise to power of their own ancestral lineages, specifically that of the Cavec who came to dominate the highland Maya region in the fifteenth century. This mixture of highland Maya, lowland Maya, and Mexican-influenced cultures ultimately gave birth to the traditions contained in the *Popol Vuh*.

The arrival of the Spaniards in the early sixteenth century resulted in the abrupt disruption of Quiché-Maya rule. Hernán Cortés, conqueror of the Aztec empire in Mexico, heard reports of rich lands to be had southward in Guatemala. He therefore sent one of his captains, Pedro de Alvarado, to subdue any resistance in that direction and claim the area for the Spanish Crown. In his first letter to Cortés, Alvarado described Guatemala as "the wildest land and people that has ever been seen.... We are so far from help that if Our Lady does not aid us, no one can" (Alvarado 1979, 105). Following a brief, yet bloody campaign, Alvarado entered the Quiché capital at Cumarcah (also known by its Nahua name, Utatlan) without resistance on March 7, 1524, at the invitation of the lords Oxib Quieh and Beleheb Tzi. Once inside the city, Alvarado suspected a trap and ordered the arrest and execution of its rulers:

> As I knew them [the Quiché lords] to have such ill will toward the service of His Majesty, and for the good and tranquility of the land, I burned them, and

I commanded to be burned the town of Utatlan to its foundations, for it was dangerous and strong.... All they that were taken prisoners of war were branded and made slaves (Alvarado 1979, 102–3).

During the early Spanish Colonial period, the population of Guatemala declined by as much as 85% as a result of war, forced labor, and disease. Fortunately, President Alonso López Cerrato, the successor to Pedro de Alvarado, was more tolerant:

> During this year [1549] the Lord President Cerrado arrived.... When he arrived, he condemned the Spaniards, he liberated the slaves and vassals of the Spaniards, he cut the taxes in two, he suspended forced labor and made the Spaniards pay all men, great and small. The lord Cerrado truly alleviated the sufferings of the people. I myself saw him, oh, my sons! (Recinos and Goetz 1953, 137).

Christianity was formally established in Guatemala in 1534 under Bishop Francisco Marroquín, who sent out priests with portable altars to the various Indian towns and villages to baptize the Maya and destroy any remnants of "idolatry" and "paganism" which might have survived the Conquest. To aid in the process of conversion, missionary priests gathered the Maya into towns, each with a church to administer Catholic rites and instruct them in the Christian faith. Because Cumarcah had been all but destroyed during the war, the remnants of its population were moved to a new settlement nearby in ca. 1555, which the Spanish authorities called Santa Cruz del Quiché (Holy Cross of the Quiché). It was likely here that the *Popol Vuh* was compiled in the form that we have today.

PRECOLUMBIAN *POPOL VUH*

In the preamble to the *Popol Vuh*, its Quiché authors wrote that the contents were based on an ancient book from across the sea (p. 64). In a later passage, the source of these writings is identified as Tulan, which they located across the sea to the east (p. 259), apparently a reference to the Maya lowlands of the Yucatán Peninsula. The Quiché lords held these "writings of Tulan" in great reverence and consulted them often (p. 287).

The Maya lowlands had a tradition of literacy dating back to at least AD 200, centered on a sophisticated hieroglyphic script. If the Precolumbian version of the *Popol Vuh* was like other ancient texts from the lowlands, it was painted on long strips of bark paper or deer skin which were given a thin coating of lime plaster to create a smooth writing surface, and then folded accordian style into a codex book. A number of such ancient painted codices were seen by the first Spanish missionaries and administrators who arrived in Guatemala. Bartolomé de las Casas saw several hieroglyphic books about 1540. He wrote that they contained the history of the people's origins and religious beliefs, written with "figures and characters by which they could signify everything they desired; and that these great books are of such astuteness and subtle technique that we could say our writing does not offer much of an advantage" (Las Casas 1958, 346).

. Las Casas was particularly impressed by the fact that the Maya could write "everything they desired." The Maya were, in fact, the only people in the New World who had a writing system at the time of the Spanish conquest which had this capability. Maya hieroglyphs are partly phonetic (glyphs which stand for individual sounds) and partly logographic (picture writing in which a glyph stands for an entire word or concept). Because of their phonetic nature, Maya glyphs may be placed together to form any word which can be thought or spoken. There is no evidence that such a script was ever developed or used in the Guatemalan highlands after the Late Preclassic, however, the authors of the *Popol Vuh* made clear that they based their writings on an imported text from the Maya lowlands. It is likely that some few scribes at the Quiché court were familiar enough with such books in their possession that they could read them in at least a cursory way.

Beginning in March 1555, a judge from the province of Mexico named Alonso de Zorita began a tour of inspection through the province of Guatemala in order to moderate tribute levies and correct administrative abuses inflicted on the local Maya population. As part of his duties, Zorita visited the ancient city of Utatlan to learn what he could about the ancient political system of the Quichés. There he was shown "paintings that they had which recorded their history for more than eight hundred years back, and which were interpreted for me by very ancient Indians" (Zorita 1963, 271–2).

There must have been hundreds of hieroglyphic books in the Maya world at the time of the Spanish conquest. It is one of the great tragedies of New World history that the vast majority of these were destroyed. Las Casas witnessed the destruction of a number of such books which were burned to "protect" the Maya from their traditional religion:

These books were seen by our clergy, and even I saw part of those which were burned by the monks, apparently because they thought [they] might harm the Indians in matters concerning religion, since at that time they were at the beginning of their conversion (Las Casas 1958, 346).

Diego de Landa was particularly zealous in his efforts to destroy any hieroglyphic books which he could find in northern Yucatán: "We found a large number of books of these characters and, as they contained nothing in which there were not to be seen superstition and lies of the devil, we burned them all, which they regretted to an amazing degree and which caused them much affliction" (Landa 1941, 78).

Only four lowland Maya codices are known to have escaped these purges. We can only add our own laments to those of the Maya over the irretrievable loss of a people's literary heritage. Of the many hieroglyphic books that once existed in the highlands, including the Precolumbian version of the *Popol Vuh*, not a single one is known to have survived.

The fact that the contents of the original *Popol Vuh* predated the Spanish conquest gave them an aura of mystery and power. Its authors referred to the ancient book upon which the *Popol Vuh* was based as an *ilb'al*, meaning "instrument of sight or vision" (p. 64; lines 51–52). The word is used today to refer to the clear quartz crystals that Quiché priests use in divinatory ceremonies. It may also be used to refer to magnifying glasses or spectacles, by which things may be seen more clearly. Thus the rulers of the Quichés consulted the *Popol Vuh* in times of national distress as a means of seeing the future:

> They knew if there would be war. It was clear before their faces. They saw if there would be death, if there would be hunger. They surely knew if there would be strife. There was an instrument of sight. There was a book. Popol Vuh was their name for it (p. 287).

Ancient Maya books were periodically displayed on state occasions as an assertion of legitimacy by the rulers who possessed them (Carmack 1973, 17–18). Diego de Landa wrote that "the most important possession that the nobles who abandoned Mayapan took away to their own country was the books of their sciences" (Landa 1941, 39). Even today the possession of old books and manuscripts is highly prestigious among the highland Maya. La Farge and Byers observed that the titles and papers of the community of Todos Santos were kept in a chest which "is highly revered, if not worshiped, by the Indians, and is carried in a solemn procession on New Year's day, when the new officials take office" (La Farge and Byers 1931, 14).

The Precolumbian version of the *Popol Vuh* has unfortunately been lost. Even the authors of the sixteenth century manuscript copy wrote that the more ancient book could no longer be seen in their day, and that what they compiled was based on the original (p. 64). It should not be assumed that this was a word for word transcription, however. The few Precolumbian Maya codices that survive, as well as the numerous inscriptions found on stelae, altars, architectural wall panels, etc., all bear texts that are highly formalized and condensed references to dates, persons, and events that briefly outline the stories they wish to tell. These are often accompanied by illustrations to further elucidate the otherwise terse prose. No known Precolumbian text contains the kind of long story-telling devices, descriptive detail, commentary, and extensive passages of dialogue found in the *Popol Vuh*. It is more likely to have been a compilation of oral traditions based to one degree or another on mythic and historical details outlined in a Precolumbian codex with their associated painted illustrations.

AUTHORS OF THE *POPOL VUH*

The authors of the *Popol Vuh* were anonymous. In the text they refer to themselves only as "we" (p. 64), indicating that there were more than one who contributed to its compilation. The anonymity of the authors is unusual since most Colonial period highland Maya documents were prepared for some official purpose, and were duly signed by their authors as testimony of their veracity. For whatever reason, those who were responsible for compiling the *Popol Vuh* did not wish their identities to be known.

The authors were traditionalists, in the sense that they recorded the history and theology of the ancient highland Maya people without adding material from European sources. The *Popol Vuh* thus contains very little direct Christian influence. By its own account it is a faithful record of the contents of the ancient *Popol Vuh* text which could no longer be seen (p. 64). Although the traditions of the book were compiled after the Conquest, "under the law of God and Christianity" (Ibid.), its Quiché authors venerated their traditional Maya gods as luminous, wise beings who brought life and light to the world through their creative works. The statement that the *Popol Vuh* was composed within Christianity immediately follows a declaration that the Maya gods "accomplished their purpose in purity of being and in truth" long before the arrival of the Christian God

(p. 63). Thus the *Popol Vuh* contrasts its "ancient word" (pp. 59, 64) which contains light and life, with that of the more recent voice of Christianity. In highland Maya society, antiquity denotes authority. A modern priest-shaman in Momostenango once told me that the Maya "Earth God" is greater than Christ and the saints because he was worshiped by his people for centuries before the arrival of the Europeans.

Such unapologetic reverence for the ancient gods would have been offensive to the Spanish missionaries. During the early decades of the Spanish conquest, the most obvious expressions of Maya religion and literature were either destroyed or forced into hiding. Old hieroglyphic books were singled out as dangerous hindrances to the conversion of the people and were actively sought out and destroyed. Those who were found in possession of such books were persecuted and even killed. As much as two hundred years later, Ximénez wrote that many ancient books were still kept in secret by the Quichés so that the Spanish authorities would not learn of them (Ximénez 1929–31, I.i.5).

It was the loss of such precious books as the hieroglyphic *Popol Vuh* which may have prompted Quiché scribes to preserve what they could of their literature by transcribing their contents into a form which would make them safer from the fiery purges of Christian authorities. The authors of the *Popol Vuh* may have recognized the danger in this and cloaked themselves with anonymity to protect themselves. The preamble to the *Popol Vuh* may hint at this when it declares that "the original book exists that was written anciently, but its witnesses and those who ponder it hide their faces" (p. 64). It is therefore he who "witnesses and ponders" the ancient book who is in hiding, perhaps an indirect reference to the authors of the *Popol Vuh* manuscript who did not wish their identities known for fear that the authorities might do harm to them or the book in their possession.

The *Popol Vuh* was likely composed in its present form at Santa Cruz del Quiché, a new city founded by the Spanish conquerors near the ruins of Cumarcah/Utatlan, the ancient capital of the Quichés. The majority of its inhabitants were members of the old ruling classes which had been resettled from Cumarcah to aid in their conversion to Christianity and to more easily supervise their activities. The authors of the text were most likely members of the Quiché nobility who may have retained some Precolumbian manuscripts from the royal archives that survived the Conquest.

The *Popol Vuh* does provide some clues as to who its authors may have been. In an extended passage placed immediately after the dynastic list of the Quiché kings themselves, the text declares that the three *Nim Ch'okoj* (Great Stewards) of the principal Quiché ruling lineages were "the mothers of the word, and the fathers of the word" (p. 305). "The word" is used in the text to describe the *Popol Vuh* itself (p. 59, lines 1,4), indicating that the *Nim Ch'okoj* were likely the authors of the book. *Nim Ch'okoj* was a relatively minor position within the Quiché nobility, charged with certain duties at royal banquets, perhaps including the recitation of tales dealing with the gods, heroes and past rulers of the Quiché nation.

The *Popol Vuh* lists don Juan de Rojas and don Juan Cortés as the contemporary Quiché kings of the ruling Cavec lineage when the manuscript was written (p. 297). These men were grandsons of the two kings burned by Pedro de Alvarado during the conquest of the Quiché nation. If the authors of the *Popol Vuh* were the three *Nim Ch'okoj* of the major Quiché lineages in the days of Juan de Rojas and Juan Cortés, then at least one of their names is known. The contemporary *Título Totonicapán* was completed during the reign of these same two kings. One of the signatories of the document was "don Cristóbal Velasco, *Nim Chocoh Cavec*" (Great Steward of the Cavec) (Chonay and Goetz 1953, 195; Carmack and Mondloch 1983, 200). Thus don Cristóbal Velasco was likely one of the elusive authors of the *Popol Vuh* as well.

Whoever they may have been, the authors of the *Popol Vuh* manuscript were trained in the use of European letters. Soon after the formal establishment of Christianity in highland Guatemala, Christian missionaries began to teach representatives of the various Maya lineages of Guatemala to read and write their languages using a modified Latin script developed by Fr. Francisco de la Parra. The first bishop of Guatemala, Francisco Marroquín strongly advocated this policy as a means of aiding the conversion effort to Christianity. The authors of the *Popol Vuh* undoubtedly learned to read and write with the Latin alphabet under the direction of Christian missionaries who were actively establishing schools for this purpose in major Maya towns, undoubtedly including Santa Cruz del Quiché.

HISTORY OF THE *POPOL VUH* MANUSCRIPT

Although the *Popol Vuh* is undated, internal evidence points to the work being completed between the years 1554 and 1558. The manuscript mentions that Juan de Rojas and Juan Cortés, grandsons of the kings burned by Alvarado during the Conquest, were alive and recognized as rulers when the *Popol Vuh* was written. The signatures of these kings appear on the last page of the *Título Totonicapán*, which is dated September 28, 1554 (Chonay and Goetz 1953, 194–5). The *Popol Vuh* must have been written prior to 1558, because by that date don Juan de Rojas had disappeared from Colonial records and had presumably died. Thus the *Royal Title of Don Francisco Izquin Nehaib*, dated November 22, 1558, is signed by Don Juan Cortés and Don Martín, kings of the Quiché at Santa Cruz (Recinos 1957, 115). The *Popol Vuh* also refers to one don Pedro de Robles as the current "Lord Magistrate" of the Nihaib lineage (p. 301). Pedro de Robles is known to have taken office soon after 1554, therefore the *Popol Vuh* must have been written sometime between the years 1554 and 1558.

This decade was one of great impoverishment in the town of Santa Cruz del Quiché. Despite a dramatic decline in population in the area following the Conquest, Spanish officials continued to drain its resources with heavy tribute levies and extortion. This became particularly severe with the accession of the Spanish king Philip II in 1556. The new king was desperate to augment royal revenues by any means possible to alleviate Spain's acute financial difficulties. As a result, the Crown sought to limit where possible the traditional tribute rights and other privileges which had been the chief means of support for the Quiché nobility, while seizing their assets (Carmack 1973, 20).

Alonso de Zorita, a judge from the *Audiencia* of Mexico, travelled through Guatemala in 1555. While there, he visited Santa Cruz del Quiché and inquired of the native rulers concerning their government. He was amazed to find that those who were at one time "lords of Utatlan" were:

> "as poor and miserable as the poorest Indian of the town, and their wives fixed the tortillas for dinner because they had no servants, nor any means of supporting them; they themselves carried fuel and water for their houses. The principal lord was named Don Juan de Rojas, the second, Don Juan Cortés.... They were all extremely poor; they left sons who were all penniless, miserable tribute-payers, for the Spaniards do not exempt any Indians from payment of tribute" (Zorita 1963, 272).

Spanish conquerors had divided up much of the land they had seized as spoils of war in the form of an *encomienda*, an institution whereby the Crown authorized Spaniards who participated in the Conquest to collect tribute and demand labor from the Indians in return for services such as military duty and providing for the spiritual welfare of Indians under their control (Orellana 1983, 137). Members of the Maya nobility protested this confiscation of their property, claiming traditional rights as rulers under Colonial law. Spanish courts tended to respect land claims and tribute rights held by important noble lineages if these could be documented based on written proof of genealogy and history. Many highland Maya texts were prepared specifically as "royal titles," and were duly signed by native rulers as legal documents. Where possible, these titles were based on Precolumbian books whose antiquity served to bolster their authenticity in court.

The Quiché lord, don Juan Cortés, travelled to Spain in 1557 to directly press his case for royal privileges at the court of Philip II. This endeavor was unsuccessful as he was judged to be unworthy of special rights, being the son of an idolator. It was also suspected that he was not whole-heartedly converted to the Christian faith, and that it would require "very little to restore their ceremonies and attract their former subjects to himself" (Tedlock 1996, 56). This reflects the general mood of the Spanish authorities in Guatemala who sought to limit the rights of native rulers. The governor of Guatemala, Alonso López Cerrato, wrote to the Spanish king on May 25, 1552, that the Maya prior to the Conquest "reverenced" their rulers "as gods, and if this were to continue, the lords could raise the land in rebellion easily" (Carmack 1973, 379. Translation by author).

The fate of the sixteenth century transcription of the *Popol Vuh* is unknown for the next 150 years. At some time during this period, it was taken from Santa Cruz del Quiché to the nearby town of Chuvila, now known as Santo Tomás Chichicastenango. Chichicastenango had long since eclipsed Santa Cruz in size and importance, and most members of the old nobility had transferred their residence there. Today it is still famed for its spectacular mountain scenery, and its preservation of traditional Quiché culture.

Between 1701 and 1704, a Dominican monk named Francisco Ximénez, the parish priest of Chichicastenango, came to obtain the manuscript. Ximénez had served since 1694 in various Maya communities where he learned a number of dialects and studied Maya grammar so that he could teach it to newly-arrived clerics. He was particularly impressed with the Quiché language, calling it the "principal one of the world."

Ximénez was interested as well in the ancient traditions of the Quichés. He noted that in his parish the people still conserved ancient "errors" which they had believed prior to the arrival of the Spaniards (Ximénez 1929–31, I.i.54). His curiosity concerning ancient Quiché history and religion may have overcome the suspicion of the guardians of the *Popol Vuh* manuscript, who allowed him to see it and make a copy. Ximénez wrote that other such texts were also in their possession:

> It was with great reserve that these manuscripts were kept among them, with such secrecy, that neither the ancient ministers knew of it, and investigating this point, while I was in the parish of Santo Tomás Chichicastenango, I found that it was the doctrine which they first imbibed with their mother's milk, and that all of them knew it almost by heart, and I found that they had many of these books among them (Ximénez 1929–31, I.i.5).

Ximénez transcribed the Quiché text of the *Popol Vuh*, and added a Spanish translation of its contents. It is unknown what happened to the sixteenth century manuscript, although presumably Ximénez returned it to its Quiché owners. It is possible that the original may still survive in the possession of village elders or in the town archives of Chichicastenango.

Ximénez's manuscript lay forgotten in parish archives until the Guatemalan Civil War of 1829 when all religious orders were expelled from the country. Books and papers formerly housed in convents and monasteries were subsequently transferred to public libraries, government repositories, or the collections of private individuals. Ximénez's copy of the *Popol Vuh* manuscript apparently ended up in the library of the University of San Carlos in Guatemala City. An Austrian traveler named Carl Scherzer saw it there in 1854 and had a copy made to take with him back to Europe. In part, Scherzer commissioned this copy to be made due to the poor condition of the manuscript. He described it as having been "written in such light ink that the original might very well become illegible and useless in a few years" (Scherzer 1856, 9). Lamentably, this faded copy of the Ximénez transcription of the *Popol Vuh* has since vanished from public records. Scherzer published Ximénez's Spanish version of the text in 1856, the first time the *Popol Vuh* had appeared in print. The book was greeted with a great deal of excitement in Europe and America, where interest in ancient cultures was widespread.

In 1861, four years after Scherzer's book, the Quiché version of the *Popol Vuh* was published for the first time, along with a rather flowery French translation by Father Charles Etienne Brasseur de Bourbourg. This publication was based on yet another copy of the Ximénez transcription which Brasseur had obtained from a Quiché man, named Ignacio Coloch, who resided in the town of Rabinal. This manuscript is of supreme importance because it is the oldest known Quiché version of the *Popol Vuh* text which has survived. Ximénez was in charge of the parish of Rabinal from 1704–1714, immediately following his years in Chichicastenango. It is unknown whether Ximénez prepared the "Rabinal Manuscript" during this period of his ministry or brought it with him from Chichicastenango.

The Rabinal Manuscript of the *Popol Vuh* bears the cumbersome title, *Empiezan las historias del origen de los Indios de esta provincia de Guatemala, traduzido de la lengua quiché en la castellana para más comodidad de los Ministros del Sto. Evangelio, por el R.P.F. Franzisco Ximénez, Cura doctrinero por el Real Patronato del Pueblo de Sto. Thomás Chuilá*

Figure 6. Initial page of the oldest known manuscript copy of the Popol Vuh, ca. 1701–4. The Quiché text appears in the left column while the Spanish translation by Ximénez parallels it on the right. Courtesy The Newberry Library, Chicago.

(Beginning of the histories of the origin of the Indians of this province of Guatemala, translated from the Quiché language to Spanish for the greater convenience of the Ministries of the Holy Gospel, by the Reverend Father Franzisco Ximénez, Parish Priest for the Royal Patronage of the Town of Santo Tomás Chuilá). It is handwritten in a clear, flowing cursive script arranged in two columns, Quiché on the left and Ximénez's Spanish translation on the right. Fortunately the ink used has remained well-preserved, and the paper is in remarkably good condition with almost no lacunae due to stains, tears or holes. It was placed at the end of a series of linguistic studies made by Ximénez which he entitled *Arte de las tres lenguas Cacchiquel, Quiché y Tzutuhil* (Art of the three languages

Cacchiquel, Quiché and Tzutuhil). These studies include a brief grammar, confessional, and Catechism in each of the three languages.

Brasseur brought the Rabinal Manuscript to Europe as part of a large corpus of native American documents which he had collected in his travels through Mexico and Guatemala. The bound volume containing the Ximénez transcription of the *Popol Vuh* was purchased after Brasseur's death by the American collector, Edward E. Ayer, who eventually donated it to the Newberry Library in Chicago, Illinois, where it is catalogued as Ayer MS 1515.

THE POETIC NATURE OF THE *POPOL VUH*

The *Popol Vuh* is not only the most important highland Maya text in terms of its historical and mythological content, it is also a sublime work of literature, composed in rich and elegant poetry. In this respect it can be compared with other great epic poems of the ancient world such as the *Ramayana* and *Mahabharata* of India, or the *Iliad* and *Odyssey* of Greece.

Quiché poetry is not based on rhyme or metrical rhythms, but rather the arrangement of concepts into innovative and even ornate parallel structures. Seldom are the authors content with expressing a single idea without embellishing it with synonymous concepts, metaphors, or descriptive epithets. The Quiché poet is much like the composer of classical music who begins with a simple melody and then weaves into it both complementary and contrasting harmonies to give it interest and depth. Thus endless variations on a given theme are possible.

Books such as the *Popol Vuh* were not simply records of dry history, but universal declarations of the purpose of the world and man's place in it. The written words were thus intended to conjure up an image in the mind, to give new life and breath to the gods and heroes each time the story was read. The beauty of the work depends not only on the story itself, but on how the story is told. As Munro Edmonson points out, Mayan texts are meant to be "read and pondered rather than skimmed over" (Edmonson 1982, xiii).

Yet the beauty of Quiché poetry may sound awkward and repetitive when translated into European languages. Some translators in the past have ignored or failed to recognize the poetic nature of the *Popol Vuh*, particularly its use of parallelism, and have tried to improve its seemingly purposeless redundancy by eliminating words, phrases, and even whole sections of text which they deemed unnecessary. While this unquestionably helps to make the story flow more smoothly, in keeping with our modern taste for linear plot structure, it detracts from the character of Quiché high literature. Welch points out that "in many ancient contexts, repetition and even redundancy appear to represent the rule rather than the exception" (Welch 1981, 12).

The first modern scholar to recognize parallelism in Maya literature was Sir J. Eric Thompson, who noticed that Precolumbian hieroglyphic texts seemed to contain redundant glyphs. Because the ancient Yucatec Maya books of Chilam Balam have similar redundancies, he concluded that these parallel glyphs were intended as a "flowing harmony," and were "interpolated to improve the cadence of a passage" (Thompson 1950, 61–62).

Miguel León-Portilla was the first translator to arrange portions of Quiché and Yucatec Maya documents into poetic verse (León-Portilla 1969, 51–55, 75, 92–93). His recognition of the literary nature of Maya texts was a significant advance over previous translations which virtually ignored the presence of poetry. Nevertheless, his criteria for separating individual poetic lines, or cola, was somewhat haphazard, and he failed to recognize the presence of most forms of parallelism in the text.

In his translation of the *Popol Vuh,* Munro Edmonson arranges the entire text into parallel couplets. He asserts that "the *Popol Vuh* is primarily a work of literature, and it cannot be properly read apart from the literary form in which it is expressed" (Edmonson 1971, xi). While he has been criticized for failing to identify other types of poetry in his work (D. Tedlock 1983, 230), it is still the only translation of the full text of the *Popol Vuh* which has emphasized the poetic nature of the text. It is also true that by far the most common arrangement in the *Popol Vuh* is the parallel couplet. Edmonson himself recognized that his arrangement of the text was not the last word on the literary structure of the *Popol Vuh*: "I am certain that my reading does not exhaust either the poetry or the sense that is expressed, and that the Popol Vuh contains more of both beauty and meaning than I have found in it" (Edmonson 1971, xiii).

For the purposes of the second volume of this monograph, I have arranged the literal translation of the *Popol Vuh* according to its poetic structure. Lines which are parallel in form or concept have been indented an equal number of spaces from the left margin of the page.

TYPES OF PARALLELISM IN THE *POPOL VUH*

1. **Identical Parallelism:** The repetition of identical elements. Example, lines 794–795:

Sooty our mouths,	**Xaq qa** chi',
Sooty our faces.	**Xaq qa** wach.

2. **Synonymous Parallelism:** The repetition of elements which are similar in meaning or significance. Example, lines 58–59:

Witness of it,	**Ilol** re,
Ponderer of it.	**B'isol** re.

3. **Antithetic Parallelism:** The contrast of one element with an opposite or antithetical element. Example, lines 730–1:

Day rain,	**Q'ijil** jab',
Night rain.	**Aq'ab'al** jab'.

4. **Associative Parallelism:** The correlation of elements which are complementary to one another. This association may be material, familial, functional, or gender-based.

   a. Material association, in which the substance of the elements is similar in nature. Example, lines 243–244:

Its **cypress groves**,	U **k'isisil**,
Pine forests its face.	U **pachajil** u wach.

   b. Familial association, in which elements are related by kinship. Example, lines 5129–5130:

First our **grandfathers**,	Nab'e qa **mam**,
Our **fathers**,	Qa **qajaw**,

   c. Functional association, in which two elements act in a similar manner. Example, lines 137–138:

Merely alone the **Framer**,	Xa u tukel ri **Tz'aqol**,
Shaper,	**B'itol**,

   d. Gender association, in which two elements are paired as male and female representatives of a parallel occupation. Example, lines 287–288:

Says the **She Who Has Borne Children**,	Kacha' ri **Alom**,
He Who Has Begotten Sons:	**K'ajolom:**

5. **Augmentive Parallelism:** Parallel elements in which one word or phrase clarifies or augments the meaning of another. Example, lines 151–152:

Thus surely there is the **sky**,	Keje' k'ut xax k'o wi ri **kaj**,
There is also **its Heart Sky**.	K'o nay puch **u K'ux Kaj**.

6. **Causative Parallelism:** Parallel elements in which the first word or phrase directly effects or precipitates the associated words or phrases. Example, lines 716–7:

He came **Striking Jaguar**,	Xpe **Tukum B'alam**,
He struck them.	**Xtukuwik.**

7. **Epithetic Parallelism:** The association of an element with a complementary noun or adjective which serves to define the nature of that element. Example, lines 591–2:

This the **grandfather**,	Are' ri **mama'**,
This **master of tz'ite**,	Are' **aj tz'ite**,

8. **Alliterative Parallelism:** Elements which parallel one another in sound when read aloud. In lines 486–7, the verbs *yoj* and *yoq'* were apparently chosen for their similar sounds, in addition to their synonymous meaning:

Then **they undid** it therefore,	Ta **xkiyoj** k'ut,
They toppled it again	**Xkiyoq'** chik

9. **Grammatical Parallelism:** Elements which are grammatically parallel in construction, such as the following example from lines 11–13, in which the same passive verb form is used as a gerund in each line of the strophe:

Its **being manifested**,	U **k'utunisaxik**,
Its **being declared**,	U **q'alajob'isaxik**,
Its **being expressed** as well,	U **tzijoxik** puch,

10. **Alternative Parallelism:** Parallelism in which elements appear in an alternating arrangement, such as the following example from lines 591–7, which is arranged ABCA'B'C'.

This the grandfather,	Are' ri mama',
This master of *tz'ite*,	Are' aj tz'ite,
Xpiyacoc his name.	Xpiyakok u b'i'.

This therefore **the grandmother,**	**Are'** k'u **ri ati't,**
Mistress of Days,	**Aj Q'ij,**
Mistress of Shaping at its foot,	**Aj B'it** chi raqan,
Xmucane her name.	**Xmuqane u b'i'.**

II. **Chiasmus, or Reverse Parallelism:** Parallelism in which the first element of a strophe parallels the last, the second element parallels the next to last, etc. This arrangement tends to focus attention on the central elements, thus asserting their importance. It is a rather common poetic form in sixteenth century Maya literature, particularly in the Guatemalan highlands, however, none of the known documents composed after 1580 contain passages of chiasmus. Several of these later texts might otherwise be expected to contain ancient poetic forms, since they include significant sections of Precolumbian history and culture. Among these are the *Título Zapotitlan*, the *Título Santa Clara*, the *Título Chauchituj* and the *Título Uchabaja*. By 1580, however, scribes who possessed ancient codices and were familiar with their contents were for the most part gone. Perhaps by this time the old poetic literary forms were already forgotten or had fallen into disuse (Christenson 1988). The first chiasm that I was able to identify within the *Popol Vuh* appears in lines 32–35:

Midwife,	**I'yom,**
Patriarch,	**Mamom,**
Xpiyacoc	**Xpiyakok,**
Xmucane, their names,	**Xmuqane**, u b'i',

The name of the "Midwife" in line 32 is Xmucane, which appears in line 35. The name of the "Patriarch" in line 33 is Xpiyacoc, which appears in line 34. The descriptions and proper names of this couple thus appear in a chiastic arrangement. Edmonson, who believed that the Popol Vuh is arranged entirely in paired couplets, was confused by the order of the names Xpiyacoc and Xmucane: "It is odd that this frequent couplet places the male first, the reverse of the usual Quiché order; indeed, if the reconstructed forms are correct, they would make better sense reversed" (Edmonson 1971, 5 n. 35). Recognition of the chiasmus in this passage clears up the confusion (see also lines 538–541 for a repetition of this arrangement).

Chiasms may appear within a single line or extend for several lines, as in the following ten line example which is placed at the conclusion of the account of the creation of the first humans (lines 5171–5180), and which is arranged in the form ABCDEE'D'C'B'A'.

Then **they were multiplied**,	Ta **xpoq'otajik**,
There at **its coming out sun**.	**Chila'** chi **releb'al q'ij**.
Truly **their names** came to be the **people**:	Qi **u b'i'** xuxik ri **winaq**:
Sovereign,	Tepew,
Ballplayer,	Oloman,
Masker,	K'ojaj,
Sun Lord,	K'enech Ajaw,
Would be called now **their names people**.	Chuchax chik **u b'i' winaq**.
There its coming out sun	**Chila' releb'al q'ij**
They were multiplied.	**Xpoq'otajik**.

Within the *Popol Vuh*, entire sections may appear in chiastic form. The account of the first creation is arranged as a single, large chiasm. Each phase of the creation is outlined in detail from primordial stillness to the formation of the face of the earth, along with its mountains and rivers. The final portion of this section then recapitulates the events of the creation in reverse order:

Creation begun with a **declaration of the first words** concerning the creation (lines 97–117)

The **sky** is in suspense and the **earth is submerged in water** (lines 118–136)

The creation is to be under the direction of **Its Heart Sky** (lines 137–192)

The **creation** of all things begun (lines 193–201)

The creation of **earth** (lines 202–232)

The creation of **mountains** (lines 233–255)

The **division of the waters** into branches (lines 256–258)

"Merely **divided** then existed **waters**," (line 259)

"Then were revealed great **mountains**." (line 260)

"Thus its creation **earth** this," (line 261)

"Then it was **created** by them" (line 262)

"**Its Heart Sky**, [who first conceived the creation]" (lines 263–267)

"It was set apart the **sky**, it was set apart also **earth within water**," (lines 268–269)

"Thus its **conception** this, when they thought, when they pondered" (lines 270–274)

12. **Envelope Parallelism:** The repetition of parallel elements at the beginning and end of a long stanza or section of poetry. This has the effect of tying together the introduction and conclusion of a passage to set it apart from that which precedes and follows it. Example, lines 5147–5148 initiate the envelope:

| These therefore their names | Are' k'u ki b'i' |
| Their wives these: | Kixoqil wa': |

This introductory couplet is followed by four couplets listing the wives of the Quiché progenitors. The section is then concluded with a parallel enveloping couplet in lines 5157–5158:

| These therefore their names | Are' k'ut u b'i' |
| Their wives. | Kixoqil. |

Such envelopes may appear at the beginning and end of much larger sections as well. The account of the second creation begins with lines 275–276, describing the formation of the wild animals of the earth:

| THEN they conceived again | TA xkino'jij chik |
| Its animals mountain, | U chikopil juyub', |

The account concludes with lines 432–3, which recapitulate the introductory couplet with a parallel envelope:

| The animals that are here | Ri chikop k'o waral |
| On its face earth. | Chuwach ulew. |

13. **Merismus:** The expression of a broad concept by a pair of complementary elements which are narrower in meaning. Thus, in lines 64–65, "sky-earth" represents all creation as a whole. Lines 240–241 use "mountain-valley" to include the face of the earth as a whole. Lines 338–339 use "deer-birds" to describe all wild animals, while lines 748–749 use "dogs-turkeys" to describe all domesticated animals.

14. **Emblematic Parallelism:** The use of simile to compare elements, often with the use of words such as "like" or "as." Example, lines 832–833:

| These therefore the spider monkeys, | Are' k'u ri k'oy, |
| Like people they would appear. | Keje' ri' winaq chiwachinik. |

15. **Combination of Parallel Arrangements:** The use of two or more types of parallelism in a single strophe. The following example from lines 4948–4956 is a combination of parallel couplets arranged into chiastic form (AABBCB'B'A'A'):

MERELY framed,	**XA** tz'aq,
Merely **shaped** they are called.	Xa **b'it** ke'uchaxik.
There was no their mother,	**Maja b'i ki chuch,**
There was no their father.	**Maja b'i ki qajaw.**
Merely lone men we would say.	Xa u tukel achij chiqab'ij.
Nor surely woman gave them birth,	**Ma na ixoq xe'alanik,**
Nor also were they begotten	**Ma nay pu xek'ajolaxik**
By the **Framer,**	Rumal ri **Aj Tz'aq,**
Shaper,	**Aj B'it,**

Lines 5063–5070 combine alternate parallelism with parallel couplets placed in the third position (ABCCA'B'C'C'):

Not therefore **good**	Ma k'u **utz**
They heard it,	**Xkita'o,**
The **Framer,**	Ri **Aj Tz'aq,**
Shaper.	**Aj B'it.**
"**Not good**	"**Mawi utz**
This they said,	**Ri' mi xkib'ij,**
Our **framing,**	Qa **tz'aq,**
Our **shaping:**	Qa **b'it:**

16. **Monocolon**: An isolated line which does not parallel any associated line, thus standing on its own. Because monocolons are relatively rare within the *Popol Vuh*, they are all the more powerful when they do occur. In general they are used when the author desires to give extra emphasis to a passage. Thus line 200 appears as an isolated declaration:

Then be it so.	Ta' chuxoq.

STROPHIC LENGTHS

The various types of parallelism in the *Popol Vuh* may appear within a pair of lines, or they may extend through multiple lines of text. While the parallel couplet is the standard poetic form in the *Popol Vuh*, it is by no means the only one. Tedlock recognized this in his work with highland Maya literature: "To measure all Mayan texts by the single standard of the couplet is to miss the very essence of Mayan verse rhythms, which move in twos, and sometimes threes, and once in a while arch over to produce a four" (D. Tedlock 1983b, 230). I would only add that such verse rhythms may also extend beyond four lines to form quintets, sextets, and even longer arrangements.

The following are examples of the various strophic types in terms of length found within the *Popol Vuh*:

1. **Parallel Couplets (Bicolon):** By far the most common strophic length in the *Popol Vuh* is the couplet, consisting of two parallel lines. Example, lines 165–166:

Then they thought,	Ta xena'ojinik,
Then they pondered.	Ta xeb'isonik.

In modern Quiché speech, formal prayers and even every-day conversation tend to utilize parallel couplets. The following selection is from a prayer made by a Quiché priest-shaman in Momostenango as recorded by Barbara Tedlock (B. Tedlock 1982, 197). The translation, orthography and punctuation have not been altered from Tedlock's transcription, although I have arranged the prayer into couplet form:

Pardon my sin God.	Sachaj la numac Tiox.
Pardon my sin Earth.	Sachaj la numac Mundo.
I am giving my fine,	Quinya'o ri numulta,
my present	nu presenta
before you God,	chiwäch la Tiox,
before you Earth.	chiwäch la Mundo.
I am giving my wax candle,	Quinya'o wa' jun nuceracandela,
my stake	nu tac'alibal
toward the legs	pa ri akän
arms of God	k'äb la Tiox
at the rising of the sun,	chirelebal k'ij,
at the setting of the sun	chukajibal k'ij
the four corners of sky,	cajxucut kaj,
the four corners of earth,	cajxucut ulew.
Come here then my work,	Sa'j la rech c'ut nuchac,
my service.	nupatan.

2. **Parallel Triplets (Tricolon):** Three parallel lines of text. Example, lines 374–376:

"Speak!	"Kixch'awoq!
Call upon us!	Kojisik'ij!
Worship us!" they were told.	Kojiq'ijila'!" xe'uchaxik.

3. **Parallel Quatrains (Tetracolon):** Four parallel lines of text. Example, lines 5034–5037:

We speak,	Kojch'awik,
We listen,	Kojta'onik,
We ponder,	Kojb'isonik,
We move.	Kojsilab'ik.

One interesting phenomenon which appears frequently within longer series of parallel lines is "gapping," in which an expected word or clause is omitted in one line, although it is implied by the parallelism of the series. Gapping is used in modern Quiché to break up the monotony of a long series of parallel elements. An example in the *Popol Vuh* appears in lines 66–69, in which the word "four" is expected in the third line, but is not expressed:

Its four cornerings,	U kaj tz'ukuxik,
Its four sidings,	U kaj xukutaxik,
Its measurings,	Retaxik,
Its four stakings,	U kaj che'xik,

4. **Longer parallel series:** The following is an example of a parallel sextet in lines 464–469:

Merely it would come undone,	Xa chiyojomanik,
Merely crumbled,	Xa tzub'ulik,
Merely sodden,	Xa neb'elik,
Merely mushy,	Xa lub'anik,
Merely fallen apart,	Xa wulanik,
Merely as well it would dissolve.	Xa pu chi'umarik.

The *Popol Vuh* is fundamentally based on these various forms of parallelism. Recognition of the presence of parallelism in a given text helps to focus attention on what the authors feel is important. By pairing each thought with complementary ones, the authors are able to develop their ideas with greater clarity. They may compare elements, contrast them, elaborate upon their significance, or add layers of meaning which would not otherwise be obvious.

Parallelism is also the primary means used by Quiché authors to give order to their thoughts. The words of the *Popol Vuh* were not arranged into sentences and paragraphs as in modern literature. The use of periods, commas, and capitalization to separate independent concepts was inconsistent at best, reflecting the authors' lack of familiarity with European devices for punctuation. Parallelism provided a means of structuring the book's ideas into distinct and coherent entities.

Much of Quiché literature was based in whole, or in part, on oral tradition. Parallelism is a common mnemonic device used in many ancient cultures to help narrators remember the flow and direction of their tale. This is particularly true of the chiastic type of parallelism, which may give order to large sections of a story. It also gives the listener an opportunity to hear a recapitulation in reverse order of what had been said, while reminding him of the central themes that are of special importance.

The presence of parallelism in the *Popol Vuh* is also a tremendous, though unintended, boon to modern translators. By comparing an ambiguous word or passage with its associated line, its general meaning is often clarified. This is especially important when interpreting a word which has more than one possible meaning, or which is poorly transcribed through scribal error.

Perhaps the most important reason that I have stressed the poetic nature of the *Popol Vuh* in this translation is the insight it gives into the mind of the ancient Quiché author. We can see how he organized his thoughts as he took pen or brush in hand to set them down in permanent form. Far from being the random musings of an unlearned story-teller, the *Popol Vuh* can be appreciated as the eloquent creation of a master poet with a sophisticated literary heritage.

ORTHOGRAPHY

The Quiché version of the *Popol Vuh* transcribed by Ximénez was written using a modified Latin alphabet to represent Quiché sounds. Thus *x* is used to represent the *sh* sound of English; *h* represents the hard Spanish *j*; and *v* represents the English *w*. For the most part, the letters used were based on those standardized by the Franciscan priest Francisco de la Parra in 1545. The orthography is therefore consistent with the writing system taught by

Christian missionaries during the early Spanish Colonial period, although the *Popol Vuh* text is much less consistent in its use of the Parra alphabet than other contemporary documents such as the *Título Totonicapán* (Carmack and Mondloch 1983) or the *Título Yax* (Carmack and Mondloch 1989). Variant spellings of words occur throughout the manuscript and glottalized sounds in particular are haphazardly distinguished at best. Even when used faithfully, however, the Parra alphabet presents a number of problems in interpretation, since the Quiché language includes several sounds which have no equivalents in this system.

Long and short vowels are treated as separate letters in Quiché and should be distinguished when written. The Ximénez transcription of the *Popol Vuh* seldom makes such distinctions. For example, the word transcribed as *vach* might be read with a long vowel *vach* ("my companion"), or with a short vowel *väch* ("my face").

The Quiché language utilizes both a palatal stop (*k*) and a uvular stop (*q*). The *Popol Vuh* manuscript uses a single letter (*c*) to represent both these sounds. In addition, each of these has a glottalized form (*k'*) and (*q'*), pronounced by occluding the vocal apparatus momentarily and then opening it forcefully to create a mildly-explosive release of sound. Because the Latin alphabet has no equivalent for glottalized sounds, Parra invented letters to represent them. The *Popol Vuh* manuscript however does not consistently use the Parra glottalized letters for the palatal and uvular consonants. In most cases it either ignores glottalization altogether, representing them with the letter *c*, or uses the letter *q* to represent both glottalized forms. As a result, the single letter "c" may have four equally plausible readings.

For example, the word *cac* might be read as *kak* (their gourd); *kaq* (red); kaq (their peccary); *kak'* (their turkey); *qak* (our gourd); *qak'* (our turkey); *qaq* (our peccary); *kaq'* (their tongues); *qaq'* (our tongues); *k'ak'* (new); *k'aq* (to throw); *q'ak* (flea); or *q'aq'* (fire). Four other combinations are possible which have no known meaning in modern usage, but which might have existed in the archaic language of the sixteenth century.

The glottalized forms of other consonants and vowels are also either ignored or used inconsistently in the Ximénez manuscript. Thus there is often no difference between the written form of *che* (toward him/her) and *che'* (tree). Imagine the difficulties for the reader when the words *tzaq* (to thrown down) and *tz'aq* (to frame or build) appear with the same spelling.

If this weren't confusing enough, words which appear to be contextually the same may appear with variant spellings. The Quiché authors who composed the text in the sixteenth century were pioneers in the use of a foreign alphabet to represent their language in written form. They did not have the luxury of officially recognized dictionaries with standardized spellings, nor did they have computers to scan for errors. In light of the enormous difficulties involved in its composition, the *Popol Vuh* manuscript is remarkably consistent, although discrepancies in spelling inevitably appear in the text.

It is impossible to know how many variant spellings crept into the text as a result of scribal errors made by Ximénez when he copied his version from the original manuscript. At one point, Ximénez copied eleven lines of the same passage of text twice (folio 8r). He caught his mistake and crossed out the repeated section. If no scribal errors were made, the two transcriptions should be identical, yet Edmonson found an average of one discrepancy every five lines in the duplicated section (Edmonson 1971, 46). Without the original document composed by the Quichés, a perfect reading of the text is impossible to verify.

Since the sixteenth century, a number of writing systems have been invented for Quiché in an attempt to avoid the confusion inherent in the Parra alphabet. Unfortunately, this has resulted in the proliferation of a great many competing systems without a consensus as to which should be the standard. Many of these utilize letters not found in the modern European alphabet, making them impossible to use with most typewriters and computer keyboards.

In 1986 the Guatemalan Ministry of Public Education set up a commission to standardize alphabets for the twenty-one recognized highland Maya languages. This standardization effort had become particularly important due to the Guatemalan government's proposed "Program of Bilingual Education" in Mayan communities, designed to improve literacy and promote native American cultures and languages. This program included the publication of bilingual dictionaries, school textbooks, and official translations of the Guatemalan Constitution in the various highland Maya languages.

The results of this commission were officially endorsed by the Guatemalan government and signed into law as Governmental Decree Number 1046–87 by President Marco Vinicio Cerezo Arévalo on November 23, 1987.

The following is a list of the modified Latin letters developed by Parra as used in the *Popol Vuh* text, along with the modern orthographic equivalents and a guide to pronunciation:

Parra	Modern	
a, aa	a	As in the *a* of "father."
a	ä	As in the *o* of "mother."
b	b'	Similar to the English *b*, but pronounced with the throat closed while air is forcefully expelled to produce a glottal stop.
ch	ch	As in the *ch* of "child."
qh, ch	ch'	Pronounced with the tongue in the same position as for the *ch*, but the throat is closed and air forcefully expelled to produce a glottalized *ch*.
e, ee	e	As in the *a* of "late."
i, ÿ, ii	i	As in the *ee* in "eel."
h	j	Pronounced like the English *h*, but deeper in the throat. Similar to the Spanish *j* or the German *ch* (as in the proper name "Bach").
c, q	k	Similar to the *k* in "king."
c, q	k'	Pronounced with the tongue in the same position as for the *k*, but the throat is closed and air forcefully expelled to produce a glottalized *k*.
l	l	Pronounced like the English *l*, but with the tongue moved forward to contact the upper incisor teeth. When appearing as the terminal letter in a word, this sound is immediately followed by the *h* as in the English word "hot."
m	m	As in the *m* of "mat."
n	n	As in the *n* of "net."
o, oo	o	As in the *o* of "home."
p	p	Pronounced like the English *p* but shortened in length.
c, q	q	Pronounced from further back in the throat than the letter *k*, similar to the *kh* in the Egyptian word *ankh*.
ε, c, q	q'	Pronounced with the tongue in the same position as for the *q*, but the throat is closed and air forcefully expelled to produce a glottalized *q*.
r	r	Similar to the Spanish *r*, pronounced with a brief tap of the tongue against the roof of the mouth.

z	s	As in the s of "sit."
t	t	Similar to the English t but shortened in length.
d, t	t'	Pronounced with the tongue in the same position as for the t, but the throat is closed and air forcefully expelled to produce a glottalized t.
tz	tz	As in the ts of "mats."
tz, q,	tz'	Pronounced with the tongue in the same position as for the tz, but the throat is closed and air forcefully expelled to produce a glottalized tz.
u, v, uu	u	As in the oo of "root"
v, u	w	As in the w of "wind."
x	x	Pronounced like the sh in "shy."
y, i	y	As in the y of "yellow." When appearing as the terminal letter in a word, it is pronounced like the ee in "eel," immediately followed by an English h as in "hot."
	'	Glottalization mark for vowels. For example a' would be similar to the pronunciation of the ott in the Scottish pronunciation of "bottle." Generally there is no equivalent for glottalized vowels in the Popol Vuh, although occasionally a double vowel may have been intended to serve this purpose.

I have used the modern alphabet in my literal translation and transcription of the Quiché text. When pronouncing Maya words, the emphasis is always on the final syllable. When pronouncing Nahua words, the emphasis is always on the next to last syllable.

Due to the haphazard nature of commas and periods in the Popol Vuh text, I have altered the punctuation to conform with modern usage, but otherwise the grammatical constructions and word order of the original manuscript have not been altered in the literal translation. In order to avoid interpretations of spelling with regard to proper names, which in many cases would be little more than a guess, I have left them in their original Parra Latin spelling. To maintain consistency in this regard, I have used Quiché throughout this book, the spelling found in the original manuscript, rather than the modern K'iche'.

POPOL VUH

PREAMBLE[1]

THIS IS THE BEGINNING[2] OF THE ANCIENT TRADITIONS[3] of this place called Quiché.[4]

HERE we shall write.[5] We shall begin[6] to tell the ancient stories of the beginning, the origin of all that was done in the citadel[7] of Quiché, among the people of the Quiché nation.[8]

[1] lines 1–96

[2] The Quiché word *xe'* (root) is used here to describe the beginning or foundation of the authors' words concerning the history of the Quiché people. The subsequent narrative is thus seen as growing like a plant from this "root" (lines 4–6).

[3] The *Popol Vuh* manuscript does not utilize capitalization or punctuation to differentiate sentences. Capitalization is, however, used to mark the beginning of what the authors consider to be the major divisions of their story. In general, only the first word of each new section is capitalized. In this translation, I have marked these divisions by capitalizing the first word of the introductory line where appropriate. In two instances (lines 1 and 97), the entire introductory line is capitalized in the manuscript. Line 1 introduces the preamble of the text, while line 97 is the first line of the body of the story itself.

[4] The authors at various times refer to the land, the nation, the capital city, and the people themselves as Quiché (K'iche' in the modern orthography of the Maya languages), meaning "many trees" or "forest." The homeland of the Quiché people in western Guatemala is mountainous and heavily forested.

[5] The authors here state that they are "writing" this history. The people of ancient Mesoamerica (roughly the area of Central Mexico southward to Guatemala, Belize, and parts of Honduras and El Salvador) were the only literate Precolumbian cultures in the New World. Following the Spanish conquest, native Americans were discouraged from using their own ancient writing systems in favor of the Latin script. The manuscript of the *Popol Vuh* was thus written in the Mayan language of the Quichés, but with a European script. It is this set of circumstances that has preserved the *Popol Vuh* in a fully readable form when so many other native American texts were either destroyed or written in an as yet incompletely decipherable glyphic form.

[6] *Tikib'a'* is literally "to plant." "The beginning," also in this sentence, is therefore literally "the planting."

[7] Based on *tinamit*, a Nahua-derived word meaning "fortified town, citadel, or fortification wall" (Campbell 1983, 85). Although in modern Quiché, *tinamit* simply refers to a town or city, the word is used in the *Popol Vuh* text to specify fortified centers occupied by ruling lineages (Carmack 1981, 23). Here the citadel of the Quiché people is also called Quiché, apparently referring to the heartland region of their nation. This would include the capital city, Cumarcah, as well as its surrounding territory.

[8] *Amaq'* may refer to a geographic entity such as a town or region, as well as the group of people who occupy that territory. It may also describe a group of people unified by a common language and/or ethnic origin, such as a lineage, clan, or tribe (Hill 1996, 64; Akkeren 2000, 24). Thus Cook defines *amaq'* as composed of endogamous landholding communities subordinate to the lord or patrilineage head centered at his *tinamit* (2000, 27). Hill and Monaghan identify the *amaq'* as an alliance of confederated lineage groups (1987, 74). *Amaq'* also implies something that is permanent, fixed, stable, secure, or settled. I have chosen to use the word "nation" as this is the currently preferred term for Native American groups as well as their territorial possessions.

Here we shall gather the manifestation, the declaration, the account
of the sowing[9] and the dawning[10] by[11] the Framer[12] and the Shaper,[13] She
Who Has Borne Children and He Who Has Begotten Sons,[14] as they are
called; along with Hunahpu Possum[15] and Hunahpu Coyote,[16] Great White

[9] The manuscript reads *euaxibal* (obscurity, that which is hidden in darkness). This is likely
a transcription error for *auaxibal* (sowing, that which is sown), a concept that is paired with
"dawning" throughout the text as a metaphor for the creation (see pp. 71, 78–82, 110, 206–
207, 227; lines 196–197, 209–210, 442–443, 543–544, 612–613, 1653–1654, 5091–5092).
[10] The primary focus of the creation is to form humanity (cf. p. 70–71; lines 213–218). The
"sowing" and "dawning" of this couplet may refer in a literal sense to a new beginning, but
may also be interpreted in human terms. In addition, *tz'uk* (germinate/sprout) is used as a
metaphor for human birth (Coto). Among the Quichés, when a woman becomes pregnant,
the event is announced by a respected elder of the community at certain lineage shrines.
This ceremony is referred to as "the sowing" of the future child (B. Tedlock 1982, 80). In Santiago Atitlán, when an infant is born it is said that "he (or she) sprouted" (Carlsen 1997, 54).
The "dawning" also refers to the dawn of humanity, as indicated by the reference to "anyone"
rather than "anything" on p. 71. In the Quiché language, to give birth is "to dawn" or "to give
light" (*-ya' saq*). In Chichicastenango children are called *alaj q'ij* (little sun) or *alaj q'ij saj* (little
ray of sun) when they are referred to in ritual contexts (Schultze-Jena 1954, 25).
[11] The following is a long list of deities, arranged in pairs, which the Quichés believed to
have participated in the creation at the beginning of time. The list consists of not only the
names of separate gods, but their titles and secondary names as well. It is thus difficult to
distinguish how many gods are really involved. In some cases, titles are definitively assigned
to individual gods later in the text. In other cases, gods can be assumed to be separate
individuals when they appear simultaneously in different locations or when they engage in
conversation as distinct entities. When these instances are taken into consideration, there
appear to be only three pairs of gods who actively participate in the creation—the Framer
and the Shaper, Sovereign and Quetzal Serpent, and Xmucane and Xpiyacoc. Without their
titles, the same six names appear together planning the creation on p. 68 (lines 137–144) and
again in connection with the creation of humankind on p. 197 (lines 4963–4968). Later in
the account, yet another god, Heart of Sky, will be named as the presiding deity who oversees
the work (pp. 70–72; lines 183–184).
[12] *Tz'aqol* (Framer) refers to one who makes something by putting things together (i.e.,
a building from stone or adobe, a meal from various ingredients, or a woven cloth from
individual threads).
[13] *B'itol* (Shaper) refers to one who makes something by modeling (i.e., pottery from clay,
or a sculpture from carved stone), thus giving shape to an otherwise amorphous substance.
The Framer and the Shaper are the most frequently mentioned gods involved in the creation
of the world and its inhabitants. Their names imply that the creation involved giving frame
and shape to matter that already existed rather than conjuring something out of nothing.
This pair of gods was so important that soon after the Spanish conquest, Father Domingo
de Vico used their Quiché names to refer to the God of the Old Testament (Carmack and
Mondloch 1983, 206).
[14] These are titles for the divine couple, Xmucane and Xpiyacoc (see p. 80; lines 557–558).
Ximénez translated their Quiché names, Alom and K'ajolom, as simply "Mother" and
"Father." A more accurate translation for Alom, however, is "She Who Has Borne Children,"
from the perfect aspect of the root verb *al* (to bear children). The name of the male god,
K'ajolom, specifically indicates his having begotten male offspring, thus "He Who Has
Begotten Sons." Fray Bartolomé de las Casas wrote in the sixteenth century that the people
of Guatemala worshiped as their principal gods "the Great Father and the Great Mother that
were in heaven," apparently referring to this divine couple (Las Casas 1967, III.cxxiv.650).

Peccary[17] and Coati,[18] Sovereign[19] and Quetzal Serpent,[20] Heart of Lake and Heart of Sea,[21] Creator of the Green Earth and Creator of the Blue Sky,[22] as they are called.

---

[15] Hunahpu Possum and Hunahpu Coyote are also likely titles for the gods Xpiyacoc and Xmucane (see pp. 79–80; lines 498–501). For a discussion of the etymology of the name Hunahpu, see footnote 163. *Wuch'* is the opossum (*Didelphis yucatanensis*), which appears later in the text presiding over the moments immediately preceding the rising of the sun (pp. 173–174; lines 4144–4151). In the Dresden Codex (Lee 1985, folios 25–28, pp. 51–52), the aged deity Mam, likely a lowland Maya version of Xpiyacoc, is depicted as a possum presiding over the five days of the Uayeb prior to the beginning of the new year. Father Thomás Coto, who compiled a dictionary of the closely related Cakchiquel-Maya language in the seventeenth century, mentions under the Spanish word *Escuridad*, that *vuch* is the darkness of night just prior to the dawn (Coto 1983, 207–8).

[16] *Utiw* is the coyote (*Canis latrans*), an animal also associated with the night.

[17] Saqi Nima Aq (Great White Peccary). The word *saqi* may be translated as "light, bright, or white." Later in the text (p. 98; line 1055), this same god is described as having very white hair due to his advanced age; thus "white" is the most likely translation here. In that same passage, "Great White Peccary" is given as one of the names or titles of the patriarchal creator god Xpiyacoc mentioned in the next paragraph. There are two species of peccary, or wild pig, living in Central America—*Peccari angulatus yucatanensis* (Collared Peccary) and *Tayassu pecari* (White-lipped Peccary). The latter is perhaps intended here because it is the larger of the two and is decorated with white facial markings.

[18] This is another name or title for the female creator goddess Xmucane, mentioned in the next paragraph (see p. 62; line 1056). The coati, or coatimundi, which inhabits tropical Central America is *Nasua narica yucatanica*. It is a raccoonlike animal with a long tail and a long, pointed, flexible snout.

[19] *Tepew* (Sovereign) is one of several words in the *Popol Vuh* that were borrowed from the central Mexican group of languages, Nahua, variants of which were spoken by both the epi-Toltec and Aztec nations. This word is the Quiché form of the Nahua *tepeuh*, meaning "conqueror" or "majesty" (Campbell 1970, 4). Coto and Basseta record that in the Colonial era, the Quichés recognized the word as referring to "majesty, dignity, lordship, power." Tedlock and Recinos translate the word as "sovereign," which I prefer to the more descriptive "majesty" used by Edmonson.

[20] Q'ukumatz may be translated as "Quetzal Serpent" or, less accurately, as "Feathered Serpent." Q'uq' refers to the quetzal bird, *Pharomacrus mocinno*, one of the most beautiful birds in the world. It inhabits the cloud forests of southern Mesoamerica between 3,000 and 4,000 feet in elevation. Both male and female have brilliantly colored iridescent blue/green feathers on their wings, tail, and crest, while their breasts are a bright crimson. The shade of blue or green depends on the angle of light striking its feathers. The male quetzal's tail feathers were highly prized by Maya royalty for their beauty and size, often reaching three feet in length. The unique coloration of the bird carried profound religious significance for the Maya. Its predominant blue/green feathers represented sky and vegetation, both symbols of life. Its red breast represented fire, the force that quickens life. *Kumatz* is a general term for "snake" or "serpent." The serpent was a common Maya symbol for regeneration or rebirth because of its tendency to periodically shed its skin to reveal a newer and brighter one. The combination of an avian lord of the skies with a serpentine lord of the earth and underworld gave this god power over all levels of the Maya universe. He is undoubtedly related to the well-known god Quetzalcoatl (Nahua for "Quetzal Serpent) worshiped by the Aztecs of Central Mexico.

[21] These are likely titles for Sovereign and Quetzal Serpent, who are associated with water

These collectively are evoked and given expression as the Midwife[23] and the Patriarch,[24] whose names are [25]Xpiyacoc[26] and Xmucane,[27] the

(see p. 68; lines 140–143; Recinos and Goetz 1953b, 76). *K'ux* may refer to either "heart" or "spirit." This pair of deities thus embodies the inward powers of large, standing bodies of water. The *Popol Vuh* states that prior to the creation the world consisted of a vast expanse of placid waters from which all things emerged (p. 67; lines 129–136).

[22] These are likely titles for Xpiyacoc and Xmucane (see p. 80; lines 565–566). They literally mean "blue/green plate" and "blue/green bowl." The Quiché language has only one word, *räx*, for both blue and green. When distinguishing between the colors, modern Quiché people are forced to say "*räx* like the sky" for blue, or "*räx* like a tree" for green. This same type of dichotomy appears here. The "blue/green plate" refers to the green surface of the earth covered with vegetation, and the arch of the sky is envisioned as an inverted "blue bowl." The earth is specifically likened to a plate on p. 71 (lines 205–206).

[23] Midwife and Patriarch are titles for Xmucane and Xpiyacoc (see p. 80; lines 536–537). I'yom may be literally translated as "She Who Has Had Grandchildren," but the word is also commonly used as an affectionate title for a midwife. I have chosen this interpretation here. The title of the goddess implies that she assists in the "birth" of the world.

[24] *Mamom* may also be translated as "He Who Has Had Grandchildren." In this case, it is more likely a title of respect for the god as a grandfatherly patriarch who oversees the creation. In modern Quiché society, *mamom* is a title used on occasion to refer to the head of patrilineage groups. They are often consulted on important family matters. They also participate directly in the rituals of marriage, the blessing and naming of children, and the consultation of dead ancestors to determine their will. Tedlock translates *Mamom* as "Matchmaker," since one of the intercessory tasks that such individuals have is to petition for the hand in marriage of a prospective bride on behalf of a member of his lineage (D. Tedlock 1996, 63, 217). This translation seems somewhat limited in its scope, however, considering the range of responsibilities held by the lineage patriarch.

[25] The names of the Midwife and Patriarch are given here as Xpiyacoc and Xmucane, but in reverse order. Throughout the *Popol Vuh*, female deities are listed before male deities when paired in parallel couplets. It thus makes little sense that Xpiyacoc, the name of the grandfather god, would be written before that of Xmucane, his female counterpart. This is an example of chiasmus, a form of reverse parallelism in which the first element of a strophe parallels the last, the second element parallels the next to last, etc. This arrangement, rather common in the text (see introductory section on poetics), tends to focus attention on the central elements, thus asserting their importance. The passage is thus arranged in the following way in lines 32–35 of the literal translation:

Midwife,	I'yom,
Patriarch,	Mamom,
Xpiyacoc,	Xpiyakok,
Xmucane, their names.	Xmuqane, u b'i'.

The name of the "Midwife" in line 32 is Xmucane, which appears in line 35. The name of the "Patriarch" in line 33 is Xpiyacoc, which appears in line 34. Edmonson, who believed that the *Popol Vuh* is arranged entirely in paired couplets, was confused by the order of the names Xpiacoc and Xmucane: "It is odd that this frequent couplet places the male first, the reverse of the usual Quiché order; indeed, if the reconstructed forms are correct, they would make better sense reversed" (Edmonson 1971, p. 5, n. 35). Recognition of the chiasmic nature of this passage clears up the confusion (see also p. 80; lines 538–541 for a repetition of this arrangement with regard to Xpiyacoc and Xmucane).

[26] Xpiyacoc is the male deity, while Xmucane serves as the divine female principal that brings about the creation. The derivation of the name Xpiyacoc is problematic. Edmonson suggests that it is based on the Nahua *yex-pa-ococc(an-e)*, which he reads as "thrice in

Protector[28] and the Shelterer,[29] Twice Midwife and Twice Patriarch, as they are called in Quiché traditions. They gave voice to all things and accomplished their purpose in purity of being and in truth.[30]

another two places," and relates it to the next phrase of the text in which this deity is referred to as "twice patriarch." Tedlock prefers that it should be read as a Quiché name, and that it is based on the verb *yekik/yakik*, which his Quiché collaborator interpreted as "to be put in order, to be lifted up" with regard to the problems of clients who are under treatment by *aj q'ij* priests. Perhaps the most likely derivation of this name is found at Rabinal where there is a design woven into textiles which locals call *piyakok* and identify as a turtle (Akkeren 2000, 207, 261–264). *Kok* is "turtle" in both lowland and highland Maya languages, making this an intriguing possibility. At Chichen Itza as well as Mayapan (both post-Classic sites likely contemporary with the early history of the Quichés), the aged grandfather earth deity (God N, Pauahtun, Bacab, Mam) wears a turtle carapace and bears up the sky (Taube 1992, 92–99; Schele and Mathews 1998, 214–218). Among the contemporary Kekchi and Pokomchi, this god is identified as the Mam (Grandfather), an earth deity who oversees the five day Uayeb period prior which precedes the beginning of the new year in the ancient calendric system. It is possible that Xpiyacoc is the Quiché version of this deity. Ultimately, a definitive etymology is impossible to determine. When proper names are passed down through generations of time, they often tend to become altered in their pronunciation, and perhaps their original meaning as well. If Xpiyacoc is derived from a Nahua original, it had certainly become mangled to the point where an Aztec envoy at the Quiché court would have had a difficult time coming up with an obvious meaning for it in his language. The same is true for Yucatec, Cholan, or Mam derivations for the name. There are similar-sounding words in each of these languages, although none are a precise fit. It is thus possible that the Quichés of the sixteenth century preserved the archaic spelling because they saw it simply as a proper name, without necessarily preserving memory of its original derivation (see also footnote 163 with regard to this phenomenon). I have chosen to leave such names untranslated.

[27] The name Xmucane may be derived from *x-* (feminine marker, diminutive) plus *muqik* (to bury, to cover, plant in the ground), thus giving a possible reading of "She Who Buries or She Who Plants," referring to the planting of a seed in the earth or a developing child in the womb. Ximénez wrote that native priests in his day called upon Xmucane and Xpiyacoc for inspiration, particularly concerning the birth of infants and midwifery (Ximénez 1929–31, I.i.6). Alternatively the name may be derived from the verb *muqunik* (to see, look). Xmucane and Xpiyacoc are referred to as seers several times in the text (see pp. 79–80; lines 511–517; 522–23). Akkeren suggests that the name should be derived from Yucatec and read as "Curved/Buried is your Tail." He associates her with a scorpion deity based on the name of a scorpion textile motif at Rabinal—*muqje* (tail in highland Maya languages is *je*, however its lowland Maya equivalent is *ne*), as well as an entry in the *Ritual of the Bacabs* referring to a scorpion entity as *bul moc a ne* (well-curved is your tail) (Arzápalo Marín 1987, 385–386; Akkeren 2000, 262–264). It may be fruitless to seek for a single meaning for such deity names as these. Particularly with regard to names and archaic words used in ceremonial contexts, Quichés derive a host of meanings from them, including puns and other word plays. Thus Barbara Tedlock points out that each named day in the traditional highland Maya calendar has a range of potential meanings, all of which are equally valid depending on context. For example, in interpreting a divinatory outcome, the meaning of the day *C'at* may be derived from *c'atic* (to burn), *pa c'at* (in nets), or *c'asaj c'olic* (to be in debt) (B. Tedlock 1982, 110). This is one reason I prefer to leave such names untranslated. Xmucane is likely the Quiché version of the grandmother goddess of the Maya lowlands (Goddess O, Chac Chel, Ix Chel). Like God N, the grandmother Goddess O is associated both with the forces of destruction and creation. On folio 74 of the Dresden Codex she is shown pouring out water from an inverted jar, symbolic of the destruction of the world by flood (Lee 1985, 77; Taube

This account we shall now write under the law of God[31] and Christianity.[32] We shall bring it forth because there is no longer the means whereby the Popol Vuh may be seen,[33] the means of seeing clearly that had come from across the sea—the account of our obscurity, and the means of seeing life clearly, as it is said. The original book exists that was written anciently,[34] but its witnesses and those who ponder[35] it hide their faces.[36]

1992, 101; Thompson 1972, 99). A skeletized version of this goddess wearing a crossed-bone skirt is paired with God N on the columns of the Lower Temple of the Jaguars at Chichen Itza. She is paired with God N as well on the upper columns of the Temple of the Warriors, suggesting a close association. Despite her destructive aspect, Goddess O is also considered the great creatrix, the principle deity of creation, divination, medicine, childbirth, midwifery, and weaving (Tozzer 1941, 129, 154; Taube 1992, 101; Akkeren 2000, 241), all aspects characteristic of the grandmother goddess Xmucane.

[28] Edmonson translated *matzanel* as "shelterer," while Tedlock translated it as "defender." A more literal translation would be "embracer," but with the implication that this embrace is meant to be protective in nature.

[29] The root verb, *ch'uq*, means "to cover." Thus, the translation "shelterer" refers to a deity who provides a protective shelter or cover.

[30] The phrase is *saqil k'olem, saqil tzij*. *Saqil* is a word laden with implied meanings in the Quiché language. These include "light, clarity, whiteness, brightness, and purity." *K'olem* is "existence, being," as well as the "nature or essence" of a thing. *Saqil tzij* is literally "white word, or truth," but it may also refer to "posterity, generation, or dynastic succession within a royal family." As a verb it means "to light" a fire or candle.

[31] *U ch'ab'al Dios* (his speech/language God). This phrase is often used in Roman Catholic sermons to refer to the doctrine, or preaching, of the Christian God. It also has a legalistic interpretation (law, declaration, proclamation), without religious overtones. The latter reading seems preferable as the *Popol Vuh* text is not written as a Christian doctrinal treatise.

[32] Here, the authors of the *Popol Vuh* confirm that they are compiling the ancient traditions of their people under the law of Christianity, imposed following the Spanish conquest. Surprisingly, *Dios* (God) and *Christianoil* (Christianity) are the only examples of Christian or Spanish-derived words in the *Popol Vuh* until the end of the text, where the arrival of the Spaniards is described. This lack of intrusive Spanish words argues for the purity of the text as an accurate record of Precolumbian cosmology and history. The *Popol Vuh* therefore stands in marked contrast to other post-Conquest highland Maya texts such as the *Annals of the Cakchiquels* and the *Título Totonicapán*, which contain numerous biblical and European cultural allusions using borrowed Spanish words. Although this passage acknowledges that the Quiché nation is subject to Christianity, the authors unabashedly describe the glory and wisdom of their ancient gods. Page 63 of the text (lines 44–45) declares that the Quiché gods act "in purity of being and in truth," perhaps indirectly contradicting the Christian missionaries of the time, who characterized such Maya deities as devils or demons.

[33] *Vuh* refers to Maya books, or codices painted on deerskin or bark paper. *Popol* is derived from the root *pop*, meaning "mat." Thus a literal translation would be "book that pertains to the mat." Within ancient Quiché society, a woven mat was used as a royal throne from which the king gave counsel to his people. The mat symbolized the power not only of the ruler, but also of his subjects. In this sense, the interlaced fibers of the mat represented the unity of the members within the community, linked inseparably in a common purpose. Thus Ximénez translated *popol* as "community," and the Motul Dictionary glosses *popol na* as a "community house." *Popol Vuh* might then be interpreted as "Book of the Community" or "Counsel Mat Book." I have chosen to leave the title untranslated, because no literal English equivalent

Great is its performance[37] and its account of the completion and germination[38] of all the sky and earth—its four corners and its four sides. All then was measured and staked out into four divisions, doubling over and stretching the measuring cords of the womb of sky and the womb of earth.[39] Thus were established the four corners, the four sides,[40] as it is said, by the Framer and the Shaper, the Mother and the Father[41] of life and all

could convey adequately its full meaning. I have kept the traditional spelling of the book's name, *Popol Vuh*, rather than the more modern orthographic spelling, *Popol Wuj*, since it is the original form used by the Quiché authors in the sixteenth century manuscript.

[34] This line apparently refers to a painted version of the *Popol Vuh* written prior to the Spanish conquest, which served as the inspiration for the text that survives today.

[35] *B'isonel* is generally "one who mourns or is unhappy." Coto notes that it may also refer to one who "ponders, considers, or has compassion."

[36] It is significant that this passage affirms that it is the "witness" and "ponderer" of the ancient book who "hide their faces," not the book itself. The authors of the *Popol Vuh* were anonymous, perhaps out of fear of persecution should the manuscript be discovered by the Spanish authorities. Edmonson suggests that the "witness" who hides his face may have been the author himself (Edmonson 1971, 7 n. 56). This reading also suggests that the Precolumbian version of the *Popol Vuh* may have still existed when the Quiché authors were compiling their alphabetic version.

[37] *Pe'oxik* refers to something which has been hired or rented. Dennis Tedlock convincingly suggests this refers to the hiring of persons to perform the text of the *Popol Vuh* as a drama (D. Tedlock 1996, 219, n. 63).

[38] *Tz'uk* is a term used for any type of birth (Coto), although it most often refers to the "birth" of plants in the form of germination or sprouting (Basseta, Varea).

[39] The gods thus laid out the extent of their creation by measuring its boundaries, driving stakes to mark its four corners, and stretching a measuring cord between the stakes. Andrés Xiloj, a modern Quiché *aj q'ij* priest who worked with Tedlock on his translation of the *Popol Vuh*, recognized the terminology of this passage and explained that the gods were measuring out the sky and earth as if it were a maizefield being laid out for cultivation (D. Tedlock 1996, 220). Vogt quoted a Tzotzil-Maya from Zinacantán as saying that the universe is "like a house, like a table," representing that which is systematic, and well-ordered (Vogt 1993, 11). Wisdom also recorded that the Chortí-Maya of Guatemala considered both the squared maize field and the shamanic altars on which traditionalist Maya priests conduct their divination rituals to be the world in miniature (Wisdom 1940, 430). By laying out the maize field, or setting up a ritual table, the Maya transform secular models into sacred space. With regard to the maize field, this charges the ground with the power of creation to bear new life. In a similar way, the divinatory table provides a stage on which sacred geography may be initimately studied, and even altered. Note that on pp. 81–82 (lines 565–623) the creator deities carry out a divinatory ceremony in an attempt to create the first human beings. A prominent Quiché *aj q'ij* priest, named Don Vicente de León Abac, described his work to me in this way: "When I am seated at my table, I am *aj nawal mesa* [of, or pertaining to, the spirit essence of the table]. My body is in the form of a cross just like the four sides of the world. This is why I face to the east and behind me is the west. My left arm extends out toward the north, and my right arm points to the south. My heart is the center of myself just as the arms of the cross come together to form its heart. My head extends upward above the horizon so that I can see far away. Because I am seated this way I can speak to Mundo [World]."

[40] Coto defines *xukut* as "side." Basseta defines it as "corner," in which case this would be synonymous with the preceding *tz'uk* (corner, angle).

creation,[42] the giver of breath[43] and the giver of heart,[44] they who give birth and give heart to the light everlasting,[45] the child of light born of woman and the son of light born of man,[46] they who are compassionate[47] and wise in all things—all that exists in the sky and on the earth, in the lakes and in the sea.

[41] When paired together, *chuch-qajaw* (mother-father) is the title for the highly respected head of a patrilineage group or the patriarchal founder of a patrilineage. If this couplet is meant as a single title, then the Framer and the Shaper are being addressed as the great founders of the family of all living. In modern Quiché society, traditionalist *aj q'ij* priests may refer to deity and ancestors as *chuch tat* (mother fathers) in their ritual prayers (Schultze-Jena 1954, 99).

[42] This word is a gerund derived from the verb *winaqirik*, which may be translated "to create or to generate." The root, *winaq*, means "people"; therefore a more literal translation would be "to people." The creation is thus seen as similar to the way people come to be, a natural process of giving birth.

[43] "Breath" is also a metaphor for "spirit," or that which constitutes a person's life force.

[44] *K'uxlanel* (literally "heartener"). The heart is the central defining essence of a person, or what might be referred to as the soul. Thus the creators are those who ensoul living things. In addition, the Quichés use "hearten" to refer to someone who provides for, looks after, tends to, or counsels someone. The verbal form of this word also has the sense of "to remember." In English this would be "bear in mind," but for the Quichés this would be conceived as "bear in heart."

[45] *Amaq'il*, when used as an adjective, is something that is "eternal, perpetual, everlasting."

[46] These are likely metaphors for the living. Thus in modern Quiché prayers, priests refer to the dead as *may k'ij may sákj*, "they who are hidden from the sun, hidden from the light" (Schultze-Jena 1954, 52).

[47] This is the same term, *aj b'is*, used to describe the "ponderer" of the *Popol Vuh* text in line 59. Coto notes that it not only describes one who ponders, but who does so with sympathy or compassion.

THE PRIMORDIAL WORLD[48]

THIS IS THE ACCOUNT of when all is still silent and placid.[49] All is silent and calm.[50] Hushed[51] and empty is the womb of the sky.

Figure 7. "Alone lies the expanse of the sea, along with the womb of all the sky." The Maya of the region consider Lake Atitlán to be the waters of creation from which all things emerged.

THESE, then, are the first words, the first speech. There is not yet one person, one animal, bird, fish, crab, tree, rock, hollow, canyon, meadow, or forest. All alone the sky exists. The face of the earth has not yet appeared. Alone lies the expanse of the sea, along with the womb of all the sky. There is not yet anything gathered together. All is at rest. Nothing stirs. All is languid, at rest in the sky. There is not yet anything standing erect. Only the expanse of the water, only the tranquil sea lies alone.[52] There is not yet

---

[48] lines 97–154

[49] The authors place the following description of the primordial world in the present tense, thus painting a picture of the stillness that existed prior to the creation as if in vision before their eyes.

[50] In the sixteenth-century Cakchiquel-Maya dictionary compiled by Francisco de Varea, *silee* refers to the calming of the wind after a storm (Varea 1929).

[51] *Lolinik* refers to hushed, undifferentiated sounds such as the rustling of leaves in the wind or the soft hum of insects in the night.

Figure 8. "Luminous they are in the water, wrapped in quetzal feathers and cotinga feathers. Thus they are called Quetzal Serpent." Serpent deity, redrawn from a Classic Maya cylinder vessel, ca. 750–850.

anything that might exist. All lies placid and silent in the darkness, in the night.

All alone are the Framer and the Shaper, Sovereign and Quetzal Serpent, They Who Have Borne Children and They Who Have Begotten Sons. Luminous[53] they are in the water,[54] wrapped in quetzal feathers and cot-

[52] This description of the world prior to the first creation is similar to Mixtec tradition as recorded by Fray Gregorio García in his *Origen de los Indios del Nuevo Mundo e Islas Occidentales*: "In the year and in the day of obscurity and utter darkness, before there were days and years, the world being in deep obscurity, when all was chaos and confusion, the earth was covered with water, there was only mud and slime on the surface of the earth" (León-Portilla 1980, 145).

[53] In his *Vocabulario de lengua quiche*, Domingo de Basseta interprets *zaktetoh* as "the brightness that enters through cracks." Thus the brightness of the gods is seen as shining between the feathers that envelop them.

[54] "Quetzal Serpent," whose Quiché name is traditionally written Qucumatz in colonial documents, is associated with water in most ancient highland Maya texts. According to the *Annals of the Cakchiquels*, a group of highland Maya called themselves Qucumatz because "they said that there was salvation only in the water" (Recinos and Goetz 1953, 59). Gagavitz, a legendary ancestor of the Cakchiquels, transformed himself into Qucumatz by throwing himself into a lake, thus causing a storm to agitate the water and form a whirlpool (Recinos and Goetz 1953, 76). Nuñez de la Vega wrote that the Quichés believed that Qucumatz is a serpent with feathers that moves in the water (Recinos 1950, 81 n. 2). The ancient Maya generally associated standing water with the underworld. Thus, the god Quetzal Serpent combines the contrasting powers of a celestial bird with a terrestrial serpent, the darkness of deep waters with the light of the upper world. Thus he transcends all levels of existence.

[55] The *räxon* (*Cotinga amabilis*), commonly known as the Lovely Cotinga, is a dovelike tropical bird with turquoise-blue plumage and a purple breast and throat. According to the *Annals of the Cakchiquels*, the highly prized feathers of the Lovely Cotinga were given as trib-

inga[55] feathers. Thus they are called Quetzal Serpent. In their essence, they are great sages, great possessors of knowledge. Thus surely there is the sky. There is also Heart of Sky,[56] which is said to be the name of the god.[57]

ute by the Cakchiquel clans to the lords of Tulan in the East (Recinos and Goetz 1953, 48).

[56] *U K'ux Kaj* (Heart of Sky—also called Huracan, cf. p. 70; lines 183–189), appears to be the principal god in the *Popol Vuh* account. He is the only deity to appear in every phase of the creation, as well as throughout the mythologic and historical portions of the text. *K'ux* refers to the heart as the source of the "vital spirit" of a thing, or that which gives it life. According to Coto's dictionary, it is also believed to be the center of thought and imagination. This deity, therefore, combines the powers of life and creativity, which are believed to exist in the midst of the heavens. During each creative period, Heart of Sky is the deity who first conceives the idea of what is to be formed. Other deities then carry out his will by giving it material expression.

[57] *K'ab'awil* (god) refers to the general concept of deity in the *Popol Vuh*. The word is used to refer to ancient gods such as Heart of Sky, as well as to the wood or stone effigies carved to represent them. Soon after the Spanish conquest, Dominicans chose the word *k'ab'awil* to refer to the Christian "God." Franciscans, on the other hand, rejected this usage of the word because of its earlier association with Precolumbian religion. This difference was a frequent point of contention between the two missionary orders during the early Colonial Period.

THE CREATION OF THE EARTH[58]

THEN came his word. Heart of Sky arrived here with Sovereign and Quetzal Serpent in the darkness, in the night. He spoke with Sovereign and Quetzal Serpent. They talked together then. They thought and they pondered. They reached an accord,[59] bringing together their words and their thoughts.[60] Then they gave birth, heartening one another. Beneath the light, they gave birth to humanity. Then they arranged for the germination and creation[61] of the trees and the bushes, the germination of all life and creation, in the darkness and in the night, by Heart of Sky, who is called Huracan.[62]

First is Thunderbolt Huracan, second is Youngest Thunderbolt,[63] and third is Sudden Thunderbolt.[64] These three together are Heart of Sky.[65] Then they came together with Sovereign and Quetzal Serpent. Together they conceived light and life:

[58] lines 155–274

[59] Literally "they found themselves."

[60] The creation is described as a unified effort by a number of gods, all acting in concert with one another after careful deliberation and planning. None can act alone without the direction and assistance of other deities. In Quiché society, lack of unity is seen as one of the chief causes of misfortune and failure. Disagreements are therefore quickly resolved through direct discussion or mediation by a respected elder.

[61] *Winaqirik*. The root of this verb is *winaq* (people), making it something like "to people." It is used however, to refer to the creation not only of humanity, but the earth, vegetation, animals, etc. Tedlock translates it as "generation" (D. Tedlock 1996, 65).

[62] The etymology of this god's name is too complex and obscure to give a definitive translation. In its simplest interpretation, *Juraqan* means "One Leg." Belief in a one-legged god was widespread throughout Precolumbian Mesoamerica. An important example was the Maya god K'awil (God GII of the Palenque Triad, who was often depicted with one anthropomorphic foot and the other a serpent), associated with kingship and the sky. *Raqan*, however, may also refer to the length or height of an object. The following line uses the name to refer to a bolt of lightning as a long flash of light. Coto interprets *raqan* as something "long or gigantic in size." According to Dennis Tedlock's Quiché collaborators, "leg" may also be used as a means of counting animate things, in the same way that we refer to the counting of "head" of cattle. "One Leg" might therefore mean "one of a kind" (D. Tedlock 1983a, 138). The god's name would thus refer to his unique nature as the essential power of the sky. In addition, the homophonous word *huracán* was used along the Gulf Coast of Mexico and the West Indies to refer to powerful swirling winds. The modern English hurricane may be derived from the Taino version of this word (Recinos 1950, 83 n. 7; Hunt 1977, 242; D. Tedlock 1996, 223). This interpretation is consistent with the god's nature as the "heart of the sky," the eye of the hurricane forming the divine axis around which time and creation revolve in endless repetitive cycles of birth and destruction.

[63] *Ch'i'p* refers to the youngest member of the family or the smallest member of a group.

"How shall it be sown? When shall there be a dawn for anyone? Who shall be a provider?[66] Who shall be a sustainer?[67]

"Then be it so. You are conceived. May the water be taken away, emptied out, so that the plate of the earth may be created—may it be gathered and become level. Then may it be sown; then may dawn the sky and the earth. There can be no worship, no reverence given by what we have framed and what we have shaped, until humanity has been created, until people have been made," they said.

Then the earth was created by them. Merely their word brought about the creation of it. In order to create the earth, they said, "Earth," and immediately it was created. Just like a cloud, like a mist, was the creation and formation[68] of it.

Then they called forth the mountains from the water. Straightaway[69] the great mountains came to be. It was merely their spirit essence,[70] their miraculous power,[71] that brought about the conception of the mountains

[64] *Räxa* (green, new, fresh, sudden). This is a sudden flash or bolt of lightning (Coto 1983, 479). It may also refer to the lightning's ability to renew or regenerate. In Santiago Atitlán, traditionalists believe that it is lightning that splits open maize seeds to allow them to germinate and bear new life (Christenson 2001, 72–74, 134).

[65] These three gods comprise the powers of the sky, symbolized by various aspects of the thunderbolt. Thunderstorms combine the elements of water (rain) and fire (lightning), which Quichés see as essential to all life. Lightning is also considered the force that fertilizes the earth and promotes the growth of crops. In modern Quiché society, lightning is believed to be the inspirational force of the sky. Modern *aj q'ij* priests take note of sensations within their bodies, which they call "lightning in the blood," and interpret them as revelatory messages (B. Tedlock 1982, 133–147). Although Quiché gods are normally named in pairs, there are occasional appearances of a trinity, as in this case. The principal gods of the three ruling Quiché lineages were Tohil, Auilix, and Hacavitz (see p. 223). Quiché temples generally had three entrances (for reconstruction drawings of such temples, see Carmack 1981, 270, 273). The idea of a trinity in Maya cosmology may be very ancient. The largest of the Maya centers built prior to the birth of Christ was El Mirador, located in the central Petén rain forest of Guatemala. Characteristic of its temples was a unique triadic pattern consisting of huge platforms, each surmounted by three pyramids.

[66] *Tzuqul* is a provider of any kind, although generally in the sense of food. Barbara Tedlock notes that one of the names for priest-shamans in Momostenango is *tzuqunel* (feeder) because he symbolically "feeds" the Mundo [Spanish "World," the principal earth deity] and his own ancestors with their ceremonies (B. Tedlock 1982, 114). A fundamental aspect of indigenous highland Maya religion is the belief that human beings stand as essential mediators between this world and that of their patron deities and ancestors. Sacred ritual, performed at the proper time and in a manner established by ancient precedent, is necessary to maintain this link or all creation runs the risk of collapse.

[67] *Q'o'l* is one who provides sustenance, primarily in the form of nourishment, but also nurtures in any other way, such as a mother caring for an infant.

[68] There is no English equivalent for the verb *pupuje'ik*. According to the colonial era dictionary compiled by Fr. Domingo de Basseta, the word means "the way in which clouds rise up from mountains."

Figure 9. "First the earth was created, the mountains and the valleys. The waterways were divided, their branches coursing among the mountains." Highland stream near Xetzak, Cunen.

and the valleys.[72] Straightaway were created cypress groves and pine forests to cover the face of the earth.

Thus Quetzal Serpent rejoiced:

"It is good that you have come, Heart of Sky—you, Huracan, and you as well, Youngest Thunderbolt and Sudden Thunderbolt. That which we have framed and shaped shall turn out well," they said.

[69] *Ju suk'.* Basseta translates this as "quickly, instantly." It literally means "one straight," somewhat like our English phrases "straightaway," or "directly."

[70] *Nawal* also has no English equivalent. In Quiché theology, all things, both living and inanimate, have a spirit essence which they call *nawal.* This spirit essence is believed to give them power to act or communicate on a supernatural plane, for example, to transform their usual form into that of a powerful animal or force of nature. Father Coto ascribes this power to the devil, defining the word *naual* as "the magical means whereby the devil spoke to the Quichés through their idols. Thus they would say that the life of the tree, the life of the stone, of the hill, is its *naual,* because they believed there was life in these objects. If a man asks his wife for something to eat or drink when there is nothing in the house, the wife would reply, *xa pe ri tin naualih?* (Do you expect me to perform miracles?)" (Coto 1983, 328, 369). Although *nawal* is borrowed from the Nahua language, where it means "to transform" (Campbell 1983, 84), the Quiché interpretation of the word is derived from the root *na',* meaning "to feel" or "to know." Thus the creation took place by means of the power of the gods' spirit essence or divine knowledge rather than by physical action.

First the earth was created, the mountains and the valleys. The waterways were divided, their branches coursing among the mountains. Thus the waters were divided, revealing the great mountains. For thus was the creation of the earth, created then by Heart of Sky and Heart of Earth, as they are called. They were the first to conceive it. The sky was set apart. The earth also was set apart within the waters. Thus was conceived the successful completion of the work when they thought and when they pondered.

[71] *Pus* is a loan word from ancient Mixe-Zoque (Campbell 1983, 83), likely the language of the Olmecs who dominated the Gulf Coast region from ca. 1500–400 BC. It refers to the cutting of flesh, and specifically to the practice of human sacrifice. In Colonial period Quiché texts, the word is often paired with the word *nawal* to describe the supernatural power of deities to accomplish what ordinary humans cannot. In the first years after the Spanish conquest, Roman Catholic missionaries adopted the word to describe the power of the Christian God to forgive sins and offer his body as a sacrament (Coto 1983, 424). This use of the word was soon abandoned, however, because of the word's association with ancient Maya gods and their ceremonies. Father Coto thus defines *pus* as "magic, enchantment, necromancy, or witchcraft," thereby associating the people's belief in the power of the Quiché gods with evil and sorcery (Coto 1983, 74, 180, 328, 369).

[72] *Juyub'-Taq'aj* (Mountain-Plain) is an example of merismus, the expression of a broad concept by a pair of complementary elements that are narrower in scope. This pairing is commonly used among present-day Quichés to refer to the earth as a whole. This not only comprises the physical contrast of elevations versus valleys, but also the notion of wilderness versus cultivated land (Cook 2000, 75).

THE CREATION OF THE ANIMALS[73]

THEN were conceived the animals of the mountains, the guardians of the forest,[74] and all that populate the mountains—the deer[75] and the birds, the puma[76] and the jaguar,[77] the serpent[78] and the rattlesnake,[79] the pit viper[80] and the guardian of the bushes.

She Who Has Borne Children and He Who Has Begotten Sons then asked:

"Shall it be merely solitary, merely silent beneath the trees and the bushes? It is well that there shall be guardians for them," they said.

Thus they considered and spoke together, and immediately were created the deer and the birds. Having done this, they then provided homes for the deer and the birds:

"You, deer, will sleep along the courses of rivers and in the canyons. Here you will be in the meadows and in the orchards. In the forests you shall multiply. You will walk on all fours, and thus you will be able to stand," they were told.

Then they established the homes of the birds, both small and great.

"You, birds, you will make your homes and your houses in the tops of trees, and in the tops of bushes. There you will multiply and increase in numbers in the branches of the trees and the bushes," the deer and the birds were told.

---

[73] lines 275–339

[74] Quichés believe that the wild animals of the forest serve as guardians and caretakers for the god of the earth, who is usually referred to as *Juyub'-Taq'aj* (Mountain-Plain) or *Dios Mundo* (Spanish for "God Earth). He is often described as a kindly, old, white-haired man who lives in the uninhabited forests. When hunting deer, drinking from a mountain stream, or clearing a field for planting crops, permission must first be obtained from the earth god and appropriate payment made in the form of prayers and offerings. If the proper offerings are not made, the earth god might send one of his wild animals to attack the ungrateful person or to raid his property.

[75] Most likely the white-tailed deer (*Odocoileus americana toltecus*).

[76] The Central American mountain lion or cougar (*Felis concolor*).

[77] *Panthera onza.*

[78] This may refer to the boa constrictor (*Constrictor constrictor*) or the venomous bushmaster (*Lechesis muta*).

[79] *Crotalus durissus.*

[80] *K'an Ti'* (Yucatec or Cholan: "Yellow Mouth") is a pit viper, likely the cantil or *fer-de-lance* (*Bothrops asper*), which is extremely poisonous (Cook 2000, 166). Its name is perhaps derived from the yellow markings around the mouth of the *fer-de-lance* (D. Tedlock 1996, 228 n. 66). Basseta records that it may be any venomous serpent and lists specifically the coral snake. I have used pit viper which covers the range of venomous vipers living in the Maya region.

When this had been done, all of them received their places to sleep and their places to rest. Homes were provided for the animals on the earth[81] by She Who Has Borne Children and He Who Has Begotten Sons. Thus all was completed for the deer and the birds.

Figure 10. "You, birds, you will make your homes and your houses in the tops of trees, and in the tops of bushes." Water bird, redrawn from a Classic Maya ceramic plate.

[81] No animals other than the deer and birds are mentioned as having received their homes and sleeping places. Thus the deer and birds represent all the animals of the earth, indicating their symbolic importance as the primary guardians of earth and sky.

THE FALL OF THE ANIMALS[82]

THEN it was said to the deer and the birds by the Framer and the Shaper, She Who Has Borne Children and He Who Has Begotten Sons:

"Speak! Call! Don't moan or cry out. Speak to one another, each according to your kind, according to your group," they were told—the deer, the birds, the pumas, the jaguars, and the serpents.

Figure 11. "Your calling will merely be to have your flesh eaten." Deer marked for death with crossed bones, redrawn from a Maya ceramic vessel.

"Speak therefore our names. Worship[83] us, for we are your Mother and your Father. Say this, therefore: 'Huracan, Youngest Thunderbolt, and Sudden Thunderbolt, Heart of Sky and Heart of Earth, Framer and Shaper, She Who Has Borne Children and He Who Has Begotten Sons.' Speak! Call upon us! Worship us!" they were told.

But they did not succeed. They did not speak like people. They only squawked and chattered and roared. Their speech was unrecognizable,[84] for each cried out in a different way.

---

[82] lines 340–433

[83] *Q'ijarisaj* (to worship) is derived from the root *q'ij* (day or sun) in a transitive imperative verb form (cause to be). If such a word existed in English, it might be something like "dayify" (to honor their day, perhaps through calendric ceremonies) or "sunify" (to glorify the gods like the glory of the sun). The gods' purpose in carrying out the creation seems to be to provide beings who will be able to speak intelligibly. Only in this way could the gods be worshiped properly—through the articulation of their names with human speech. Page 80 (lines 534–535) emphasizes that "words" are the gods' support.

When they heard this,[85] the Framer and the Shaper said, "Their speech did not turn out well."

And again they said to each other:

"They were not able to speak our names. We are their Framer and their Shaper. This is not good," said She Who Has Borne Children and He Who Has Begotten Sons to each other.

They were therefore told:

"You shall be replaced because you were not successful. You could not speak. We have therefore changed our word. Your food and your sustenance, your sleeping places and your places to rest, that which belonged to you, shall be in the canyons and the forests.

"Nevertheless, because you have not been able to worship us or call upon us, there will yet be someone else who may be a worshiper. We shall now make one who will give honor. Your calling will merely be to have your flesh eaten. Thus be it so. This must be your service,"[86] they were told. Thus were commanded the animals, both small and great, that were upon the face of the earth.

Then they wanted to test again their fate. They wanted to make another attempt. They wanted to try again to arrange[87] for those who would worship them.

The speech of the animals could not be understood. Because of the way they were made, they were not successful.[88] Therefore their flesh was brought low. They were made to serve. The animals that were on the face of the earth were eaten and killed.

[84] Literally "not appeared its face their speech."

[85] Literally "try again their day." *Q'ij* (day, sun) has a host of associated meanings. As Barbara Tedlock writes, "each day has 'its face,' its identity, its character, that influences its events; a person's luck of the moment, or even his fate in general, is called 'the face of his day' (B. Tedlock 1982, 2).

[86] *Patan* in this context is a required service, the same word being used for tribute payments.

[87] *Nuk'* is to arrange for something, but it also means "to experiment or test," implying a level of uncertainty that matches the previous two phrases, forming a triplet.

[88] The principal reason for the downfall of the first created beings was their inability to communicate in human speech, so the gods could not be worshiped with intelligible words. Each subsequent unsuccessful creation will be destroyed for the same reason.

THE CREATION OF
THE MUD PERSON[89]

THUS there was another attempt to frame and shape man by the Framer and the Shaper, by She Who Has Borne Children and He Who Has Begotten Sons:

"Let us try again before the first sowing, before the dawn approaches. Let us make a provider, a sustainer for us. How shall we then be called upon so that we are remembered upon the face of the earth? We have already made a first attempt with what we have framed and what we have shaped. But we were not successful in being worshiped or in being revered by them. Thus, let us try again to make one who will honor us, who will respect us; one who will be a provider and a sustainer," they said.

Then was the framing, the making of it. Of earth and mud was its flesh composed. But they saw that it was still not good. It merely came undone and crumbled. It merely became sodden and mushy.[90] It merely fell apart and dissolved. Its head was not set apart properly.[91] Its face could only look in one direction. Its face was hidden. Neither could it look about. At first it spoke, but without knowledge.[92] Straightaway it would merely dissolve in water, for it was not strong.

Then said the Framer and the Shaper:

"We have made a mistake; thus let this be merely a mistake.[93] It cannot walk, neither can it multiply. Then let it be so. Let it be merely left behind as a thing of no importance,"[94] they said.

---

[89] lines 434–517

[90] *Lub'anik* refers to vegetables that have been boiled so long they have become soft and mushy.

[91] The fact that the head was not placed apart from the body indicates that it did not have a neck with which to turn its head.

[92] When the first Spanish missionaries arrived among the Maya they vigorously suppressed Precolumbian documents such as the *Popol Vuh* and replaced them with doctrinal treatises based on the Bible. Many of these, such as the *Theologia Indorum* by Domingo de Vico, stressed the creation account of Genesis. I can't help but wonder if the first Maya to hear these sermons found it strangely logical that these foreign priests, who burned their books and did not speak their language, were declared to be "formed from the dust of the ground," made soft by a mist that "watered the whole face of the ground" (Genesis 2:6–7). Did the Maya think, "Ah, they're mud people. They speak but without knowledge and understanding."

[93] *Lab'e* is a "mistake, fault, defect, deformed child, or monster." It is also used to indicate a bad omen.

[94] According to Coto, *na'oj chi ri'* means "leave behind; of little importance."

Therefore they undid it. They toppled what they had framed, what they had shaped.

Then they said again:

"How then will we truly make that which may succeed and bear fruit; that will worship us and that will call upon us?" they asked.

Then they thought again:

"We shall merely tell Xpiyacoc and Xmucane, Hunahpu Possum and Hunahpu Coyote, 'Try again a divination,[95] a shaping,'" said the Framer and the Shaper to each other.

Then they called upon Xpiyacoc and Xmucane, and in this manner were the seers[96] addressed: "Grandmother of Day, Grandmother of Light!" In this way, they were addressed by the Framer and the Shaper, for these are the names of Xpiyacoc and Xmucane.

Figure 12. "Of earth and mud was its flesh composed. But they saw that it was still not good. It merely came undone and crumbled." Terra cotta head of a Classic Maya lord, San Antonio Museum of Art.

[95] *Q'ijixik*, which might be translated "dayification," refers to a divinatory ceremony in which a handful of *tz'ite* beans or grains of maize (cf. 573–574) are cast and then interpreted by a sequential counting of the days of the Quiché ritual calendar. Thus the outcome of the creation is to be ritually determined through a divinatory "counting of days." This practice was apparently widespread in ancient Mesoamerica. The Codex Borbonicus from Central Mexico depicts two aged deities casting seeds of maize or *tz'ite* in a divinatory ceremony (folio 21). Calendar divination is still a common practice among the highland Maya.

[96] According to Basseta, *nicvachinel* refers to a "soothsayer, diviner, fortuneteller," based on the root verb *nicoh* (to see, or look ahead). Coto adds that a *niq vachinel* is one who sees well, or divines by means of lots, which, in fact, Xpiyacoc and Xmucane practice on pp. 81–82 (lines 583–623). The implication is that Xpiyacoc and Xmucane were able to see with divine foresight.

THE CREATION OF THE
EFFIGIES OF CARVED WOOD[97]

HURACAN, along with Sovereign and Quetzal Serpent, then spoke to the Master of Days[98] and the Mistress of Shaping, they who are seers:

"It shall be found; it shall be discovered how we are to create shaped and framed people who will be our providers and sustainers. May we be called upon, and may we be remembered. For it is with words that we are sustained, O Midwife and Patriarch, our Grandmother and our Grandfather, Xpiyacoc and Xmucane. Thus may it be spoken. May it be sown. May it dawn so that we are called upon and supported, so that we are remembered by framed and shaped people, by effigies[99] and forms[100] of people. Hearken and let it be so.

"Reveal your names, Hunahpu Possum and Hunahpu Coyote, Great She Who Has Borne Children and Great He Who Has Begotten Sons, Great Peccary and Great Coati, Jeweler and Worker in Precious Stones, Sculptor and Wood Worker, Creator of the Green Earth and Creator of the Blue Sky, Incense[101] Maker and Master Artist,[102] Grandmother of Day and Grandmother of Light. Thus shall you all be called by that which we shall

---

[97] lines 518–679

[98] *Aj q'ij* is still the title used by Quiché priests who divine the will of deity through a ritual counting of the days in the sacred calendar. The title means literally "he/she of days," or "master of days," although modern ethnographers often refer to them as "daykeepers." Because Xmucane and Xpiyacoc assisted in the creation of the universe at the beginning of time, thus setting in motion the endless cycles of day and night, birth and death, sowing and harvest, they stand as the ideal interpreters through divination of these cycles.

[99] *Poy* is any type of created image that resembles a human— an effigy, doll, manikin, scarecrow, etc.

[100] According to Basseta, *anom* is something that is created in the image of something else, a "model or form," often made by means of a mould. It is also used to refer to a "fool, buffoon, or someone who is lightminded and unserious." These words presage the falseness and lack of intelligence characteristic of the wooden effigies that are soon to be created.

[101] *Q'ol.* This is tree sap, the most common source of incense among the Maya. This word most commonly refers to pine resin incense, although it may be used for other types as well.

[102] The Quiché title *Aj Toltecat* is given to anyone who is highly skilled in art, science, religion, and creative endeavors in general. *Toltecat* refers specifically to the ancient Toltecs, who, under the legendary priest-ruler Topiltzin Quetzalcoatl, founded the city of Tula in Central Mexico in the tenth century a.d. Although the city fell some two centuries later, the fame of its people was passed from generation to generation, undoubtedly embellished significantly with each retelling. At the time of the Spanish conquest, the ancient Toltecs had achieved an almost mythic reputation as masters in all the arts. The Aztecs gave the following description in folio 172v of the Codex Matritensis:

Figure 13. "Thus began the divination ceremony, the casting of grains of maize and of tz'ite, the revelation of days and of shaping." Divination ceremony using grains of maize at Chutinamit, near Santiago Atitlán.

frame and shape. Cast[103] grains of maize and tz'ite[104] to divine how what we shall make will come out when we grind and chisel out its mouth and face in wood,"[105] so it was said to the Masters of Days.

> The Toltecs were a skillful people;
> all of their works were good, all were exact,
> all well made and admirable.
>
> Their houses were beautiful, with turquoise mosaics,
> the walls finished with plaster,
> clean and marvelous houses, which is to say
> Toltec houses, beautifully made,
> beautiful in everything...
>
> Painters, sculptors, carvers of precious stones,
> feather artists, potters, spinners, weavers,
> skillful in all they made....
>
> The Toltecs were truly wise;
> they conversed with their own hearts....
> They played their drums and rattles;
> They were singers, they composed songs
> and sang them among the people;
> They guarded the songs in their memories,
> they deified them in their hearts. (León-Portilla 1980, 207)

Thus began the divination ceremony, the casting of grains of maize and of tz'ite, the revelation of days and of shaping. Then spoke the one Grandmother and the one Grandfather to them.

For this was the Grandfather, the Master of the Tz'ite, Xpiyacoc by name. And this was the Grandmother, the Mistress of Days[106] and Mistress of Shaping who is at the foot,[107] who is called Xmucane.

Thus they began to speak, to carry out their divination ceremony:

"May it be discovered. May it be found. Say it! Our ears hear you. Speak! Tell it! May the tree be found that is to be carved and chiseled out by the Framer and the Shaper. If this is to be the provider and the sustainer, then may it now be sown that the dawn may come. You, grains of maize, and you, tz'ite; you, days, and you, the shaping—you are called,[108] you are summoned."[109] Thus it was said[110] to the grains of maize and the tz'ite, to the days and the shaping.

"Bring it to a conclusion, [111] O Heart of Sky. Do not punish them further.[112] Do not cause any more suffering for Sovereign and Quetzal Serpent," they said.

Then they spoke straight to the point:[113]

---

[103] *Mala'* (to cast) refers not only to the scattering of the grains of maize or *tz'ite*, but also to the act of gently passing the hand over the pile of grains to mix them prior to their use in divination ceremonies (for a description of this ceremony see Schultze-Jena 1954; B. Tedlock 1982).

[104] *Tz'ite* is the bright-red beanlike seed of the coral tree (Spanish: *palo de pito* tree; *Erythrina corallodendron*). The seeds are used in divination ceremonies. Just as in the *Popol Vuh* manuscript, modern Quiché *aj q'ij* priests may use maize kernels or *tz'ite* seeds for such divinations. *Tz'ite* seeds are often referred to metaphorically as maize as well (Schultze-Jena 1954, 84; B. Tedlock 1982, 84).

[105] Each of the first three creative attempts used a different class of material—animal (wild beasts and birds), mineral (mud), and vegetable (wood).

[106] In Momostenango the ideal is for married couples to act as the agents in such ceremonies, similar to the tradition of Xpiyacoc and Xmucane (B. Tedlock 1982, 85).

[107] *Chi raqan* may mean either "at the foot" or "at the leg" since the Quiché language does not distinguish between the foot and the leg. Although Dennis Tedlock translates this phrase somewhat inaccurately as "who stands behind others," I agree with his interpretation that Xmucane in her role as a female *aj q'ij* (daykeeper) positions herself at the feet of the petitioner so as to give assistance "as a daykeeper does when praying and giving offerings on behalf of a client, or a midwife does when assisting a birth" (D. Tedlock 1996, 234 n. 70).

[108] According to Basseta, *chokonik* refers to "calling," in the sense of being called upon to carry out an errand.

[109] *Taqentaj* is "to be summoned, commissioned, dispatched, given a task to fulfill, or be sent out as a messenger."

[110] Modern *aj q'ij* priests also speak directly to the *tz'ite* as they carry out their divinatory ceremonies, urging them to give an accurate and true answer to their petition.

[111] *K'ix* is "to complete, finish, conclude, or come to a solution" (Varea). As a noun, the word refers to a thorn, spine, or insect sting. When used as a verb, it is one of the words used to describe drawing blood in auto-sacrificial ceremonies. In this passage, it is possible that

"May these effigies of wood come out well. May they speak. May they communicate there upon the face of the earth. May it be so," they said.

And when they had spoken, straightaway the effigies[114] of carved wood were made. They had the appearance of people and spoke like people as well. They populated the whole face of the earth. The effigies of carved wood began to multiply, bearing daughters and sons.

Nevertheless, they still did not possess their hearts nor their minds. They did not remember their Framer or their Shaper.[115] They walked without purpose.[116] They crawled on their hands and knees and did not remember Heart of Sky. Thus they were weighed in the balance. They were merely an experiment, an attempt at people. At first they spoke,

Figure 14. "And when they had spoken, straightaway the effigies of carved wood were made." Classic Period wooden figure from Tabasco, Metropolitan Museum of Art.

both meanings are intended. In Mesoamerican theology, gods of the creation often sacrifice themselves in order to provide the sacred blood necessary to produce new life.

[112] The phrase *mak'ajisaj u chi', u wach* (don't grind up his mouth, his face) is a common expression meaning something like "don't punish him" or "don't teach him a hard lesson." Heart of Sky is thus being counseled not to cause Sovereign and Quetzal Serpent any more grief with further failures to successfully create beings who can worship and support them. Perhaps a bit of frustration at the gods' lack of success up to this point is evident in this address by Xpiyacoc and Xmucane to Heart of Sky. The Quichés are known for their directness in prayer. When a perceived injustice takes place in the life of a petitioner, he/she may well complain directly to the god who has responsibility for that malady and insist bluntly that things be made right. Bunzel suggests that Quiché deities are generally neutral entities, and thus "subject to bribery, cajolery and threats" (Bunzel 1952, 267). I heard one farmer bitterly accuse the earth god of taking a tool of his, even though the man had made all the appropriate offerings, and demand that it be returned immediately. Modern *aj q'ij* priests repeatedly admonish the gods to tell the truth and not *b'an tzij* (make words or lie).

[113] Literally "they spoke its straightness."

[114] *Poy* refers to any effigy fashioned in the likeness of a human, such as a doll or scarecrow. Tedlock translates the word as "manikin," Recinos as "figure," and Edmonson as "doll."

[115] Again, the cause of the downfall of this attempt at humanity is their failure to *remember* the gods and thus worship them properly.

[116] According to Basseta, *xaloq'* is something "without cause, without purpose, in vain." Tedlock's Quiché collaborator remarked that this phrase indicates that the wooden effigies were "like animals," because humans must ask permission of the gods to travel any significant distance (D. Tedlock 1996, 234, n. 70).

but their faces were all dried up. Their legs and arms were not filled out. They had no blood or blood flow[117] within them. They had no sweat or oil. Their cheeks were dry, and their faces were masks.[118] Their legs and arms were stiff. Their bodies were rigid.[119] Thus they were not capable of understanding[120] before their Framer and their Shaper, those who had given them birth and given them hearts. They were the first numerous people who have lived here upon the face of the earth.

[117] The text lists two parallel words here, *kik'el* and *komajil*, both of which mean "blood." Basseta mentions that *komaj* may specifically refer to menstruation, or menstrual blood flow.

[118] Quichés consider the face to be the symbol for the personality or essence of a person. The fact that the wooden effigies had masks rather than faces implies that they were false by nature.

[119] The word *yeyoj* means both "rigid" as well as "stubborn."

[120] *Na'wik.* This is the capacity to understand, notice, observe, perceive. Thus it is the wooden effigies' inability to learn and grow in knowledge that destroys them. *Na'b'al* (understanding, knowledge, memory) is a uniquely human trait. A resident of Santiago Chimaltenango noted that even a newborn baby has *naab'l*. But although animals may have a kind of awareness, they lack *naab'l* (Watanabe 1992, 82). Watanabe suggests that the notion of *naab'l* includes the larger concepts of soul, socialization, learning, and conventions of Chimalteco morality (Ibid., 100). Thus, the effigies of wood lack the essential awareness, and understanding that are characteristic of human beings. In this sense, they are like the animals who were not able to remember or honor the gods properly and were thus destroyed.

THE FALL OF THE
EFFIGIES OF CARVED WOOD[121]

THEN came the end of the effigies carved of wood, for they were ruined, crushed,[122] and killed. A flood was planned by Heart of Sky that came down upon the heads of the effigies carved of wood.[123]

The body of man had been carved of tz'ite wood[124] by the Framer and the Shaper. The body of woman consisted of reeds[125] according to the desire of the Framer and the Shaper. But they were not capable of understanding and did not speak before their Framer and their Shaper, their makers and their creators.

Thus they were killed in the flood. There came a great resin down from the sky.[126]

There came the ones called Chiselers of Faces, who gouged out their eyes.[127] There came Death Knives,[128] which cut off their heads. There came Crouching[129] Jaguar, who ate their flesh. There came Striking[130] Jaguar, who struck them. They smashed their bones and their tendons.[131]

Figure 15. "A flood was planned by Heart of Sky that came down upon the heads of the effigies carved of wood." The destruction of the world by flood, from the Dresden Codex, p. 74 (Villacorta and Villacorta 1930).

---

[121] lines 680–837

[122] *Q'utuxik* is "to be crushed or pulverized," generally with reference to dried vegetables like chili peppers.

[123] The destruction of the earth by flood prior to our present age was a widespread tradition in Mesoamerica: "There was among them information of the flood and of the end of the world, and they called it Butic, which is the word which means flood of many waters and means 'judgment,' and so they believe that another Butic is about to come, which is another flood and judgment, not of water, but of fire, which they say would be the end of the world,

Their bones were ground up. They were broken into pieces. Their faces were ground up[132] because they proved to be incapable of understanding before the face of their mother and the face of their father, Heart of Sky, Huracan by name.[133]

in which all the creatures would reprove, especially those which serve man, like the stones on which they grind their corn and wheat, the pots, the vessels, giving to understand that they will turn against man, and that the moon and sun would be eclipsed, saying that they would be eaten" (Las Casas 1967, III.ccxxxv.507; cf. III.cxxiv.650. Translation by author). The Yucatec Maya *Book of Chilam Balam of Chumayel* records that the people of that age "were buried in the sand at the shore of the sea, in the waves. Then in a great sheet of water the waves came. When the great serpent was taken away, the heavens fell and the earth was submerged" (León-Portilla 1969, 50; cf. Roys 1967, 170). Aztec tradition also has the inhabitants of the fourth age of the earth destroyed by flood: "These are those who lived in the fourth Sun, called 4–Water. They lived 676 years, until they were destroyed. They were swallowed up by the waters and became fish. The heavens collapsed upon them and in a single day they perished" (Velázquez 1945, 119–120). Although the *Popol Vuh* has the wooden effigies destroyed in a flood (see also p. 85; lines 706–709, 728–731), lines 710–723 have them crushed and devoured by monstrous beasts, while lines 736–823 describe their ruin at the hands of their own domesticated animals, grinding stones, utensils, and other possessions.

[124] In highland Guatemala, the wood of the *tz'ite* (coral tree) is still considered to have extraordinary power, including the ability to speak (Orellana 1984, 98). In the Tz'utujil-Maya village of Santiago Atitlán, traditionalists venerate an effigy carved of *tz'ite* wood that they call Maximon (Ancient One Who Is Bound) or alternatively Mam (Ancient One). The trunk of this effigy is approximately 2.5 feet in height and 6–8 inches thick, with separate pieces of wood attached to form the head and legs. A carved mask with a roughly hewn face is tied about the head (cf. p. 84; lines 668–669). This effigy is said to be more ancient than Christ, having been created "in the beginning of time, or of the world" (Mendelson 1959, 58, 60). Maximon is considered old and often malignant, standing in opposition to the established order of the community. He is thus associated with forgetfulness (B. Tedlock 1982, 101; cf. p. 83; lines 652–653, 656–657), hunger, sterility, sexual depravity (Thompson 1970, 299; Mendelson 1958b, 9), and opposition to life deities. He is particularly prominent during Easter celebrations, in which he presides over the death and entombment of Jesus Christ (Mendelson 1959, 1965; Tarn and Prechtel 1997; Christenson 2001, 176–191). The Maximon figure may be a remembrance of the chaotic world prior to the creation of humankind, when the gods were not remembered or worshiped properly by effigies carved from *tz'ite* wood. Cook suggests that Maximon's opposition to Christ represents a kind of "underground survival of powers from earlier, superseded epochs" (Cook 2000, 139–140).

[125] This is the type of reed commonly used for weaving mats in Guatemala (*Typha angustifolia*).

[126] Some confusion appears in the text as to the nature of the flood that destroyed the wooden effigies. Here the flood is composed of resin, sap, or turpentine (secretions of pine trees). Page 87 (lines 728–731) however describes a watery flood caused by heavy rainfall.

[127] *U b'aq' u wach* (its seed his/her face) refers to the eyes.

[128] *Lotz* is a knife used in butchering or surgery, although the word may also refer to the act of cutting flesh.

[129] "Crouching," as if lying in ambush.

[130] *Tukuj* is "to strike something violently, with the intention of breaking it."

[131] *Ib'och'il* may refer to "tendons, blood vessels, or nerves." I have chosen "tendons" because this word best parallels bones as a stiff supporting structure of the body.

[132] To "grind someone's face" is a metaphor for inflicting punishment.

[133] The violent destruction of the wooden effigies is perhaps commemorated in the dis-

Thus they caused the face of the earth to be darkened, and there fell a black rain,[134] a rain that fell both day and night. The small and the great animals came in upon them.[135] Their faces were crushed by the trees and the stones. They were spoken to by all their maize grinders and their cooking griddles,[136] their plates and their pots, their dogs[137] and their grinding stones.[138] However many things they had, all of them crushed their faces.

Their dogs and their turkeys[139] said to them:

"Pain you have caused us. You ate us. Therefore it will be you that we will eat now."

Then the grinding stones said this to them:

"We were ground upon by you. Every day, every day, in the evening and at dawn, always you did *holi, holi, huki, huki*[140] on our faces. This was our

membement of the Maximon figure at Santiago Atitlán (see previous note on the *tz'ite*-wood figures). Maximon is a figure of carved *tz'ite*-wood prominently displayed at times of crisis, such as during the death of Christ at Easter or at harvest time, when the crops are ceremonially "killed." When Christ rose from the dead and life restored to the world at the climax of such festivals, Maximon was ritually defeated by disassembling the wooden pieces of his body, removing his mask, and placing it upside down so that he cannot harm anyone and so that he will be left "without power of speech" (Mendelson 1965, 123). In other highland Maya communities, figures representing Maximon are torn apart, hung from trees, or burned. I saw one particularly evil-looking Maximon near the town of Sololá slashed repeatedly with a machete and thrown out onto a highway so that cars and buses would run over it.

[134] "Black" in the sense that the storm was so severe that the sky was darkened with clouds.

[135] The implication is that the wild animals of the mountains entered into the houses of the wooden effigies. The Quichés believe that when a wild animal enters their home it is to deliver a message from the earth god, who is the master of the animals. In this case, the message is a foreshadowing of the destruction that is soon to come upon the wooden effigies.

[136] *Xot* (griddle) is a round, flat clay piece upon which tortillas or slices of steamed maize dough are cooked.

[137] There were very few domesticated animals in Precolumbian Mesoamerica. Those that have been documented are the dog, turkey, and honeybee. The dog mentioned here is a small, fat, nearly hairless variety that does not bark and that was eaten in addition to being kept as a pet.

[138] This is the *metate*, upon which maize and other grains are ground. It is usually made from a single block of heavy volcanic stone, quadrangular in shape, and supported by three short stone legs.

[139] In modern Quiché usage, *ak'* refers to chickens, which were introduced by the Spaniards soon after the Conquest. The Precolumbian *ak'* was the domesticated turkey (*Meleagris ocellata*). Colonial period dictionaries often refer to the turkey as *kitzih ak'* (true *ak'*) to distinguish it from the chicken introduced from Europe. The dog and turkey together represent those domesticated animals raised by the Quichés and thus under their direct care and supervision. The wooden effigies thus reaped the vengeance of their own animals as a result of their cruelty and thoughtlessness.

[140] The phrase *holi, holi, huqui, huqui* has been translated in a variety of ways in the past. Raynaud translates it as "strip, strip, tear, tear." Edmonson interprets it as "Crunch, crunch! Scrape, scrape!" Tedlock uses "R-r-rip, r-r-rip, r-r-rub, r-r-rub." *Juk'i* may, in fact, be translated "scrape" or "rub," but *jol* has no relevant meaning in this passage. I have chosen to leave the

Figure 16. "This day, therefore, you shall try the teeth that are in our mouths. We shall eat you," said the dogs to them." Dog, redrawn from a Classic Maya Vase (Coe 1973, 99).

service for you who were the first people. But this day you shall feel our strength. We shall grind you like maize. We shall grind up your flesh,"[141] said their grinding stones to them.

Then their dogs said this to them:

"Why was it that you didn't give us our food? All we did was look at you, and you chased us away. You threw us out. You raised sticks against us to beat us while you ate.[142] Thus you have spoken to us.[143] We could not speak; therefore we received nothing from you. How could you not have understood this?[144] You did understand. We were forgotten because of you. This day, therefore, you shall try the teeth that are in our mouths. We shall eat you," said the dogs to them. Thus their faces were crushed.

Then spoke also their griddles and their pots to them:

"Pain you have caused us. Our mouths and our faces are sooty. You were forever throwing us upon the fire and burning us. Although we felt no pain, you now shall try it. We shall burn you," said all of their pots. Thus their faces were all crushed.

The stones of the hearth flattened them. They would come out from the fire, landing on their heads and causing them pain. They fled. They hurried

phrase untranslated, because I believe the authors intended the words to convey the sound that is produced when maize is ground on a *metate* stone. The initial h of each of the words is pronounced harshly, like a Spanish j or a German ch, creating a coarse sound remarkably like that of stone scraping rhythmically against stone.

Figure 17. It is said that the spider monkeys that are in the forest today are descendents of these people." Spider monkeys at La Venta Park, Villahermosa.

away. They wanted to climb up on top of the houses, but the houses would fall apart beneath them and they were thrown off. They wanted to climb up to the tops of the trees, but the trees would not support them. They wanted to hide in caves, but the mouths of the caves closed up before their faces.

Thus the framed people, the shaped people, were undone. They were demolished and overthrown as people. The mouths and the faces of all of them were ruined and crushed.

[141] It is poetic justice that each of the household possessions of the wooden effigies chose to punish their owners with the same torments that they had suffered previously at their hands. Thus the grinding stones grind the faces of the wooden people in the same way that their own faces had been ground upon day in and day out (p. 87; lines 767–769). The dogs who had been eaten now eat their masters (p. 88; lines 784–789). The griddles and pots, which had been placed on the fire each day, now throw their owners into the fire to be burned (p. 88; lines 799–800). The stone tools and hearthstones pound the heads of the wooden effigies as they had been beaten upon (pp. 88–89; lines 800–807).

[142] Even today domesticated dogs are often treated very carelessly among the Quichés. Most are emaciated and in constant fear of beatings and harsh words.

[143] The purpose of the creation has been to create people who were capable of speech in order to sustain the gods. The dogs are pointing out that, instead, their speech has been limited to beatings and violence. Thus the wooden effigies have also failed in their purpose.

[144] *Na'wik* is to "understand, know, notice, observe, or perceive." Any of these might fit this context. Pages. 84–86 (lines 673, 724–725) assert that it was the lack of ability in the wooden effigies to "understand" that condemned them.

It is said that the spider monkeys[145] that are in the forest today are descendents[146] of these people. This was their heritage because their flesh was merely wood when it was created by the Framer and the Shaper. Therefore the spider monkeys appear like people, descendents of one generation of framed and shaped people. But they were only effigies carved of wood.

[145] *K'oy* refers to the spider monkey (*Ateles vellerosus* or *Ateles geoffroyi*). Central Mexican traditions are remarkably similar. The *Anales de Cuauhtitlan* relate the tradition that in the fourth age of the earth "people were turned into monkeys. They were scattered over the mountains, and the monkey-men lived there" (León-Portilla 1980, 138).

[146] *Etal* is generally used to mean "sign, symbol, or manifestation." Coto notes that it may also refer to "descendents, son, heritage, or succession." The latter interpretation seems to fit the context better in this passage.

THE PRIDE OF SEVEN MACAW
BEFORE THE DAWN [147]

WHILE the face of the earth was only a little brightened,[148] before there was a sun, there was one who puffed himself up[149] named Seven Macaw.[150] There was a sky and an earth, but the faces of the sun and moon were dim.[151] He therefore declared himself to be the bright sign for those who were drowned in the flood.[152] He was like an enchanted person in his essence.

[147] lines 838–907

[148] This translation is based on the Quiché word *natatic*, which refers to the first faint rays of light at dawn. Basseta likens it to the dim light cast by the moon.

[149] *Nimarisaj rib'* (to aggrandise self) is a common Quiché expression for pride or boastfulness. The *Popol Vuh* repeatedly describes this as forbidden or evil (see for example pp. 94,96; lines 915–916), and those who are guilty of it are severely punished under the direction of the god Heart of Sky.

[150] The scarlet macaw (*Ara macao*) is a large species of parrot with beautiful, bright-red plumage. Seven Macaw is portrayed as a boastful individual whose ultimate downfall is ordained by Heart of Sky because of the excessive pride he had in his glorious appearance.

[151] The verb *moymot* (dim) refers to something giving off a dim or shadowy light, such as a sputtering candle flame or the sky at twilight.

[152] The account of Seven Macaw is set at the time prior to the flood that destroyed the wooden effigies, as described in the previous section (see also p. 93; lines 901–902). This episode may have political overtones as well. According to the *Books of Chilam Balam* the founder of Izamal, one of the principal Yucatec centers in the Postclassic period, was a semi-deified lord named Kenech Kakmo (Resplendent Macaw) (Roys 1967, 82, 141, 160 n. 2; Craine and Reindorp 1979, 83–84 n. 78). This lord was also the ancestor of a number of the principal lineages of Yucatán who worshiped him as a god. So important was this god/ruler that the *Chilam Balam of Maní* refers to him as the personification of all northern Yucatán (Craine and Reindorp 1979, 156). Cogolludo wrote of him: "They had another temple on another mount in the northern part of the city, and this, from the name of an idol which they worshiped here, they called Kinich Kakmo, which means the sun with a face. They say that the rays were of fire and descended at mid-day to consume the sacrifice, as the vacamaya flies through the air (which is a bird something like a parrot, though larger in size, and with finely colored feathers). They resorted to this idol in time of mortality, pestilence, or much sickness, both men and women, and brought many offerings. They say that at mid-day a fire descended and consumed the sacrifice in the sight of all. After this the priest replied to their inquires about the sickness, famine, or pestilence, and thus they learned their fate (Cogolludo 1957, IV.8.198; cited in Craine and Reindorp 1979, 83 n. 78). Izamal was eventually conquered by Kak-u-Pacal (Fire His Shield) of Mayapan. Gaspar Antonio Chi wrote that "in course of time the inhabitants of the said town (Izamal) were conquered by Kak-u-Pacal and a hundred valorous captains formerly of the town of Mayapan, and that those who founded this place were called Kinich-Kabul, Kinich Kakmo and others from whom descend the Xool, Mo and Coyi <families>, Indians so named in this province" (cited in Roys 1967, 160 n. 2). Mayapan is a good candidate for the Tulan mentioned in the *Popol Vuh* as the sacred city from which the ancestors of the Quiché rulers derived their authority to rule (pp. 210–213). Thus this account of the boastfulness of a sun-faced/eyed macaw who declared

"I am great. I dwell above the heads of the people who have been framed and shaped. I am their sun. I am also their light. And I am also their moon.[153]

"Then be it so. Great is my brightness. By the brilliance of my silver and gold[154] I light the walkways and pathways[155] of the people.

"My eyes sparkle with glittering blue/green jewels.[156] My teeth as well are jade stones,[157] as brilliant as the face of the sky. This, my beak, shines brightly far into the distance like the moon.[158]

"My throne is gold and silver. When I go forth from my throne, I brighten the face of the earth.

himself to be a sun and moon god, but who ultimately fell at the hands of the ancestors of the Quichés (who eventually became apotheosed as the true sun and moon—see p. 191) may be a mythic recollection of this historical incident. It is perhaps significant as well that the conquest of Izamal was carried out by Kak-u-pacal (Fire His Shield), while the titular god of the Quichés, Tohil, was primarily a fire deity (pp. 213–217). In addition, the progenitors of the Quiché ruling lineages bore the title K'enech Ajaw (Resplendent Lord—see p. 203 n.505), the legitimate sun lords as opposed to the false sun of Seven Macaw.

[153] Although the predominant emphasis in this passage is on the light of the sun and moon, the authors of the text apparently also meant to emphasize that Seven Macaw saw himself as the means of marking the passage of time. Q'ij means both sun and day; Ik'il may refer to the moon, but more often this form of the word refers to month. Calendrics are a vital part of highland Maya culture and ritual because passages of time are believed to be manifestations of deity. Notice that at the end of the chapter the authors refer to the "days and months" before the sun and moon could be seen.

[154] Puwaq refers to any type of precious metal. In modern usage, the word requires a color modifier to determine its specific type—q'an puwaq (yellow precious metal) for gold or copper, saq puwaq (white precious metal) for silver, etc. In this case, Seven Macaw compares his brilliance to that of shiny metal.

[155] B'inib'al (walkway) and the parallel word chakab'al (pathway) both end in the suffix -b'al, which indicates a facilitative object. The root of b'inib'al is b'inik (to walk); therefore, the word may refer to anything which facilitates the act of walking. This may be a well-cleared walkway, a walking stick, or a torch to illuminate one's path in darkness. Chakab'al has a similar usage, although its root, chakanik, refers to the act of walking on all fours, or crawling. The same two verbs are used to describe the travel of animals (p. 74; lines 312–314), as well as that of the wooden effigies before their destruction in the flood (p. 83; lines 654–655). Tedlock's collaborator, Andrés Xiloj, indicated that these two words "are in the prayers we say at the warabal ha [patrilineage shrines], to ask permission for anyone who goes out of the house to whatever place" (D. Tedlock 1985, 261). Seven Macaw is thus boasting that he stands as the only "way and light" for all creation in the darkness of the predawn world.

[156] K'uwal may refer to any rare gemstone. It is derived from a root word meaning "to be hidden or covered up." Colonial period dictionaries often give "emerald" as the specific definition of the word, and emerald appears to be the blue/green jewel described here.

[157] Xit is the word for greenstone. Green or blue stones like jade, serpentine, nephrite, and turquoise were highly prized in ancient Mesoamerica, their value surpassing that of gold. Maya lords often decorated their teeth with jadeite or nephrite inlays as a token of their power and prestige. Such inlays were so meticulously carved and fitted into prepared incisor teeth that no significant gaps between tooth and stone are detectable.

[158] The scarlet macaw has a shiny white beak.

"Thus I am the sun. I am the moon as well for those who are born in the light, those who are begotten in the light.

"Then be it so. My vision[159] reaches far," said Seven Macaw.

Now Seven Macaw was not truly the sun, but he puffed himself up in this way because of his plumage and his gold and his silver. His vision did not reach beyond where he sat. It did not really reach everywhere beneath the sky.

Thus Seven Macaw puffed himself up in the days and months before the faces of the sun, moon, and stars could truly be seen. He desired only greatness and transcendence before the light of the sun and moon were revealed in their clarity. This was in the era when the flood was made because of the effigies of carved wood.

Now we shall tell how Seven Macaw died; how he was defeated at the time when people were made by the Framer and the Shaper.

---

[159] *Wach.* I base this reading on various compounds of the word that refer to vision or sight, such as *solwachij* (to gaze, stare fixedly). *Wach*, however, is a complex word that comprises all the aspects of a thing that give it its essential nature. As such it may be translated as "face, countenance, image, or visage." Vision is one of the primary aspects of this nature because it is the means by which knowledge is gained (see pp. 197–200; lines 4983–5123).

THE FALL OF SEVEN MACAW
AND HIS SONS[160]

THIS is the beginning of his defeat. This is the shaking[161] of the day of Seven Macaw by the twins,[162] named Hunahpu[163] and Xbalanque.[164] They were simply gods. As a result they saw evil in this prideful one who acted according to his own desires before the face of Heart of Sky.[165]

---

[160] lines 908–984

[161] *Yiqoxik* is literally "to be shaken," but with the implication of being troubled, disturbed, harassed, disquieted, or fearful.

[162] Literally "two sons/boys." *K'ajol* (son) is often used in the text to refer to a young man or boy without necessarily emphasizing the parentage of the individual.

[163] Here we are introduced for the first time to the twin heroes, Hunahpu and Xbalanque, who will be the central focus of much of the remainder of the mythological portions of the *Popol Vuh*. Hunahpu has generally been translated in the past as "One Master of the Blowgun" or "One Blowgun Hunter" on the assumption that *pu* is a shortened version of *[p]ub'* (blowgun). This may well be the original etymology of the name. In this section of the text, Hunahpu is described as a great blowgun hunter. On the other hand, the authors of the *Popol Vuh* text consistently wrote the word for blowgun as *ub'* or *wub'*, not *pu*. It is therefore unlikely that the Quiché authors of the text had "blowgun" in mind when they wrote the name of this deity. If the Quiché scribes had meant to make it clear that he was a "blowgunner," they would have used the word currently in use at the time. I believe that they remembered the name as it was handed down to them over the generations and simply preserved the archaic spelling because that was simply his proper name. Hunahpu is treated as a single proper name elsewhere in the text, much like Taylor and Cooper are used as family names without necessarily calling to mind the professions of clothier or barrel maker. The father of the culture hero Hunahpu is named Hun Hunahpu, which if translated literally would mean "One One Master of the Blowgun," a needlessly redundant reading unless Hunahpu were meant to be read as a single untranslated name. Schele and Mathews have proposed an alternative reading based on a Cholan-Maya language etymology, the language of the Classic Maya (ca. AD 250–900) that dominated the lowland region from Palenque and Calakmul as far south as Copan (Schele and Mathews 1998, 74, 295). Inscriptions from this period refer to the Central Mexican city of Teotihuacan as *Puh* (Place of Cattail Reeds). This is the Maya language version of *Tollan* (Nahuatl for "Place of Cattail Reeds), the legendary founding place of the arts and sciences, as well as of political power and legitimacy. This title was given to a number of major centers, including Teotihuacan, Cholula, Chichen Itza, and Tenochtitlan. It is likely that the concept is even older, dating to Olmec traditions in the southern Gulf Coast region, tied to legends of the birth of the world from the primordial sea. The reeds represent the first life to emerge from this place of origin (Schele and Mathews 1998, 200). If *Hunahpu* is related to this concept, the title could be interpreted as "One/First He of the Place of Cattail Reeds," meaning that the deity pertains to the legendary founding place of Mesoamerican civilization, or the place of original creation. Hunahpu is also one of the named days of the 260–day sacred calendar still used by the Quichés. This day is associated with the underworld realm of the dead and with rebirth from that realm. I have chosen to leave the name untranslated, as it is used in this context as a proper name, rather than a descriptive term.

[164] The derivation of the name Xbalanque is problematic. The prefix *x-* is a diminutive as well as a feminine indicator. Thus, depending on the context, it may mean "young, small,

Thus the boys said:

"Good shall never come of this. People will never be able to live here on the face of the earth. Thus we will try to shoot him with our blowguns.[166] When he flies over his food, we will shoot him, thus causing him to be afflicted. Then his jade, his gold and silver, his jewels, his glittering things, and all things over which he keeps vigil, will come to an end.

"May it be done thus, for people cannot be created where only gold and silver are glory.[167] Then be it so," said the boys. And each one shouldered his blowgun.

Now this Seven Macaw had two sons. His firstborn was Zipacna,[168] and his secondborn was Cabracan.[169] Chimalmat[170] was the name of their mother, the wife of Seven Macaw.

little," or it may be used as a female title, such as "lady." The latter usage has led to some speculation that Xbalanque may have been the twin sister of Hunahpu, acting as the female counterpart to the male powers of the hunter. This theory is not supported by the text, however, which consistently refers to the twins as "sons" or "boys." Hunahpu himself often carries the x- prefix, although not as consistently as his brother (see lines 4307, 4550, 4576, 4586, 4646, 4725). B'alan is undoubtedly an archaic spelling of b'alam (jaguar), m/n letter substitutions being fairly common in Quiché. Indeed, Vico transcribed the name in his Theologia Indorum as Xbalamquej (Carmack and Morales Santos 1983, 6–8). Known for its ferocity and cunning, the jaguar is the largest predator in Mesoamerica. Rulers decorated their thrones with jaguar symbols and wore jaguar pelts to emphasize lordly power. In addition, the jaguar is associated with ritual powers of transformation and prophecy. The terminal ke is more difficult to interpret. The most likely derivations are kej (deer) or q'ij (sun or day). The latter possibility is intriguing. The Maya closely identified the jaguar with the sun, particularly in its journey through the underworld at night. The story of Xbalanque and his brother focuses on their passage through the underworld, where they defeat the lords of death, ultimately to become the apotheosed sun and moon in the sky. Father Bartolomé de las Casas was told in the sixteenth century that Exbalanquen was a god from the area of the Guatemalan Alta Verapaz who made war with the lords of hell and returned as a great ruler (Las Casas 1958, 427). The word for sun in the Kekchi-Maya dialect of the Alta Verapaz region is q'e, and Xbalamq'e is still remembered by the Kekchi as a sun god (D. Tedlock 1996, 239 n. 77). If this name is purely of Kekchi origin, Balamq'e may be read in that language as "hidden sun, or the night sun" (Ibid.). The most likely translation of the name would therefore be "Young Hidden/Jaguar Sun."

[165] The text makes it clear that the twin heroes Hunahpu and Xbalanque did not act alone or without authority. All their actions were first ordained by the god Heart of Sky (also called Huracan—cf. p. 70; lines 183–189), and were carried out under his direction.

[166] The shooting of a bird deity by twin boys armed with blowguns is a frequent subject of Maya art at least as far back as the Early Classic period (AD 200–600), indicating that the theological foundation of this incident is of great antiquity.

[167] Q'aq'al is a word laden with culturally-significant implications. Literally it is derived from the root q'aq' (fire, flame), but in this form it refers to "glory, power, majesty." Thus the twins suggest that the creation of human beings cannot be successful when material wealth such as gold and silver are the sole source of glory and power in the world.

[168] Zipacna is most likely derived from the Nahuatl cipactli, a monstrous crocodile whose spiny back symbolized the mountainous earth floating on the primordial sea. This

Zipacna was he that sustained the great mountains—Chigag,[171] Hunahpu,[172] Peculya,[173] Xcanul,[174] Macamob,[175] and Huliznab.[176] These are the names of the mountains that existed at the time of the dawn. In a single night, they were created by Zipacna.

Cabracan was he who would shake the mountains, both small and great, causing them to tremble.

But it was only the pride of the sons of Seven Macaw:

"This is what I am. I am the sun!" said Seven Macaw.

"This is what I am. I am the maker of the earth!" said Zipacna.

"And I am he who fells the sky and causes the earth to tumble down!" said Cabracan. Now these, the children of Seven Macaw, received their greatness from their father. The boys, Hunahpu and Xbalanque, therefore saw evil in them before the creation of our first mother and our first father. Thus the boys planned their deaths and their loss.

probability is consistent with the *Popol Vuh* account in which Zipacna declares himself to be the caretaker of the mountains and creator of the earth. Cipactli is also a day on the Central Mexican calendar, suggesting that like other names in the *Popol Vuh*, this character has calendric associations. This is a long hill in the center of the Rabinal valley roughly the shape of a crocodile. It is still called Sipac and the people of Rabinal associate it with a crocodile (Akkeren 2000, 60).

[169] The Quiché name *Kab'raqan* may be literally translated "Two His Legs." In modern usage, this is the common word for "earthquake," and this interpretation fits Cabracan's role as a shaker of mountains (p. 96; line 961). Together, the brothers Zipacna and Cabracan comprise a dichotomy of opposites, the one claiming to create the mountains and the other destroying them.

[170] Chimalmat is almost certainly derived from the Nahuatl *chimalmatl*, meaning "shield bearer," a fairly common name for female deities. In Aztec legend, she was the mother of the Toltec priest-ruler Ce Acatl Topiltzin Quetzalcoatl. Chimalmat is also one of the names for the mother of the Aztecs' patron god, Huitzilopochtli, as well as the female bearer of cult objects in Aztec migration accounts. Alternatively, the name may be Quiché in origin, consisting of *chi* (preposition "at, in, to, on, from," etc.) and *malmat* (Basseta: to walk with haste) or *malmot* (Coto: "to appear unexpectedly," particularly with regard to a phantasm).

[171] "Mouth Fire," a volcano in the district of Sacatepequez, Guatemala, nineteen kilometers southeast of Antigua. It is better known by its Spanish name, Volcán de Fuego (Volcano of Fire).

[172] Edmonson and Recinos identify this volcano as Volcán de Agua (Spanish: Volcano of Water), also located in the district of Sacatepequez, southeast of Antigua. Tedlock identifies it with Volcán de Acatenango, located in the same district (D. Tedlock 1996, 241 n. 77). In either case, it must be a volcano located near Chigag as the *Annals of the Cakchiquels* describes it as "standing abreast" of Chigag (Recinos and Goetz 1953, 61).

[173] Volcán Acatenango, in the district of Sacatepequez, located southwest of Antigua. Tedlock suggests that this is Volcán de Agua (D. Tedlock 1996, 241 n. 77).

[174] Volcán Santa María, southwest of Quetzaltenango, Guatemala. *Xkanul* is also a general term for volcano in Quiché.

[175] Volcán Zunil in the district of Quetzaltenango, Guatemala.

[176] The identity of this mountain is unknown. Edmonson identifies it with Tajumulco, a volcano in the district of Huehuetenango, Guatemala (Edmonson 1971, 36 n. 938).

THE DEFEAT OF SEVEN MACAW[177]

THIS, then, is the blowgun shooting of Seven Macaw[178] by the twins.[179] We shall now tell the story of the defeat of each of the prideful ones.

This is Seven Macaw and a great nance tree.[180] This, then, is the food of Seven Macaw. Each day he would rise up to the top of the tree to knock down some of the fruit of the nance tree, and it is there that he was seen by Hunahpu and Xbalanque.

The twins watched for him beneath the tree, hidden in its leaves. At length Seven Macaw perched on the nance tree to feed and was shot by them. Hunahpu[181] directed a pellet straight from his blowgun into his jaw. Seven Macaw cried out,[182] sailing over the top of the tree and landing on the ground.

Quickly, Hunahpu ran out to seize him. But instead Seven Macaw tore off the arm of Hunahpu. He wrenched it back, bending it back at the shoulder until it was torn free from Hunahpu.

Still, it was good what they did. This first episode will not result in their defeat by Seven Macaw, even though he took away the arm of Hunahpu.

So then Seven Macaw went to his home, holding his jaw in his palms.

"What have you got there?" asked Chimalmat, the wife of Seven Macaw. "What is it?"

"Two demons[183] shot me. My jaw was dislocated by them,[184] and now my teeth torment me with pain. This I have brought to hang over the fire. It

---

[177] lines 985–1188

[178] At the beginning of this section, the authors point out certain elements of the story as if they could be seen by the reader. This feature may be evidence that in the Precolumbian version of the *Popol Vuh* the text was accompanied by painted illustrations.

[179] Literally "two sons or boys."

[180] The nance (*Byrosinima crassifolia*) is a smooth-skinned, yellow tropical fruit about the size of a cherry.

[181] Throughout this section on the shooting of Seven Macaw, the authors of the text refer to the first of the twins as One Hunahpu, which is also the name of his father. To avoid confusion, the authors generally shortened the name of the son to Hunahpu or Xhunahpu (Little Hunahpu). For the same reason, I have left the name as Hunahpu.

[182] Literally "he broke open his mouth," a common Quiché expression meaning "to scream, shout, or cry out." In this case, it is a play on words as well, considering Seven Macaw's broken jaw.

[183] *K'axtok'* (demon, deceiver) is a derrogatory term for harmful beings, either human or supernatural, particularly when the harm is some form of deception or trickery. In the colonial period, Christian missionaries used the word to refer to devils, and this is still the most common usage in modern Quiché communities. "Demon" or "rascal" is perhaps closer to

Figure 18. "At length Seven Macaw perched on the nance tree to feed and was shot by them." Bird deity being shot by twins with blowguns, redrawn from an Early Classic Maya plate.

will dangle over the fire until they come to take it back again. Truly they are demons," said Seven Macaw as he hung the arm of Hunahpu.

Then Hunahpu and Xbalanque planned again. They went to speak to the first Grandfather, whose hair was now truly white, and also the first Grandmother, who was now truly humble. They were people who now walked bent over with age. Great White Peccary was the name of the Grandfather, and Great White Coati was the name of the Grandmother.

The boys then spoke to the Grandmother and the Grandfather:

"We would like you to accompany us to retrieve our arm from Seven Macaw. We will just follow along behind you. You will say to him, 'Suffer these our grandsons that accompany us. Their mother and father are dead, thus they follow along there behind us. We provide for them by removing worms from teeth,[185] which is our profession.' Thus Seven Macaw will see us merely as children, even while we are giving you our instructions," said the twins.

"Very well," they said.

Thus they came to where Seven Macaw was seated on the edge of his throne. The Grandmother and the Grandfather passed below the home of the lord while the twins played behind them.

___

the ancient authors' intent, since "devil" carries inappropriate European religious overtones. Tedlock uses the word "trickster."

[184] Perhaps this incident is meant to explain the peculiar bent beak of the macaw, as well as the fact that the lower beak is much smaller than the upper beak.

[185] *Chikopil* is the collective term for any type of animal. I have chosen "worm" because the Maya believe that toothaches are caused by parasitic worms or insect larvae. Perhaps this is a result of the wormlike appearance of dental pulp seen within broken teeth.

Now Seven Macaw was crying out because of his teeth. When he saw the Grandfather and Grandmother journeying together, he asked them:

"From where do you come, our grandfather?" he asked.

"We are just making a living, thou[186] lord," they replied.

"How do you make your living? Are not those your children that accompany you?"

"They are not, thou lord. These are our grandsons. But surely we take pity on them and give them a portion. We give them our scraps, thou lord," said the Grandmother and the Grandfather.

The lord was by then nearly finished off because of the pain in his teeth. Therefore it was with great effort that he spoke again:

"I beg of you, take pity on me. What medicines[187] would you make? With what medicines would you cure?" asked the lord.

"We would merely remove worms from teeth, cure eye ailments, and set bones,[188] thou lord," they replied.

"Very well. Cure then my teeth, for truly they ache constantly, and I can no longer bear it. I cannot sleep because of them, and the same goes for my eyes. Two demons shot me with a blowgun, and since then I have not been able to eat because of it. Thus take pity on me, for my jaw and my teeth cause me anguish."

"Very well, thou lord. It is a worm that causes the pain. We will merely replace them. Thy teeth will have to come out."

"It is perhaps not a good thing that my teeth come out, for it is only because of them that I am lord. My teeth, along with my eyes, are my finery."

"We shall replace them then with this ground bone."

But instead of ground bone, they were mere white grains of maize that were to be placed.

"Very well then, take them out. Help me," he said therefore.

[186] Throughout the following passage, Seven Macaw is addressed using the formal *lal* (somewhat akin to the English "thou"), rather than the more familiar *at* ("you"). In modern usage, this is a mode of speech reserved for respected officials, lineage patriarchs, or the elderly. Thus the "grandparents" are at least feigning recognition of Seven Macaw's lordly status. Seven Macaw addresses the elderly grandparents using the familiar "you," indicating he considers himself more important.

[187] The word *ki'* may be translated as "medicine, sweet, *pulque*, alcoholic beverages, poison, or venom." Only by looking at the context can its meaning be discerned.

[188] Bonesetters are still an important group of ritual specialists in many highland Maya communities. In addition to setting bones, they are generally also initiated *aj q'ij* (daykeeper) priests (B. Tedlock 1982, 57, 74).

So then the teeth of Seven Macaw were taken out. As a substitute they placed mere white grains of maize, mere shiny white grains of maize, and immediately his face fell. No longer did he appear as a lord. At length all of the brilliant blue/green jewels in his mouth were removed.

Then the eyes of Seven Macaw were treated. His eyes were plucked,[189] thus completely removing the precious metal from them. He surely felt no pain. He just stared instead.

Thus the basis for his pride was completely taken away according to the plans of Hunahpu and Xbalanque. When at length Seven Macaw died, Hunahpu retrieved his arm. Then also Chimalmat died, the wife of Seven Macaw.

Thus the wealth of Seven Macaw was lost, for the healers took it away—the jewels, the precious stones, and all that which had made him proud here upon the face of the earth.[190] It was truly the enchanted Grandmother and the enchanted Grandfather that did it. Then the boys retrieved their arm and implanted it back into its socket, making it whole again.

They had desired the death of Seven Macaw, and they were able to do it. For they saw pride as evil[191] and went to do these things according to the word of Heart of Sky.

---

[189] As a butcher trims meat, or a barber trims hair. It may also refer to the plucking of feathers from a chicken prior to cooking, which is likely the meaning in this passage. This is an explanation for the large white eye patch and unusually small eyes of the scarlet macaw, which appear as if something had been taken away.

[190] The *Popol Vuh* makes it clear that the power and authority of Seven Macaw were based on his wealth rather than his own abilities. When his riches were taken away, he was susceptible to defeat.

[191] *Itzel*. It is difficult to discern how this word was understood prior to the Spanish conquest. Colonial dictionaries associate it with witchcraft and evil, and this is still a major connotation of the word in modern Quiché usage. This interpretation likely has Spanish Christian influences, however, which did not exist in Precolumbian Quiché culture. Coto also lists under this word "falseness, filth, ugliness, error, perversion, and worthlessness." Basseta simply interprets it as "bad."

THE DEEDS OF ZIPACNA AND
THE FOUR HUNDRED BOYS[192]

THESE now are the deeds of Zipacna, the firstborn son of Seven Macaw.

"I am the maker of mountains," said Zipacna.

Now this Zipacna was bathing on the banks of a river when there passed by four hundred boys,[193] dragging a tree to be used as a supporting beam for their hut. These four hundred were walking along, having cut down a great tree for its lintel.[194]

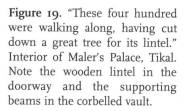

Figure 19. "These four hundred were walking along, having cut down a great tree for its lintel." Interior of Maler's Palace, Tikal. Note the wooden lintel in the doorway and the supporting beams in the corbelled vault.

---

[192] lines 1189–1385

[193] The Maya system of numbers is vigesimal, based on twenty. *O' much'* is literally five sets of eighty, or four hundred.

[194] The lintel of a structure is ritually significant. The world is conceived by the Maya as a great house, its corners being the four cardinal points, its roof the sky, and its foundation the underworld (Vogt 1976, 58). The lintel represents the principal access point of the interior space and was often ornately decorated in Precolumbian times. Such beams are therefore seen as endowed with great power, particularly those used in the homes of spiritual leaders. Zipacna's brazen usurpation of the great wooden beam may indicate that he is taking upon himself the power of this sacred access point without authority or ritual preparation. If this interpretation is correct, Zipacna's ultimate destruction as ordained by the creator god, Heart of Sky, is more understandable.

Zipacna therefore came to the four hundred boys and asked them:

"What are you doing, boys?"

"It's just this tree; we cannot lift it to our shoulders to carry it."

"I will carry it on my shoulders. Where does it go? What use does it have in your hearts?"

"It is to be the lintel for our hut."

"Very well," he said therefore.

Thus he carried it on his shoulders up to the doorway[195] of the hut of the four hundred boys.

"Stay with us, boy. Do you have a mother or a father?"

"There is no one," he replied.

"Surely we beseech you then to help us, for tomorrow another tree will be raised as a supporting beam for our hut."

"Fine," he said again. Then the four hundred boys made their plans:

"This boy, what will we do to him? We will kill him. For it is not good what he does, just lifting the tree all by himself. Let us therefore dig a great hole, and then we shall abandon[196] him there. We will say to him, 'Go dig out the earth from the bottom of the hole.' And when he is bent over down there in the hole, we will hurl down the great tree, and thus he will die there in the hole," said the four hundred boys.

And so they dug a great hole that went down very deep. Then they sent for Zipacna:

"We entrust you to go now to dig in the ground, for we are not able to do it," he was told.

"Very well," he replied.

Thus he went down into the hole.

"Call when you have finished digging up the earth, for you must go down deep," he was told.

"Fine," he replied.

Then he began to dig in the hole. But this hole was to be his own salvation. He had learned that he was to be killed, and therefore he had dug a branching hole to one side. It was in this secondary hole that he was saved.

"How far are you into it?" he was asked by the four hundred boys.

---

[195] Literally "its mouth hut."

[196] *Tzaq* may mean "to throw down, to lose, or to abandon" something. The latter interpretation is closer to what actually occurred.

"I am digging it quickly. When I shall call up to you there, then the digging will have been successfully completed," called Zipacna from the hole.

But he did not dig his own tomb there at the bottom of the hole; rather he dug the means for his own salvation. Therefore, when Zipacna called up, he had already saved himself there inside the hole:

"Come and take the earth away—the dirt that I have dug up from the hole. Truly deep have I dug down. Can you not hear my call? Your voices just echo away as if you were a long way off when I hear them," said Zipacna from his hole.

Thus he was already sheltered when he called up from inside the hole. The boys then dragged over the great tree and hurled it down into the hole.

"He is no more. He does not speak. When he cries out, we will know that he shall be dead," they whispered to each other.

For they each hid their purpose when they hurled down the tree.

So when he spoke he cried out with a loud voice, he called out one more word when they dropped down the tree.

"Aha, we have succeeded! Truly good! We have done it to him. He died. What kind of omen would it have been if he had persisted in carrying out his deeds, his work? Then he might have become first among us, placing himself over us, even us the four hundred boys," they said.

And so they rejoiced:

"For three days we will merely make sweet drink.[197] And when three days have passed, we will drink to our dwelling, to our hut, even us the four hundred boys!" they said.

---

[197] *Ki'y* may refer to an alcoholic beverage, something sweet, medicine, poison, or even snake or insect venom. In this context, *ki'y* refers to an intoxicating drink, likely some form of *chicha*, a home-made fermented drink popular in the Guatemalan highlands made from various fruits, berries, cane, or maize. Alternatively it may be *pulque*, made from the fermented sap of the maguey (agave, or century plant). *Pulque* is viscous, milky-white, and slightly foamy. It ferments very quickly, generally within twelve hours and has an alcohol content of 6%, approximately the same as the average beer. A distilled form of this ancient drink is sold today as mezcal or tequila, although the distillation process was not known prior to the Spanish conquest. In Aztec mythology, *pulque* is personified by gods known as the Centzon Totochtin (400 Rabbits), who appear frequently in painted manuscripts such as the Codex Magliabechiano. These gods are also associated by the Aztecs with the four hundred youths slain by the god Huitzilopochtli as ritual sacrifices. The deaths of the four hundred youths in the *Popol Vuh* account may thus have had ritual significance. The beverage referred to could also possibly be *balche*, made from fermented honey and the bark of the *balche* tree. Alcohol is a prevalent part of highland Maya society, used both socially as well as a necessary component of ceremonial observances.

"Tomorrow and the next day we will see if ants don't come forth from the ground when he begins to stink and decompose. Then will our hearts be comforted, when we will drink our sweet drink," they said.

But Zipacna heard this down there in the hole when they said this. And on the second day, the ants assembled themselves. They walked about. They swarmed beneath the tree. Everywhere they carried in their teeth the hair as well as the nails of Zipacna.

Now when the boys saw this, they said to each other:

"The demon is finished. Look at the ants. They have gathered together. They have assembled here, and everywhere they carry his hair in their teeth. Surely they can be seen carrying his nails. We have done it at last," they said to each other.

But Zipacna was still alive. He had merely cut the hair off his own head and gnawed off his own nails to give to the ants. Thus the four hundred boys thought that he had died.

On the third day, they started in on their sweet drink. All the boys became drunk. All four hundred boys thus were drunk and didn't feel anything when Zipacna collapsed their hut down upon their heads. As a result, all of them were finished, struck down every one of them. Not even one or two of the four hundred boys were saved.

Such was the death of these four hundred boys at the hands of Zipacna, the son of Seven Macaw. It is said that they became the constellation known as the Pleiades,[198] but perhaps this is merely a fable.[199]

Now we will tell the story of the defeat of Zipacna by the twins, Hunahpu and Xbalanque.

[198] *Motz.* The Pleiades are a cluster of stars in the constellation of Taurus (composing a spot on the Bull's shoulder). It is derived from the word meaning to gather together in large numbers.
[199] Literally "whiteness word." This is a play on words, fable, or fantastic story.

THE DEFEAT OF ZIPACNA[200]

THIS now is the overthrow and death of Zipacna. He was defeated by the twins, Hunahpu and Xbalanque, whose hearts were offended by the deaths of the four hundred boys at the hands of Zipacna.

Now this Zipacna would spend each day wandering in search of his food, only fish and crabs, which he looked for in the rivers. By night, however, he would carry mountains on his back.

Thus Hunahpu and Xbalanque transformed for him a great crab. For this purpose, they used a bromelia flower,[201] the kind of bromeliad that may be picked in the forests, to make the open claws. For its shell and backside, they used a hollowed-out stone. This shell they placed at the bottom of a cave below a great mountain. Meauan[202] was the name of this mountain where he was defeated.

When the boys came, they found Zipacna by the river:

"Where are you going, boy?" they asked Zipacna.

"I'm not going anywhere. I'm just searching for my food," replied Zipacna.

"What is your food?"

"Only fish and crabs, but I haven't found any yet. It has been two days since I have eaten, and now I cannot bear the hunger," said Zipacna to Hunahpu and Xbalanque.

"There is a crab there below the canyon. It is truly a great crab. Why don't you try your luck with it?" asked Hunahpu and Xbalanque. "Perhaps you will be able to eat it. It merely bit us when we tried to catch it, so we are afraid of it. But he will not go away and you could catch it."

"Take pity on me. Guide me there, boys," said Zipacna.

"We do not want to. Just go along yourself. There is no way that you will get lost if you just follow the course of the river until you reach the base

---

[200] lines 1386–1524

[201] *Ek'* (bromelia) is a parasitic tropical flower. It grows from the branches of trees and has long, pointed red petals that look somewhat like the legs of a crab. The Quichés today use bromelia flowers to decorate festive arches and the shrines of Christian saints.

[202] Meauan was identified by Brasseur and Recinos as a mountain west of Rabinal, Guatemala (Brasseur 1858, 128; Recinos 1950, 102 n. 3). It is likely the mountain known today as Miagua, located some 20 km. northwest of Rabinal and bordering the Chixoy River (Akkeren 2000, 299). If this identification is correct, Akkeren suggests that Meauan may be a contracted form of *me'al ajaw* (daughter lord), the Quiché version of the Kekchi origin of the town's name, *Rab'inal* (Place of the Lord's Daughter) (2000, 60, 66).

of the great mountain. There it will be, situated below the canyon. Just go along over there," said Hunahpu and Xbalanque.

"Please take pity on me. I will never find it, boys. You go first as my guides. I know where there are many birds that you could shoot with your blowguns," said Zipacna.

He humbled himself before them, promising to reward them. He wept before them.

"Perhaps you will not be able to catch it. Then you would return like we did. Because not only were we not able to eat it, but it would straightaway bite us. We went in there headfirst on our stomachs,[203] but it became frightened. A little later we went in lying on our backs, but we couldn't find it again. Thus it would be good if you went in lying on your back," he was told.

"Very well," replied Zipacna.

Thus they left, accompanied by Zipacna. At length they arrived below the canyon where the crab was placed, its surface bright red there at the base of the canyon. This was their deception.[204]

"That's good," rejoiced Zipacna.

He wanted to put it straight in his mouth because he was truly famished and wanted to eat it. He just wanted to go in headfirst on his stomach.[205] But the crab climbed high up, and Zipacna came back out.

"Didn't you get it?" he was asked.

"No. It climbed high up and after awhile I couldn't find it again. Perhaps it would be good then if I went in again lying on my back," he said therefore.

---

[203] *Jupulik* is to lie face down/on one's stomach. It may also be used to indicate "headfirst." Both meanings are likely applicable in this context.

[204] The word used here is *kumatzij*, which is a pain caused by cramps, arthritis, etc. It is derived from *kumatz* (serpent, twisted). My reading is based on the assumption that the word is actually a contraction of two words, *kumatz tzij* (twisted word—deception, lie).

[205] The implication of the story is that the Twins had tried to get Zipacna to enter the cave on his back where he would be prone and helpless. If Zipacna was a crocodile, as his name implies (Zipacna is likely derived from the Nahuatl *cipactli*—crocodile), he would be helpless because crocodiles cannot move well when flipped over on their backs. Despite the Twins' admonition, however, Zipacna did the natural thing and rushed headlong on his belly into the cave to reach the crab. Just as the Twins had predicted, the crab was frightened and climbed up high out of his reach. In this position he could not look up nor lift his arms above his head. Zipacna thus took the Twins' original advice to go back in and try again on his back, perhaps giving him hope that he could then reach up to grab the crab as it climbed upward. When the mountain settled down on his prone form, he was unable to flip back over again.

Then he went back in again lying on his back. He went all the way in until only his kneecaps showed outside. Thus he was completely swallowed up. The mountain then settled down onto his chest so that he could not turn over again. Zipacna became stone. Thus was the defeat of Zipacna at the hands of the boys, Hunahpu and Xbalanque.

Such is the ancient account of the first son of Seven Macaw, the Maker of Mountains, as he was called, who was defeated beneath the mountain called Meauan.[206] It was merely enchantment by which this second prideful one was defeated.

Now we shall tell the tale of another.

Figure 20. "The mountain then settled down onto his chest so that he could not turn over again. Zipacna became stone." Stucco crocodile, Comalcalco.

---

[206] This association between Zipacna and earthquakes continued well-after the Conquest. Coto wrote the following under the heading of estremesçerse (Spanish: tremor): "*Cabrakan* [Quiché: earthquake] is the tremor of the earth. They once believed, and continue to believe today, that beneath the earth there is a giant who holds up the earth who they call Çipacnay, and when he moves the earth trembles, and that this is the god of earthquakes" (Coto 1983, 224. Translation by author). In the contemporary Rabinal version of the myth, a hungry creature who moved mountains and volcanoes without any effort was lured into a cave by a woman from Coban where there was a crab hiding. Once inside, the mountain collapsed on him and he became the hill visible today (Shaw 1971, 46–51; Akkeren 2000, 70).

THE DEFEAT OF CABRACAN[207]

THE third prideful one was the second son of Seven Macaw, Cabracan by name.

"I am the wrecker of mountains," said he.

It was simply because of Hunahpu and Xbalanque that Cabracan was defeated. Then Huracan, Youngest Thunderbolt, and Sudden Thunderbolt spoke to Hunahpu and Xbalanque, saying:

"According to my word, the second son of Seven Macaw must also be defeated. For it is not good what they have done upon the earth. They surpass the sun in greatness and importance,[208] and this is not as it should be. Thus, lure him away there to the East, where the sun rises," said Huracan to the twins.[209]

Figure 21. "I am merely a feller of mountains. I will wreck them as long as there is sun and light." All of the mountains mentioned in the text were volcanoes like this one, Volcán San Pedro, near Santiago Atitlán.

[207] lines 1525–1720

[208] Literally "weightiness." According to Basseta, *nimal* (greatness) and *alal* (weightiness, importance) together form a couplet that refers to "power."

[209] Thus it is Huracan (also known as Heart of Sky) who directs the actions of the twins in overthrowing the pride of Seven Macaw and his two sons.

"Very well, thou lord. It has always been thus, that we do not approve of him.[210] For he is not lifted up where thou art, thou Heart of Sky," the boys replied when they received the word of Huracan.

Now this Cabracan occupied himself as a wrecker of mountains. He would simply tap his foot a little on the surface of the earth, and straightaway mountains, both small and great, would tumble down.[211]

Then he was met by the twins:

"Where are you going, boy?" they asked Cabracan.

"I'm not going anywhere. I am merely a feller of mountains. I will wreck them as long as there is sun and light,"[212] he said when he spoke to them.

Then Cabracan spoke again to Hunahpu and Xbalanque:

"Where have you come from? I do not know your faces. What are your names?" asked Cabracan.

"We have no names.[213] We have just been blowgunning and trapping in the mountains. We are just poor orphans, for there is nothing that is ours, boy. We just wander in the mountains, both small and great. There is one great mountain that we saw that keeps growing until truly high it ascends. It simply rises up, far above the peaks of all the mountains. We could not catch even one or two birds before its face. Is it really true that you fell all mountains, boy?" asked Hunahpu and Xbalanque of Cabracan.

"Is it true that you saw this mountain of which you speak? Where is it? You shall surely see that I will fell it. Where did you see it?"

"There it is in the East, where the sun rises," said Hunahpu and Xbalanque.

"Good. You lead the way,"[214] the twins were told.

"No, you just take the middle place between us, one on your left and one on your right hand. We have our blowguns, and if there are any birds, we will shoot them," they said.

They rejoiced that they could practice their shooting. But there were no clay pellets in their blowguns. When they shot them, they merely blew at

---

[210] Literally "not good we see them," a common Quiché expression for "not liking or disapproving" of something.

[211] *B'ulij* describes the mountains cascading or tumbling down like water from a mountain spring.

[212] This is a common Quiché expression still used today in a somewhat shortened form, *chi b'e q'ij saq*, meaning roughly "as long as there is sun and light" or simply "forever."

[213] In many ancient cultures, revealing one's name was not taken lightly; it was believed that to do so was to relinquish power.

[214] Literally "take our road" or, as paraphrased in a somewhat similar English phrase, "lead the way."

the birds. Thus Cabracan was amazed.

Then the boys used a twist drill to make their fire, upon which they roasted the birds. They covered the skin of one of the birds with quicklime until it was coated with white earth.

"We will give this to him when he becomes ravenous with hunger.[215] When he savors the aroma of our birds, he will be defeated. We will put earth on its skin. We will cook it in earth. In the same way, therefore, he himself will be buried in the earth. This must be if the great sage, the one to be framed and shaped, is to be sown and to have his dawn," the boys said.

"Cabracan shall desire with all his heart[216] to eat what we will cook. This shall be the desire of the heart of Cabracan," said Hunahpu and Xbalanque to each other.

Then they roasted the birds until they had been cooked to a golden brown. They would drip with fat from their skins and give off a fragrant aroma. Thus Cabracan desired to be fed. His mouth watered. He just gulped and drooled saliva and spittle because of the fragrance of the birds.

Thus he begged of them:

"What is it that you are eating? Its aroma is truly delicious to smell. Give me a little," he said therefore.

Then they gave to Cabracan a bird, and this was his defeat. When he had finished the bird, they went on their way again until they arrived in the East. There they came to the great mountain.

But by now the legs and arms of Cabracan had become weak.[217] Never again would he be strong because of the earth coated on the skin of the bird he had eaten. He could no longer do anything to the mountains. He did not succeed in causing them to fall apart.

Then the boys tied him up. They tied his hands behind his back. The boys were mindful to make sure that his hands were well bound. They also tied his ankles[218] together. Then they hurled him down into the earth and buried him.[219]

Thus Cabracan was defeated at the hands of Hunahpu and Xbalanque. Innumerable were their deeds here on the face of the earth.

[215] *Jiq'onoq* is "to be ravenous, gluttonous, excited with desire."
[216] *K'uxilal* is a "longing for something with all one's heart, a desire for something above all else."
[217] The word is often used to describe old or wornout clothing in addition to something that is weak.
[218] Literally "its neck his legs." In Quiché phraseology, the neck of the arm is the wrist, and the neck of the leg is the ankle.

Now we shall tell of the birth of Hunahpu and Xbalanque, having first given the account of the defeat of Seven Macaw along with Zipacna and Cabracan here upon the earth.

---

[219] Even today the Quichés associate earthquakes with a bound giant buried beneath the mountains. The following story was recorded by Ruth Bunzel at the Quiché town of Chichicastenango: "They say of the earthquake, that there is a giant under the earth, bound by his hands and feet, and when there is a slight tremor, it is because he has moved his hands or feet a little; and when he turns over on the other side is when there are strong earthquakes" (Bunzel 1952, 428).

THE TALE OF THE FATHER OF
HUNAHPU AND XBALANQUE[220]

WE shall now name the name of the father of Hunahpu and Xbalanque. We shall retell it.[221] We shall merely repeat the tale, the account of the engendering of Hunahpu and Xbalanque. But we shall tell only the half of it, the smallest part of the tale of their father.

---

[220] lines 1721–1732

[221] Literally "we shall retell its head." This is a problematic passage. Tedlock follows Edmonson, who believes that the verb used in the text, *camuh*, is a scribal error and should be *cumuh* (to drink), implying that the authors of the text are proposing a kind of toast to the telling of the story of the fathers of Hunahpu and Xbalanque (Edmonson 1971, 58; D. Tedlock 1996, 91, 249 n. 91). Tedlock used this passage as evidence that the authors of the *Popol Vuh* were "Toastmasters" (D. Tedlock 1985), or "Masters of Ceremonies" (D. Tedlock 1996). I prefer to read the verb as a shortened version of *camuluh* (to retell, review, repeat, go over again).

THE DEEDS OF ONE HUNAHPU AND
SEVEN HUNAHPU ABOVE XIBALBA[222]

THIS, therefore, is the account of they whose names are One Hunahpu[223] and Seven Hunahpu. For thus they are called. It was in the darkness, in the night, when One Hunahpu and Seven Hunahpu were born to Xpiyacoc and Xmucane.

Now this One Hunahpu had two children, both sons. One Batz[224] was the name of his firstborn, and One Chouen[225] was the name of his secondborn. The name of their mother was Xbaquiyalo.[226] Thus she was called, the wife of One Hunahpu.

But Seven Hunahpu had no wife. He was merely a companion, merely secondary. By his nature, he was like a servant[227] to One Hunahpu. They were great thinkers, for great was their knowledge. They were seers here upon the face of the earth. They were good by their nature, and in their birth as well.[228]

They revealed their talents[229] to One Batz and One Chouen, the sons of One Hunahpu. Thus One Batz and One Chouen became flautists and singers, writers and sculptors, jade workers and precious metalsmiths.[230]

As for One Hunahpu and Seven Hunahpu, they would merely play dice and ball everyday. The four of them would pair off to oppose each other.

---

[222] lines 1733–1918

[223] *Junajpu* is a day on the traditional highland Maya calendar, dedicated to the memory of ancestors.

[224] *B'atz'* is the Quiché word for the howler monkey. It is also one of the named days from the traditional highland Maya calendar.

[225] *Chouen* is derived from the Yucatec Maya word *chuen*, meaning "howler monkey." In addition, *aj chuen* is a title meaning "artisan" (Barrera Vásquez 1995, 110), a reading consistent with the artistic nature of these twins. Twin monkey scribes appear frequently in Classic Maya art as patrons of writing. It is also the Yucatec Maya day name that corresponds to the day B'atz' in the Quiché calendar.

[226] Xbaquiyalo. The likely etymology of this name is *x-* (lady), *baqi* (bone), *ya'* (water/river), *lo* (perhaps), yielding Lady Bone Water. Tedlock notes that in Yucatec, *bak ha'* (also "bone water") is the snowy egret or snowy heron, and thus translates the name as "Egret Woman" (D. Tedlock 1996, 250 n. 91).

[227] *K'ajol* is literally "son," or "boy," but it is a common metaphor used throughout the text for servant, which seems to be the meaning in this context.

[228] *Yake'ik* (to arise) is also a metaphor for birth, which is likely the connotation here.

[229] *Na'wikil* is "talent, ingenuity, genius, skill, cleverness, inventiveness."

[230] Tedlock believes that this list of six occupations should be divided into two sets of poetic triplets, thus grouping writers with flautists and singers as performing artists. Such a grouping would imply that the composition of literary texts such as the *Popol Vuh* is based

Figure 22. "Now it was on the path leading to Xibalba where they played ball." Ancient ballcourt at Copan.

When they gathered together to play in the ballcourt, the Falcon would arrive to watch over them. This Falcon was the messenger of Huracan, Youngest Thunderbolt, and Sudden Thunderbolt. The face of the earth was not far for him. Nor was Xibalba[231] far for him. In an instant, he could return again to the sky with Huracan.

Thus they tarried here upon the earth. By then the mother of One Batz and One Chouen had died.

Now it was on the path leading to Xibalba where they played ball. Thus the lords of Xibalba, One Death and Seven Death,[232] heard them:

more on an oral tradition than carved or painted inscriptions (D. Tedlock 1985, 269). I come to the opposite conclusion. The more likely arrangement for the list would be three sets of couplets, the preferred type of parallelism throughout the text. In addition, writers and carvers are paired without question on pp. 141, 147 (lines 2568–2569, 2714–2715). Thus the authors of painted codices are closely associated with those who carve inscriptions on stone monuments. Far from suggesting that the *Popol Vuh* is based on an oral tradition, this passage implies that the authors consider ancient writers to have set down their literary creations in a manual process. This implication strengthens the view that the *Popol Vuh* is based on a painted text.

[231] *Xib'alb'a* (Place of Fear) is the Quiché name for the underworld, ruled by lords of death and disease. Modern Quichés still use the word to describe an underground hell inhabited by demons who cause sickness.

[232] *Kame* (Death) is a named day on the highland Maya calendar. The death lords thus both bear calendric dates as their names.

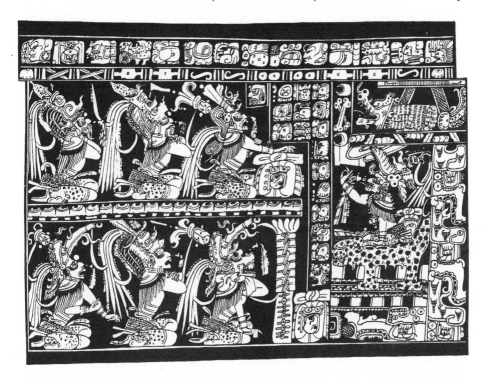

Figure 23. "These, therefore, were the great judges, all of them lords. Each was given his task and his dominion by One Death and Seven Death." View of the gods in the darkness of the underworld at the time of first creation from a Classic Maya vase (Drawing from Coe 1973, 109).

"What is happening on the surface of the earth? They are just stomping about and shouting. May they be summoned here therefore. They shall come to play ball, and we shall defeat them. They have simply failed to honor us. They have neither honor nor respect. Certainly they act arrogantly[233] here over our heads," said therefore all those of Xibalba.

Then they whose names were One Death and Seven Death gathered all of their thoughts.

These, therefore, were the great judges, all of them lords. Each was given his task and his dominion by One Death and Seven Death:

These are the lords named Flying Scab[234] and Gathered Blood.[235] Their task is to sicken people in their blood.

---

[233] *Jikik* is to "act arrogantly, act insolently, insult, or mock".

[234] *Pat* is a "snare, trap" in Quiché. Campbell, however, suggests that this is likely a loan word from Kekchi, meaning "scab, crusted sore" (Campbell 1983, 82). This reading fits the context better in that it parallels the paired demon, Gathered Blood.

These, then, are the lords Pus Demon and Jaundice Demon.[236] Their dominion is to swell people up until pus oozes from the skin of their legs, and the skin of their faces becomes yellow with jaundice, as it is said. Thus this is the dominion of Pus Demon and Jaundice Demon.

These, then, are the lords Bone Staff and Skull Staff, the staff bearers[237] of Xibalba. Their staffs are mere bones. These staff bearers are they who skeletize people until they are truly bones and skulls. As a result, they would die having received only emaciated bones, bloated with starvation.[238] These are they whose names are Bone Staff and Skull Staff.

These, then, are the lords whose names are Sweepings Demon[239] and Stabbings Demon.[240] Their task is simply to overtake people if they abandon sweepings and trash in back or in front of their houses.

Figure 24. "These, then, are the lords Bone Staff and Skull Staff, the staff bearers of Xibalba. Their staffs are mere bones." Death god bearing a staff, redrawn from a Classic Maya vase.

[235] *Kuchuma Kik'* (Gathered Blood) is still known by Quiché storytellers as a cruel lord of the underworld who gathers blood shed upon the ground as a result of injury, illness, or violence. This blood is then served to his fellow lords at a banquet.

[236] *Ajal Puj, Ajal Q'ana. Ajal* is likely a loan word from Chol, meaning "evil spirit" (Campbell 1983, 81). *Puj* is "pus," and *q'ana* is "yellowness, jaundice."

[237] As emblems of office, Quiché political and religious leaders carry staffs that are often topped with ornate silver carvings symbolizing divine power.

[238] "Emaciated bones, swelling he will receive." This couplet refers to the end stages of starvation. Most of the body becomes emaciated, while the belly becomes distended from fluid collecting in the tissues due to a lack of protein. This latter condition is called ascites.

[239] In modern usage, *mes* refers to "trash or garbage," but more literally it refers to "sweepings." The trash produced by Quichés is that which is swept away from a floor, pathway, or porch while cleaning. Thus a broom is referred to as a *mesb'al* (instrument of sweepings). Tedlock's collaborator, Andrés Xiloj, pointed out that the best way to keep away the demons of Xibalba was to keep one's house swept clean and not allowing trash to accumulate (D. Tedlock 1996, 253, n. 92). Diego Chávez, a prominent artist in Santiago Atitlán related the following story with regard to a carved wooden panel in his home that depicts a *cabecera* (head elder within the traditional confraternity system) administering justice: "It reminds me of the old days when people respected the Maya confraternity officials and we had no need for jails. Now all people know is killing and thievery. In this panel I show a woman accused of not respecting her family. At that time if she were found guilty, the *cabecera* would send her to sweep all of the dust around the church. In this way she would remember to

These would be overtaken and stabbed by them until they fall face down upon the earth and die. This, therefore, is the dominion of Sweepings Demon and Stabbings Demon, as they are called.

These, then, are they whose names are Lord Wing[241] and Packstrap.[242] Their dominion is the people who die on the road as a result of sudden death, as it is called. Blood would come to their mouths, and they would die vomiting blood. Each one has his task, the burden he carries on his shoulders. They would simply wear out the necks and the hearts of these people so that they die on the road. They would cause this to happen outside. When people go out walking, they would come upon them. This, then, is the dominion of Wing and Packstrap.

These, therefore, gathered together their thoughts when One Hunahpu and Seven Hunahpu were persecuted and harassed.[243] For the Xibalbans desired the gaming things of One Hunahpu and Seven Hunahpu—their leathers, their yokes,[244] their arm protectors,[245] their headdresses, and their face masks—the finery of One Hunahpu and Seven Hunahpu.

Figure 25. "Each one has his task, the burden he carries on his shoulders. They would simply wear out the necks and the hearts of these people so that they die on the road." Deity wearing a packstrap, from Copan Stela D (drawing by Linda Schele).

sweep the uncleanness from her own life even as she swept the church for the benefit of the town" (Christenson 2000, 194).

[240] Based on the root *toq'* (to stab, to gore).

[241] The manuscript reads *xic*. If this is to be interpreted as *xik'*, this is "wing"; alternatively, if it is to be understood as *xik*, it is a "hawk." I prefer the former reading only because hawks do not have underworld or malevolent associations in contemporary highland Maya communities.

[242] *Patan* is the tumpline or pack strap (Spanish *mecapal*) worn by porters across the forehead to secure burdens carried on the back. This lord causes the sudden death of people carrying heavy burdens on the road. Having myself carried loads in this way over miles of mountain trails, I have had many an opportunity to curse this particularly malevolent underworld lord.

[243] Contemporary Quichés also believe that illness is caused by various underworld lords. The following is from a prayer for protection in which the lords of illness and death are

Now we shall tell of their journey to Xibalba. One Batz and One Chouen, the sons of One Hunahpu, remained behind. Their mother had died. Later One Batz and One Chouen will be defeated by Hunahpu and Xbalanque.

invoked and propitiated with offerings at a shrine in the cemetery at Chichicastenango. Among these are the "lord of sickness and pain, of death and destruction in the roads and trails, of death and destruction through *aguardiente*, of death and destruction from food poisoning, of death and destruction from vomiting, of death and destruction from strain and exertion—come hither, be seated before this World of the cemetery! And also the master of pain and misfortune, of wounds from pistols and knives and cutlasses, from Remingtons and Mausers, come hither, be seated before this World of the cemetery! And also the lord of vomiting and indigestion, the lord of fever and dysentery, and also the lord of cold sweat (malaria) and green chill (tuberculosis), of swellings of the abdomen (cancer), of influenza and bronchitis, and also the lord of all the minor illnesses; and also the lord of smallpox, come hither before this mountain shrine of the cemetery! Be seated here, however many may be your manifestations; look upon us here before this World. Be seated, all of you. Lords, pardon my trespass" (Bunzel 1952, 390).

[244] Unfortunately *b'ate* does not appear in any early colonial dictionaries, perhaps because the ballgame ceased to be played soon after the Spanish conquest. Thus the names for the equipment used in the game fell out of usage. From the description found later in the *Popol Vuh* text, the ball bounces off of this article in the process of playing the game. I have chosen to translate the word as "yoke," a well-known article of ballgame equipment throughout Precolumbian Mesoamerica. It is a U-shaped apparatus worn about the hips and used for striking the ball to keep it in play. Yokes were probably made of wood, although intricately carved stone replicas have been found in many parts of ancient Mesoamerica, particularly along the Gulf Coast of Veracruz.

[245] Depictions of Precolumbian ballplayers in ancient Maya art often show the lower arms wrapped with a protective device.

THE SUMMONS OF ONE HUNAHPU
AND SEVEN HUNAHPU TO XIBALBA[246]

THEN was the arrival of the messengers of One Death and Seven Death:

"Go you war councilors[247] to summon One Hunahpu and Seven Hunahpu. Tell them when you arrive, 'Thus say the lords: They must come, say the lords to you. They must come here to play ball with us that we may be invigorated by them. Truly we are amazed greatly at them. Thus they must come, say the lords. May they bring hither their implements—their yokes, their arm protectors, and their rubber ball[248] as well. Thus say the lords,' tell them when you arrive there," the messengers were told.

These messengers were the owls[249]—Arrow Owl, One Leg Owl, Macaw Owl, and Skull Owl—for so the messengers of Xibalba were called.

This Arrow Owl was like the arrow, piercing.[250]

This One Leg Owl merely had one leg, but there were his wings.

This Macaw Owl had a red back, and there were also his wings.

Now this Skull Owl only had a skull with no legs; there were merely wings.

The burden[251] of these four messengers was to be the war councilors.

Thus they arrived there from Xibalba. They arrived suddenly, perching atop the ballcourt.[252] One Hunahpu and Seven Hunahpu were playing ball at the court that was called Honor and Respect[253] at Carchah[254] when they

---

[246] lines 1919–2032

[247] *Raj pop achij* (he of the mat of warriors). *Aj pop* is a title given to lords or rulers, as well as to those who sit on ruling councils. *Achij* is literally "man" but is generally used in the *Popol Vuh* text to refer to soldiers/warriors.

[248] *Kik'* is the vital fluid of any living thing (blood for animals, sap for trees, etc.). Rubber, as well as a ball made from rubber, is also called *kik'* since it is made from the sap of the rubber tree (*Castilla elastica*).

[249] Owls continue to be regarded as heralds of sickness and death by the Quichés, and they are extremely unwelcome anywhere near homes (Oakes 1951, 46; Bunzel 1952, 272, 343; Schultze-Jena 1954, 84; Watanabe 1992, 68).

[250] Based on the root *kopij*, *kopkik* is something that "strikes, pierces, or causes harm." In this context, "pierce" fits the arrow analogy best.

[251] *Eqalem*, is a burden carried on the back. Metaphorically, the Maya use the word for "burden" (Spanish *cargo*) to refer to an "office or responsibility."

[252] Maya ballcourts were generally bounded by high stone walls. The owls apparently alighted on top of one of these.

[253] *Nim* (Honor) *Xob'* (Respect). Notice that on page 115 (lines 1818–1819), the lords of Xibalba complained that those who were playing ball above their heads did not give them

came. The owls, therefore, alighted atop the ballcourt, where they delivered in order the words of One Death and Seven Death, Pus Demon and
Jaundice Demon, Bone Staff and Skull Staff, Flying Scab and Gathered
Blood, Sweepings Demon and Stabbings Demon, Wing and Packstrap. For
these are the names of all the lords. Thus the owls repeated their words.

"Are these not the words of the lords One Death and Seven Death?"

"Those are the words that they said," replied the owls. "We shall surely be
your companions. 'You shall bring all the gaming things,' say the lords."

"Very well. But wait for us while we leave instructions behind with our
mother," they said.

Figure 26. "The owls, therefore, alighted atop the ball-
court, where they delivered in order the words of One
Death and Seven Death." Death owl, redrawn from a
Classic Maya vase.

proper "honor" or "respect," the same two words which comprise the name of the ballcourt
in these lines. Nimxor is listed in the *Annals of the Cakchiquels* as a place near Carchah in the
Alta Verapaz region, thus this is likely a play on words (Recinos and Goetz 1953, 64).

[254] Kar Cha'j (Fish Ballcourt/Ashes). This may be a play on words between ashes (*chaj*) and
ballcourt (*cha'j*). It is likely a reference to the Kekchi-Maya town now known as San Pedro
Carchá located near Cobán, a city east and somewhat north of Quiché territory. Modern
Quichés have vague notions of the entrance to the underworld being located in the Alta
Verapaz region inhabited by the Kekchis. It is perhaps significant that later in the story
the sons of One Hunahpu also descended into Xibalba to confront the lords of death in the
underworld ballcourt. They ultimately died by hurling themselves into a furnace. Their ashes
were then cast into a river which resulted in their being revived as "people-fish."

Thus they went to their home to speak to their mother, for their father had died:

"We must surely go, our mother. The messengers of the lord have just arrived to take us. 'They must come,' we were told. Thus the summoners have spoken. But this, our rubber ball, shall remain behind," they said.

Then they went to tie it up above the house.

"We will surely return to use it again. Until then, merely play the flute and sing, write and carve." In this way One Batz and One Chouen were instructed. "Thus you shall warm our home, and you shall warm the heart of your grandmother."

But their mother, Xmucane, wept bitterly.[255]

"We must go, but we will not die. Do not grieve," said One Hunahpu and Seven Hunahpu as they left.

---

[255] The manuscript reads *quz quz*. Coto writes that the expression ɛuzɛuh *que'in oɛ* means to "cry much, with great pain."

THE DESCENT OF
ONE HUNAHPU AND SEVEN
HUNAHPU INTO XIBALBA[256]

THEN went One Hunahpu and Seven Hunahpu, guided by the messengers as they descended along the path to Xibalba. They went down steep steps until they came out again upon the banks of turbulent river canyons. Trembling Canyon and Murmuring Canyon were the names of the canyons that they passed through.

They also passed through turbulent rivers. They passed through Scorpion River, where there were innumerable scorpions. But they were not stung.

Then they arrived at Blood River. They were able to pass through it because they did not drink from it.

Then they arrived at Pus River, which was nothing but a river of pus. Neither were they defeated here but simply passed through it as well.

At length they arrived at a crossroads,[257] and it was here at the four crossing roads that they were defeated. One was Red Road and another was Black Road; White Road was one while another was Yellow Road.[258] Thus there were four roads.

Now this, the black road said:

"Me! Take me, for I am the lord's road." Thus spoke the road.

But it was there that they were defeated. They started then on the road to Xibalba. At last they arrived at the council place of the lords of Xibalba, and there again they were defeated.

They who were seated first in order were mere effigies of carved wood, adorned[259] by the Xibalbans. It was these, then, that they greeted:

---

[256] lines 2033–2267

[257] Crossroads are considered to be extremely dangerous by the Maya because they are focal points for the unseen powers of all directions. Ximénez wrote that the ancient Quichés ceremonially collected the sins of their community and abandoned them at crossroads (Ximénez 1929–31, pp. 84–85).

[258] The Maya associated the cardinal directions with colors. The Quichés associated white with north, red with east, yellow with south, and black with west. Modern rituals often begin by placing candles with these corresponding colors at the cardinal directions in order to symbolically delimit the corners of the world. Thus the brothers were tricked into following the black, or west, road—a premonition of their defeat and death since this is the road that the sun takes when its sinks into the underworld.

[259] *Wutalik* is "adorned, dressed up, fitted out."

"Morning,[260] One Death," they said to the first effigy.

"Morning, Seven Death," they said again to the carved wood.

Thus they did not prevail. Instead, the lords of Xibalba roared[261] with laughter. They merely roared with laughter, all the lords, because they had completely prevailed. In their hearts, they had defeated One Hunahpu and Seven Hunahpu.

And after they had laughed, One Death and Seven Death spoke:

"It is good that you have come. Tomorrow you shall put to use your yokes and your arm protectors," they were told.

"Sit down on our bench,"[262] they were told.

But the bench that they were offered was nothing but a very hot stone, and they were burned when they sat on it. Truly they spun around on top of it. Neither did they find relief. Truly they leaped up when their seats[263] were burned.

Thus the Xibalbans laughed again. They laughed until their insides hurt and their chests became cramped from their laughter.[264] All the lords of Xibalba grabbed themselves and rolled around in their laughter.

"Now just go to the house. Someone will come to deliver your torch[265] and your cigars[266] there at the sleeping place," they were told.

Thus they arrived in the House of Darkness. There was nothing but darkness inside that house.

Then the Xibalbans gathered their thoughts:

"Tomorrow we will merely sacrifice them. They only have to make a mis-

---

[260] The greeting *q'ala'* means literally "be it clear." It is somewhat akin to the common Quiché greeting at the beginning of the day, *saqirik* (it brightens or it dawns), referring to the arrival of morning.

[261] *Jumujub'* (to roar) is based on *jumumik*, which denotes the sound of an earthquake, a passing truck, or a powerful wind.

[262] *Tem* is a long, flat wooden or stone bench. Rooms of ancient Maya palaces contained such benches arranged along their interior walls. The seating arrangements along these benches were determined by rank within the ruling hierarchy.

[263] Literally "sitters, or means of sitting."

[264] Literally "serpent laughter." *Kumatz* (serpent) is used here to refer to cramps in the body, an association still current among modern highland Maya. The lords of Xibalba thus laughed so hard that they were getting side aches.

[265] These are pine wood torches. Such torches are still used today and are made from a very resinous pine wood called *ocote* in Spanish. The resin of the wood is easy to ignite and keeps the torch burning without rapidly consuming the wood itself.

[266] Smoking tobacco is a very ancient Maya tradition and carries important religious significance. Stone carvings and painted codices frequently depict gods and humans smoking cigars that could be grotesquely huge in size. The English word "cigar" is likely derived from the verb *sik'arik* (to smoke).

take and straightaway they will die by means of our gaming things that we use to play ball," said the Xibalbans to each other.

For their ball was merely a round blade. White Dagger[267] was the name of the ball of Xibalba. Their ball was sharp, shattered bones pierced through the ball of Xibalba.

Thus One Hunahpu and Seven Hunahpu entered into the House of Darkness. At length one came to give them their torch, which was already lit. It had been sent by One Death and Seven Death, along with cigars for each of them which had also already been lit.

These, then, were sent by the lords to One Hunahpu and Seven Hunahpu. They were seated cross-legged there in the darkness when the courier arrived to give to them their torch and their cigars. The torch was brightly burning when it arrived, and with it were lit each one of the cigars:

"These are to be returned at dawn. They are not to be used up. Instead, they are to be collected again intact. Thus say the lords to you," they were told.

Therefore they were defeated. For they used up the torch as well as the cigars that had been given to them.

Figure 27. "Therefore they were defeated. For they used up the torch as well as the cigars that had been given to them." Individual smoking a cigar, from Madrid Codex, p. 86b (Villacorta and Villacorta 1930).

Xibalba is crowded with trials, for there are many kinds of trials there.

The first of these is the House of Darkness, where nothing but darkness exists within.

The second is named Shivering House, for its interior is thick with frost. A howling wind clatters[268] there. An icy wind whistles through its interior.

The third is named Jaguar House, where there are nothing but jaguars

[267] The name of this dagger implies that it is a sacrificial knife (see p. 132; lines 2409–2410).

[268] The wind clatters because it is laden with frost and hail. The verb used refers to the sound of grains falling on a hard surface or hail falling on a roof.

inside. They bare their teeth, crowding one another, gnashing and snapping their teeth together. They are captive jaguars within the house.

The fourth trial is named Bat House, for there are none but bats inside. In this house they squeak. They shriek as they fly about in the house, for they are captive bats and cannot come out.

The fifth, then, is named Blade House,[269] for there are only blades inside—row upon row of alternating blades that would clash and clatter there in the house.

Thus there are many trials in Xibalba. One Hunahpu and Seven Hunahpu did not enter into them. These are merely the names of each of the houses of trial.

Thus One Hunahpu and Seven Hunahpu came out and appeared before One Death and Seven Death:

"Where are my cigars and my torch that were given to you last night?" they were asked.

"We finished them off, O lord."

"Very well then, now your day is at an end. You are to die."

Thus they were lost. They were broken as well.

"Here your faces shall be hidden, for you are to be sacrificed," said One Death and Seven Death.

Then they were sacrificed and buried. It was at the place named Crushing[270] Ballcourt that they were buried. The head of One Hunahpu was cut off, while the rest of his body was buried with his younger brother.

---

[269] These are blades made of either flint or obsidian, a dark volcanic glass that when properly flaked can produce a razor-sharp edge. Obsidian blades were a major trade item throughout the history of ancient Mesoamerica, being one of the principal materials used in weapons, cutting tools, mirrors, sacrificial knives, and bloodletting instruments.

[270] *Puk'b'al* (Crushing). The root verb for *puk'b'al* has a variety of possible interpretations. It may mean "to crush, to grind to a very fine consistency, to kick up dust, to sift, to beat, to spill, to spread abroad, to scatter, to disentangle, or to card wool. *Puk'b'al* may thus refer to the dustiness of the ballcourt or the tendency to kick up dust during vigorous play. It may also imply that this ballcourt is where opponents are "ground down, beaten, or sifted." This latter interpretation is intriguing, because "to crush" is often used in the text to refer to the destruction or violent death of people (pp. 85, 87–88, 291; lines 682, 743, 789, 801, 8454). Father Coto notes that a synonymous word for "to crush," *k'ajb'ik*, refers specifically to human sacrifice, which is the likely implication here as well. It is also possible that the word should be read as *pukb'al*, which also has a variety of meanings depending on context. It means literally "to fall from overripeness or decay (fruit, flowers, teeth), or to be plucked out (hair, feathers)." Metaphorically the word when applied to humans means "crestfallen, melancholy, disdained, contemptible, or scorned." In this case such an interpretation may refer to the humiliation and misery of those who lose in the ballcourt. Both interpretations may apply here considering the Maya's fondness for plays on words and puns. Alternatively,

Figure 28. "The head of One Hunahpu was cut off, while the rest of his body was buried with his younger brother." On the left is a sacrifice by beheading in the court of an underworld lord, from a Classic Maya vase (Coe 1973, 92).

"Place his head in the midst of the tree that is planted by the road," said One Death and Seven Death.

Now when they went to place his head in the midst of the tree, the tree bore fruit.[271] The tree had never borne fruit until the head of One Hunahpu was placed in it. This was the tree that we now call the calabash.[272] It is said to be the head of One Hunahpu.

One Death and Seven Death marveled at the fruit of the tree, for its round fruit was everywhere. Neither could the head of One Hunahpu be seen clearly, for his face had become identical in appearance with the calabashes.

This was seen by all Xibalba when they came to look at it. In their hearts, they perceived the greatness of the essence of that tree, for it was accom-

the word may be a scribal error for *puzbal* (place of sacrifice), a reading which fits the context of this passage well.

[271] Contemporary Tz'utujil burial practices at Santiago Atitlán may be related to this mythic account. Once placed in the grave, Atitecos raise a small mound of earth over the body and plant a tree on top which represents the soul of the dead reborn to new life. The community cemetery has long rows of graves bearing trees, giving the appearance of a great orchard or grove. Ximénez described a similar practice in highland Guatemala at the beginning of the eighteenth century and noted that persons were frequently buried in the maize fields, an indication that the dead were reborn as maize (1929–1931, I, 100). This is particularly significant with regard to Atiteco traditions of one of their principal culture heroes, Francisco Sojuel, who is believed to have set the pattern for many of the contemporary ritual practices

plished immediately when the head of One Hunahpu entered into its midst.

Thus the Xibalbans spoke one to another, "Let no one cut the fruit, nor enter beneath the tree," they said.

Thus they restricted themselves. All the Xibalbans restrained themselves. For the head of One Hunahpu was no longer clear, having become identical with the fruit of the tree whose name is the calabash. Great is the account of it.

Now a maiden heard of it. Thus we shall now tell of her arrival there.

Figure 29. "Now when they went to place his head in the midst of the tree, the tree bore fruit. The tree had never borne fruit until the head of One Hunahpu was placed in it." Fruitful tree from the Panel of the Foliated Cross, Palenque (drawing by Linda Schele).

observed today: "When Francisco Sojuel was being persecuted by his enemies they tried to kill him by cutting him into little pieces and sprinkling them with lemon juice and salt. But when they came back the next day they found that his coffin was empty and from it grew a griant zapote tree filled with fruit. People plant zapote trees over the graves of their family in memory of Francisco Sojuel because he did not die" (Christenson 2001, 207). The association between ancestors and fruit trees is also characteristic of ancient Maya thought. The sides of the sarcophagus of K'inich Janab Pakal at Palenque depict ten of the king's ancestors emerging out of a cleft in the groundline marked with *kaban* (earth) signs. Behind each ancestor is a fruit-bearing tree, indicating that they are rising from their graves in a fashion parallel to the sprouting of world trees (Schele and Freidel 1990, 221; McAnany 1995, 43).

[272] The calabash tree (*Crescentia cujete*) yields a large gourd with a hard, bonelike rind that is sometimes dried to make bowls. When dried, the gourd is whitish in color and approximately the size of a human skull.

THE MAIDEN LADY BLOOD AND
THE TREE OF ONE HUNAHPU[273]

THIS, therefore, is the account of a maiden, the daughter of the lord named Gathered Blood.

A MAIDEN, the daughter of a lord, had heard of it. Gathered Blood was the name of her father, while the name of the maiden was Lady Blood.[274]

When she heard the account of the fruit of the tree as told by her father, she was amazed by the tale:

"Can I not come to know it by seeing the tree that has been spoken of? I hear that its fruit is truly delicious," she said.

Thus she went alone beneath the tree that was planted at Crushing Ballcourt:

"Ah! What is the fruit of this tree? Is not the fruit borne by this tree delicious? I would not die. I would not be lost. Would it be heard if I were to pick one?" asked the maiden.

Then spoke the skull there in the midst of the tree:

Figure 30. "A maiden, the daughter of a lord, had heard of it." Classic Maya figurine of a noblewoman, National Museum of Anthropology, Mexico City.

"What is it that you desire of this? It is merely a skull, a round thing placed in the branches of trees," said the head of Hunahpu when it spoke to the maiden. "You do not desire it," she was told.

---

[273] lines 2268–2374

[274] In Maya society, blood is the most precious substance because it bears within itself the spirit or essence of the ancestors and thus, by extension, of the founding deities from whom they descended. It is therefore the repository of life which transcends individuals to include the ancestral dead. It is consistent with this view that "Lady Blood," daughter of an underworld lord, is the means by which the skull of One Hunahpu is able to produce new life out of death.

"But I do desire it," said the maiden.

"Very well then, stretch out hither your right hand[275] so that I may see it," said the skull.

"Very well," said the maiden.

And so she stretched upward her right hand before the face of the skull. Then the skull squeezed out some of its saliva, directed toward the hand of the maiden. When she saw this, she immediately examined her hand. But the saliva from the skull was not in her hand.

"My saliva, my spittle, is merely a sign that I have given to you. This head of mine no longer functions, for it is merely a skull that cannot work.[276] The head of a truly great lord has good flesh upon his face. But when he dies, the people become frightened because of his bones. In like manner, his son is like his saliva, his spittle. He is his essence. If his son becomes a lord, or a sage, or a master of speech, then nothing will have been lost. He will go on, and once more become complete. The face of the lord will not be extinguished nor will it be ruined. The warrior, the sage, the master of speech will remain in the form of his daughters and his sons.[277]

[275] The Quichés associate the right side of the body with maleness and the left with femaleness. Lady Blood's impregnation through her right hand is thus destined to produce male offspring.

[276] I base this reading on *chak* (work), which is consistent with the previous phrase and thus serves as a couplet of ideas, the most common poetic form in the *Popol Vuh*. Sam Colop suggests that it should rather be *ch'aq'* (flesh), thus reinforcing the idea of a fleshless skull (Colop 1999, 68 n. 165). Either reading is consistent with the context of One Hunahpu's discourse, and possibly it is meant to be a play on words.

[277] Seeds are referred to as small bones or skulls in many highland Maya languages. The reverse is also true, human bones are seen as seeds, the source of new life as expressed in succeeding generations. Thus Schultze-Jena wrote, "when they [Quichés] ask for a young girl in marriage, they refer to progeny and make mention of human bones. It is probable that they have in mind the comparison of bones with the seeds of plants, and that human bones are bearers of life in the succession of the generations" (Schultze-Jena 1954, 52. Translation by author). Ruth Bunzel noted that the Quichés of Chichicastenango claimed that their formalized speech and ceremonies were attributed to ancient ancestral precedent and that this is a means of preserving the lives and knowledge of their ancestors: "And now this rite and custom belongs to the first people, our mothers and fathers.... This belongs to them; we are the embodiment of their rites and ceremonies" (Bunzel 1952, 232, 238). When performed at appropriate times and under appropriate circumstances, such ceremonies are perceived as a means for dead ancestors to manifest themselves. In Santiago Atitlán, a priest extracts certain garments that once belonged to the ancestors and wears them as he dances to the four cardinal directions to recreate the limits of the cosmos. Following the perform-ance of this dance in 1998, the priest sought me out to ask if I had seen "the ancient *nuwals* [revered, powerful ancestors] giving birth to the world." He explained that they had filled his soul with their presence as he danced, guiding him in his steps, and now everything was new again. In the eyes of the priest, the dance was not a symbol of the ancestral dance, but a genuine creative act in which time folded inward on itself to reveal the ancestors themselves (Christenson 2001, 24). In a more literal sense, highland Maya see their descendents as their

"Thus may it be so, as I have done to you. Climb, therefore, up there to the face of the earth. You will not die, for you have entered into a promise. Thus be it so," said the skull of One Hunahpu and Seven Hunahpu.

Now in this they merely carried out the thoughts and words of Huracan, Youngest Thunderbolt, and Sudden Thunderbolt.

Thus the maiden returned again to her home, having been given many instructions. Straightaway her children were created in her womb[278] by the mere saliva. Thus was the creation of Hunahpu and Xbalanque.

Now when the maiden had arrived at her home and six moons were completed, she was noticed by her father, Gathered Blood by name.

"replacements." Carlsen writes that much of Tz'utujil society is based on the principle of change as manifested in the transition from birth to death and back again (Carlsen 1991, 26; 1997, 50–55). Generational changes represent the transferral of life from the grandparents to their grandchildren. Thus when a baby is born, Tz'utujils say "he/she sprouted," or "he/she returned," implying that the spirit of a dead ancestor, like a newly-sprouted plant from the dead husk of a maize kernel, has returned to occupy a new body. In most highland Maya languages, the word for grandfather, *mam*, is also the word for grandchild, suggesting an equivalent relationship (Cook 2000, 257 n. 22, 260 n. 35). It is common for parents to name their children after their grandparents to reinforce this idea of substitution. Houston and Stuart also note that among the Classic Maya royal names tend to skip one or more generations, perhaps an allusion to this principle of generational substitution (Houston and Stuart 1996, 295). On a panel from Palenque now housed in the Dumbarton Oaks collection in Washington D.C., K'an Hok' Chitam dances out of the underworld in the guise of the god Chak Xib Chak. He is named in the accompanying text as the *k'exol* ("replacement") of an ancestor with the same name who died 92 years earlier (Schele and Miller 1986, 274). At Santiago Atitlán, this principle of substitution may be applied to single generation changes: "One's child is sometimes actually addressed as 'parent,' and males will address their fathers as *nuk'jol*, or 'my son.' Likewise, a woman will often call her father *wal*, which translates as 'child.' As replacements are necessary for the grandparents' regeneration, the *k'ex* naming pattern has more than superficial significance" (Carlsen 1997, 55).

[278] The cycle of birth, death, and rebirth is one of the most prominent motifs in ancient Mesoamerican art and literature. The Maya saw death as a necessary part of life. For maize to grow and produce, a seed must first die and be buried in the earth. It was thus necessary for One Hunahpu to descend into the underworld to die before a new generation could appear and be capable of overcoming death. The maiden, Lady Blood, stood as an intermediary. As the daughter of one of the principal lords of death, she belonged to the darkness of the underworld. As the consort of One Hunahpu, she had the potential to create new life from death.

THE ASCENT OF LADY BLOOD
FROM XIBALBA[279]

THEN the maiden was discovered[280] by her father, for he saw that she was now with child. Thus all the lords, One Death and Seven Death along with Gathered Blood, gathered their thoughts:

"This my daughter is with child, O lords. It is merely the result of her fornication,"[281] said Gathered Blood when he met with the lords.

"Very well then. Question her[282] about this, and when she doesn't tell, she will be sacrificed. She will go far away to be sacrificed."

"Very well, ye lords," he replied.

He therefore questioned his daughter:

"Who is responsible for the child that is in your womb, my daughter?" he asked.

"I have no child, my father," she replied. "I have not known the face of any man."[283]

"Very well then. It is true that you are a fornicator."[284]

"Sacrifice her,[285] you war councilors," the four owls were told. "Then bring back her heart inside a bowl so that the lords may examine it this day."

---

[279] lines 2375–2509

[280] *Na'tajik* is generally "to recall, remember," but it may also refer to the discovery of something secret, a more appropriate reading for this context.

[281] This is glossed by Basseta as "bastard."

[282] Literally "dig at her mouth." This is a common Quiché expression for questioning or interrogating a person closely. Thus the father will try to dig the truth out of his daughter's mouth.

[283] This is a polite expression for sexual intercourse. Quichés in traditional communities are very prudish when it comes to sexual matters, rarely referring to sex directly and seldom engaging in public displays of affection. Lady Blood's statement is accurate both figuratively (she never having engaged in sexual intercourse) and also literally. As Tedlock points out, she never saw the living face of One Hunahpu, only his skull (D. Tedlock 1996, 262 n. 100).

[284] *Joxol ch'ek* (scratcher knee). This is a play on words, a particularly prevalent Maya practice when referring to sexual things as a way of speaking about it indirectly. *Jox* is "to have sex," and also "to hoe or to scratch." A "knee scratcher" is a fornicator, prostitute, or one who wishes to seduce someone to have sex. The more common expression today is "leg burner" which also means seductress or prostitute.

[285] Violations of custom with regard to adultery and other forms of illicit sex are considered very serious in traditional Quiché society, although in most cases punishment is left in the hands of the ancestors or deity: "The Quiché Indians have a firm belief and conviction that the ancestors punish adultery on behalf of the man, as well as his spouse if she tolerates it in her house, with sickness, affliction, and even death" (Schultze-Jena 1954, 23. Translation by author). Sexual transgressions in particular are believed to subject those involved to the

And so they went, carrying the bowl and lifting up the maiden in their talons. They took with them the White Dagger, the instrument of her sacrifice.

"You will not succeed in killing me, you messengers, for this that is in my womb was merely created and is not the result of fornication. Rather it is the result of my admiration for the head of One Hunahpu which is at Crushing Ballcourt. Thus do not sacrifice me, you messengers," said the maiden when she spoke.

"But what shall we give as a substitute for your heart? For we were told by your father, 'Bring hither her heart so that the lords may examine it and be satisfied with its form. Bring hither the bowl quickly, and place her heart inside it.' Were we not told this? Therefore, what will we put in the bowl? For above all else, we do not want you to die," said the messengers.

Figure 31. "And so they went, carrying the bowl and lifting up the maiden in their talons." Woman borne by an underworld owl, from the Dresden Codex, p. 17b (Villacorta and Villacorta 1930).

"Very well. The heart will not be theirs. At the same time, your homes will no longer be here. No longer will you lure people by force to their deaths.[286] Only the true fornicator will be subject to One Death and Seven Death. Mere croton tree sap[287] will be theirs henceforth. Thus be it so. It

whims of the lords of various illnesses who live in the underworld and who "feed" on the lives of those who do not live in accordance with societal rules.

[286] According to Basseta, chi'j is "to forcefully lure, lead away, or captivate."

[287] Thus the lords will receive not human blood, but rather the red sap of the croton tree (Croton sanguifluus; Spanish: Sangre de Dragón—Dragon's Blood Tree). Vázquez de Espinosa wrote that "there is a tree in this province of Chiapa and of Guatemala that is called dragon. It is tall like the almond tree; the leaves are white and the stems are of the same color, and if it is struck with a knife it weeps blood, as natural as if it were human" (Vázquez de Espinosa 1969, 1st.I.iv.590, p. 147. Translation by author). Both blood and tree sap have the same name, kik', in Quiché.

will be this that you shall burn before their faces. It will not be this, the heart, that you will burn before their faces. Thus be it so. Take what the tree produces," said the maiden.

Then the red secretions[288] of the tree were collected in the bowl. There it congealed and became round. The red tree, therefore, oozed forth the substitute for her heart. The sap of the red tree was thus like blood when it came out. It was the substitute for her blood.[289]

Thus she collected the sap, the secretion of the red tree. Its surface became like bright red blood in the bowl when the maiden cut open the tree called the Sacrifice Red Tree.[290] She named this "blood," and blood croton it is still called.

"There on the face of the earth you will be esteemed, for it is become yours," she said therefore to the owls.

"Very well then, you maiden. We shall go then upward to hide you. But first we shall give the substitute for your heart before the faces of the lords," said the messengers.

And so they arrived before the faces of the lords, who were all awaiting them expectantly.[291]

"Was it not successful?" asked One Death.

---

[288] *Wa'l* is the general Quiché term for the liquid secretions or fluid content of plants and animals. Thus *u wa'l baq'wach* (its secretions eyes) are tears, *u wa'l pix* (its fluid tomatoes) is tomato sauce, *u wa'l alanxax* (its fluid oranges) is orange juice, and here *u wa'l che'* (its secretions tree) is another word for tree sap.

[289] Offerings, including blood sacrifices from chickens or turkeys, are still seen as "substitutes" for the offerer so that deity will not take them through illness or death (Bunzel 1952, 360). Landa wrote that in the Yucatec month of Mac, the pre-Conquest Maya "took out a great many of the hearts of the animals and birds and threw them into the fire to burn. And if they were unable to get large animals like tigers (jaguars), lions (pumas) or crocodiles, they made their hearts out of their incense; but if they had killed them, they brought their hearts for that fire" (Landa 1941, 163). It is likely that following the Spanish conquest, incense continued to represent a substitute for the blood sacrifice Precolumbian Maya once offered to deity. At the beginning of the eighteenth century Fray Antonio Margil recorded an incident in which a sick man consulted a Quiché shaman after falling ill in a forest. The shaman informed him that the "Lord of the Forest" had made him ill, but that there was a remedy: "Do not worry, because I go now to pray to the Lord of the Forest for you, and will take him his food [copal incense] in your name" (Hill 1992, 144). The shaman thus used incense to purchase the health of the man by offering it as a replacement to assuage the appetite of the Lord of the Forest.

[290] *Chuj* is the Yucatec Maya word for "sacrifice." If this is the correct reading of the word, it would serve as further evidence that significant elements of the early mythology recorded in the *Popol Vuh* have a lowland origin. Alternatively, if the word is to be read as *ch'u'j*, this is the Quiché word for the scarlet-colored dye made from the cochineal insect, *Coccus axin*. In this case, the word would modify *kaq* (red), indicating that it is a bright, vivid red.

[291] *Tz'elewachin* is "to await, expect" (Coto).

"It was successful, O lords. This is surely her heart here in the bottom of the bowl."

"Very well. I would see it therefore," said One Death.

Then he lifted it up with his fingers,[292] dripping with blood from its surface. It was bright red with blood.

"Stir well[293] the face of the fire and place it over the fire," said One Death.

Then they dried it over the fire, while the Xibalbans savored its fragrance. They all rose up to lean over it, for truly delicious was the smell of the blood to them.

Now while they were bent over, the owls went to guide the maiden up to the hole leading above the earth. Then the guides returned back down again.

Thus the lords of Xibalba were defeated, for the maiden had tricked them all.[294]

---

[292] *Chuyej* is "to lift something with one's fingers" (Basseta).

[293] *Lu'* is "to stir a fire to revive it" (Basseta).

[294] *Moywachixik* (to be blinded faces) is a Quiché expression meaning "to be tricked, deceived."

LADY BLOOD AND THE
MIRACLE OF THE MAIZE[295]

THIS, therefore, is the mother[296] of One Batz and One Chouen.

Then arrived the woman, Lady Blood by name, who came to the mother of One Batz and One Chouen. Her children were still in her womb, however, it wasn't long before the birth[297] of Hunahpu and Xbalanque.

So then the woman came to the Grandmother. She said to the Grandmother:

"I have come, thou lady,"[298] she said when she arrived there with the Grandmother. "I am thy daughter-in-law and thy child,[299] thou lady."

Figure 32. "So then the woman came to the Grandmother." Grandmother goddess (Goddess O), redrawn from a Classic Maya vase (Taube 1992, fig. 51c).

[295] lines 2510–2663

[296] Actually she is their grandmother, but because the real mother of One Batz and One Chouen had died by this time (p. 118; line 1913), Xmucane is acting as their mother.

[297] Literally *yake'ik* (they arise), which is glossed as a metaphor for birth in Coto.

[298] *Chichu'* (lady) simply means "woman, female." It is most commonly used, however, in titles of respect, such as *ajawinel chichu'* (ruler female, queen) or *alib' chichu'* (parent-in-law female).

[299] Traditionally, a new bride moves into the home of her mother-in-law, at least temporarily, to get acquainted and to ensure that she learns the skills necessary to run a household. By declaring herself to be the daughter-in-law and child of Xmucane, she is presenting herself as a claimant to familial hospitality. In contemporary Quiché households, marriage severs a woman permanently from her parent's influence, suggesting that Lady Blood really had nowhere else to go: "When the girl leaves for her husband's house, she takes with her noth-

"From where have you come? Do my children yet exist? Did they not die in Xibalba? Only these two are left as their sign and their word.[300] One Batz and One Chouen are their names. If you see that you have come, go back the same way,"[301] the maiden was told by the Grandmother.

"But it is true that I am thy daughter-in-law. These are surely his. These that I am carrying belong to One Hunahpu. One Hunahpu and Seven Hunahpu are alive. They are not dead. That which they have done is merely a manifestation of their light,[302] thou mother-in-law. Thus you shall see it. You shall see his face in these that I am carrying," she told the Grandmother.

Now One Batz and One Chouen gloried in these things:[303] Only the flute and song did they do. Only writing and carving was their work every day. And so they comforted the heart of the Grandmother.

Thus the Grandmother spoke to her:

"I do not want you. You are not my daughter-in-law. It is merely the result of your fornication that is in your womb. You are a deceiver. My children that you spoke of have died," the Grandmother said again.

"They are truly his, I say to you."

"Very well then, I hear you that you are my daughter-in-law," the maiden was told. "Go then to get food that these may eat. Go and harvest a great netful of maize and return with it.[304] Then you will surely be my daughter-in-law, just as you have said."

"Very well," she replied.

Then she went to the maizefield[305] that belonged to One Batz and One

ing but her personal clothing.... Theoretically, the girl is now completely cut off from her blood kin. In going from her father's side she forfeits her rights to inherit. She is discouraged from visiting her parents, and her relations with her family assume a purely formal character. It is assumed that she will never again return to their house" (Bunzel 1952, 28).

[300] Both of these terms are also metaphors for "descendents, progeny."

[301] Edmonson sees this as a humorous response to the common Maya greeting, "I have arrived" (Edmonson 1971, 81 nn. 2451–2452). The polite response is "you have arrived," but in this case, the grandmother turns the answer around and orders her to go away.

[302] "Merely his self-manifestation light." In other words, One Hunahpu and Seven Hunahpu will show themselves once again in the light when their sons are born. "To appear in the light" is a common Quiché metaphor for birth.

[303] Literally "inflames," with the implication that it gives glory, power, majesty.

[304] It is customary in Quiché society for a new bride to be given heavy tasks by her in-laws to prove her ability to provide for a family. In this case, Lady Blood is given a great net which is to be used to carry the maize for the family's food. In Maya theology, the net is a significant symbol for the divine order of the universe. Its fixed pattern represents the regularity of the seasons in the fabric of time. Thus Maya goddesses are often depicted weaving on a cosmic loom.

[305] Ab'ix may refer to the maizefield or a single maize plant, as in line 2604.

Chouen, along the path that had been cleared by them. The maiden thus started out and arrived there at the maize-field. But there was only a single ear[306] of maize[307] in the field. There was not even one or two or three more. Although there was maize there, it was but a single ear that had been produced.

Then the heart of the maiden sank:[308]

"See, I am a sinner![309] I am a debtor![310] Where shall I obtain the netful of food that is asked for?" she asked.

Thus she called upon the guardians of the food:

"Come, arise. Come, stand up Lady of the Day Toh,[311] and Lady of the Day Canil,[312] Lady Cacao[313] and Lady of the Day Tzi,[314] you the guardians of the food of One Batz[315] and One Chouen," said the maiden.

Figure 33. "But there was only a single ear of maize in the field. There was not even one or two or three more." Maize plant from Chutinamit, near Santiago Atitlán.

[306] *Wi'* (head). The Maya think of ears of maize as "heads."

[307] *Jal* is an ear of maize, dry and ready to harvest.

[308] Literally "finished therefore her heart."

[309] *Makol* (sinner). Modern Quiché prayers and ceremonies generally begin with a long litany of sacred beings and objects who are invoked to be present. This is followed by the phrase *sacha' la nu mak* (take away my sin), often repeated several times. This is not a reference to specific sins, but a request to take away any flaws in the body or character of those present that might taint the results of the ceremony. I recorded this prayer by an *aj q'ij* priest at a healing ceremony in Momostenango in the late 1970s: "We call upon you Earth, we ask you Lord of the Day 11 *No'j*, we ask you Lord 5 *No'j*... We ask a favor of you; we ask you a favor because there is sickness among us, there is a sick little girl. Take away my sin, King of the World, Savior of the World, so that you may speak—the Seven Skies, the Seven Earths. Take away my sin that there may be light, that there may be clarity. Take away my sin I ask you, the great mountains and the small mountains; the great plains and the small plains; the great animals who are lords of the mountains and you small animals who are in the mountains. Take away my sin, our people, our mothers and fathers, our grandmothers and our grandfathers. Take away my sin and witness us here today at this table. It has its service, to bring out the transformation, to bring out the mother-fathers. This is its service. Take away my sin."

[310] *K'asb'ol.* According to Father Coto, *qazbal* means "sinner, transgressor, debtor" In modern usage, the term refers to a person who is indebted to someone else, either financially or socially. This is perhaps the reason why the day name *Toj* is listed first in the following passage, a day associated with the payment of debts. Coto also lists *qazbol macol,* obviously related in some way to the paired couplet here, and notes that the two words taken as a pair refer to the merchant trade.

Then she took hold of the corn silk, the corn silk atop the ear of ripe maize,[316] and pulled it upward. She did not pick the ear of maize, but it multiplied there in the net until the great net overflowed. Then when the maiden returned, the animals carried the net for her as she returned. But when she arrived and saw her grandmother, they gave back her pack frame,[317] and she perspired as if she had carried it.

[311] This passage likely refers to female manifestations of three of the days in the traditional highland Maya calendar—*Toj*, *Q'anil*, and *Tz'i'* (Ruud van Akkeren, personal communication). These are consecutive days, although the order should be *Q'anil*, *Toj*, and then *Tz'i'*. Modern *aj q'ij* priests invoke the days of the calendar in their prayers and ceremonies as lords and attribute to them specific power to bless or to punish. Thus they conceive of the days as living beings with personalities and specific spheres of influence. *Toj* is "tribute or payment." Metaphorically it may also be "punishment or illness" caused by sin. In her note on *Toj*, as one of the named days in the traditional Quiché calendar, Ruth Bunzel quotes an *aj q'ij* priest collaborator: "*T'oj* (*enfermedad*, sickness). Symbolizes the suffering which is caused by sin. 'This is a bad day, a day of sickness. On the day *t'oj* one burns incense in the house for the Lord of Sickness. *T'oj* is also a day for calling sickness to punish an enemy. If divination comes out in 7 *qanil*, 8 *toj*, 9 *ts'i'* it is bad. These are bad days. The content of *qanil* is corn, or the milpa, *toj* is sickness, *ts'i'*, "dog," some shameless act. When one has a sickness of the body that is like a worm eating the flesh, we call this *xu jut qanil*, which is a worm that is found sometimes in the *milpa* [maizefield]. When this worm gets into the body and eats at the flesh then it is because of these days. For this sickness comes from stealing corn or else it may be due to sorcery, for they are the days of sorcery also. For instance, if a man finds that his *milpa* has been robbed he goes to his *milpa* at midnight, breaks off an ear of corn and places a candle between the two halves, and asks San Jacinto and San Augustín, the patrons of the *milpa* to punish the robber, and he calls the days 7 *qanil*, 8 *t'oj*, 9 *ts'i'* to punish him. Then after a time the man who has stolen the corn will suffer from this disease, which is like cancer and ulcers. This is the meaning of these days" (Bunzel 1952, 282–283).

[312] *Q'anil*, Literally "Yellowness," referring specifically to the yellow of ripe maize, and is sometimes used as a metaphor for the fruitfulness of the earth in general. Bunzel: "*Qanil* (*milpa*, cornfield). Symbolic of the regeneration of the earth, of rebirth after, death, as exemplified in the growth of corn. '*Qanil* is the day of the milpa, a good day. It is a day to give thanks for one's *siembres* [plantings], for harvest and planting. After the harvest one waits for the day *qanil*, either 2 or 3 *qanil*, to give thanks. And likewise after planting. This is optional. But it is obligatory for all people to give thanks for their food and their land on the day 8 *qanil*. And each year one does this, until one dies'" (Bunzel 1952, 55, 282). Barbara Tedlock adds that one of the mnemonics used for this day by *aj q'ij* priests in Momostenango is *cak'anaric uwäch ulew* ("harvest"—literally, "the face of the earth becomes yellow"), and adds that "on these days, the lineage priest-shaman, depending on whether planting or harvest time is closer, passes seeds saved from the previous year, or else fresh corn ears that have been chosen as seed ears for the next year, through the copal smoke. In so doing, he is symbolically feeding (*tzukunic*) both the Mundo [Spanish "World," the principal earth deity] and his own ancestors" (B. Tedlock 1982, 114).

[313] *Kakaw* is the true cacao (*Theobroma cacao*) from which chocolate is made. Cacao was highly prized in Precolumbian Mesoamerica, where it was used to make a spiced chocolate beverage. So precious was the bean of the cacao that it was used as the most common form of currency in purchasing goods and services. Ruud van Akkeren (personal communication) notes that one of the prime areas of cacao cultivation in the region is Tiquisate/Nahualate on the Pacific coast. This is also the area of the Toj and Q'anil lineages. Several highland Maya documents mention the taking of women as captives from these lineages. There are also

Now when the Grandmother saw the food, the great netful, she said:

"Where did you come by this food? From where was it stolen? I will surely go to see if you have finished off the maize plant and brought it all here,"[318] said the Grandmother.

Thus she went to see the maize plant. But there was the single ear of maize still on the maize plant, and it was clear where the net had been placed beneath it.

The Grandmother thus rushed back to her home and said to the maiden:

"This is but a sign that you are in truth my daughter-in-law. I will surely watch your deeds, for they that are to be my grandchildren are enchanted already," the maiden was told.

several *terra cotta* renderings of women with cacao pods growing from their body found in this area that are now located in the *Popol Vuh* Museum in Guatemala City.

[314] *Tz'i'a* (Dog) is a metaphor for shamelessness. Bunzel: "*T'si'* (*chucho*, dog). This symbolizes sin, especially sexual impurity. '*t'si*', 'dog,' a bad day, the worst of all. The day of shameless and beastly actions (especially sexual). This is the meaning of *t'si'* in the divinations. There are no ceremonies for this day, because it is evil. But if one wishes to ask forgiveness of one's evil acts, one asks it on the next day (9 *bats*)'" (Bunzel 1952, 283).

[315] Perhaps it is not a coincidence that the day immediately following *Q'anil*, *Toj*, and *Tz'i'*, is *B'atz'* in the traditional calendar.

[316] *Jal* is a dried ear of maize ready to be harvested.

[317] *Ko'k* is a wooden boxlike frame used to haul things on the back.

[318] It is still customary among contemporary Quichés to carry harvested maize in large nets and to bring them home at one time wherever possible: "The whole harvest from a field is brought in at one time even if extra laborers must be hired to carry it. If it must be carried any distance, the bearers run the whole way, shouting. When they enter the house, the owner and his wife meet them. When the harvest from the large estate of Don Náches, a wealthy Ladino was brought into his town house more than fifty bearers were hired for the occasion. They ran into town in single file, shouting, encircled the plaza before taking the corn to the owner's house, and the church bells were rung" (Bunzel 1952, 51). The arrival of the harvested maize is always an important event, even in smaller households. This episode suggests that Lady Blood had brought an entire harvest, though the Grandmother knew that no such field of maize existed in her family's plot.

HUNAHPU AND XBALANQUE IN THE
HOUSE OF THE GRANDMOTHER[319]

NOW we shall relate the tale of the birth of Hunahpu and Xbalanque.

THIS, therefore, is the account of their birth that we shall tell. When the day arrived, the maiden Lady Blood gave birth. The Grandmother did not see it when they were born, for these two arose[320] suddenly. Hunahpu and Xbalanque were their names. They arose in the mountains, but when they were taken into the house they did not sleep:

"Take them away and abandon them, for truly shrill are their mouths," said the Grandmother.

Thus they were placed on an anthill, and there they slept blissfully.

Then they were taken out again and placed on a thornbush. This was done by One Batz and One Chouen, for they would have had them die there on the anthill and on the thornbush.[321] They wanted this because of the treachery[322] and jealousy[323] of One Batz and One Chouen.

Thus at first their younger brothers were not accepted in the house. They were not known. Therefore they just grew up in the mountains.

Now One Batz and One Chouen were great flautists and singers. They had grown in greatness. They had passed through great affliction and mis-

---

[319] lines 2664–2899

[320] *Xeyake'ik* (they arose). This is a metaphor for birth according to Coto.

[321] This treatment of the twin sons of One Hunahpu and Lady Blood is a serious breach of highland Maya attitudes toward children, particularly infants. Despite poverty and private concerns, children are always accepted as a "gift" in Quiché homes and treated with patience and indulgence. Infants and small children are never left alone under any circumstances. Whenever possible babies accompany their mothers, who carry them on their backs everywhere as they go about their work. Toddlers and small children are cared for solicitously by their older siblings who also carry them about wherever they go. "[Quichés] care for them tenderly and reproach themselves if the child falls ill. There is no infanticide; that would be a violation of all their moral ideas" (Bunzel 1952, 99). This attitude is so pervasive in highland Maya society that it is difficult to believe that it would have been otherwise at the time the *Popol Vuh* was composed. It is likely that the "treachery" of One Batz and One Chouen toward their half-brothers would have been recognized as sufficient grounds for the punishment they later received when they were turned into monkeys. It is significant in this regard that monkeys were earlier described as descendents of the wooden people who "did not possess their hearts nor their minds," "walked without purpose," "did not remember Heart of Sky," and "were not capable of understanding" (pp. 83–90). It was the cold and dry hearts of the wooden people that had led to their ultimate destruction.

[322] *Ch'aqimal* is "treachery, lies, calumny, slander, falsehood, or mockery." Basseta wrote that it may also refer to the loud shouting of young men. In modern usage it suggests something that festers and spreads, such as an abscess, gangrene, or smallpox.

[323] Literally "red or fiery countenance," a common Quiché expression for jealousy.

fortune, and thus they had become great. They were sages. They were not only flautists and singers, but they had also become writers and carvers. Everything they did was successful for them.

For they knew of the circumstances of their birth, and certainly they were ingenious. They were the substitutes for their father who had gone to Xibalba and had died. Thus One Batz and One Chouen were great sages. In their hearts, they knew everything from the first, even before their younger brothers were created.

But nothing ever came of these enchanted abilities[324] because of their envy. The abuses[325] born in their hearts merely fell upon their own backs and nothing came of them.[326]

Thus they were ignored[327] by Hunahpu and Xbalanque, who went out every day to hunt with their blow-

Figure 34. "Thus at first their younger brothers were not accepted in the house.... Therefore they just grew up in the mountains." Twin youthful deities, redrawn from a Classic Maya vase (Taube 1992, fig. 58c).

guns. They were not loved by their grandmother, nor by One Batz and One Chouen. Nor were they given any food. When meals were prepared for them, One Batz and One Chouen would eat it all before they returned.

[324] *Na'wikil* is derived from the word for enchantment, or unusual power of knowledge. It is also used to refer to extraordinary abilities or talents.

[325] *Yoq'* is an "abuse, insult, or affront."

[326] Tedlock's Quiché collaborator, Andrés Xiloj, commented on this passage: "We see a person; we speak behind his back and he doesn't hear what we are murmuring. Then this murmur doesn't fall upon that person, but we are the ones who pay for it" (Tedlock 1996, 265 n. 105). Bunzel recorded the following explanation from a Quiché seeking justice from a slander inflicted on him: "Now I have a clean heart, my wife is satisfied, and the woman also has set everything right. Now I can go before the ancestors to ask justice. But if I go before them with my sins still upon me, and quarreling with my wife or relatives, then I shall die at once, before my enemy, for the justice which I ask for him will fall upon me" (Bunzel 1952, 376).

[327] The root of this verb is derived from *poy*, which has been used previously to describe the wooden effigies that were destroyed. Today the word is used for scarecrows, dolls, or statues. Each of these is something that resembles reality but is false. Basseta writes it is to be "discounted, ignored, displeased, dissatisfied" as well as to be "perverted, corrupted."

But they did not become enraged[328] or angry. They tolerated it, for they knew their own nature, and this was a light by which they could see.

Thus when they returned each day, One Batz and One Chouen would take away their birds and eat them. They did not give anything to the twins, Hunahpu and Xbalanque. One Batz and One Chouen merely played the flute and sang.

Then one day Hunahpu and Xbalanque returned without bringing any birds. The Grandmother was enraged because of this:

"What is the reason that you have not brought any more birds?" Hunahpu and Xbalanque were asked.

"This is why, our grandmother. Our birds are just stuck up in the top of the tree," they said. "There is no way to climb to the top of the tree to reach them, our grandmother. Therefore we would like our older brothers to go with us to bring down the birds," they said.

"Very well," said their older brothers. "We will go with you at dawn."

Thus they were defeated. The two of them had planned for the defeat of One Batz and One Chouen:

"We shall merely overturn their nature. This is the essence of our words. Thus be it so, for great is the affliction that they have caused us. If it had been according to their desires, we, their younger brothers, would have died and been lost. In their hearts, we are looked upon as slaves, as if we worked for them. Instead, we shall make of them an example," they said one to another.

Thus they went there below the tree whose name is Yellow Tree,[329] in company with their older brothers. As they went, they began to shoot with

[328] Literally "inflamed." The tolerance of the twins to the injustice of their older siblings is characteristic of Quiché practice. There are certainly rivalries among family members. Bunzel noted that the calm that prevails in all households is somewhat superficial, often hiding bitterness and discord with a "smooth surface of respectful courtesy" (Bunzel 1952, 12). Particularly among older family members, there is often an atmosphere of intense rivalry and mistrust. This antagonism seldom if ever erupts into open conflict, however, for fear of retribution from deceased ancestors who do not tolerate such behavior: "The ancestors and 'the idols' stand ready to punish the blows or harsh words that violate the sanctity of the house. The injured 'weep before the idols' demanding revenge, and the ever present fear of sorcery stays the free expression of antagonism. Within the house quiet and dignity prevail. All intercourse is marked by elaborate etiquette" (Ibid., 120). Thus one of her collaborators who was preparing for a ceremony told her: "It is better that I go out of the house before I am provoked to retort. There is nothing I can do, I must not quarrel or argue. For I am asking justice before the spirits, and if I do anything, they will immediately drag me out of this life" (Ibid., 380). Children are seldom chastened by their parents in traditional Quiché households, but it is made clear from a very early age that open expressions of anger or physical abuse between siblings is not tolerated and that when it does occur such behavior invites retribution by the ancestors in the form of illness or even death.

their blowguns, for there were innumerable birds in the top of the tree singing riotously. Their older brothers marvelled at this when they saw the birds. But not one of these birds that they saw fell down beneath the tree:

"Our birds do not fall down here. Just go and bring them down," they said to their older brothers.

"Very well," they said.

And they climbed up to the top of the tree. But the tree began to grow larger. It swelled in size. Thus when they wanted to come back down, One Batz and One Chouen couldn't climb down from the top of the tree.[330]

They therefore called down from the top of the tree:

"What can we say, our younger brothers? Take pity on us. This tree is truly frightening to see, our younger brothers," they called down from the top of the tree.

Thus Hunahpu and Xbalanque called back to them:

"Loosen your loincloths[331] and retie the long end below your bellies. Pull out the tail end[332] behind you. Then you will be able to walk freely," they were told by their younger brothers.

"Fine," they said.

And so they pulled out the ends of their loincloths,[333] and these immediately became tails. They appeared just like spider monkeys. Thus they went up into the tops of the trees there in the small mountains and the great mountains. They went out into the forests, howling and chattering loudly in the branches of the trees.

Thus was the defeat of One Batz and One Chouen at the hands of Hunahpu and Xbalanque. It was merely by their enchantments that it was done.

[329] *Can Te* (Lowland Maya: Yellow Tree). Recinos (1950, 128 n. 6) and Campbell (1983, 82) identify this as *Gliricidia sepium*, known in Central America as *Madre de cacao* (Spanish: Mother of Cacao). The Maya extracted a yellow dye from this tree (Roys 1967, 161 n. 8).

[330] Akkeren (2000, 65, 303–304) suggests that this tale is the origin of the famous *Palo Volador* in which dancers dressed as monkeys climb a tall pole, tie long ropes to their ankles, and spin downward as the ropes gradually unwind (Cook 2000, 107–118). In many communities this popular dance has been banned because of the danger involved.

[331] Ximénez identifies *we'x* as short trousers worn by men, but likely they were loincloths prior to the Spanish conquest based on the description in the text of their being loosened and retied. *Weexj* is the name for the traditional white trousers worn in Santiago Chimaltenango (Watanabe 1992, 93)

[332] This is a good example of a play on words. The text uses the term *je'* here to describe the end of the brothers' loincloths. While *je'* may be used to refer to the end of something, it also means "tail," presaging the transformation that would soon take place.

[333] *To'q*. This word is still in use in the highlands as a generic term for underwear (Mondloch, personal communication).

Now when they arrived back at their home, they spoke with their grandmother and mother:

"Our grandmother, something has happened to our older brothers. Their faces have changed.[334] They go about like animals now," they said.

"If you have done something to your older brothers, you will cause me misery and anguish. Let this not be what you have done to your older brothers, my grandsons," said the Grandmother to Hunahpu and Xbalanque.

They replied then to their grandmother:

"Do not grieve, our grandmother. You shall see again the faces of our older brothers. They will come back. But this is a test for you, our grandmother. Please do not laugh, for we will test their fate," they said.

Thus they began to play the flute. They played "Hunahpu Spider Monkey" on the flute.

---

[334] *Rax ki wach* (new their faces). This is a physical reality, in that the brothers now have monkey faces, but it also has a host of implied meanings. Basseta records that this suggests "without shame." Coto adds that it refers to one that has "gone astray, lost self-control, is impudent, outside the bounds of justice, talks nonsense, babbles, or chatters."

THE FALL OF ONE BATZ
AND ONE CHOUEN[335]

THEN they began to sing, to play the flute, and to play the drum.[336] And when they had taken up their flute and their drum, the Grandmother sat down with them as well. Thus they played the flute, calling them with the music. In song they called out their names, with the music whose name is "Hunahpu Spider Monkey."

Then arrived One Batz and One Chouen, dancing as they came. But when the Grandmother looked at them, she saw their ugly faces[337] and laughed, for she could not contain her laughter.

Therefore they immediately went away. Their faces could not be seen anymore, for they had gone back into the forest.

"What now will you do, our grandmother? We shall try it four times in all. Only three times more we shall call them with flute music and song. But you must truly contain your laughter when we try it again," said Hunahpu and Xbalanque.

Then they played the flute again, and again they came dancing in the middle of the house patio. Animatedly they did it, tempting their grandmother to laughter.

Thus immediately the Grandmother began to laugh again. For the faces of the spider monkeys were truly funny. They were paunchy[338] and naked below their chests.[339] And when they came, she laughed a great deal, which made them depart again into the mountains.

"Surely, what more can we do, our grandmother? This third time we shall try it again," said Hunahpu and Xbalanque.

Thus they played the flute again, and again they came dancing. But this time the Grandmother was able to contain well her laughter. They therefore scampered on the wall.[340] Their mouths were very red, and their faces were

[335] lines 2900–3023

[336] *Q'ojom* is a general term for any kind of percussion instrument, although "drum" is the most common interpretation in colonial dictionaries. In most modern Quiché communities, the word refers to the marimba, which has become extremely popular but which most likely did not exist in Precolumbian Guatemala. The flute and drum are still the instruments used to accompany traditional native dances and processions.

[337] *Itzel u wach* (evil his face) and *k'ax u wach* (painful his face) are common expressions used by the Quichés to describe an ugly person.

[338] *Xiririk –pam* is "pot-bellied, big bellied, paunchy" according to Basseta.

[339] A polite way of saying that their genitals were exposed. This is a sign of disgrace, or dishonor among the ancient Maya.

foolish.[341] Their mouths were puckered[342] and bushy.[343] Their faces were silly, and they snorted[344] at them. Now when she saw this, the Grandmother again burst out laughing. Never again were their faces seen because of the laughter of their grandmother.

"But this once more, our grandmother, we shall call upon them."

Thus for the fourth time they played their flutes again, but this time they did not come back. Instead they remained out in the forest.

Thus they spoke to their grandmother:

"We tried, our grandmother, and at first they came back. We have tried to call them back again. But do not grieve. We are your grandsons, and we are here. Just love[345] our mother, O grandmother.

"Our older brothers will be remembered. Thus be it so. They were given names and also given titles. One Batz and One Chouen shall be called upon," said Hunahpu and Xbalanque.

Figure 35. "The ancient ones also called upon them, they who were the writers and the carvers." Monkey scribe, redrawn from a Classic Maya vase.

[340] *Tz'aq* is a wall or a large building.

[341] *Tak* denotes someone who is "foolish, stupid, crazy, hard of hearing, or quick to anger."

[342] *Mutzuma'q* is "rounded," in this case describing the brothers' mouths as similar to the appearance of monkeys when they pucker their lips.

[343] *Chik'imal* (bushy) is used to describe unkempt or uncombed hair that sticks out away from the head or face.

[344] *Joq'ij* is to make sounds through the nose.

[345] *Loq'oj* is to "love, esteem, appreciate, value, honor, or regard." Thus the twins seek to replace the treachery and jealousy of the household with love and respect. In Quiché view, this is not merely the establishment of a more comfortable home environment, but an essential prerequisite for the proper expression of divine will. In contemporary Quiché thought, ancestors and deity do not tolerate open anger, jealousy, or pride and punish such severely. Until these characteristics are eliminated from the house of their mother and

And since that time they have been called upon by the flautists and the singers. The ancient ones also called upon them, they who were the writers and the carvers.[346] A long time ago, they became animals. They became spider monkeys because of their pride, for they had abused their younger brothers according to the dictates of their hearts. Thus they were ruined. One Batz and One Chouen were lost, becoming animals. Thus their community and their home is now among the flautists and the singers. For great were their accomplishments when they dwelt with their grandmother and their mother.

Figure 36. "Then they began to sing, to play the flute, and to play the drum." Maya elder playing a traditional flute and drum, Santiago Atitlán.

grandmother, the twins would not be able to act in concert with Heart of Sky, identified in the text as the inspiration for the twins subsequent actions in defeating death and restoring their father/ancestor to power. Note that even in victory, Hunahpu and Xbalanque show a degree of honor and respect for the legitimate accomplishments and titles of their older siblings, acknowledging that they will be remembered.

[346] Las Casas wrote that in the early Colonial period, these two brothers were the patrons of all the arts: "All the skilled artisans, such as painters, featherworkers, carvers, silversmiths, and others like them, worshiped and made sacrifices to those younger sons called Huncheven and Hunahan, so that they would grant them the skill and mastery to carry out their work in an accomplished and perfect way; but although they worshiped them as divine men, they were not held as gods in general, nor superior to all others" (Las Casas 1967, III.ccxxxv, 506. Translation by author).

HUNAHPU AND XBALANQUE
IN THE MAIZEFIELD[347]

THEN they began again to accomplish their deeds, to manifest themselves before the face of their grandmother and before the face of their mother. First they worked the maizefield:

"We are going to farm the maizefield, our grandmother and our mother," they said.

"We are the substitutes for our older brothers," said Hunahpu and Xbalanque.

Thus they took up their axes and their hoes,[348] carrying them on their shoulders. Each of them also shouldered his blowgun and departed their home, having first left instructions with their grandmother to bring their food:

"At midday come to give us our food, grandmother," they said.

"Very well then, my grandsons," said their grandmother.

Then they arrived there to farm

Figure 37. "Then they arrived there to farm the maizefield. They merely stuck the hoe into the ground, and it truly began to plow the earth." Andrés Xiloj, a prominent aj q'ij from Momostenango, working his maizefield with a hoe (photo by Garrett Cook).

the maizefield. They merely stuck the hoe into the ground, and it truly began to plow the earth. All by itself the hoe did the plowing for them.

As for the axe, they just stuck it into the fork[349] of a tree, and by its own strength it would fell it. Thus the one axe chopped and felled all the trees and bushes, feverishly working to cut down the trees all by itself.

Now this, the hoe, would break up countless stalks and briars. Just the one hoe would clear countless mountains, both small and great, as it went.

[347] lines 3024–3272
[348] Mixk'ina'. A wooden hoe according to Basseta.
[349] Literally the "armpit" of the tree.

Then they gave instructions to an animal, Turtle Dove by name. Hunahpu and Xbalanque placed it atop a great stump and spoke to it:

"When you see our grandmother coming to bring our food, immediately cry out that she has arrived. Then we will take up the hoe and the axe."

"Very well," said the Turtle Dove.

Thus they merely hunted with their blowguns. They didn't truly farm the maize. And when the Turtle Dove cried out, they came quickly, the one taking up the hoe while the other one took up the axe.

They would then put field debris on their heads and rub dirt on their hands. The one would dirty his face as if he had truly farmed the maizefield, while the other one would scatter wood chips on his head as if he had truly been cutting down trees.

In this way they were seen by the Grandmother, and thus they were given to eat. They did not truly farm the maize, and so it was unmerited that she went to give them their food.

And when they returned home they would say, "We are truly tired, our grandmother." And they would rub and stretch their legs and arms in front of their grandmother to deceive her.

But on the second day, they arrived at the maizefield to find that all the trees and bushes had been raised up again. All the stalks and briars had again fastened themselves together.

"Who is playing tricks on us?"[350] they asked therefore.

Now it was all the animals, both great and small, that had done it—the puma and the jaguar, the deer and the rabbit, the fox and the coyote, the peccary and the coati, the small birds and the great birds. These had done it. In a single night they did it.

Thus they began again to farm the maize. Again the earth was broken up. The trees were cut down. There they gathered their thoughts, over by the cut trees and the broken ground:

"We will just watch over our maizefield tonight, and thus we will discover whatever it was that has done this," they said when they gathered together their thoughts.

So when they returned to the house, they said:

"Someone perhaps has been playing tricks on us, our grandmother. When we arrived a while ago at our maizefield, we found that it had

[350] Literally "who is plucking at us?" Metaphorically this is to deceive or to play a trick on someone, although not in a playful way.

become a great field of grass and a great forest once again," they said to
their grandmother and their mother.

"Therefore we shall go back and watch over it by night. For it is not good
what has been done to us," they said.

Thus they concealed themselves. They went out again to cut down the
trees, and then they hid themselves there, taking cover.

At length all the animals gathered together, coming together[351] as one.
All the small and great animals arrived in the very heart of the night,[352] chattering as they came. And this was their speech:

"Arise trees; arise bushes," they said when they came.

Thus they congregated beneath the trees and the bushes, emerging
where they could be seen before their faces.

The first of these were the puma and the jaguar. The boys wanted to seize
them, but they would not give themselves up.

Then emerged the deer and the rabbit. They grabbed them by their tails,
but these just broke off, leaving the tail of the deer behind in their hands
along with the tail of the rabbit. Thus they still have shortened tails.[353]

Neither would these give themselves up—the fox or the coyote, the peccary or the coati. All the animals just passed on by in front of Hunahpu
and Xbalanque.

Thus their hearts were troubled because they weren't able to catch any
of them.

But one more came along behind all the rest. He scurried when he came,
and they netted him. They snared the rat in a net. They caught him and
squeezed him behind the head. According to their desire, they strangled
him and burned his tail over a fire. Because they did this to the tail of the
rat, their tails still do not have hair on them. And their eyes are the way they
are because the boys, Hunahpu and Xbalanque, strangled him.

"I must not die by your hands. Your task is not to be maize farmers. But
there is something that is yours," said the rat.

"Where is that which is ours? Speak then," the boys said to the rat.

"Will you first let me go?" asked the rat. "My word is here in my belly.[354]
I will tell it to you if you first give me a little food."

"We will give you your food later, but tell us first," he was told.

[351] This is to join together disparate pieces, or gather in a mixed group.
[352] Literally "zenith its heart night," meaning midnight.
[353] The Guatemalan varieties of the white-tailed deer (*Odocoileus americana*) and cottontail
rabbit (*Sylvilagus floridanus yucatanicus*) both have short tails. They are paired in this couplet
because they were the most commonly hunted game animals in the Maya area.

"Very well then. It is what belonged to your fathers, One Hunahpu and Seven Hunahpu by name, who died in Xibalba. They left behind their gaming things hanging above the house[355]—their yokes, their arm protectors, and their rubber ball as well. Your grandmother did not show these to you, for it was because of them that your fathers died."

"Is it not true? Do you truly know this?" the boys asked the rat.

Thus they rejoiced in their hearts when they heard from the rat the news about the rubber ball.

This, therefore, was given to the rat as his food—grains of maize, squash seeds, chili peppers, beans, pataxte, and cacao.

"These, then, are yours. If anything has been swept out with the trash and has become exposed, then it is yours. You shall gnaw on it," said Hunahpu and Xbalanque to the rat.

"Very well then, boys. But what will I say if your grandmother sees you?" he asked.

"Don't be disheartened,"[356] they said to the rat. "We are here. We know what to say to our grandmother. We will lift you up onto the corner of the house to fetch them. Straightaway you will go up to where the things are hanging. We will be able to see it in the rafters of the house, reflected in our sauce."[357]

Thus Hunahpu and Xbalanque gathered their thoughts and instructed him all night. And when it was truly midday,[358] they arrived.

---

[354] The implication is that the rat's information cannot be expressed until his belly has been satisfied with something to eat.

[355] This would be the rafters beneath the roof. This is a common place for storing tools, old clothing, and harvested maize. I have passed many a night sleeping in the "maize loft" as a guest in Quiché homes. The rat would know lofts are storage places since rats are to be found in every loft I have ever been acquainted with. On cold nights, they like to share bedding as uninvited sleeping companions.

[356] Literally "may it not fall your heart."

[357] Ti' (bite) as in a bite to eat. This refers to a snack, rather than a full meal. This turns out to be a bowl of mashed chili sauce.

[358] Literally "zenith sun."

HUNAHPU AND XBALANQUE
DISCOVER THE GAMING THINGS[359]

THE rat they carried could not be seen clearly when they arrived. While one went into the house, the other went around to the corner of the house and immediately lifted up the rat.

Then they asked their mother for their food:

"Just prepare for us a bite to eat," they said. We desire chili sauce, our grandmother."

Thus their bite was prepared, and a plate of sauce was placed before them. But this was just a trick they were playing on their grandmother and their mother. They drained the water jug dry:

"We are truly thirsty. Bring us something to drink," they said to their grandmother.

"All right," she replied.

Thus she left, leaving them behind to eat. But it was not true that they were hungry. It was merely a deception so that they could see the rat reflected in their chili sauce. There the rat was, behind the rubber ball where it hung above the house. This they saw reflected in their chili sauce.

Then they sent forth a mosquito.

Figure 38. "Thus the water that she had raised leaked out from the front of the jug. Try as she might, the face of the jug would not be sealed." Grandmother goddess with a flowing jug, redrawn from the Dresden Codex, p. 39b (Villacorta and Villacorta 1930).

The mosquito is an insect similar to a small biting fly.[360] It went to the river and pierced the front of the Grandmother's jug.

Thus the water that she had raised leaked out from the front of the jug. Try as she might, the face of the jug would not be sealed.[361]

[359] lines 3273–3338

[360] *Us.* Both *xa'n* (mosquito) and *us* may refer to mosquitos, but they can also be the small biting flies that congregate on the banks of rivers.

"What is our grandmother doing? We are gasping for water. We are parched with thirst!" they said to their mother.

Thus they sent her away.

Then the rat clawed at the ropes that held the rubber ball from the thatch roof above the house until it fell, along with the yokes, the arm protectors, and the leathers. They carried them away and hid them along the road leading to the ballcourt.

Then they went back to where their grandmother was at the river, and there they found their grandmother and mother busily trying to seal the face of the jug. Thus they arrived at the river, each carrying his blowgun:

"What have you been doing? Our hearts became weary, so we came," they said.

Figure 39. "Then the rat clawed at the ropes that held the rubber ball from the thatch roof above the house until it fell." Rat holding a bound rubber ball, from a Classic Maya stucco panel at Tonina (drawing by Linda Schele).

"Look at the front of my jug. It cannot be sealed off," replied their grandmother.

Immediately then they sealed it, and together they returned once more, leading the way before their grandmother.

Thus was the discovery of this rubber ball.

---

[361] The ancient lowland Maya worshiped an aged female deity named Ixchel (Goddess O of the codices), who is often depicted with a jug from which she pours out water in the form of rain. Ixchel was also a patroness of medicine, fertility, childbirth, midwifery, and the art of divination. The grandmother goddess Xmucane was apparently the Quiché equivalent of Ixchel, associated with the powers of creation (pp. 60–62; line 35), divination (pp. 79–82; lines 569–599), midwifery (p. 62; lines 32, 38), medicine (p. 99; lines 1112–1119), childbirth (p. 113; lines 1736–1742), and now the leaking water jug.

THE SUMMONS OF HUNAHPU
AND XBALANQUE TO XIBALBA[362]

AND so they went rejoicing as ballplayers to the ballcourt. For a long time they played ball there alone, sweeping clear the ballcourt of their father.

Figure 40. "And so they went rejoicing as ballplayers to the ballcourt. For a long time they played ball there alone, sweeping clear the ballcourt of their father." Ballcourt at Iximche, Guatemala.

Then the lords of Xibalba heard it:

"Someone has begun to play again over our heads. Have they no shame, stomping about up there? Did not One Hunahpu and Seven Hunahpu die when they desired to puff themselves up before us? Go then to summon them here once again," said One Death and Seven Death, along with all the lords.

"Summon them here," they said to their messengers. "Tell them, 'They must come, say the lords. Here we shall play ball with them. In seven days, we will play, say the lords.' Tell them this when you arrive there," the messengers were told.

[362] lines 3339–3469

Thus they came along the great cleared pathway, the road that led to the home of the boys. The messengers pursued[363] them into the home of the Grandmother, but the boys were still playing ball when the messengers of Xibalba arrived.

"The lords say, 'They must surely come,'" said the messengers of Xibalba.

Then the messengers of Xibalba set the date:

"In seven days, they will be expected." Such was the word left with Xmucane.

"Very well then," replied the Grandmother. "They shall go as summoned, you messengers."

Thus the messengers returned again, leaving the Grandmother heartbroken:

"How shall I tell my grandsons of their summons? Were these not truly from Xibalba? They are just like the messengers who arrived in the past when their fathers went away to die," said the Grandmother.

Thus she wept bitterly in the house alone.

Then a louse fell down on her. It itched, so she picked it up and put it in her hand. The louse scuttled as it went along.

"My grandchild," she asked the louse, "would you like me to send you to summon my grandsons at the ballcourt?"

Thus he left as a summoner with this message:

"Messengers have arrived with your grandmother saying that you are to come. The messengers of Xibalba declare, 'In seven days you are to come,' says your grandmother."

Such was the message given to the louse. And so he went, scuttling along the way. Now sitting in the road was a youthful toad by the name of Tamazul.[364]

"Where are you going?" asked the toad of the louse.

"I am going to give the boys a message that is in my belly," said the louse to Tamazul.

"Very well then, but I see that you are not going very fast," the toad said to the louse. "Wouldn't you like me to swallow you? Then you would see how fast I could go. We would get there quickly."

---

[363] *Toq'oj* is to pursue with the intention of importuning, persecuting, harassing, or vexing someone.

[364] The name Tamazul is derived from the Nahuatl *tamasolli* (toad), perhaps indicating a Central Mexican origin for portions of this tale.

"Very well," said the louse to the toad.

Thus he was licked up by the toad, who went hopping along his way. But he did not go fast. Presently, he was met by a great snake whose name was White Life.[365]

"Where are you going, boy Tamazul?" asked White Life.

"I am a messenger with a message in my belly," said the toad to the snake.

"But I see that you aren't going very fast. Perhaps I would arrive there more quickly," said the snake to the toad.

"Go right ahead," he was told.

Thus the toad was swallowed up by White Life. The snake, then, received his food and they still swallow toads today.

Now this snake went quickly along his way. Then again the snake was met by the falcon, a great bird.[366] And the snake was swallowed by the

Figure 41. "When the falcon arrived, he alighted atop the edge of the ballcourt while Hunahpu and Xbalanque were rejoicing and playing ball." The Laughing Falcon (Sutton, 1951, 198).

---

[365] *Saqiq'as* (White Life) is identified as a large snake by Varea.

[366] *Wak.* The name of this bird is closely related to the Nahuatl word for falcon, *oactli.* It is likely the bird known as the Laughing Falcon (*Herpetotheres cachinnans*), which makes a sound similar to this call (Tedlock 1996, 270 n. 114). Bassie-Sweet points out that the call of the laughing falcon is an indication of the coming of the rains in Mesoamerica (personal communication). She suggests that the twins' clearing of the maize field implies the dry season when the fields are cleared for burning. The subsequent descent into Xibalba would coincide with this period of death and sterility. The call of the laughing falcon may presage the return of rain and agricultural rebirth.

[367] This humorous story may have prophetic significance as well. The louse represents corruption and decay. The toad is associated with the watery underworld and the fertility of the earth's interior as a source of renewal. The serpent is a common symbol of regeneration because of its tendency to periodically shed its old skin to uncover a new one. Finally, the falcon is a common symbol of the reborn sun at dawn. Thus the sequence of animals may presage the death and corruption of the twins in the underworld, followed by their rebirth to new life and apotheosis as the sun and moon. Literally then, death would be swallowed up by the ultimate triumph of Hunahpu and Xbalanque.

falcon.[367] Then he arrived atop the ballcourt. Thus the hawk received his food, so that he still eats snakes in the mountains.

When the falcon arrived, he alighted atop the edge of the ballcourt while Hunahpu and Xbalanque were rejoicing and playing ball.

Then the falcon cried out:

"Wak-ko! Wak-ko!" was the cry of the falcon.

"What is that which is crying out? To our blowguns!" they said.

HUNAHPU AND XBALANQUE RECEIVE
THE SUMMONS TO XIBALBA[368]

SO then they shot the falcon. The pellet from the blowgun buried itself straight into his eye,[369] knocking him down. Thus he fell, and they went out to seize him and question him:

"Why have you come?" they asked the falcon.

"I have a message in my belly.[370] But surely you must first cure my eye, and then I will tell it," said the falcon.

"Very well then," they replied.

So they took off a little of the surface of their rubber ball and put it in the face of the falcon.[371] This they called Sliced Rubber. Immediately he was cured by them, making good again the sight of the falcon.

"Tell it then," they said to the falcon.

Thus he vomited the great snake.

"Speak!" they said again to the snake.

"All right," he replied. And so he vomited the toad.

"What is your errand? Speak!" the toad was told.

"My message is here in my belly," said again the toad.

Then he tried to throw up, but he did not vomit. His mouth just drooled. He tried, but nothing did he vomit. Thus the boys wished to beat him.

"You are a deceiver," he was told.

Then they squashed his rear end with their feet, crushing the bones of his backside with their feet.

Again he tried, but he just salivated at the mouth. So they pried open the mouth of the toad. It was pried open wide by the boys. They searched in his mouth and found that the louse was merely stuck in front of the toad's teeth. He was just in his mouth. He hadn't really been swallowed. It was merely as if he had been swallowed.

Thus the toad was defeated. As a result, it is not obvious what food was given to him. He could not go fast; thus he merely became spoil for the snake.

---

[368] lines 3470–3556

[369] This is a play on words in the original Quiché, since "eye" is *u b'aq' u wach* (its pellet or seed his face).

[370] The irony is that this expression is literally true, since the message is contained in the animals that he had swallowed.

[371] The laughing falcon has a black patch around the eyes.

"Speak!" the louse was told.

Thus he spoke his word:

"The Grandmother says to you boys, 'Go and summon them. Messengers have arrived from Xibalba, the messengers of One Death and Seven Death. 'In seven days[372] they will come here to play ball with us. They must bring their gaming things—the rubber ball, yokes, arm protectors, and leathers. They will liven up this place, say the lords.' 'This is their word that has come,' says your grandmother. 'Thus you must come,' the Grandmother truly says. Your grandmother weeps. She calls out that you must come."

"Is it not true?" they asked in their hearts when they heard this. And immediately they returned to advise their grandmother.

[372] The number seven has ritual significance in Maya theology. In this case, it may refer to the seven levels of the earth that were believed to exist above the underworld (Thompson 1971, 214). Thus the twins were allowed a day to pass through each of these layers on their journey downward into Xibalba. It may also refer to the seven sacred directions of the Maya universe—the four cardinal directions plus the sky, center, and underworld.

THE DESCENT OF HUNAHPU AND XBALANQUE INTO XIBALBA[373]

"SURELY we must go, our grandmother. But first we will advise you. This is the sign of our word that we will leave behind. Each of us shall first plant an ear of unripe maize[374] in the center of the house.[375] If they dry up, this is a sign of our death. 'They have died,' you will say when they dry up. If then they sprout again, 'They are alive,' you will say, our grandmother and our mother. This is the sign of our word that is left with you," they said.

Thus Hunahpu planted one, and Xbalanque planted another in the house. They did not plant them in the mountains or in fertile ground. It was merely in dry ground, in the middle of the interior of their home, that they planted them.

Then they left, each with his blowgun, and descended to Xibalba. They quickly went down the steps, passing through various river canyons. They passed through the midst of many birds. "Flocks" was the name of the birds.

And again they passed over Pus River and Blood River. In their hearts, the Xibalbans had intended these as traps. But they were not troubled. They just passed over them, floating on their blowguns.

When they came to the four crossroads, they already knew the roads of Xibalba—the Black Road, the White Road, the Red Road, and the Blue/Green Road.

Then they sent an insect named Mosquito. They sent him on ahead to obtain for them what he could hear:

"You shall bite each one of them in turn. Bite the first one seated there and then keep on biting them until you have finished biting all of them. It

---

[373] lines 3557–3993

[374] *Aj*. This is an ear of unripe maize, or maize that is still soft on the cob. Alternatively, it may also refer to the stalk of the maize plant.

[375] Although this incident seems odd, it is consistent with the ancient Maya conception of the universe in which all creation is seen as a house. The four corners represent the cardinal directions while its walls and ceiling form the vault of the sky. The foundation posts thus form the boundaries of the underworld. The maize plant is often depicted as a divine axis mundi standing at the center point of the universe with its roots extending downward into the underworld while its stalk reaches into the sky. The ancient Maya often erected colossal stone monuments of their revered kings decorated with tree and maize elements to emphasize the rulers' identity with this sacred living center. Thus the Quichés would see nothing odd in the twins identifying themselves with a maizestalk planted at the center of a divine household.

will be truly yours then to suck the blood of people on the road," the mosquito was told.

"Very well then," said the mosquito.

So then he went along the Black Road until he alighted behind the effigies of carved wood. The first ones were all dressed up. He bit the first one, but there was no response. Then he bit the second one seated there, but he did not speak either.

Next he bit the third one seated there, who was One Death—"Ouch!" said each one when he was bitten. "What?" was their reply:

"Ow!" said One Death.

"What, One Death? What is it?"

"I am being bitten!"

"It's just . . . Ow! What was that? Now I am being bitten!" said the fourth one seated there.

"What, Seven Death? What is it?"

"I am being bitten!"

Next, the one seated fifth said, "Ow! Ow!"

"Flying Scab," asked Seven Death, "what is it?"

"I am being bitten!" he said.

Then the sixth one seated there was bitten. "Ow!"

"What, Gathered Blood? What is it?" asked Flying Scab.

"I am being bitten!" he said.

Next, the seventh one seated there was bitten. "Ow!" he said.

"What, Pus Demon? What is it?" asked Gathered Blood.

Figure 42. "Thus they came to where the Xibalbans were." Death God, from the Dresden Codex, p. 13b (Villacorta and Villacorta 1930).

"I am being bitten!" he said.

Then the eighth one seated there was bitten. "Ow!" he said.

"What, Jaundice Demon? What is it?" asked Pus Demon.

"I am being bitten!" he said.

Then the ninth one seated there was bitten. "Ow!" he said.

"What, Bone Staff? What is it?" asked Jaundice Demon.

"I am being bitten!" he said.

Then the tenth one seated there was bitten. "Ow!"

"What, Skull Staff? What is it?" asked Bone Staff.

"I am being bitten!" he said.

Then the eleventh one seated there was bitten. "Ow!" he said next.

"What, Wing? What is it?" asked Skull Staff.

"I am being bitten!" he said.

Next, the twelfth one seated there was bitten. "Ow!" he said.

"What, Packstrap? What is it?" asked Wing.

"I am being bitten!"

Next was bitten the thirteenth one seated there. "Ow!"

"What, Bloody Teeth? What is it?" asked Packstrap.

"I am being bitten!" he said.

Then the fourteenth seated one was bitten. "Ow!"

"What, Bloody Claws? What is it?" asked Bloody Teeth.

"I am being bitten!" he said.

Thus their names were named. Each of them revealed the name of the other. Each of the individuals in order of their rank had his name revealed by the one who sat next to him.[376] Not one of their names was missed until all of the names were named when they were bitten by a hair that Hunahpu had plucked from the front of his knee. It wasn't really a mosquito that had bitten them. And so Hunahpu and Xbalanque heard the names of all of them.

Thus they came to where the Xibalbans were.

"Hail these lords who are seated there," said a tempter.

"These are not lords. These are merely effigies carved of wood," they said. Then they hailed each one of them:

"Morning, One Death. Morning, Seven Death.[377]
Morning, Flying Scab. Morning, Gathered Blood.
Morning, Pus Demon. Morning, Jaundice Demon.
Morning, Bone Staff. Morning, Skull Staff.

[376] There is a definite hierarchy among the lords of Xibalba, exemplified by the order in which they are seated on the palace bench. In traditional Maya confraternity houses, such as at Santiago Atitlán, there is a bench where, on ceremonial occasions, elders sit in the order of their rank of authority.

[377] The greeting in each case is *q'ala ta*. *Q'ala* is a shortened version of "it is clear," related to the common modern Quiché greeting in the morning, *saqirik* (it has dawned). *Ta* may simply mean "then," a frequently used word in the text. It may also be a shortened form of *tat* (father), a term commonly used when addressing highly ranked or older persons.

Morning, Wing.   Morning, Packstrap.

Morning, Bloody Teeth.   Morning, Bloody Claws," they said
when they arrived there.

All of them had their faces revealed, for all of their names were named.
Not one of their names was missed. When they were called upon, they gave
the names of each one without leaving any of them out.

"Sit down here," they were told, for it was desired that they sit on top of
the bench. But they didn't want to:

"This isn't a bench for us. It is merely a heated stone," said Hunahpu and
Xbalanque. Thus they were not defeated.

"Very well then, just go into that house," they were told.

So then they entered into the House of Darkness. But they were not
defeated there either. In their hearts, the Xibalbans ordained that they
would be defeated there in this, the first of the trials of Xibalba.

Thus they entered first into the House of Darkness. There the messenger
of One Death gave to them a torch, already burning, and a cigar for each of
them. And the messenger said when he arrived:

"Thus says the lord: 'Here is their torch. It must be given back at dawn
along with the cigars. They must return them.'"

"Very well," they replied.

But they didn't light the torch. They just placed the red tail feather of a
macaw on it as a substitute for flame. Thus the night watchmen saw it as
if it were burning.

As for the cigars, they just put fireflies on their tips. All night they would
glow brilliantly because of them.

"We have defeated them," said the night watchmen.

But the torch was not used up, for it was only an illusion. Neither did the
cigars have anything burning on them. It was merely an illusion as well.
Thus they returned them whole to the lords:

"What becomes of them? Where did they come from? Who begat them?
Who gave them birth? Truly our hearts are troubled, for it is not good what
they are doing to us. Their appearance as well as their nature are unique,"
they said one to another.

Then they summoned all of the lords:

"Let us play ball, boys," they were told.

But first they were questioned by One Death and Seven Death:

"Where did you really come from? Would you tell us, boys?" they were
asked by the Xibalbans.

"We must have come from somewhere, but we don't know." Only this they said. They told them nothing.

"Very well then. We will just go and play ball,[378] boys," the Xibalbans said to them.

"Fine," they replied.

"Here is our rubber ball that we will use," said the Xibalbans.

"No, we will use ours," said the boys.

"Not so. We will use this one that is ours," said again the Xibalbans.

"Very well," said the boys.

"It appears to be a skull, but it is merely drawn on the ball,"[379] said the Xibalbans.

Figure 43. "As for the cigars, they just put fireflies on their tips. All night they would glow brilliantly because of them." Firefly, redrawn from a Classic Maya vase (Coe 1973, 99).

"It is not. It is a skull we tell you," said the boys.

"Not so," replied the Xibalbans.

"Very well then," said Hunahpu.

Thus the Xibalbans threw down their rubber ball, which landed before the yoke of Hunahpu. And when the Xibalbans saw this, the White Dagger

[378] The ballgame was played throughout Mesoamerica beginning at least by the time of the Olmecs ca. 1500 B.C. Although the rules varied over time and from region to region, it generally involved opposing teams of two or more players attempting to bounce a solid rubber ball without the use of hands through a ring placed vertically along the ballcourt's walls. Sahagun described a similar type of ballgame among the Aztecs in the sixteenth century:

> These balls... were solid, of a certain resin or gum which is called *ulli* [rubber] which is very light in weight and bounces like an inflated ball.... The ballgame was called *tlaxtli* or *tlachtli*. The court consisted of two walls with some twenty or thirty feet of distance between them and each was up to forty or fifty feet in length. The floor and walls were heavily plastered, the latter having some one and a half *estados* [nearly ten feet] in height. In the middle of the court was a line made especially for the game; and in the middle of the walls, halfway down the playing stretch, were two stones like millstones perforated in the middle, facing each other, and they each had holes wide enough that the ball could fit into each of them. And whoever placed the ball there won the game. They did not play with their hands but hit the ball with their flanks. For playing they wore gloves on their hands and a leather apron on their flanks to hit the ball (Sahagún 1938, II.viii.10, pp. 297–298).

[379] The verb root, *juch'* means "to draw lines or to adorn with figures" according to Coto. Thus the Xibalbans try to convince the twins that their ball looks like a skull only because it has had skull-like features drawn on it.

came out of their rubber ball. It clashed about over the ground of the entire ballcourt, threatening the boys.

"What is that?" asked Hunahpu and Xbalanque. "You just want death for us. Did we not answer your summons when your messenger came? Have pity on us. We will just go, then," said the boys to them.

It was their desire that the boys would straightaway die there because of the blade. They were to have been defeated. But it was not so. It was the Xibalbans who were now defeated by the boys.

"Don't go, boys. We will just play with your ball," the boys were told.

"Very well then," they replied.

Thus they took out their rubber ball, and it was thrown down. Then their prizes were chosen:

"What will we win?" the Xibalbans asked.

"Surely it is your choice," the boys said.

"Our prize[380] shall be merely four bowls of flowers," said the Xibalbans.

"Very well. What kinds of flowers?" the boys asked the Xibalbans.

"One bowl of red petals,[381] one bowl of white petals, one bowl of yellow petals, and one bowl of the large ones," said the Xibalbans.

"Very well," replied the boys.

So then the ball was dropped

Figure 44. "It appears to be a skull, but it is merely a drawing." Skull within a rubber ball, from a wall panel in the Great Ballcourt at Chichen Itza (drawing by Linda Schele).

into play. They were equal in strength, but the boys made many plays with the ball for they played with all their hearts. At last, the boys gave themselves up to be defeated, and the Xibalbans thus rejoiced at their defeat:

[380] This is likely a play on words between ch'ako'n (prize, spoils) and related words such as ch'akom (cuttings of flowers or plants), and chakaj (bouquet, bunch of flowers according to Varea).

[381] This reading for much'ij is based on much' (to break apart, crumble, break into pieces). Flower petals are commonly given as offerings in modern highland Maya ceremonies, often broken off the flower as part of the ceremony as prayers are made. It would be much easier for the ants to carry away petals than whole flowers. Alternatively, it may be related to muchechen, which Basseta defines as "a fragrant flower," and a "sign of love."

Figure 45. "So then the ball was dropped into play. They were equal in strength, but the boys made many plays with the ball for they played with all their hearts." Ballplayer lunging for the ball, from a Classic Maya panel from Site Q (drawing by Linda Schele).

"We have done well. We have already defeated them at the first attempt," said the Xibalbans. "Where shall they go to get the flowers?" they asked in their hearts.

"You will give to us the flowers as our prize early in the morning," the boys Hunahpu and Xbalanque were told by the Xibalbans.

"Very well. We will play ball again early in the morning," they said. Then they made their plans together.

Thus the boys entered into Blade House, the second trial of Xibalba. Here it was desired that they would be sliced apart by the blades. They were to have died quickly in their hearts. But they did not die. They spoke to the blades, instructing them in this way:

"Yours shall be the flesh of animals," they said to the blades.

Thus they stopped moving. As one they all lowered the points of their blades.

And while they were passing the night in Blade House, they called out to all the ants:

"Cutting ants,[382] conquering ants, come! Go and get flower blossoms as prizes for the lords."

"Very well," they said.

Then the ants went to get flowers from the garden of One Death and Seven Death. Now the Xibalbans had previously instructed the guardians of their flowers:

"Look after our flowers with all vigilance. Do not allow them to be stolen. For by these we have defeated the boys. What if they were able to obtain these as our prize? Thus do not sleep all night."

"Very well," they said then.

But the guardians of the garden did not notice anything. They would just cry out aimlessly in the branches of the trees. They just toddled along through the garden repeating their song:

"Shpurpuwek, shpurpuwek,"[383] said the one when he called.

"Puhuyu, puhuyu," said the other, the whippoorwill by name, when he called.

These two were the guardians of the garden of One Death and Seven Death. They didn't notice the ants stealing that which they were guarding. They swarmed[384] and thronged, carrying away the flowers. They went to cut down flowers from the tops of trees, gathering them together with those from below the trees. All this they did while the guardians were crying out, not noticing that their tails and wings were being gnawed on as well.

The flowers were thus loosened until they fell down to be gathered up. The four bowls were thus quickly filled with their flowers. By dawn they had all been collected.

Then the messengers arrived to summon them:

"'Come!' says the lord. 'May they straightaway bring hither our prize,'" the boys were told.

"Very well," they answered.

For they had collected the flowers into the four bowls. Thus they went, arriving before the lords. Now the lords received the flowers with woeful faces. Thus the Xibalbans were defeated. The boys had just sent ants, and in one night they had collected the flowers in the bowls. Thus the Xibalbans all turned pale. Their faces were pallid because of the flowers.

And so they summoned the flower guardians:

---

[382] These are large, leaf-cutting ants, known in Guatemala as *zompopos*.

[383] Tedlock interprets this as the call of the whippoorwill (D. Tedlock 1996, 274 n. 123). Interestingly enough, the Quiché version of the call is phonetically very similar to the English name for the bird as well as to its song.

[384] *B'olowik* is literally "to boil." It is also used to describe the swarming of insects according to Coto.

"For what reason have you allowed our flowers to be stolen? These flowers that you see are ours," the guardians were told.

"We noticed nothing, O lords. But our tails have surely suffered[385] for it," they replied.

Then their mouths were split open[386] as punishment for allowing that which they were guarding to be stolen. Thus One Death and Seven Death were defeated by Hunahpu and Xbalanque. And this is the reason why the mouths of whippoorwills gape wide open to this day.

Then the ball was dropped into play again, but the game was even. And when they had finished playing ball, they planned together once more:

"At dawn again," said the Xibalbans.

"Very well," said the boys when they had finished.

---

[385] *Kuyu* is "to suffer, or endure." It is also used to describe something "bent, crooked, crippled, or lame." Either reading would be applicable here. Whippoorwills have very short wing and tail feathers.

[386] This is apparently meant as a play on words. The whippoorwills are said to have "cried out," in song when they should have been guarding the gardens of Xibalba. The Quiché phrase is "they broke open their mouths." Now the Xibalba lords "split open their mouths" as the punishment chosen to match the birds' crime.

HUNAHPU AND XBALANQUE
IN THE HOUSE OF COLD[387]

AND so they now entered the House of Cold. The cold here was immeasurable. The interior of the House of Cold was thick with hail.

But straightaway the boys caused the cold to dissipate.[388] They did it in. They ruined and destroyed the cold. Thus they did not die, but rather were alive when it dawned again. The Xibalbans had wanted them to die there, but this was not to be. Instead they were just fine when the dawn came.

So then their guardians came again to summon them.

"What is this? Haven't they died?" asked the lords of Xibalba.

And again they marveled at the deeds of the boys, Hunahpu and Xbalanque.

---

[387] lines 3994–4017
[388] *Tzaj* is to "evaporate, dry up, dissipate, exhaust."

HUNAHPU AND XBALANQUE
IN THE HOUSE OF JAGUARS[389]

NEXT they entered into Jaguar House, which was crowded inside with jaguars:

"Do not eat us. We will give you what is yours," the jaguars were told.

Then they scattered bones before the beasts, who voraciously crunched them.[390]

The hearts of the night watchmen found this sweet, saying, "They are finished. They have given themselves up. They have eaten their hearts, and now these are their skeletons that are being gnawed upon."

But they didn't die. They were just fine when they came out again from Jaguar House.

"What kind of people are these? Where have they come from?" asked all the Xibalbans.

Figure 46. "Next they entered into Jaguar House, which was crowded inside with jaguars." Underworld jaguar surrounded by waterlilies, redrawn from a Classic Maya vase.

---

[389] lines 4018–4037

[390] *Paq'aq'ik* refers to the sound of crunching, gnawing, or eating rapidly. It is also used to describe the sound of walking over dry leaves. Alternatively it may also refer to the sound of something being rent or split.

HUNAHPU AND XBALANQUE
IN THE HOUSE OF FIRE[391]

NEXT they went into the fire, for there was a House of Fire. There was nothing but fire inside. But they were not burned. They were to have been roasted and set aflame. Instead they were just fine when dawn came. It had been desired that they would straightaway die when they passed through there, but it was not so. Thus all the Xibalbans lost heart as a result.

[391] lines 4038–4051

HUNAHPU AND XBALANQUE
IN THE HOUSE OF BATS[392]

NEXT they were put inside Bat House, which had only bats inside. It was a house of death bats. These were great beasts with snouts like blades that they used as murderous weapons.

When they arrived there, they were to be finished off. They had to crawl inside their blowguns to sleep so that they would not be eaten there in this house.

Nevertheless, it was because of a single death bat that they gave themselves up in defeat. It came swooping down. But this was merely a way to manifest themselves when it occured.

Thus they pleaded for wisdom all that night as the bats made a din with their flapping wings.

"Keeleetz! Keeleetz!" they said all night long.

At length things quieted a little, and the bats became motionless.

Thus one of the boys crawled to the end of his blowgun. Xbalanque said, "Hunahpu, do you see the dawn yet?"

"I will go and see for certain if has happened," he replied.

Hunahpu truly wanted to look out of the mouth of his blowgun to see the dawn. But when he did so, his head was cut off by the death bat,[393] leaving the greater part of his body behind.

"What? Hasn't it dawned yet?" asked Xbalanque. But Hunahpu did not move.

"What is going on? Hunahpu wouldn't have left. What then has he done?"

But nothing moved; only the rustling of wings was heard. Thus Xbalanque was ashamed:

"Alas,[394] we have given in already," he said.

At the word of One Death and Seven Death, the head was placed atop the ballcourt. Thus all the Xibalbans rejoiced because of the head of Hunahpu.

[392] lines 4052–4177
[393] The ability of bats to cut down fruit from trees while in flight associated them in the mind of the ancient Maya with decapitation sacrifice. Bats are often seen painted on ancient Maya vessels as underworld denizens of death, decorated with crossed bones and extruded eyeballs that have their optic nerves still dangling from them.
[394] Ximénez translates *akarok* as "Ay! Ay!" In English the more common expression of lament would be "Alas!"

Then Xbalanque summoned all of the animals—the coati and the peccary, and all the animals both small and great—while it was still dark, early in the morning. He then entreated them for their food:

"I send each of you to bring the food that belongs to you," said Xbalanque to them.

"Very well," they said.

Then they all went to obtain what was theirs. When they returned they were many. One brought back rotten things, another brought leaves, another brought stones, and yet another brought dirt. Thus the animals, both small and great, each brought their various foods.

Figure 47. "'Blacken it again with soot, old man,' the possum was told." Opossum deity bearing torches, from the Dresden Codex, p. 39a (Villacorta and Villacorta 1930).

Now after many had come, the coati arrived last of all bringing a chilacayote squash. She[395] came rolling it along with her nose. This was to be transformed into the head of Hunahpu. Immediately its eyes were carved upon it. Numerous sages came down from the sky. For Heart of Sky, he who is Huracan, appeared here. He arrived here in Bat House.

But the face wasn't completed successfully in time. Only its beautiful covering had appeared. It only had the ability to speak by the time the horizon of the sky began to redden, for it was about to dawn.

"Blacken it again with soot, old man,"[396] the possum[397] was told.

---

[395] The coati is consistently associated with females in the text, just as the peccary is associated with males. They are particularly identified as the grandmother and grandfather deities respectively (pp. 60–61, 80, 98; lines 22–23, 559–560, 1055–1056). Akkeren cites a possible ethnographic survival of this association between the coati and gourds. In the Yucatec village of Xcacal, a ceiba tree is cut down in the forest and re-erected as a "tree of abundance" in the center of the main plaza. An actor dressed as a coati climbs the tree and scatters squash seeds while tying fruit to its branches (Akkeren 2000, 296).

[396] *Ama'* is a general term for "male," whether human or animal. In this case, it is used as a nickname for the aged possum deity. Because of the possum's gray coat, awkward gait, and snaggly teeth, the Maya associated this animal with old age (Miller and Taube 1993, 128).

[397] Father Coto lists under the Spanish word *Escuridad*, that *vuch* (possum) is the darkness of night just prior to the dawn (Coto 1983, 207–8). This is perhaps a manifestation of the creator deity Xpiyacoc, one of whose principal titles is Hunahpu Possum (Karen Bassie-Sweet, personal communication; see pp. 60, 79–80; lines 20, 500, 555). In the Tzotzil area, a grandfather possum, called "Old Man Possum," is associated with the dawn at the beginning of the planting season, and that the red light of the east is said to be one of his manifestations: "'Uch [Possum] is greatly respected, because it has fire, because at dawn it

"Fine," replied the Grandfather.

And he blackened the sky with soot until it was dark again. Four times the Grandfather blackened it with soot. Thus today people say, "The possum blackens it with soot."

Finally the sky succeeded in turning red, and then blue when it began its existence.

"Is it not good?" Hunahpu was asked.

"Yes, it is good," he replied.

For his head was well supported. It became just like a true head. Then they planned a deception;[398] they took counsel together:

"Don't play ball. Just look threatening. I will surely be the one to accomplish it," said Xbalanque to him.

Then he instructed a rabbit:

"Be there at the head of the ballcourt in the tomato patch,"[399] the rabbit was told by Xbalanque. "And when the rubber ball comes your way, hop away until I accomplish my task," the rabbit was told. Thus he was given his instructions there in the night.

And when it dawned, the both of them were well.[400]

lights up the hills. It is not the sunlight, for the sun rises later.... 'Uch is as God because it has light, a red light, that later disappears to give place to the God, the sun. Neither 'Okinahual nor 'Uch are evil, but they must be respected as a God. God must be respected, but he is not bad. Perhaps he punishes when he is overlooked" (Guiteras-Holmes 1961, 195–197; cf. 33, 206, 292). Akkeren compares this passage with the New Years pages of the Dresden Codex in which a possum deity presides over the five days of the Wayeb at the close of the annual cycle. In the *Popol Vuh* account, however, the possum is associated not with the annual change of the solar year, but "the moment of the new Sun-era" (Akkeren 2000, 290).

[398] *Xkib'an ki tzij* (they made their words). To "make" words is to deceive or to lie.

[399] There is some confusion as to where the rabbit was told to be. The manuscript here reads *pixc*, which Tedlock reads as *pixik'* (acorn or oak). This is contradicted, however, by lines 4197 and 4217, which read *pix* (tomatoes, or tomato patch), a reading given by most translators. The confusion may be due to a play on words, a practice beloved by the Maya. *Pixk'onik* is the verb for "to hop (like a rabbit or flea)," while the rabbit is *pixab'ax* (instructed) in lines 4164 and 4174.

[400] Literally "good their faces both of them," the standard way of saying that they were "fine," but also in this context a clever play on words considering the newly-made "face" of Hunahpu.

THE HEAD OF HUNAHPU
IS RESTORED[401]

SO the ball was again dropped into play. The head of Hunahpu was first placed atop the ballcourt.

"We have already triumphed. You are finished. You gave in, so give it up," they were told.

But Hunahpu just called out:

"Strike[402] the head as if it were a rubber ball," they were told. "No harm will come to us now, for we are holding our own."

Thus the lords of Xibalba threw down[403] the ball where it was met by Xbalanque. The ball landed before his yoke and bounced away. It sailed clear over the ballcourt. It just bounced once, then twice, landing in the tomatoes. Then the rabbit came out, hopping along.[404] All the Xibalbans thus went after him. The Xibalbans all went after the rabbit, shouting and rushing about.

Thus the twins were able to retrieve the head of Hunahpu, replacing it where the chilacayote squash had been. They then placed the chilacayote

Figure 48. "The ball landed before his yoke and bounced away. It sailed clear over the ballcourt. It just bounced once, then twice, landing in the tomatoes. Then the rabbit came out, hopping along." Ballplayer with a rabbit, from a Classic Maya vessel (drawing by Linda Schele).

[401] lines 4178–4241

[402] The action referred to is, unfortunately, not clear. According to Coto, k'aqa may be "to strike, to throw," or even generally "to play ball."

[403] This is a case where the limitations of the Latin alphabet in which the manuscript was written are apparent. The text reads xetzacou. If this is to be read as xetzaqow, it would mean that the Xibalbans "threw out" the ball into play. Alternatively, if it is to be read as xetzak'ow, it would mean that the Xibalbans "struck" the ball. It is impossible to know which of these alternatives is correct, although it would be helpful to our understanding of how the game was played.

[404] The hopping of the rabbit thus confuses the lords of Xibalba into thinking it is the bouncing ball.

squash on the ballcourt, while the true head of Hunahpu was his once more. Therefore they both rejoiced again. While the Xibalbans were out searching for their rubber ball, the twins retrieved it from the tomato patch. And when they had done so, they called out:

"Come on! We found our rubber ball!" they said. Thus they were carrying the round ball[405] when the Xibalbans returned.

"What was it that we saw?" they asked.

And so they began again to play ball, both teams making equal plays until at last Xbalanque struck the chilacayote squash, strewing it all over the ballcourt. Thus its seeds were scattered before them.[406]

"What is this that has been brought here? Where is he that brought it?" asked the Xibalbans.

Thus the lords of Xibalba were defeated by Hunahpu and Xbalanque. They had passed through great affliction, but despite everything that had been done to them, they did not die.

---

[405] *Ki k'olem* (they were carrying a round thing). This is undoubtedly a reference to the ball, although it is not specified (James Mondloch, personal communication).

[406] A play on words is made here between *saqiram* (scattered) and *saqilal* (squash seeds). If one did not recognize the pun in the original Quiché, the choice of words would be confusing.

THE DEATHS OF
HUNAHPU AND XBALANQUE[407]

THIS, then, is the memorial to the deaths of Hunahpu and Xbalanque. We shall now tell it in memory of their death.

What they had planned to do, they had done despite all their afflictions and misfortunes. Thus they did not die in the trials of Xibalba. Neither were they defeated by all the ravenous beasts that lived there.

And then they summoned two seers. Visionary persons they were. The names of these sages were Descended[408] and Ascended:

"The lords of Xibalba may inquire of you concerning our death. They are even now putting together their thoughts on the matter, because we have not yet died. We have not been defeated. We confounded their trials. Nor have the animals seized us. This, therefore, is the sign that is in our hearts. Heated stones will be the means by which our murder will be accomplished. Thus when all Xibalba has gathered together to determine how to ensure our death, this shall be the idea that you will propose. If you are asked about our death when we are burned, this is what you shall tell them, you, Descended and you, Ascended, if they should speak to you about it:

"'Wouldn't it perhaps be good if we scatter their bones in the canyon?'

"Then you are to say, 'This would not be good, for they would merely arise again to new life.'[409]

"Then they will say to you, 'Perhaps it would be good to merely hang them in the top of a tree?'

"You will then reply, 'Certainly that would not be good, for you would see their faces before you.'

"Then the third time they will say, 'Would it be a good thing if we merely scatter their bones in the course of the river?'

"If then you are asked this, you will reply, 'It is good that they should die. And it would be good if their bones were ground upon the face of a stone like finely ground maize flour. Each one of them should be ground

---

[407] lines 4242–4365
[408] The Colonial period Varea dictionary lists *Xulu* (Descended) as "[spirit] familiars appearing alongside rivers." Basseta lists *ah xulu* as "a diviner," consistent with the statement in the *Popol Vuh* that he is a visionary seer. The paired figures "Descended" and "Ascended" likely refer to the common modern expression "to go down and up," which means to "go all over, or everywhere" (Jim Mondloch, personal communication).
[409] Literally "would be revived their faces."

separately. Then these should be scattered there in the course of the river. They should be sprinkled on the river that winds among the small and great mountains.'

"This, then, is what you will say. Thus will be made manifest what we have said to you in counsel," said Hunahpu[410] and Xbalanque.

For when they had thus counseled them, they already knew of their death. The Xibalbans were even then putting together the great heated stones in the form of a pit oven,[411] placing large hot coals within it.

Then came the messengers of One Death and Seven Death to accompany them:

"The lords say to us: 'May they come! Bring them so that they may see what we have cooked up for them.'[412] This is the word of the lords unto you, boys," they were told.

"Very well," they replied.

Thus they went quickly to the mouth of the pit oven. There the Xibalbans wanted to force them into playing with them:

"Let us jump over this our sweet drink. Four times each of us will go across it, boys," they were told by One Death.[413]

Figure 49. "There the Xibalbans wanted to force them into playing with them." Ceramic figurine of an underworld demon from Tapijulapa, Regional Museum of Tabasco, Villahermosa.

---

[410] The manuscript reads Xhunahpu (Little Hunahpu) which is the diminutive form of Hunahpu. It is perhaps used in this section to distinguish him from his father One Hunahpu, who had also died in Xibalba.

[411] *Chojib'al* (pit oven) is dug into the ground and filled with hot stones or coals to roast meat.

[412] This is a play on words. *Chojij* means "to cook, broil, or set fire to something"; but it also means "to straighten out, take a direct route, or rectify something." Thus the Xibalbans were trying to trick the twins by saying that they were going to settle things, while at the same time hinting at the means by which they intended to kill them.

[413] The Xibalbans are lying about the purpose of the pit. They are suggesting that it is an underground vat for making some intoxicating drink, whereas in reality it is a pit oven into which they hope to trick the twins into falling.

"You cannot trick us with this. Do we not already know the means of our death, O lords? You shall surely see it," they said.

Then they turned to face one another, spread out their arms and together they went into the pit oven. Thus both of them died there. Then all the Xibalbans rejoiced at this. They contentedly shouted and whistled:

"We have defeated them. None too soon have they given themselves up," they said.

Then they summoned Descended and Ascended, with whom word had been left by the boys. And the Xibalbans divined of them what was to be done with their bones. Thus according to their word, the bones were ground up and strewn along the course of the river. But they did not go far away; they just straightaway sank there beneath the water. And when they appeared again, it was as chosen boys, for thus they had become.

THE RESURRECTION OF
HUNAHPU AND XBALANQUE[414]

ON the fifth day they appeared again. People saw them in the river, for the two of them appeared like people-fish. Now when their faces were seen by the Xibalbans, they made a search for them in the rivers.

And on the very next day, they appeared again as two poor orphans.[415] They wore rags in front and rags on their backs. Rags were thus all they had to cover themselves. But they did not act according to their appearance when they were seen by the Xibalbans. For they did the Dance of the Whippoorwill and the Dance of the Weasel. They danced the Armadillo and the Centipede.[416] They danced the Injury, for many marvels they did then. They set fire to a house as if it were truly burning, then immediately recreated it again as the Xibalbans watched with admiration.

Then again they sacrificed themselves. One of them would die, surely throwing himself down in death. Then having been killed, he would immediately be revived. And the Xibalbans simply watched them while they did it. Now all of this was merely the groundwork for the defeat of the Xibalbans at their hands.

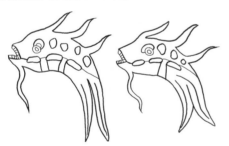

Figure 50. "People saw them in the river, for the two of them appeared like mere people-fish." Fish, redrawn from a Classic Maya vase.

[414] lines 4366–4398

[415] *Meb'a'* literally means "poor," but it may also apply to one who has met with misfortune, such as an orphan, widow, or beggar. The twins reappear as youths that have no parents (p. 182; lines 4459–4468), suggesting that "orphan" may be an appropriate translation. On the other hand, they are obviously poor (p. 182; line 4428–4430), dressed in rags (p. 180; lines 4373–4375), and in need of resources (p. 182; lines 4489–4490). I have chosen "poor orphans" because it includes both meanings.

[416] *Xtz'ul* is a centipede. The Varea dictionary lists *xts'ul* as "a dance with small masks and macaw tail feathers." During this dance, participants put sticks down their throats (like sword swallowers), bones in their noses, and give themselves hard blows on their chests with a large stone. Basseta also defines this as a dance, in which masked performers with tortoiseshell rattles put sticks or daggers in their mouths (like sword-swallowers). A variant name for centipede is *Q'uq'kumatz* (Feathered Serpent), indicating that this may be a dance in honor of that creator deity (Coto 1983, 128).

THE SUMMONS OF HUNAHPU AND XBALANQUE BEFORE THE LORDS[417]

AT length the news of their dances came to the ears of the lords One Death and Seven Death. And when they had heard of it, they said:

"Who are these two poor orphans? Is it truly delightful? Is it true that their dancing and all that they do is beautiful?"

For the lords were delighted with the account when they heard it. Thus they entreated their messengers to summon them to come:

"Say this to them: 'May they come so that we may watch them, for we marvel at them,' say the lords."

Thus the messengers went to the dancers and repeated the words of the lords to them.

"We don't want to, for in truth we are timid. We would be ashamed to enter into such a lordly house! Our faces are truly ugly,[418] and our eyes are just wide in poverty. Don't they see that we are merely dancers? What then would we say to our fellow orphans? We have responsibilities. They also desire our dances, for they revive their faces with us. It is not right that we should do the same with the lords. Therefore we do not want to do this, O messengers," said Hunahpu and Xbalanque.

But they were pestered, threatened with misfortune and pain. And so they went with apprehension,[419] for they didn't want to be going any too soon. Many times they had to be prodded because they just walked along slowly, making little progress, while the messengers who brought them led the way to the lords.

---

[417] lines 4399–4447
[418] Literally "evil/bad/filthy our faces," a common expression for "ugly" among modern Quichés as well.
[419] Literally "red misfortune they went."

HUNAHPU AND XBALANQUE DANCE BEFORE THE LORDS OF XIBALBA[420]

AT length they arrived before the lords. They pretended to be humble,[421] prostrating themselves[422] when they came. They humbled themselves, stooping over and bowing. They hid themselves with rags, giving the appearance that they were truly just poor orphans when they arrived. Then they were asked where their home mountain was[423] and who their people were. They were also asked about their mother and their father:

Figure 51. "They danced the Armadillo." Armadillo dancer, redrawn from a Classic Maya vase.

"Where do you come from?" they were asked.

"We do not know, O lord. Neither do we know the faces of our mother or our father. We were still small when they died," they just said. They didn't tell them anything.

"Very well then. On with the spectacle. What do you want us to give you as payment?" they were asked.

"We don't want anything. Truly we are frightened," they said again to the lord.

"Do not be afraid or timid. Dance! First you will do that dance in which you sacrifice yourselves. Then burn down my home. Do everything that you know. We would watch this, for it was the desire of our hearts that you be summoned. Because you are poor orphans, we will pay whatever you ask as your price," they were told.

Thus they began their songs and their dances, and all the Xibalbans came until the place was overflowing with spectators.[424] They danced

---

[420] lines 4448–4573

[421] *Moch'och'ik* is "to humble one's self hypocritically" (Basseta).

[422] "To throw one's face on the ground" (Basseta).

[423] The Quichés still give directions by indicating which mountain is located nearby the destination. It is not uncommon to ask the location of a town or a person's house and be told, "go two mountains to the west and one to the north."

everything. They danced the Weasel. They danced the Whippoorwill. They danced the Armadillo.

Then the lord spoke to them:

"Sacrifice my dog, then revive him again," they were told.

"All right," they replied.

So they sacrificed his dog and then revived him once more. The dog was truly happy when they revived him. He vigorously wagged his tail when they brought him back to life.

Then the lord spoke again to them:

"Now you must surely burn my home," they were told.

So then they burned the home of the lord. The house was overflowing with all the lords, yet none were burned. Immediately it was restored again. Thus the home of One Death was not lost after all.

All the lords marveled, therefore, and greatly rejoiced at their dances. The lord thus spoke again to them:

"Now kill a person. Sacrifice him, but not so that he really dies," they were told.

"Very well," they said.

So they seized a person and sacrificed him. They extracted the heart of one of them and placed it before the lords. Now One Death and Seven Death marveled at this, for immediately that person was revived again by them. When he had been revived, his heart greatly rejoiced. And again the lords marveled at it:

"Now sacrifice yourselves. We would see this. Truly it is the desire of our hearts that you dance," said again the lords.

"Very well then, O lord," they replied.

So then they sacrificed themselves. Hunahpu was sacrificed by Xbalanque.

---

[424] The *Título Pedro Velasco* records that prior to the Spanish conquest, the highland Maya of Guatemala conducted dances in special "guest houses" in which their rulers danced in honor of their gods: "Each of the lineages had a house to hear the word and to administer judgment. There the lords danced the Junajpu C'oy and the Wukub Cak'ix, the Awata Tun, and the Jolom Tun. Each lineage had divisions, each with a house" (Carmack and Mondloch 1989, 178). Fray Gerónimo de Mendieta wrote that "one of the principal things which existed in this land were the songs and dances, to solemnize the festivals of their demons which they honored as gods, as well as to rejoice and find solace. The house of each principal lord thus had a chapel for singers and a place for dances. The great dances were held in the plazas or in the house patios of the great lords, for all had large plazas" (Mendieta 1993, 140). These special houses are likely analogous to confraternity houses today, where traditionalist Maya continue to conduct dances in honor of deity.

[425] *Tz'alik* is a leaf used for wrapping maize tamales. The implication is that the heart was placed on a leaf prior to wrapping it as an offering. An alternative reading would have this word derived from *tz'alam* a flat stone or altar.

Each of his legs and arms was severed. His head was cut off and placed far away. His heart was dug out and placed on a leaf.[425] Now all these lords of Xibalba were drunk at the sight, as Xbalanque went on dancing.

"Arise!" he said, and immediately he was brought back to life again. Now the lords rejoiced greatly. One Death and Seven Death rejoiced as if they were the ones doing it. They were so involved that it was as if they themselves were dancing.

Figure 52. "One Death and Seven Death rejoiced as if they were the ones doing it. They were so involved that it was as if they themselves were dancing." Death God dancing at an underworld sacrifice, from a Classic Maya vase (Coe 1973, 99).

THE DEFEAT OF
THE LORDS OF XIBALBA⁴²⁶

FOR it was the desire of the lords to abandon their hearts to the dances of Hunahpu and Xbalanque. Then came the words of One Death and Seven Death:

"Do it to us! Sacrifice us!" they said.

"Sacrifice us in the same way,"⁴²⁷ said One Death and Seven Death to Hunahpu and Xbalanque.

"Very well then. Surely you will be revived. Are you not death? For we are here to gladden you, O lords, along with your vassals and your servants,"⁴²⁸ they said therefore to the lords.

The first to be sacrificed was the very head of all the lords, One Death by name, the lord of Xibalba. He was dead then, this One Death. Next they seized Seven Death. But they didn't revive them. Thus the Xibalbans took to their heels when they saw that the lords had died. Their hearts were now taken from their chests. Both of them had been torn open as punishment for what they had done. Straightaway the one lord was executed and not

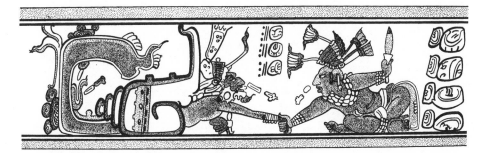

Figure 53. "Next they seized Seven Death. But they didn't revive them." Young deity sacrificing an underworld lord, from a Classic Maya vase (Coe 1973, 47).

---

⁴²⁶ lines 4574–4639

⁴²⁷ The manuscript reads *junal taj* ("the same way" or possibly "one by one"). The particular form of this word is somewhat odd. It seems to be a play on words with *junalik/junelik* (forever), thus hinting that the sacrifice would not be so much "the same" as was done before, but would be permanent. A further pun is seen in the phrase at the beginning of this section, "it was the desire of the lords to abandon their hearts," thus foreshadowing the means of their death.

⁴²⁸ Literally your "child of mother" and your "sons of men." In this case, these are metaphors that are used frequently in the text for vassals and servants.

revived. The other lord had then begged humbly, weeping before the dancers. He would not accept it, for he had become disoriented:

"Take pity on me," he said in his regret.

Then all of their vassals and servants fled into the great canyon. They
packed themselves into the great ravine until they were piled up one on top
of the other. Then innumerable ants swarmed into the canyon, as if they
had been driven there. And when the ants came, the Xibalbans all bowed
themselves down, giving themselves up. They approached begging humbly
and weeping. For the lords of Xibalba were defeated. It was just a miracle,
for the boys had transformed themselves before them.

And then they declared their names. They revealed their names before
all Xibalba.

THE MIRACULOUS MAIZE OF
HUNAHPU AND XBALANQUE[429]

"HEAR our names![430] We shall now declare them. We shall also declare the names of our fathers to you. We are they whose names are Hunahpu and Xbalanque. Our fathers are they who you killed, One Hunahpu and Seven Hunahpu by name. We are the avengers of the misfortune and affliction of our fathers. For this reason, we have endured all the tribulations that you have caused us. Thus we shall now destroy you all. We will kill you, for none among you shall now be saved," they were told.

Then all Xibalba begged humbly, weeping.

"Take pity on us, you, Hunahpu and Xbalanque. Truly we have wronged your fathers that you have named—they who are buried at Crushing Ballcourt," they said.

"Very well. Here then is our word that we declare to you. Hearken all you of Xibalba; for never again will you or your posterity be great. Your offerings also will never again be great. They will henceforth be reduced to croton sap.[431] No longer will clean blood be yours.[432] Unto you will be given only worn-out griddles and pots,[433] only flimsy[434] and brittle things.

"You shall surely eat only the creatures of the grass and the creatures of the wastelands. No longer will you be given the children of the light, those begotten in the light. Only things of no importance[435] will fall before you.

"Only the sinner and the malevolent, the wretch and the molester who clearly have sinned, will be given to you. No longer will you be able to seize

---

[429] lines 4640–4772

[430] It was traditional in Mesoamerican societies to declare one's name when a victory has been won in battle or when superiority has been established.

[431] This fulfills the prophecy of Lady Blood, in which she declared that the lords of Xibalba would no longer be allowed to receive human hearts in sacrifice but rather would have to accept the red sap of the croton tree (pp. 132–133; lines 2444–2445).

[432] The ancient Maya offered their own blood to the gods to give them a portion of their life force. This would be fresh, clean blood. Tedlock's collaborator, Andrés Xiloj, commented that the Xibalbans are allowed to collect only blood that has been spilled on the ground (through injury, illness, or violence), thus making it dirty (D. Tedlock 1996, 283 n. 138).

[433] At the end of each ritual year, broken bits of pottery are left at shrines to symbolize the passing of one age to another. New pots and utensils represent a new beginning and an opportunity for a fresh start in life.

[434] The adjective *ch'uch'* describes something that is soft and flimsy and thus unable to hold its shape.

[435] According to Basseta, these are "things of no importance," or "abandoned things."

suddenly just any person.[436] You will be called upon only over the sap of the croton," they were told, all they of Xibalba.

Thus began their devastation, the ruin of their being called upon in worship. Their glory was not great in the past, for they wanted only conflict with the people of ancient times. Surely they were not true gods. Their names merely inspired fear, for their faces were evil.[437] They were strife makers, traitors,[438] and tempters to sin and violence.[439] They were also masters of deception,[440] of the black view and the white view. They were called masters of harm[441] and vexation. Fundamentally their faces were hidden. Thus their greatness and glory were destroyed. Never again would their dominion become great. This was the accomplishment of Hunahpu and Xbalanque.[442]

Now at the same time, the Grandmother was weeping, crying out[443] before the ears of unripe maize that had been left planted. They had sprouted, but then they dried up when they were burned in the pit oven. Then the ears of maize had sprouted once again, and the Grandmother had burned copal incense[444] before them as a memorial. The heart of their grandmother rejoiced when the maize sprouted a second time.[445]

---

[436] The Quichés believe that the lords of Xibalba have power only over those who have truly committed punishable offenses and have thus submitted themselves to the powers of the underworld.

[437] *Itzel ki wach* may mean "evil their faces," or "ugly their faces."

[438] *Aj tukur.* Basseta records that *ah tucur* (literally "owl master") is "traitor." The name may also refer to the inhabitants of the Alta Verapaz region, which was called the "land of the owls" or Tecolotlán (Recinos 1950, 114 n. 6).

[439] *Lab'al* is "war, violence, offense." In modern Quiché society it refers to a savage or violent person.

[440] Literally "masters of the buried heart."

[441] *Mox wach* is "left face" or "crazy face." In modern usage it may refer to insanity, however Coto and Basseta both relate this to "violence, harm, or mischief."

[442] Las Casas recorded a similar myth that he collected in the Verapaz region of Guatemala: "Among other tales, they say that he [*Exbalanquén*], went to hell to make war, fought with all the people there, defeated them, and captured the king and many of his army. Upon his return to earth, *Exbalanquén* brought the king of hell with him, but when they were only three or four steps from the light, he begged not to be taken away; and so the victorious *Exbalanquén*, with much anger, gave him a kick and said to him, 'Go back and may yours be all that is rotten, discarded, and stinks'" (Las Casas 1967, III, cxxiv, p. 650. Translation by author).

[443] The verb roots in this couplet, *oq'* (to weep) and *sik'ij* (to call), when used together in this order imply fervent prayer, such as is done by priests at native altars (D. Tedlock 1996, 284 n. 139). As a goddess of fertility and the seasons, the weeping of Xmucane may have been associated by the Quichés with life-giving rains that helped the dry maizestalks to sprout again.

[444] *Pom* (copal incense) is made from the resin of the *palo jiote* tree (*Bursera verrucosa*). Copal is still burned by the Quichés as an offering to both Christian and traditional Maya deities.

Thus they were deified by their grandmother. She named it Center House, Center Ancestral Plot,[446] Revitalized Maize, and Leveled Earth.

She named it Center House and Center Harvest for it was in the very center of the interior of their home where they had planted the ears of maize.

She named it Leveled Earth and Revitalized Maize for it was upon level ground that the ears of maize had been planted. She named it Revitalized Maize because the maize had sprouted again. These names were given by Xmucane to what Hunahpu and Xbalanque had left planted. This was a memorial to them by their grandmother.

Now their fathers, One Hunahpu and Seven Hunahpu, had died long ago. They now went, therefore, to see the face of their father there at Xibalba. Their father spoke to them when Xibalba was defeated.

---

[445] This incident is perhaps paralleled by contemporary agricultural practices among the highland Maya. The following is a description of a traditional planting ceremony as told by Nicolás Chávez Sojuel, a Tz'utujil Maya from Santiago Atitlán:

> After preparing the ground, but before planting, four candles are placed at the corners of the maize field representing the four directions of the earth—in the east so that light will shine on the seeds; in the west so that the maize won't be burned by the sun; in the north so that the maize seed will be protected; and in the south so that the harvest will be abundant.... At the center he then places a special kind of maize ear called yo'x (twins) which splits at the end to form extra little cobs. These have been previously blessed by a shaman in the Confraternity of San Juan where the ruk'ux way (heart of food) is kept in a wooden chest. Many yo'x cobs hang from the ceiling there because that is where maize is born. These cobs are burned and their ashes are buried beneath the ground so that they can come back to life and make more maize (Christenson 2001, 117).

The hole in the center of the maizefield into which the ashes of the yo'x maize cobs are buried is called the rumuxux (navel), the same name applied to a small hole in the nave of the town's church which the Tz'utujil believe to be an access point to the underworld realm of the dead. The Atiteco practice of first burning and then burying split cobs of maize, which they call "twins," recalls the history of the twins in the Popol Vuh who also descended into the underworld where they were burned to ashes and eventually rose to new life, parallel with the maize plants in the grandmother's household.

[446] This reading is based on the work of Adrián Chávez, a prominent Quiché scholar who understood b'ichok as a solar, the Spanish word for an ancestral dwelling, or the plot of land once owned by ancestors (Chávez 1997, 63).

THE APOTHEOSIS OF
THE SUN, MOON, AND STARS[447]

HERE now is the adornment of their father by them, along with the adornment of Seven Hunahpu. For they went to adorn them at Crushing Ballcourt.

Figure 54. "Here now is the adornment of their father by them." The resurrection of the Maize God assisted by his twin sons, from a Classic Maya plate (drawing by Linda Schele).

They merely wanted his face to be restored. Thus they asked him to name everything—his mouth, his nose, and his eyes. He was able to recover the first name, but then little more was said. He did not say the corresponding names for that which is above the mouth.[448] Still, this had been said, and thus they honored him.

---

[447] lines 4773-4821
[448] The skull of One Hunahpu would have had a mouth, but not a nose or eyes, which would have been only empty holes and sockets.

Thus the heart of their father was left behind at Crushing Ballcourt. His sons then said to him:

"Here you will be called upon. It shall be so."

Thus his heart was comforted.

"The child who is born in the light, and the son who is begotten in the light shall go out to you first. They shall worship you first. Your name shall not be forgotten.[449] Thus be it so," they said to their father when they comforted his heart.

"We are merely the avengers of your death and your loss, for the affliction and misfortune that were done to you." Thus was their counsel when they had defeated all Xibalba.

Then they arose as the central lights. They arose straight into the sky. One of them arose as the sun, and the other as the moon. Thus the womb of the sky was illuminated over the face of the earth, for they came to dwell in the sky.

The four hundred boys who had died at the hands of Zipacna also rose up to become their companions. They became a constellation of the sky.

---

[449] Hunahpu is one of the twenty named days of the Quiché calendar. It is dedicated especially to the memory of ancestors. When there is a death within the family, the patrilineage priest goes to the family shrine on a Hunahpu day that falls after the day of death to pray for the person's soul (La Farge and Byers 1931, 157–165, 173–175; Bunzel 1952, 280; Schultze-Jena 1954, 71; B. Tedlock 1982, 124–125; D. Tedlock 1996, 286 n. 141). Hunahpu days are also the chosen times to visit the graves of relatives and leave offerings of food, drink, flower petals, or incense. The twins are instituting this practice, beginning with the burial place of One Hunahpu himself.

THE CREATION OF HUMANITY[450]

THIS, then, is the beginning[451] of the conception of humanity, when that which would become the flesh of mankind was sought.[452] Then spoke they who are called She Who Has Borne Children and He Who Has Begotten Sons, the Framer and the Shaper, Sovereign and Quetzal Serpent:

"The dawn approaches, and our work is not successfully completed. A provider and a sustainer have yet to appear—a child of light, a son of light. Humanity has yet to appear to populate the face of the earth," they said.

Thus they gathered together and joined their thoughts in the darkness, in the night. They searched and they sifted. Here they thought and they pondered. Their thoughts came forth bright and clear. They discovered and established that which would become the flesh of humanity. This took place just a little before the appearance of the sun, moon, and stars above the heads of the Framer and the Shaper.

---

[450] lines 4822–4861

[451] Literally "planting."

[452] The Aztecs of Precolumbian Central Mexico believed that the earth had passed through five separate creations, each with the intent of forming beings capable of human expression. Only the fifth and final attempt was successful. *The Annals of Cuauhtitlán* records the Aztec version of the fifth creation: "Thus it is told, it is said: There have already been four manifestations and this one is the fifth age. So the old ones knew this, that in the year 1–Rabbit heaven and earth were founded. And they knew this, that when heaven and earth were founded there had already been four kinds of men, four kinds of manifestations. Also they knew that each of these had existed in a Sun, an age" (León-Portilla 1980, 137). The *Popol Vuh* is consistent with this tradition in describing five separate creation attempts—the mountains and rivers, the animals and birds, the mud person, the wooden effigies, and now humankind.

THE DISCOVERY OF MAIZE[453]

IT was from within the places called Paxil[454] and Cayala[455] that the yellow ears of ripe maize and the white ears of ripe maize came.[456] THESE were the names of the animals that obtained their food[457]—fox and coyote,[458] parakeet and raven.[459] Four, then, were the animals that revealed to them the yellow ears of maize and the white ears of maize. They came from Paxil and pointed out the path to get there.

---

[453] lines 4862–4939

[454] *Paxil* means "broken, split, or cleft." Father Coto wrote that it refers in particular to the breaking in two of an ear of maize. *Paxil* is described as an "excellent mountain" filled with the maize that would eventually be used to form the flesh of humanity (p. 194; lines 4886–4889). This was a widespread belief in ancient Mesoamerica, particularly among the Maya (Freidel, Schele, and Parker 1993, 138–139). According to the Central Mexican *Codex Chimalpopoca*, it was Quetzalcoatl himself who brought the first maize out of the mountain Tonacatepetl (the mountain of our flesh or our sustenance) from which he created the first men (León-Portilla 1980, 122 n. 42). The Pipil of Guatemala relate that maize was discovered when the mountain in which it was hidden was split open by the youngest of the rain dwarfs (Schultze-Jena 1935, 31–33). Contemporary Mam still identify one of their local mountains as Paxil, saying that it is "where a flea brought the first grains of maize through a narrow crevice to give their ancestors corn" (Wagley 1941, 20; Oakes 1951, 244; Watanabe 1992, 67).

[455] *K'ayala'* means "bitter or stagnant water." This is perhaps related to the notion of the primordial waters of creation which the highland Maya often associate with seawater or brackish ponds, out of which the first mountains emerged. Among modern Quichés, *k'ayala'* is the water mixed with lime that women use to add to ground maize dough (Akkeren, personal communication).

[456] These are the dry ears of maize, ready for harvest. Colors carry great symbolic significance in highland Maya theology. Yellow is associated with the south, misfortune, death, and the dry season (Gossen 1974, 33; Tarn and Prechtel 1990, 75; Watanabe 1992, 131, 232 n. 6; Carlsen and Prechtel 1994, 85, 92). White is associated with the north, new life, and the rainy season. This passage may therefore refer to the inauguration of the agricultural cycle of harvest and new growth. This maize ultimately is used to create the flesh of mankind. As a result, the color of the grains may presage man's destiny to live and die in endless cycles. Modern Quichés also see yellow and white corn as representing female and male identities. Thus at Chichicastenango yellow and white ears are never left lying together to dry in the patio lest they "cohabit" and produce speckled offspring (Bunzel 1952, 45, 50). This passage may thus suggest that the different colored ears will be used to produce the flesh of males and females.

[457] The word *echa'* (food) refers to the principal or staple food upon which a person or animal depends for survival. In the case of the Quichés this would be maize, by far the most important part of their diet.

[458] Both the fox and coyote are cunning nocturnal animals that the Quichés associate with discovering and digging up hidden or secret things.

[459] The bright blue/green parakeet may be connected with the blue sky of day as well as the living green of growing maize. The black raven, in contrast, represents the darkness of night and the interior of the earth where the maize seed is planted, germinates, and first begins to grow.

Thus was found the food that would become the flesh[460] of the newly framed and shaped people. Water was their blood.[461] It became the blood of humanity. The ears of maize entered into their flesh by means of She Who Has Borne Children and He Who Has Begotten Sons.

Thus they rejoiced over the discovery of that excellent mountain that was filled with delicious things, crowded[462] with yellow ears of maize and white ears of maize. It was crowded as well with pataxte[463] and chocolate, with countless zapotes[464] and anonas,[465] with jocotes[466] and nances,[467] with matasanos[468] and honey.[469] From within the places called Paxil and Cayala came the sweetest foods in the citadel. All the small foods and great foods

[460] When a male child was born, the seventeenth century Maya of Guatemala burned blood shed from its severed umbilical cord and passed an ear of maize through the smoke. The seeds from this ear were then planted in the child's name in a specific area of the maize field. Parents used the maize from this small patch of land to feed the child "until he reached the age when he could plant form himself, saying that thus he not only ate by the sweat of his brow but of his own blood as well" (Fuentes y Guzmán 1932–33, I.281. Translation by author). Mothers in Santiago Atitlán place an ear of maize into the palm of their newborns and eat only dishes made from maize while breast-feeding to ensure that the child grows "true flesh." Once the child is weaned, it is given only food prepared with maize for several months. The Quichés refer to themselves as *qas winaq* (true people) and consider that they are literally of a different flesh than those who do not eat maize. Fuentes y Guzmán noted the extreme importance of maize in the cultural life of the Maya: "Everything they did and said so concerned maize that they almost regarded it as a god. The enchantment and rapture with which they look upon their maize fields is such that on their account they forget children, wife, and any other pleasure, as though the maize fields were their final purpose in life and the source of their happiness (1932–33, I.xii.3. Translation by author).
[461] Humankind is distinguished by having blood, in contrast to the wooden effigies, which lacked it (cf. p. 84; lines 664–665).
[462] *Tzatz* means "thick," like a particularly concentrated beverage or porridge. It is also used to refer to a room crowded with people or a chest tightly packed with objects.
[463] *Pataxte (Theobroma bicolor)* is an inferior grade of cacao (from which chocolate is made) used to sweeten foods and drinks, such as the maize-based drink *chorote.* Its name is derived from the Nahuatl *pataxtli.*
[464] The *zapote (Lucuma mammosa)* is a sweet tropical fruit which grows in warm, lowland areas of southeastern Mexico as well as the Guatemalan coast. It is oblong in shape, measuring 10–15 cm in length. Its skin is tough and brownish-red, while its meat varies from dark red to brown and has a delicious, aromatic flavor. Based on Quiché traditions of its association with the creation and because of its abundant fruit, Father Domingo de Vico chose the *zapote* to represent the paradisiacal Tree of Life in his writings (Carmack and Mondloch 1983, 207–208).
[465] The *anona* is the collective name for a variety of tropical fruits of the genus *Anona.* It has a yellowish-green skin with a very sweet yellowish-white pulp and black seeds.
[466] *Spondias purpurea.* A species of sour yellow plum. Its Spanish name, *jocote,* is derived from the Nahuatl *xocotl* (sour).
[467] *Byrosinima crassifolia.* A smooth, yellow fruit about the size of a cherry.
[468] *Casimiroa edulis.* A sour tropical fruit.
[469] Honeybees were domesticated by the ancient Maya and are still raised by the Quichés, particularly in the mountain villages surrounding Momostenango.

were there, along with the small and great cultivated fields. The path was thus revealed by the animals.

The yellow ears of maize and the white ears of maize were then ground fine with nine grindings[470] by Xmucane.[471] Food entered their flesh, along with water to give them strength.[472] Thus was created the fatness of their arms. The yellowness[473] of humanity came to be when they were made by they who are called She Who Has Borne Children and He Who Has Begotten Sons, by Sovereign and Quetzal Serpent.

Thus their frame and shape were given expression[474] by our first Mother and our first Father. Their flesh was merely yellow ears of maize and white ears of maize.[475] Mere food were the legs and arms of humanity, of our first fathers. And so there were four who were made, and mere food was their flesh.

Figure 55. "The yellow ears of maize and the white ears of maize were then ground fine with nine grindings by Xmucane." Quiché woman grinding maize near Momostenango.

[470] Maize is usually ground two to four times, depending on the fineness of dough desired. To grind the maize nine times would make an extremely fine consistency of dough. The number also carries great ritual significance to the Maya, being the number of moons (months) required to form a human child in the mother's womb.

[471] Xmucane acts as the creative power that prepares the maize dough and forms it into a suitable framework to contain the essence of mankind. This is the only instance in which Xmucane acts alone in a creative act without her consort Xpiyacoc. The unique ability of the female to form living flesh is thus emphasized.

[472] *Openal* is "vigor, strength, force, energy."

[473] *Q'anal* (yellowness) is a metaphor for "abundance, richness, health." In this case it is likely a metaphor for fatness, paralleling the previous line (Mondloch, personal communication).

[474] Literally "placed in words," an indication that the creators were able to bring their creation to successful completion by means of expressing words, just as in the creation of the earth at the beginning of the account.

[475] In Nahuatl, the language of the Aztecs, "our flesh" is *tonacoyotl*, which is a phrase also used to refer to "maize" (León-Portilla 1980, 122 n. 41).

THE FIRST FOUR MEN[476]

THESE are the names of the first people who were framed and shaped: the first person was Balam Quitze,[477] the second was Balam Acab,[478] the third was Mahucutah,[479] and the fourth was Iqui Balam.[480] These, then, were the names of our first mothers and fathers.[481]

[476] lines 4940–4947

[477] B'alam Quitze. B'alam is a relatively common Maya name, even today. In its most literal sense, b'alam means "jaguar"; however, when used as a title, it carries with it a host of implicit meanings. Because of the nature of the jaguar as the largest and fiercest animal of the Guatemalan jungle, b'alam is used to refer to anything powerful or mighty. The ancient Maya believed that four balams acted as supernatural protectors in the night (Roys 1967, 152 n. 8). B'alam is also the title used by Itzá-Maya priests who continued to worship the ancient gods after the introduction of Christianity (Roys 1967, 163 n. 2). In addition, balam is sometimes used to refer to priests or rulers with unusual spiritual or magical powers. Kitze appears to be the Mam form of K'iche', meaning "forest," and the Mam may have played a decisive role in the founding of the Quiché confederation (Akkeren 2000, 155). Thus the name of this progenitor may mean something like "Jaguar Forest," "Jaguar Quiché," or "Mighty Quiché." The etymology of all the progenitors' names is obscure, however, and I have therefore chosen to leave them untranslated. Balam Quitze was the ancestor of the most powerful Quiché lineage, the Cavecs, from which the ah pop, or principal lord, was chosen.

[478] B'alam Aq'ab'. "Jaguar Night" or "Mighty Night." Ancestor of the Nihaib lineage of the Quichés.

[479] Majukutaj. The meaning of the name of this progenitor is problematic. Carmack believes that it is derived from the lowland Maya word for "Traveler," or "One Who Does Not Stay" (Carmack 1981, 49). Tedlock translates it as "Not Right Now" based on the Quiché ma, "not," and jukotaj, "right away/in a moment" (Basseta). Akkeren (personal communication) suggests that the name is derived from the Mam jukotaj (elder, eminent one). Coto lists hu cotah as "one crown, ring, or similar round object" (Coto 1983, 474). In many highland Maya languages, such as Tz'utujil, the prefix Ma may be honorific, meaning something like "mister, or sir."

[480] Ik'i B'alam. If this name is derived from lowland Maya languages, which is probable, it would be read as "Black/Dark Jaguar." If it is derived from Quiché, it should likely be read as Iq'i B'alam, "Wind Jaguar" or "Wind Mighty." No lineage was founded by this man. Although the Popol Vuh names his wife as Caquixaha, the Título Totonicapán records that he had no wife and therefore had no offspring (Carmack and Mondloch 1983, 175).

[481] Although the four progenitors were male, they are referred to as "our first mothers and fathers." In modern Quiché communities, the highest ranking and most revered patriarchs hold the title of chuch-qajawab (mother-fathers) and are charged with the spiritual well-being of entire family lineages or villages.

THE MIRACULOUS VISION
OF THE FIRST MEN[482]

IT is said that they were merely given frame and shape. They had no mother. They had no father. They were merely lone men, as we would say. No woman gave them birth. Nor were they begotten by the Framer or the Shaper, by She Who Has Borne Children or He Who Has Begotten Sons. Their frame and shape were merely brought about by the miraculous power and the spirit essence of the Framer and the Shaper, of She Who Has Borne Children and He Who Has Begotten Sons, of Sovereign and Quetzal Serpent.

Thus their countenances appeared like people. People they came to be. They were able to speak and converse.[483] They were able to look and listen. They were able to walk and hold things with their hands. They were excellent and chosen[484] people. Their faces were manly in appearance. They had their breath, therefore they became. They were able to see as well, for straightaway their vision came to them.

Perfect was their sight, and perfect was their knowledge of everything beneath the sky. If they gazed about them, looking intently, they beheld that which was in the sky and that which was upon the earth. Instantly they were able to behold everything. They did not have to walk to see all that existed beneath the sky. They merely saw it from wherever they were. Thus their knowledge became full. Their vision passed beyond the trees and the

---

[482] lines 4948–5010

[483] The Maya perceive themselves as "maize people" and foreigners who eat bread as "wheat people." Maya language is intimately bound with this concept. To be a *qas winaq* (true person) and speak the Maya language properly, a person must eat maize. This notion implies that the power of human speech is not merely a means of communication that may be imitated by memorizing grammar and vocabulary, but a function of the physical essence of the Maya as a people. Vogt noted the belief among the Tzotzil-Maya of Chiapas that "unless people eat maize tortillas, they are never fully socialized, nor can they ever speak BAZ'IK'OP (real word—the Tzotzil language) (Vogt 1976, 50). When I first began working as an ethnographer in Quiché communities, I found it curious that when I struck up a conversation in the Quiché language with someone I didn't know, that person would sometimes interrupt me in mid-sentence and ask what I ate, specifically if I ate tortillas or bread. When I affirmed that I ate what they ate, including tortillas, they would nod as if that explained a great deal. After a number of such experiences I asked a friend why people were curious about what I ate. He replied, "I've never heard of anyone that isn't Maya that can speak our language. I wondered if it was because you ate maize from here. If so then you have the flesh of the ancestors in your flesh and therefore can speak what they spoke."

[484] *Cha'om* (chosen), in the sense of being "beautiful" in appearance or "pure" (Coto).

rocks, beyond the lakes and the seas, beyond the mountains and the valleys. Truly they were very esteemed people, these Balam Quitze, Balam Acab, Mahucutah, and Iqui Balam.

THE GRATITUDE OF THE FIRST MEN [485]

THEN the Framer and the Shaper asked them: "What is the nature of your existence? Do you know[486] it? Do you not look and listen? Are not your speech and your walk good? Behold now, therefore, and see that which is beneath the sky. Are not the mountains clear? Do you not see the valleys? Try it then," they were told.

Thus their vision of everything beneath the sky was completed, and they gave thanks to the Framer and the Shaper:

"Truly we thank you doubly, triply that we were created, that we were given our mouths[487] and our faces.[488] We are able to speak and to listen. We are able to ponder and to move about. We know much, for we have learned that which is far and near. We have seen the great and the small, all that exists in the sky and on the earth. We thank you, therefore, that we were created, that we were given frame and shape. We became because of you, our Grandmother, and you, our Grandfather," they said when they gave thanks for their frame and shape.

Their knowledge of everything that they saw was complete—the four corners and the four sides, that which is within the sky and that which is within the earth.

But this did not sound good to the Framer and the Shaper:

"It is not good what they have said, they that we have framed and shaped. They said, 'We have learned everything, great and small.'"

---

[485] lines 5011–5071

[486] Na' is "to know, sense, feel." For the Quichés, to know and to sense something are the same concept. Thus the creators ask the first humans about their knowledge by determining what they see, hear, and feel.

[487] Literally "we were mouthed." In receiving their mouths, the Quiché progenitors thank the creator gods for giving them the means of expressing themselves. It is the ability to speak with intelligible words that distinguishes these new creations from the animals and the failed attempts at humanity which had previously been destroyed.

[488] Literally "we were faced." In Quiché, wach (face, countenance) carries the connotation of individual "self." If something is pleasing to a person, it is said to "fall well upon the face" (utz kaqaj chuwach). To ask, "How are you?" the question would be phrased, "Is it good your face?" (La utz a wach?). Thus the first people thank the gods for having given them their identity, or sense of self. It is also intimately tied to vision. In the previous section, the first men's extraordinary vision is what gave them their ability to gain knowledge.

THE DISPLEASURE OF THE GODS[489]

THUS their knowledge was taken back by She Who Has Borne Children and He Who Has Begotten Sons:

"What now can be done to them so that their vision reaches only nearby, so that only a little of the face of the earth can be seen by them? For it is not good what they say. Is not their existence merely framed, merely shaped? It is a mistake[490] that they have become like gods.

"But if they do not multiply or are increased, when will the first planting be? When will it dawn? If they do not increase, when will it be so? Therefore we will merely undo them a little now. That is what is wanted, because it is not good what we have found out. Their works will merely be equated with ours. Their knowledge will extend to the furthest reaches, and they will see[491] everything."

Thus spoke Heart of Sky and Huracan, Youngest Thunderbolt and Sudden Thunderbolt, Sovereign and Quetzal Serpent, She Who Has Borne Children and He Who Has Begotten Sons, Xpiyacoc and Xmucane, the Framer and the Shaper, as they are called. Thus they remade the essence of that which they had framed and shaped.

[489] lines 5072–5115
[490] *Lab'e* is a "mistake, error, or bad omen."
[491] *Kilon* (they see). This form of the verb also has the implied meaning of "acquire, attain."

THE CREATION OF THE MOTHERS
OF THE QUICHÉ NATION[492]

THEIR eyes[493] were merely blurred by Heart of Sky. They were blinded like breath upon the face of a mirror. Thus their eyes were blinded. They could see only nearby; things were clear to them only where they were.[494] Thus their knowledge was lost. The wisdom of the first four people was lost there at their foundation, at their beginning.[495] Thus were the framing and the shaping of our first grandfathers and fathers by Heart of Sky and Heart of Earth.

Then their companions, their wives, also came to be.[496] It was the gods alone who conceived them as well. As if it were in their sleep they received

[492] lines 5116–5360

[493] *U b'aq' ki wach* (its seed their faces) refers to the eyes. Thus the gods clouded the eyes of the first men so that their vision would be limited.

[494] Although the creator gods eventually clouded the vision of the first men, the progenitors of the Maya and their descendants nevertheless believe themselves to bear within their blood the potential for divine sight. Present-day *aj q'ij* priests believe that their divine ancestors, who set the pattern for contemporary rituals, continue to operate through them as conduits. It is this ancestral vision that allows the *aj q'ij* to "see" beyond the limits of time and distance. Evon Vogt noted that the Tzotzil-Maya of Zinacantán believe that anciently their people could see inside sacred mountains where the ancestors live. Today only shamans are recognized to have this ability (Vogt 1993, 205). Among the Maya there is no institutional religion to sanction the qualification of a person to become an *aj q'ij*. Every Maya man and woman potentially has this ability because it is inherent in their blood. The approach that experienced *aj q'ij* priests take in training their apprentices is to teach how to interpret signs and spirit communication, often described as lightning in the blood, that they had always received since young childhood but had not the experience to understand properly. In other cases, the *aj q'ij* receives no formal training. This account is from an *aj q'ij* from Santiago Atitlán: "When I was born, I already knew how to do these things. I had no teacher. I speak with the ancestors and ancient kings and they speak with me. They help me to know how to heal and solve problems for people." Non-Maya do not necessarily have this kind of ability, because their blood does not originate from the same visionary ancestral source. In my own experience working with *aj q'ij* priests in Momostenango in the late 1970s, my frequent displays of ineptitude in learning divinatory and calendric skills was interpreted as the lack of Maya blood in my veins. I was not able to see with ancestral vision in the same way because I had a different lineage, likely not a very divine one.

[495] *U xe', u tikarib'al* (their root, their planting).

[496] Marriage is considered essential in highland Maya society. No significant office may be held by a man or woman who is not married: "Only a married man is regarded as a complete person. On all strictly formal occasions, such as the rituals in the *cofradías* a man is invariably accompanied by his wife, even when the woman has no part in the ceremonies.... An extreme expression of this sentiment of unity between husband and wife is found in the initiation ceremonies of a *chuchqajau* ["mother-father," the principal priest within a lineage]. The profession of *chuchqajau* is a sacred profession; the practitioner must have a vocation which has been manifested in dreams and in sickness, he is believed to have personal occult power in divination. But at the concluding ceremonies in which the sacred bundle is finally

them. The women were truly beautiful who were with Balam Quitze, Balam Acab, Mahucutah, and Iqui Balam. Thus when the men were brought to life, their wives truly came to be as well. At once their hearts rejoiced because of their mates.

These, then, are the names of their wives: Cahapaluna[497] was the name of the wife of Balam Quitze. Chomiha[498] was the name of the wife of Balam Acab. Tzununiha[499] was the name of the wife of Mahucutah. Caquixaha[500] was the name of the wife of Iqui Balam. These, therefore, were the names of their wives, they who came to be our rulers. These were they who multiplied the nations both small and great.

This, therefore, was our foundation, we the Quiché people. There were many who came to be bloodletters[501] and sacrificers.[502] There are no longer

delivered and the final sacrifices are performed, his wife participates in all the ceremonies, not as an assistant, but as an initiate. Throughout the ceremonies they are referred to as 'the young couple who are to receive the *vara* [sacred bundle]'" (Bunzel 1952, 122–123; cf. B. Tedlock 1982, 85). The death of one spouse causes significant "soul loss" for the other, often resulting in the widow or widower following their loved one to the grave soon after. Note that the creation of the world itself was carried out by the joint efforts of the female Xmucane and the male Xpiyacoc. They are not described as carrying out separate roles, but acting in concert and speaking with one voice (see pages 62, 79–82, 200).

[497] *Kaja Palu Na* (Sky Sea House). The *Título Totonicapán*, also composed in the sixteenth century by Quiché scribes, lists this wife's name as *Cakapaluma* (*Kaqa Paluma*, "Red Sea Turtle") (Carmack and Mondloch 1983, 175). Each of the wives of the progenitors include the word for "house" in their names, indicating that each is the founder of a lineage group. It is perhaps significant that Cahapaluna uses the lowland Maya spelling of the word for house, *na*, rather than the Quiché form of the word, *ja*. The preservation of this spelling may indicate the dimly recalled memory of the royal marriage of their most important Quiché ancestor with a royal princess from lowland Maya lands.

[498] *Chomi Ja* (Shrimp House). This reading is based on *chom*, "shrimp, large thing, thick thing" (Basseta). If the reading of "shrimp" here is correct, it would parallel the "sea turtle" name of the previous wife based on the account in the *Título Totonicapán* (Carmack and Mondloch 1983, 175).

[499] *Tz'ununi Ja* (Hummingbird House).

[500] *Kaqixa Ja* (Macaw House). No lineage group was founded by this couple. According to the *Título Totonicapán*, Caquixaha was the wife of Mahucutah, the third progenitor, while Iqui Balam was unmarried (Carmack and Mondloch 1983, 175). This is also the name of a Cakchiquel lineage.

[501] *Aj k'ixb'* may literally be translated as "he of the spines"; however, it refers here to the practice of letting blood by auto-sacrifice, paralleling the performance of sacrifice in the next line of the couplet. This was generally accomplished with a sharp spine, such as the tip of a maguey leaf or a stingray spine. Like most Mesoamerican groups, the ancient Maya offered their own blood as an offering to the gods. They believed that by so doing they returned a portion of their life force to the powers of the cosmos. Colonial dictionaries also gloss this as "penitent, confessor, shameful persons." Such auto-sacrificial acts were performed in an effort to cleanse impurities as a penitential ritual. Although auto-sacrifice is no longer performed, this concept of doing penance, confession, and pleading for cleansing of personal impurities accompanies most offerings of candles, incense, flowers, sacrificed animals, etc. in modern-day Quiché rituals.

merely four now, but four were the mothers of the Quiché people. Each of the people had different names when they multiplied there in the East. Truly these became the names of the people—Sovereign, Ballplayer,[503] Masker,[504] and Sun Lord.[505] These are the titles of the people. It was there in the East that they multiplied.

The beginning of the Tamub and the Ilocab[506] is known. As one they came from there in the East.

[502] *Aj k'ajb'* (sacrificers). *K'ajb'* is specifically blood sacrifice. Coto lists the word as referring to the type of human sacrifice performed by the Maya prior to the Spanish Conquest, but it may also be a sacrifice of one's own blood (Coto 1983, 502–503). A related verb may be *k'ajij* (to wound the knee). When the progenitors perform auto-sacrifice before their gods, it is by pricking their ears and their elbows. Thus this term and the one that precede it likely refer to auto-sacrificial rites whereby a person's own blood is offered to deity. Ximénez translates *k'ajb'* as "punishment." The related word in Classic Maya texts, *ch'ahb'*, has two related meanings with regard to war contexts. In one sense, it refers to the punishment of captives, and at the same time the notion that captives destined for sacrificial death represent a kind of penitence by proxy. Thus Classic Maya lords saw in the person of the war captive their own penance and self-denial. In this way bloodletting and sacrifice represent a kind of penitence by proxy (Stephen D. Houston, private communication). Sacrificial victims were thus seen by the ancient Maya as substitutions for the sacrificer in payment for penitential blood debt (Taube 1994, 669–74).

[503] *Oloman* (place of rubber) is derived from the Nahua word for rubber, *ol* (Campbell 1983, 84). I base my reading on the fact that for the Quiché, rubber and the rubber ball used in their games is the same word, *kik'*. There is likely a lineage component here as well, indicating that the ancestors of the Quichés came from, or were related in some way to people who inhabited, the "Place of Rubber." At the time of the conquest, this was the name commonly used by Nahua speakers to refer to the southern coast of the Gulf of Mexico. Schele and Mathews suggest that the Oloman are related to the Olmeca-Xicalanca, a group centered in the Gulf Coast region who conquered Cholula in the eighth century (Historia Tolteca-Chichimeca), and built Cacaxtla (perhaps Xochicalco as well) as their capital (Schele and Mathews 1998, 293, 383 n. 4).

[504] Masks were used by the Quichés in many of their ceremonies and are still worn in ritual dances. By wearing the mask of a god or legendary hero, the dancer takes upon himself the character and power of that figure.

[505] *K'enech Ajaw* (Yucatec: "Sun-eyed/faced Lord") is the Lowland Maya title given to the principal sun deity (Thompson 1970, 207, 228–229; Morley, Brainerd, and Sharer 1983, 470; Taube 1992, 50–56; Miller and Taube 1993, 106). *K'enech Ajaw* symbolized the sun's daily journey across the sky and had been closely associated with the various Maya royal dynasties for more than a thousand years (Miller and Taube 1993, 106; Baudez 1996). In contemporary Yucatán, a deified ruler named Kinich Kakmo (Sun-faced Fire Macaw) was remembered as the founding ancestor of Izamal (Roys 1967, 82, 160 n. 2; Craine and Reindorp 1979, 83–84 n. 78). Apparently, Quiché lords also saw themselves as earthly manifestations of the sun deity. The use of this archaic, non-Quiché title may indicate the antiquity of the concept as well as the origins of its Cavec authors.

[506] At the time of the Spanish conquest, there were three main branches of Quiché people: The ruling Nima Quichés (Great Quichés), descendents of the four first human beings just mentioned. They consisted of the Cavec, Nihaib, Ahau Quichés, and the Zaquic; the Tamub Quichés who lived in the area between Santa Cruz el Quiché and Patzite; and the Ilocab Quichés near present-day San Antonio Ilotenago (Carmack and Mondloch 1983, 309 n. 15). The –ab suffix in Ilocab functions as a pluralizer, however, I have chosen not

Balam Quitze was the grandfather, the father of nine great houses of the Cavecs.[507] Balam Acab was the grandfather, the father of nine great houses of the Nihaibs. Mahucutah was the grandfather, the father of four great houses of Ahau Quichés. Thus there were three divisions of lineages[508] that existed. The names of their grandfathers and their fathers were not forgotten—they who multiplied and proliferated there in the East.

The Tamub and the Ilocab came as well, along with the thirteen allied nations, the thirteen houses:[509] The Rabinals,[510] the Cakchiquels,[511] and the Ah Tziquinahas;[512] as well as the Zacahs[513] and the Lamacs,[514] the Cumatz[515]

to write the name of this lineage as "Ilocs" because the original derivation of the name is likely *ilolkab'* (beekeeper), an occupation characteristic of this group (Akkeren, personal communication).

[507] There were three major divisions of ruling Nima Quichés (Great Quichés), each descendents of one of the progenitors—the Cavecs, descendents of Balam Quitze who became the dominant ruling lineage of the Quichés centered at their capital at Cumarcah; the Nihaib (or Nim Haib—Great Houses), descendents of Balam Acab who settled the area of Momostenango; and the Ahau Quichés (Lord Quichés), descendents of Mahucutah. The *Popol Vuh* does not mention any descendents for the last progenitor, Iqui Balam, although a fourth lineage group of Nima Quichés, the Zaquic, is sometimes mentioned. Their founding ancestor is not named in the *Popol Vuh* text.

[508] *Chinamit.* This is a Nahua-derived word meaning literally "fence," although it is used to in the Maya highlands as "lineage, family, tribe, or confraternity" (Campbell 1970, 3).

[509] *Tecpan.* This is a Nahua term meaning "house," or "royal palace" (Carmack and Mondloch 1983, 233 n. 191). Metaphorically it may also refer to a noble or royal line, as well as the town in which it resides. The remaining groups are non-Quichés, but related highland Maya groups. The principal alliance consisted of four groups—the Quichés, Rabinals, Cakchiquels, and Ah Tziquinahas. The Rabinals live in the area surrounding the modern town of Rabinal.

[510] *Rab'inal.* Akkeren (2000, 248; cf. Campbell 1983, 82) translates the name of this lineage as "Place of the Lord's Daughter," based on the Kekchi *rab'in* (daughter of male/ princess) and *-al* (place of). Their principal center of occupation was in the area around present-day Rabinal.

[511] At the time of the Spanish conquest, the Cakchiquels were centered at their capital city of Iximche'. The Tlaxcalan allies of the Spaniards called this citadel *Quauhtemallan*, from which the present-day name of the country, Guatemala, is derived.

[512] *Aj Tz'ikina Ja* (They of the Bird House) was the dominant lineage of the people today known as the Tzutuhils, who occupied the land from the southern shores of Lake Atitlán south to the cacao-growing land of the Pacific Coast. Their capital was Chiya' (now called Chutinamit), located on a small hill at the base of San Pedro Volcano just across the bay to the northwest of the modern community of Santiago Atitlán. The group was likely composed of two separate lineage groups (the *Ah Tziquinahas* and the *Tzutuhils*), which were at times openly hostile to one another (Orellana 1984, 81; Carlsen 1997, 75). The authors of the *Annals of the Cakchiquels* stated that the Tzutuhils succeeded in temporarily expelling the Ah Tziquinahas from their citadel south of Lake Atitlán in 1521 (Recinos and Goetz 1953, 117).

[513] *Saq Aj* (White Ear of Unripe Maize).

[514] The Lamacs, like the Cumatz with whom they are paired in this passage, apparently settled the area of present-day Sacapulas (Recinos 1950, 171 n. 6; Fox 1978, 76). There is a site known as Lamak-Zacapulas approximately five leagues north of Sacapulas (Villacorta and Villacorta 1930, 94; Fox 1978, 90).

and the Tuhalhas,[516] the Uchabahas[517] and the Ah Chumilahas,[518] along with the Ah Quibahas[519] and the Ah Batenahas,[520] the Acul Vinacs[521] and the Balamihas,[522] the Can Chahels[523] and the Balam Colobs.[524]

Of these we shall speak only of the nations that became great among the allied nations. They who became great we shall declare.[525] There were many others that came out of the citadel after them, each one of them a division. We have not written their names, but they also multiplied there in the East. Many people arrived in darkness in the days of their increase, for the sun was yet to be born. There was no light in the days of their increase. They were all as one, crowded together as they walked there in the East. There was no one to provide for their sustenance. They would merely lift up their faces to the sky, for they did not know where to go.

This they did for a long time there among the magueys; among the black people and the white people, the people of many appearances and many

---

[515] *Kumatz* (Serpent). The Cumatz also settled near the present-day town of Sacapulas (Recinos 1950, 171 n. 6). The Cumatz settlement may be the site of Chutixtiox, located on a hill at the center of the Sacapulas basin approximately three kilometers west of the modern town of Sacapulas (Fox 1978, 71–77). The Cumatz were subjugated by the Quichés early in the fifteenth century as part of Lord Quicab's campaign of expansion (Recinos and Goetz 1953, 93; Recinos 1957, 141).

[516] The *Tujal Ja* (Sweatbath House) occupied the area surrounding the modern community of Sacapulas (Recinos 1950, 171 n. 6; Fox 1978, 76). Fox suggests that the settlement of this lineage may be identified with the ruins of Chutinamit, located just across the river and north of present-day Sacapulas, which once controlled the valuable salt springs nearby (Fox 1978, 81). The Tujalhas were conquered by Lord Quicab in the early fifteenth century at the same time as the rest of the Sacapulas Valley (Recinos and Goetz 1953, 93; 1957, 141–143; Carmack 1973, 369–371).

[517] *U Ch'ab'a Ja.* The name of this lineage could be "House of Arrows" (based on *ch'ab'*), or "House of Speech" (based on *ch'ab'al*). These also settled somewhere in the Sacapulas valley (Recinos 1950, 171 n. 6). Fox suggests that their principle settlement was the site of Pacot, approximately nine kilometers west of Sacapulas at the far edge of the Sacapulas Valley (Fox 1978, 84–87).

[518] *Aj Ch'umila Ja* (They of the Star House).

[519] *Aj Q'iba Ja* ("They of the Clever House). *Q'ib'* is "sharp, clever, student."

[520] *Aj B'atena Ja* (They of the Ballgame Yoke House).

[521] *Akul Winaq* (Acul People).

[522] *B'alami Ja* (Jaguar House). This lineage is clearly identified as the inhabitants of Aguacatán in a 1739 land-dispute document (Carmack 1978, 207). Their principal Precolumbian settlement was Tenam, located approximately three kilometers east of Aguacatán (Fox 1978, 101–107). This area was conquered by Lord Quicab at the same time as his campaign in and around Sacapulas (Carmack 1953b, 188; 1957, 145).

[523] *Kan Chajeleb'* (War Captive Guardians).

[524] *B'alam Kolob'* (Jaguar Rope).

[525] It is important to remember that the *Popol Vuh* was written by representatives of the Nima Quiché nobility and there was little attempt at objective "history" in the modern sense. The authors' purpose in compiling this record is, at least in part, to bolster the legitimacy and traditions of their own lineages, often at the expense of their neighboring rivals.

tongues.[526] They were destitute in their existence at the edge of the sky's foundation. And there were mountain people. They were hidden, and without homes. Only among the small mountains and the great mountains did they go. It is as if they were lacking in direction,[527] as they used to say. It is said that in those days they quarreled with the mountain people.

There they looked for the coming forth of the sun, when they had one common language. They did not yet call upon wood or stone.[528] They remembered the word of the Framer and the Shaper, of Heart of Sky and Heart of Earth, it was said. They would merely plead for their heartening, their sowing and their dawning.[529] These were people of esteemed words, of esteem, of honor, and of respect.[530] They would lift up their faces to the sky as they pleaded for their daughters and their sons:

"Alas, you, Framer, and you, Shaper: Behold us! Hear us! Do not abandon us. Do not allow us to be overthrown.[531] You are the god in the sky and on the earth, you, Heart of Sky, Heart of Earth. May our sign, our word,[532] be given for as long as there is sun and light.[533] Then may it be sown, may it dawn. May there be true life-giving[534] roads and pathways. Give us steadfast light that our nation be made steadfast. May the light be favorable that our nation may be favored. May our lives be favored so that all creation[535] may be favored as well. Give this to us, you, Huracan, Youngest Thunderbolt,

---

[526] I take this passage to mean that the area in which the progenitors lived was cosmopolitan, with diverse ethnic and language groups. It is unlikely that this is a description of the Quichés themselves because in the next section they describe themselves as being unified, with a common language.

[527] Ch'u'j refers to someone who is "wayward, erratic, insane, or mad."

[528] As described later in the text, the gods did not manifest themselves as wooden or stone images until after the first dawn (pp. 229–230; lines 6137–6140).

[529] This triplet recalls the purpose of the creation in which the creator deities were described as "hearteners" or "they who remember" (p. 66 n.44; lines 83–85), providing the foundation for the ultimate "sowing" and "dawning" of mankind (p. 71; lines 196–197).

[530] In the creation account, the gods hoped to be able to provide people on the earth who would "honor and respect" them (p. 78; lines 454–455). This is another indication that the progenitors fulfilled the requirements set forth by the gods that successful people should have the capacity to worship them in an appropriate manner. "Honor and Respect" were also the names given to the ballcourt of Hun Hunahpu (p. 119; lines 1969–1972).

[531] Pisk'alij is "to turn inside out" (Basseta).

[532] Etal (sign) and tzijel (word, as well as the act of lighting a candle or torch) when paired together refer to the posterity of children and grandchildren (Coto).

[533] This is a common Quiché expression for "eternity" or "forever."

[534] Raxal. Literally "greenness" in the sense of being invigorating, refreshing, or life-giving.

[535] Winaqirem may refer to "humanity," but it is also the name given to "creation" itself, including the mountains, rivers, and animals. On pp. 65–66 (lines 80–81), it is paired with "life" as the ultimate goal of deity.

and Sudden Thunderbolt,[536] Youngest Nanavac and Sudden Nanavac,[537] Falcon[538] and Hunahpu,[539] Sovereign and Quetzal Serpent,[540] She Who Has Borne Children and He Who Has Begotten Sons,[541] Xpiyacoc and Xmucane, Grandmother of Day and Grandmother of Light.[542] Then may it be sown. Then may it dawn," they said.

Then they fasted and cried out in prayer. They fixed their eyes firmly on their dawn, looking there to the East. They watched closely for the Morning Star,[543] the Great Star that gives its light at the birth of the sun. They looked to the womb of the sky and the womb of the earth, to the pathways of framed and shaped people.

Then spoke Balam Quitze, Balam Acab, Mahucutah, and Iqui Balam: "We shall surely await the dawn," they said.

They were great sages and wise men,[544] bloodletters and honorers, as they are called. There did not exist then wood or stone to watch over our first mothers and fathers. They were therefore weary in their hearts as they awaited the dawn.

There were many nations then, there with the Yaqui people,[545] the bloodletters and sacrificers.

[536] These three deities combined are referred to as "Heart of Sky" (see p. 70; lines 183–189).

[537] The name is likely derived from the Nahua *a* (water), and *nawak* (near, close), giving the reading of "close to water" (Campbell 1983, 84). Schultze-Jena identified Nanavac with the Mexican god Nanahuac/Nanahuatzin, a lightning deity who opened a cleft in the sacred mountain Tonacatepetl (Mountain of our Sustenance) to reveal maize (1944, 187; León-Portilla 1980, 142–143; Edmonson 1971, 5188–5192; D. Tedlock 1996, 294). This mountain is analogous to the mountain Paxil, wherein was discovered the maize that would become the flesh of the first humans (pp. 193–194; lines 4862–4881). Nanahuac was also the name of the ugly god who threw himself into the divine fire at Teotihuacan in order to be transformed into the fifth sun, or the sun of this present age. In this latter role, he was closely related to Quetzalcoatl (León-Portilla 1963, 43–44; 1980, 143 n. 86; Akkeren 2000, 162, 333; Townsend 2000, 128–129).

[538] This is likely a reference to the falcon deity, a messenger from Heart of Sky, that watched over One Hunahpu and Seven Hunahpu at their ballcourt (see p. 114; lines 1786–1796).

[539] One of the Hero Twins, brother of Xbalanque.

[540] Two of the creator deities (see pp. 61, 68–70; lines 24–25, 139–154).

[541] Titles for the ancestor couple, Xmucane and Xpiyacoc (see p. 200; lines 5107–5110). They are arranged in reverse order, or as a chiasm, with the names of the grandparent deities that follow.

[542] These are titles for the grandmother goddess Xmucane (see pp. 79–80; lines 508–517).

[543] *Ik'oq'ij* (passes before sun) is the planet Venus as morning star.

[544] *Eta'manel* (sage) is one who understands or knows by means of thinking; *na'onel* (wise person, knower) is one who knows by means of the senses. We might use the terms "thinking" and "sensing," but for the Quichés these are both related aspects of "to know."

[545] *Yaqui* is the Quiché name for the inhabitants of ancient Mexico.

"Let us go and search, to look for one who may protect us. We may find one before whom we may speak. For here we only feign existence and there is not a guardian for us," said therefore Balam Quitze, Balam Acab, Mahucutah, and Iqui Balam.

They heard news of a citadel and there they went.

THE ARRIVAL AT TULAN[546]

THIS, then, is the name of the mountain that they went to. Balam Quitze, Balam Acab, Mahucutah, and Iqui Balam, along with the Tamub and the

Figure 56. "Balam Quitze, Balam Acab, Mahucutah, and Iqui Balam... arrived at Tulan Zuyva." City surrounded by water, from a mural in the Temple of the Warriors, Chichen Itza (drawing by Ann Axtell Morris).

[546] lines 5361–5374

[547] *Tulan* (Nahua *Tullan* or *Tollan*: "Place of Cattail Reeds"). In the Quiché language, *tulan* is a "palace, or manor-house" (Basseta), while *tolan* is a city or house that has been abandoned, perhaps referring to the ruins of once great cities that dot the region and that belong to the legendary ancestors of the Maya people. In Aztec theology, Tollan was a mythic place located near Coatepec (Snake Mountain) where the ancestors of the Mexica received their patron god Huitzilopochtli. In this myth, Tollan was inhabited by the Toltecs, great sages who invented the sciences of astronomy, calendrics, agriculture, and medicine, as well as the arts of writing, painting, sculpture, metalwork, jade carving, and weaving (see footnote 102). Throughout Mesoamerica in the late Postclassic era (ca. 1200–1524), the legendary Toltecs were the bearers of political legitimacy. The Aztecs used the name *Tollan* to refer to their own legendary place of origin, as well as a general term for "city." Thus *Tollan* was an alternative name for the ancient Aztec capital city Tenochtitlan, as well as Tula in Hidalgo, Teotihuacan, Cholula, and Chichen Itza (Schele and Mathews 1998, 38–39; Akkeren 2000, 62, 88). The Tulan mentioned here was likely either Chichen Itza, a major center of power during the Terminal Classic (800–900) and Early Postclassic (900–1200) periods, or its successor Mayapan (Recinos 1950, 63–69; Recinos and Goetz 1953, 65 n; Fox 1978, 1–2,

Ilocab, arrived at Tulan[547] Zuyva.[548] Seven Caves and Seven Canyons[549] was the name of the citadel. There they arrived to obtain their gods.

119–121; Carmack 1981, 46–48). Both would have been "across the sea" (the Gulf of Mexico) with respect to the Guatemalan highlands as described in the Popol Vuh (see pp. 221, 255–256, 259).

[548] *Suywa* (Nahua: "Bloody Water"; Yucatec: "Confusion"). *Suy*, in lowland Maya languages, is a "whirlpool," or something twisted. *Suywa* is "confusion," and *suywa t'an* is "figurative or rhetorical language." In the *Book of Chilam Balam of Chumayel*, the "language of Suywa" refers to a series of riddles and plays on words that only true lords are able to solve to prove their legitimacy (Roys 1967, 88–98). In Nahua, *Zuyua* is "Bloody Water," a reading that is specifically recognized elsewhere in the *Chilam Balam of Chumayel* (Edmonson 1986, 172 lines 3580–3582). The *Annals of the Cakchiquels* agrees with the *Popol Vuh* in locating this area with the "Tulan in the East" (Recinos and Goetz 1953, 53). In the Yucatec Maya *Books of Chilam Balam*, Zuyua is identified with Xicalanco, an ancient port city on the shores of the Laguna de Términos in the Mexican state of Tabasco (Recinos and Goetz 1953, 53, 216; Campbell 1970, 7; Carmack 1981, 46).

[549] The equivalent in Central Mexican mythology is Chicomoztoc (Seven Caves), the legendary origin place of the Early Postclassic Toltecs and the many Nahua groups who claim Toltec ancestry (Davies 1977, 35–37; Tezozomoc 1975, 14–15; Torquemada 1969, I.xiv.36–38). In all likelihood the Seven Caves legend predates the Toltec era. Beneath the Pyramid of the Sun at Teotihuacan is a partially-artificial cave consisting of a central tunnel and six branches that represents in physical form the ancient place of origin (Heyden 1975, 1981; Taube 1986; Millon 1993, 20–22).

THE PROGENITORS
RECEIVE THEIR GODS[550]

THEY arrived there at Tulan, all of them. Innumerable people they were when they arrived. They walked in crowds when the gods came out to them in succession. First among them were Balam Quitze, Balam Acab, Mahucutah, and Iqui Balam, who rejoiced:

"We have found that for which we have searched," they said.

The god named Tohil[551] went out first, carried in his pack frame by Balam Quitze.

Then went out the god named Auilix,[552] carried by Balam Acab.

Next was Hacavitz,[553] the name of the god received by Mahucutah.

---

[550] lines 5375–5413

[551] *Tojil.* In the Quiché language, *tojil* refers to a "payment, debt, obligation, or tribute." This is consistent with this god's demand for tribute and sacrifice. Toj is one of the named days in the highland Maya calendar. During divination ceremonies the day Toj implies the need to pay a debt in a metaphoric sense. Barbara Tedlock notes that if a divination falls on the day Toj, this "indicates that one owes (*tojonic*) in the customs of the Mundo [Spanish "World"] or the ancestors, and by extension one may owe a favor, work, or money to another person. If the client is ill, this means that the pain (*c'äx*) is a punishment for this debt; the only way to cure it is to pay (*tojonic*) the Mundo, ancestors, or creditor what is owed, plus a penalty for the neglect" (B. Tedlock 1982, 115). Another possible derivation of the word is from Mixe-Zoque. In that language, *toh-mel* refers to "thunder" (Campbell 1983, 83). In the *Annals of the Cakchiquels*, the Quichés are called "thunderers" because they worship this god, supporting this latter reading:

> Then we asked: "Where is your salvation?" Thus we said to the Quichés. "Since it thunders and resounds in the sky, in the sky is our salvation," they said. Wherefore they were given the name of *Tohohils* (Recinos and Goetz 1953, 58).

[552] *Awilix.* In the Quiché language, this would read "you are watched over/cared for/ commissioned." Throughout the text, the Quichés promise to watch over and care for their gods, providing them with offerings, sustenance, and worship (p. 290; lines 8344–8346, 8379–8388). Tedlock suggests that it may be derived from the Kekchi, *kwilix/wilix*, "swallow" (the bird) and reads the full name as Lord Swallow (D. Tedlock 1996, 297 n. 152). More recently, Akkeren (personal communication) has suggested that the Nihaib lineage originally came from the Pico de Orizaba area, known anciently by its Nahua name Awilizapan. It is possible that Awilix, the patron deity of the Nihaib derived the name of their god from this region and its principle mountain which bore the same name.

[553] *Jakawitz. Witz* is the lowland Maya word for "mountain." In the *Título Yax* (Carmack and Mondloch 1989, folio 2r, 107 n. 135), which is far more consistent in their use of the modified Latin alphabet developed by Father Francisco de la Parra in the sixteenth century and used by scribes throughout highland Guatemala, the name of this deity is *Q'aq'awitz* (Fire Mountain). This suggests that Hacavitz, like Tohil, is primarily a fire deity. This reading is also consistent with the description of his mountain, *nima q'aq' ja* (great fire house) (see p. 224; line 5905). Another support for this reading is that xq*'aqwitz* means "yellow wasp" in Mam (Akkeren 2000, 173–174), and the wasp is one of the principle symbols of this god

Nicacah Tacah[554] was the name of the god received by Iqui Balam.

Together with the Quiché people, the Tamub also received Tohil. This is the name of the god received by the grandfathers and fathers of the Tamub, as these lords are known today.

Third, then, were the Ilocab: Tohil was also the name of the god received by the grandfathers and fathers of the Ilocab, as these lords are known today.

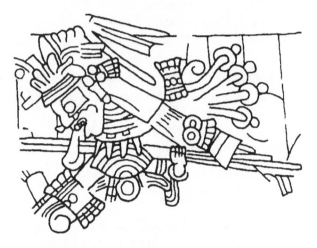

Figure 57. "There they received their gods." A highland Maya god, from a mural at Iximche (drawing by Linda Schele).

and the lineage of Mahucutah (see p. 245; lines 6783–6787). Alternatively, the authors of the *Título Totonicapán* write the name as *Jaq'awitz* (Lying Down/Recumbent Mountain).

[554] *Nik'akaj Taq'aj* (Center/Middle Plain/Valley). Because Iqui Balam failed to produce offspring, and thus a nation of descendents, this god does not appear again in the *Popol Vuh* account. The gods of the progenitors are listed as a trinity (Tohil, Auilix, and Hacavitz) subsequent to this passage.

THE PROGENITORS LEAVE TULAN[555]

THUS was the naming of the three Quichés. But in this they freed themselves because it was the same god's name, Tohil Quiché, for all of them. It was Tohil for the Tamub as well as for the Ilocab. There was only one name for god among them. Therefore the three groups of Quichés were not divided.

Three were they who were truly great in their nature: Tohil, Auilix, and Hacavitz.

Then all the nations entered therein—the Rabinals, the Cakchiquels, and the Ah Tziquinahas, along with the Yaqui people, as they are called today. It was there that the languages of the nations were changed. Their languages came to be different. They did not hear each other clearly when they came from Tulan, thus they split apart.

They came in crowds from the East. They were alike in the hides that they wore as coverings, for their dress was very poor. They had nothing of their own, but they were enchanted people in their essence when they came from Tulan Zuyva, the Seven Caves and the Seven Canyons, as they are called in the ancient account.

They did not have fire, only Tohil. This was the god of the nations when fire was first created. It was not clear how it was created, for the fire was already burning when Balam Quitze and Balam Acab saw it.

"Alas, fire has not come to be ours. We shall die of cold," they said.

Then Tohil spoke:

"Do not mourn. The fire shall be yours again should you lose it. I have spoken," Tohil said to them.

"Are you not truly god? You are our provider and strengthener. You are our god." they said when they gave thanks.

And Tohil replied:

"Very well, I am truly your god. Then be it so. I am your lord. Then be it so," the bloodletters and sacrificers were told by Tohil.

This therefore was the glory[556] of the nations, and they rejoiced because of their fire.

---

[555] lines 5414–5485

[556] Q'aq'al, derived from q'aq' (flame), means "glory, majesty, power." This incident with the fire thus has far greater implications than simple comfort. It refers to the divine source of power for the Quiché people. Offerings made by contemporary Quiché aj q'ij priests are generally burned, transforming them into smoke that rises into the sky and is suitable for reception by divinity.

THEN it began to rain while the fire of the nations[558] burned brightly. Hail fell thickly on the heads of all the nations and their fire went out because of the hail. Thus their fire came to nought. Then Balam Quitze and Balam Acab pleaded again for their fire:

"O Tohil, truly the cold has finished us," they said to Tohil.

"Very well. Do not mourn," said Tohil.

Then he brought forth fire. He twist drilled[559] inside his shoe. Thus Balam Quitze, Balam Acab, Mahucutah, and Iqui Balam rejoiced as they warmed themselves.

But the fire of the nations was extinguished and the cold had nearly finished them. Thus they came to plead for fire from Balam Quitze, Balam Acab, Mahucutah, and Iqui Balam. They could no longer bear it because of the cold and the hail. They shuddered and trembled. There was no life in them because of the shivering of their legs and their arms. Neither could they hold on to anything when they arrived:

Figure 58. "Then he brought forth fire. He twist drilled inside his shoe." A god makes new fire by means of a twist drill, from the Dresden Codex, p. 6b (Villacorta and Villacorta 1930).

---

[557] lines 5486–5601

[558] At this point the text refers to the *Amaq'* (Nations) as a distinct entity from the Nima Quiché lineages consisting of an alliance of groups who become the enemies of the Quichés. These are likely a general term for the Poqom and Kekchi speakers of the Verapaz region (Recinos 1950, 171 n. 6; Akkeren 2000, 137), and perhaps the Mam speakers further west who had dominated the Guatemalan highlands prior to the rise of the Quichés. In the *Título Totonicapán*, they are called the *Vucamag* (Seven Nations/Tribes).

[559] An ancient means of starting new fire, by spinning a wooden stick or drill on a hard wooden surface in order to produce sufficient heat to ignite kindling.

"Truly we are not ashamed to come before you to ask for just a little bit of your fire," they said when they arrived.

But they were not welcomed, and the nations cursed in their hearts. For now the language of Balam Quitze, Balam Acab, Mahucutah, and Iqui Balam was different.

"Alas, is our language now abandoned? What have we done? We are lost. Where were we deceived? We had but one language when we came from Tulan. We had but one origin[560] and creation. It is not good what we have done," said all the nations beneath the trees and beneath the bushes.

Then a person[561] revealed himself before Balam Quitze, Balam Acab, Mahucutah, and Iqui Balam. This messenger from Xibalba said to them:

"Truly Tohil is your god. He is your provider. He is also the substitute and remembrance of your Framer and your Shaper. Do not give, therefore, fire to the nations unless they first give something to Tohil in return. It is not to you that they shall give. Rather your desire must be to go before Tohil. Ask him what they shall give in return for the fire," said the person from Xibalba. He had wings like the wings of a bat. "I am a messenger from your Framer and your Shaper," said the person from Xibalba.

Thus they rejoiced. Tohil, Auilix, and Hacavitz became great in their hearts when the person from Xibalba spoke to them. Then suddenly he disappeared before their faces, although he was not destroyed.

Then the nations arrived. The cold had nearly finished them. It was thick with hail, with dark storms, and with hoar frost. The cold was too much to be conceived. All the nations covered themselves up, bending over, and crawling on their hands and knees because of the cold when they arrived before Balam Quitze, Balam Acab, Mahucutah, and Iqui Balam. They were greatly troubled[562] in their hearts. Sorrowful were their mouths and their faces.

[560] Literally "germination."

[561] Father Ximénez, who transcribed the *Popol Vuh* manuscript, inserted at this point his only commentary anywhere in the text: *Demonium loquens cis* (Latin: "Demon speaking from here on").

[562] *Q'atat* is "preoccupied, afflicted, troubled."

THE NATIONS ARE DECEIVED
INTO OFFERING THEMSELVES[563]

THUS they arrived as thieves before the faces of Balam Quitze, Balam Acab, Mahucutah, and Iqui Balam.

"Truly, will you not take pity on us? We shall only ask for a small bit of your fire. Has it not been discovered? Has it not been found? Were we not of the same home? We were of the same mountain when you were framed and when you were shaped. Take pity therefore on us,"[564] they said.

"What then will you give to us if we were to take pity on you?" they asked.

"Very well then, we will give precious metal to you," the nations replied.

"We do not want precious metal," said Balam Quitze and Balam Acab.

"What then do you truly want? We plead of you," said therefore the nations.

"Very well, we will first inquire of Tohil, then we shall tell you," they were told.

Then they asked Tohil:

"What are the nations to give, O Tohil?" asked Balam Quitze, Balam Acab, Mahucutah, and Iqui Balam. "They have come to ask for your fire."

"Very well then. This is what you will say: 'Do they not want to give the breast[565] beneath their shoulders and their armpits? Do they not desire in their hearts to embrace me—I, Tohil? If they do not want this, then I will not give to them their fire, says Tohil,' you will say to them. 'It will have a beginning, but it will not be today that they will give the breast below their shoulders and their armpits, he says to you.' This is what you will say." This is what Balam Quitze, Balam Acab, Mahucutah, and Iqui Balam were told.

Thus they spoke the word of Tohil to the nations.

"Very well then. The breast shall be given. It is good that we are to embrace him," they replied.

---

[563] lines 5602–5774

[564] Literally "pity then our faces."

[565] This deception is based on a play on words that also works in English. The verb here is *tu'nik* (to give breast, to suckle, to nurture). On one level, the nations thought they had agreed to support or nurture the progenitors, which might logically be interpreted as a regular tribute of food and other necessities. As will soon become apparent, however, Tohil meant this much more literally in the sense that the nations were to offer their breasts/chests in the form of sacrifice by heart extraction.

In this way they responded, accepting the word of Tohil. Thus they were never again to increase. "Fine," they said straightaway.

Thus they received fire and they were warmed. There was only one group that stole away the fire from within the smoke. This was the Zotzilaha.[566] Chamal Can[567] is the name of the god of the Cakchiquels. His image was merely that of a bat. They passed by in the smoke, moving stealthily as they passed. Thus when they arrived to take the fire, the Cakchiquels did not ask for it. They did not give themselves up in defeat as all the nations had done who were defeated.[568]

Figure 59. "All the nations were to be sacrificed before him. Their hearts were to be carved out from beneath their shoulders and armpits." Sacrifice by heart extraction, from a gold disk, Chichen Itza (Lothrop 1952, fig. 1. Copyright by the President and Fellows of Harvard College).

[566] *Sotz'ila Ja* (Bat House), one of the principal lineages of the Cakchiquels.

[567] Tedlock suggests that this name should be interpreted as "Snake Tooth," derived from lowland Maya Cholan or Yucatec languages: *Cha'am* (molar) and *Kan* (snake) (D. Tedlock 1996, 300 n. 156).

[568] This incident may have been included in the text in part to explain the independence and, from the Quiché viewpoint, treachery of the Cakchiquels who rebelled against the

Thus the nations gave their breasts beneath their shoulders and beneath their armpits. This, then, was the breast-giving spoken of by Tohil—all the nations were to be sacrificed before him. Their hearts were to be carved out from beneath their shoulders and armpits. This thing had not heretofore been attempted. Thus Tohil foresaw the seizure of glory and majesty by Balam Quitze, Balam Acab, Mahucutah, and Iqui Balam.

Now when they came from Tulan Zuyva, they did not eat. They fasted continuously. Yet they fixed their eyes on the dawn, looking steadfastly for the coming forth of the sun. They occupied themselves in looking for the Great Star, called Icoquih,[569] which appears first before the birth of the sun. The face of this Green Morning Star[570] always appears at the coming forth of the sun.

When they were there at the place called Tulan Zuyva, their gods came to them. But it was surely not then that they received their ultimate glory or their lordship. Rather it was where the great nations and the small nations were conquered and humiliated when they were sacrificed before the face of Tohil. They gave their blood, which flowed from the shoulders and the armpits of all the people.

Straightaway at Tulan came the glory and the great knowledge that was theirs. It was in the darkness, in the night as well, that they accomplished it. Thus they came. They were pulled up like weeds as they came out from there, leaving the East behind.

"This is not our home. Surely let us go to see where we shall begin,"[571] said Tohil. He truly spoke to Balam Quitze, Balam Acab, Mahucutah, and

Quichés in the time of Lord Quicab. Subsequent to this rebellion, the Quichés were in a state of nearly constant warfare with the Cakchiquels, their former allies (p. 278; lines 7975–7987; Recinos and Goetz 1953, 94–118). The Cakchiquels garnered further animosity by allying themselves with the invading Spaniards under Pedro de Alvarado against the Quichés and other highland Maya groups in 1524 (Recinos and Goetz 1953, 119–121).

[569] *Ik'oq'ij* (Accompanies/Bears/Passes Before Sun). This is the planet Venus as morning star. Las Casas wrote that "after the sun, which they held as their principal god, they honored and worshiped a certain star (I could not learn which star this was) more than any other denizen of the heavens or earth, because they held it as certain that their god, *Quezalcóvatl*, the highest god of the Cholulans, when he died transformed into this star" (Las Casas 1967, III, clxxiv, p. 201). Las Casas further noted that the Indians awaited the appearance of this star in the East each day, and that when it appeared their priests offered "many sacrifices and ceremonies," including incense and their own blood (Ibid.). Although Las Casas could not identify which star this was, native Mesoamerican sources identify the Feathered Serpent deity Quetzalcoatl with Venus (Roys 1967, 159 n. 7; Nicholson 2001, 16, 47, 251–252).

[570] *Raxa Ik'oq'ij. Rax* is "green, new, fresh, sudden, regenerated, revived." It is unclear whether this refers to the green color of the planet Venus, or whether it refers to the life-generating power of the Morning Star to assist in the birth of the sun.

[571] *Kojtike'* (we plant, we begin).

Iqui Balam. "You shall first give thanks. You shall carry out your responsibilities first by piercing[572] your ears. You shall prick[573] your elbows. This shall be your petition, your way of giving thanks before the face of god."

"Very well," they said.

Then they pierced their ears. They wept as they sang of their coming from Tulan. They wept within their hearts as they came, weeping for Tulan:

"Alas, it is not here that we shall see the dawn, when the sun will be born to illuminate the face of the earth," they said as they came.

They merely stayed on the road. The people of each of the

Figure 60. "You shall carry out your responsibilities first by piercing your ears. You shall prick your elbows." Deity holding the instruments of bloodletting, from the Madrid Codex, p. 86b (Villacorta and Villacorta 1930).

nations remained sleeping and resting together on the road. Yet always they looked for the star, the sign of the sun, the sign of the dawn in their hearts when they came from the East. They were truly united[574] as they made their journey here, passing through Honor and Respect,[575] as it is said today.

---

[572] *Jutik* in modern usage is "to insert or pierce," such as a thread through the eye of a needle, or a string through a series of beads.

[573] *T'is* is "to pierce with a needle," such as a piece of cloth while sewing.

[574] Literally "same face."

[575] This is the place where Hun Hunahpu and his sons played ball (see p. 119; lines 1969–1972). Thus the origin of the progenitors is defined as the homeland of the patron heroes described in the first half of the *Popol Vuh* text.

THE PEOPLE GATHER ON
THE MOUNTAIN CHI PIXAB[576]

THEN they arrived atop a mountain. All the Quiché people gathered together, along with the nations. There they all came and counseled one with another. The mountain today is called Chi Pixab.[577] This is the name of the mountain. Here they gathered together and here they gave to one another their names:

"I am this: I am a Quiché person."

"You, then, are this: Tamub your name shall come to be," the Tamub were told.

Then the Ilocab were addressed:

"You are Ilocab. This is the name that shall come to be yours. We, the three Quichés, will not be lost, for our word is one," they said when their names were given.

[576] lines 5775–5796

[577] "Place of Counsel or Instruction." Carmack identifies this as a mountain on the border between San Andrés Sajcabaja and San Bartolomé Jocotenango (Carmack 1981, 66). Here the nearby territory was divided between the major lineage groups—the Quichés, Tamub, and Ilocab settled the region to the north, centered on the mountain of Hacavitz; the Ah Tziquinahas (Tz'utuhils) settled the coastlands around Lake Atitlán; the Rabinals chose the mountains of the Rabinal basin to the east. The Cakchiquels at this time served as a lineage of vassal warriors and occupied a band of territory situated between the Quichés and the Ah Tziquinahas, centered on the mountains above Chichicastenango. These mountain redoubts were apparently chosen for their defensive potential.

THEIR SUFFERING ON
THE MOUNTAIN CHI PIXAB[578]

Then the Cakchiquels were given their name. Cakchiquels came to be their name. Also Rabinals came to be the name of that people. And Ah Tziquinahas was the name by which that people are known today.

These, then, were the names of they who spoke together. It was there that they came to await the dawn. They would look for the first appearance of the star that precedes the face of the sun when it is born.

"We came from there, but we were split apart," they said among themselves.

This is what preoccupied their hearts as they passed through their great afflictions. They did not have food or sustenance. They would only sniff the bottoms of their staffs to feel as if they were eating. But they did not eat when they came.

It was not clear how they passed over the sea to come here. It was as if there were no sea that they had to pass over.

Figure 61. "They would look for the first appearance of the star that precedes the face of the sun when it is born." This is the anthropomorphic god of the morning star, Venus, descending head-first from a sky band. The hieroglyph for Venus forms his head while the glyph for the sun rests on his right foot, from the Dresden Codex, p. 58b (Villacorta and Villacorta 1930).

They merely passed over on the tops of stones for there were stones on the sand. Thus they named it "Lined Up Stones"; and "Piled up Sand" was also its name. Over these they made their passage here from within the sea. The water divided itself and through it they made their passage here.

They were preoccupied in their hearts when they took counsel together, for they had no food. They would drink only atole[579] made of maize grains

[578] lines 5797–5870
[579] *Uk'* is any kind of drink other than water. In this case the text specifies that it is a drink made from maize, or in other words, an atole. Maize atole is the principal drink offered on

which they had borne to the top of the mountain named Chi Pixab. They had carried only Tohil, Auilix, and Hacavitz. Thus Balam Quitze observed a great fast along with his wife, named Cahapaluna; the same also did Balam Acab with his wife, named Chomiha; along with Mahucutah, who observed a great fast with his wife, named Tzununiha; and also Iqui Balam and Caquixaha, which was the name of his wife. Thus they fasted in the darkness, in the night. Great was their sorrow when they were atop the mountain which is called Chi Pixab today.

Then spoke the gods there.

ceremonial occasions in contemporary highland Maya society (Bunzel 1952, 45, 233–234; B. Tedlock 1982, 65–66). At Santiago Atitlán, this ceremonial atole is called *maatz'*. Unlike the usual type of maize drink which is made from watered-down corn dough, *maatz'* is made from grain that has been toasted and then ground fine before it is mixed with two handfuls of ash and placed in a boiling pot of water. This procedure, the only time that Atitecos grind maize kernels into dry flour, or allow maize to come into direct contact with fire, matches the Popol Vuh description of the underworld lords grinding the burned bones of Hunahpu and Xbalanque "like finely ground corn flour" (Carlsen 1997, 57–59). Because traditionalist Atitecos believe that the preparation of *maatz'* is fraught with danger, it is carried out under the direction of the Xo', the wife of the head of the confraternity in which it is to be consumed. A confraternity elder blesses her beforehand so that she will not be burned in the process. I was told by a prominent Atiteco that drinking *maatz'* symbolizes victory over "death and the fires of the underworld (Christenson 2001, 123–124)." The resulting mixture is sometimes addressed as mother's milk or sperm, both associated with rebirth and regeneration (Freidel et al. 1993, 180). Although confraternity members frequently share food and drink in an atmosphere of informality sometimes bordering on the raucous, they drink *maatz'* with great solemnity. The highest-ranking confraternity elder present distributes it to those present in order of their rank. As he does so he addressed each by name and title and calls on the patron saint of the confraternity to bless the recipient so that person's feet, knees, heart, arms, head, and thoughts will have power and nothing untoward will happen to the individual during the year. The great Atiteco culture hero Francisco Sojuel is said to have called *maatz'* the true *ruk'ux way* (heart of food) and refused to eat anything else when carrying out important ceremonies (Mendelson 1957, 139).

THE PROGENITORS
AWAIT THE FIRST DAWN[580]

THEN spoke Tohil, Auilix, and Hacavitz to Balam Quitze, Balam Acab, Mahucutah, and Iqui Balam:

"We must go now. We must rise up. For we are not meant to be here. Place us in hiding, for does not the dawn now approach? Would you not be pitiable if we should become the spoils of warriors?[581] Make for us a place that we may be with you, O bloodletters and sacrificers, and place each of us there," they said when they spoke to them.

"Very well. Let us arise and search in the forests,"[582] they all said.

Then each of them took his god to be carried on his back. Auilix was taken into a canyon named Hidden Canyon, a great canyon in the forest. Pa Auilix[583] is its name today. There he was left. He was left in the canyon by Balam Acab. He was the first to be left.

---

[580] lines 5871–6043

[581] *Aj lab'al* (warriors) is now the word for "savages" in contemporary Quiché usage.

[582] Las Casas wrote that the Maya were accustomed to keep their deity images in "rugged places, dark and secret caves" in order to keep them in greater reverence by not having them constantly on public display. On special occasions, the images were carried in procession to the temples where they were placed in sanctuaries (Las Casas 1967, III.clxxvii, 216). It is likely that ancient temples themselves were conceived as effigy mountains and that their elevated sanctuaries represented the cave-like homes of the gods (Vogt 1969, 595; Hill 1992, 6, 91; Stone 1995, 27, 35–36; Bassie-Sweet 1996, 111–131; Schele and Mathews 1998, 43, 417). With the destruction of such temples in the Guatemalan highlands at the time of the Spanish conquest, as well as the subsequent evangelization efforts by Christian missionaries, the more obvious public forms of Precolumbian ceremonialism ceased abruptly in most communities. This did not, however, preclude the continued veneration of traditional Maya deities in cave shrines and other remote locales (Bassie-Sweet 1991, 78–79; Peterson 1993, 175–177; Cervantes 1994, 35). Fuentes y Guzmán lamented in the seventeenth century that the innumerable gods that were once worshiped in highland Maya temples and houses were still venerated in mountain caves where they were given offerings of incense and animal sacrifices (Fuentes y Guzmán 1932–33, 44). Thomas Gage discovered one such deity image in 1635 while serving as a priest in Mixco, Guatemala. The image was sequestered in a cave near a spring and a large pine tree:

> When we came to it, we made very little more search, for near at hand was the cave, which was dark within, but light at the mouth. We found there more earthenware, with ashes in them, which assured us some frankincense had been burned. We knew not how far the cave might reach within, nor what might be in it, and therefore with a flint we struck fire and lighted a couple of candles and went in. At the entrance the cave was broad, and went a little forward, but when we were in, we found it turn on the left hand towards the mountain, and not far, for within two rods we found the idol standing upon a low stool covered with a linen cloth. The substance of it was wood, black shining like jet, as if it had been painted or smoked; the form was of a man's

Then Hacavitz was left on top of a great fire house.[584] Hacavitz is the name of the mountain today.[585] This they made their citadel, and this was where the god's dwelling came to be. Hacavitz it was called. Mahucutah did not leave his god behind, therefore.[586] This was the second god that was hidden by them. It was not in the forest that Hacavitz dwelt, but rather it was on a cleared[587] mountain where Hacavitz was hidden.

head unto the shoulders, without either beard or mustachios. His look was grim with a wrinkled forehead and broad startling eyes (Gage 1958, 280–281).

The image was surrounded by offerings of money, plaintains and other fruits, candles, pots of maize, honey, and little dishes of incense, the same offerings the Maya gave to the saints' images in the community church. Gage removed the image and publicly destroyed it the following sabbath, to the horror of those who worshiped it. Maya cave rituals remained for centuries a parallel theological system with that of the Roman Catholic church's pantheon of saints and deities and it continues to be an important element of traditional Maya worship in some communities (La Farge 1947, 124–128; Oakes 1951, 7; Vogt 1970, 13; B. Tedlock 1986, 128; Christenson 2001, 78–91).

[583] *Pa Awilix*. "Place of Auilix."

[584] The manuscript reads *hun nima caɛ ha* (a great fire/red house). This is likely not a proper name because of the initial article *hun* (a, one), which indicates that this is a descriptive phrase. Tedlock suggests that this is a pyramid temple (D. Tedlock 1996, 159). This is a good reading, particularly because the ancient Maya often painted their temples red and considered them to be effigy mountains. I am not wholly convinced, however, that this wasn't a true mountain, or in this case a volcano (fiery mountain) as the authors suggest that it existed in their day as a recognized and named mountain place, identified in the same way as the mountains of the other two gods, Tohil and Auilix. Carmack and Fox identify this mountain with the site of Chitinamit, a fortified settlement located on a high hill at the western edge of the Chujuyup Valley overlooking the Queca River (Fox 1978, 57–58; Carmack 1981, 65). Although separate hilltop sites, Hacavitz, Pa Tohil, and Pa Auilix are mutually visible from one another. The Chujuyup region is rugged and relatively poor for agriculture, suggesting that it was chosen more for its defensive potential. Akkeren concurs that Pa Tohil and Pa Auilix were located in the Chujuyup Valley, however, he suggests that Hacavitz was located south of Chichicastenango (Akkeren 2000, 42).

[585] *Jakawitz* in Cholan languages means "First/Beginning Mountain" tying it to the first mountain of creation. In Quiché, the verb *jaq* means "to open," which may recall the mountain of Paxil (Split Mountain) that contained the maize used to create the first human beings (see pp. 193–194; lines 4862–4939). In the *Título Yax* (Carmack and Mondloch 1989, folio 2r, 107 n. 135), which is far more consistent in their use of the modified Latin alphabet developed by Father Francisco de la Parra in the sixteenth century and used by scribes throughout highland Guatemala, the name of the deity placed on the mountain is *Q'aq'awitz* (Fire Mountain). This suggests that Hacavitz, like Tohil, is primarily a fire deity. This reading is also consistent with the description of his mountain, *nima q'aq' ja* (great fire house).

[586] The god Hacavitz was not left behind, because his sanctuary was located within the settlement of the Quiché people, rather than in the mountains and forests as the other two gods had been.

[587] *Saq*. This may be "white, clear, pure." Although there are a great number of white mountains in the highlands, due to the prevalence of lime deposits in the soil, this is more likely to be read as "cleared or bald," since it has already been described as red in color. The first citadel of the Quichés was built atop this mountain, necessitating the clearing of its trees and undergrowth if it was not deforested already.

Then came Balam Quitze. He arrived there in the great forest to hide Tohil. Pa Tohil[588] is the name of this great mountain today. Then they named the hidden canyon Healing Tohil.[589] It was crowded with snakes as well as jaguars, rattlesnakes and pit vipers. There in the forest they were, hidden by the bloodletters and sacrificers.

They were as one, Balam Quitze, Balam Acab, Mahucutah, and Iqui Balam. As one they awaited the dawn there on top of the mountain called Hacavitz.

Nearby was the god of the Tamub, along with the god of the Ilocab. Amac Tan[590] was the name of the place where the god of the Tamub was. There it dawned. Amac Uquincat[591] was the name of the place where the Ilocab dawned. The god of the Ilocab was there on a nearby mountain.

There all the Rabinals,[592] the Cakchiquels,[593] and the Ah Tziquinahas,[594] all the small nations and the great nations, arose as one. There was but one dawn. As one they awaited the coming forth of the Great Star, named Icoquih.

"First it will come forth before the face of the sun. Then it shall dawn," they said.

They were as one, Balam Quitze, Balam Acab, Mahucutah, and Iqui Balam. They did not sleep. They did not rest. Greatly did they weep in their hearts, in their bowels, for the dawn and for clarity. They came there surely as penitents, in great sorrow and great humility. They trembled because of the afflictions that they had passed through.

---

[588] "Place of Tohil." This is likely the mountain still known today as Pa Tojil, located on the south side of Chujuyup Valley (Fox 1978, 58; Carmack 1981, 65).

[589] "Healing/Medicine Tohil." Quiché *aj q'ij* priests frequently go to mountain shrines to perform healing ceremonies at specific shrines dedicated to certain deities, or the lords of days of the traditional calendar.

[590] *Amaq' T'an. Amaq'* is "nation;" *T'an* is "bald, lacking plumage." Most likely, however, this is an alternate or archaic spelling for the Tamub lineage. Thus the name of the place is simply "Nation of the Tamub." The Tamub lineage has a significant Pokom component, and in that language, Tamub may be read simply as "the descendents" (Akkeren 2000, 125). Carmack identifies this site with a series of ruins known as Cruz Che located along a slope of Telec'uch Mountain west of Hacavitz. The remains of a deity shrine still known by its ancient name, Saqirib'al (Place of Dawn), is located on a peak of the mountain (Carmack, Fox, and Stewart 1975, 66–70; Fox 1978, 57; Carmack 1981, 65).

[591] *Amaq' U Q'in K'at* (Nation Its Frame Net). Carmack suggests that this site was located on a slope of Telec'uch Mountain, separated from *Amaq' T'an* by a river canyon (Carmack 1981, 65).

[592] The Rabinals in this era settled the mountains above Joyabaj.

[593] At this phase of their history, the Cakchiquels occupied the mountain region above the present-day town of Chichicastenango.

[594] It is likely that this lineage had already begun to settle the southern shores of Lake Atitlán, which would remain the center of their territory into modern times.

Figure 62. "But these, the gods, were comforted in the canyons and the forests. They were placed in bromelia flowers and hanging moss rather than on altars." Stone deity image in the forested mountains near Chichicastenango. The deity is surrounded by a rough stone enclosure filled with offerings of flower petals, candles, and other offerings.

"Our coming has not been sweet. Alas! Would that we could behold the birth of the sun. What have we done? We were united in our mountains, but our natures have been changed," they said.

They spoke a great deal among themselves concerning their sorrow, their humility, and their fervent prayers.[595] Thus they spoke, for their hearts had yet to be comforted in the dawn.

But these, the gods, were comforted in the canyons and the forests. They were placed in bromelia flowers and hanging moss[596] rather than on altars.[597] Tohil, Auilix, and Hacavitz spoke from the first. Great was their day, their breath, and their spirit, above all the gods of the nations. Manifold were their spirit essences, their pathways, and their victorious means of chilling and frightening the very existence and hearts of the nations.

[595] Literally "weeping and crying out." This is a standard couplet used by contemporary Quichés to refer to ritual prayer.

[596] *Atz'iaq* (hanging moss/Spanish moss). An epiphytic plant (*Tillandsia usneoides*) that forms long grayish green filaments that hang from trees in tropical environments. It is in the same family of plants as the bromeliads.

[597] *Tz'alam* (Flat boards, flat stones). Most highland Maya altars constructed in the mountains consist of slabs of flat stones arranged into a table-like form, or alternatively, wooden tables.

Balam Quitze, Balam Acab, Mahucutah, and Iqui Balam gave comfort to the gods. They were not unhappy, nor did they bear ill will in their hearts for the gods that they had carried. These they had carried when they came from Tulan Zuyva, there in the East. But they were in the forest. There was the place of dawning on Pa Tohil, Pa Auilix, and Pa Hacavitz, as they are called today. It was there that our grandfathers and fathers were sown, when they dawned.

Now we shall tell of the dawning and the appearance of the sun, moon, and stars.

THE APPEARANCE OF
THE FIRST DAWN[598]

THIS therefore is the dawn,[599] the appearance of the sun, moon, and stars.

GREATLY they rejoiced, Balam Quitze, Balam Acab, Mahucutah, and Iqui Balam, when they saw the Morning Star. It came forth glittering before the face of the sun.

Then they unwrapped their copal incense, for the sun was to come forth. They unwrapped it with victory in their hearts. There were three types of incense that they burned as a means of expressing the gratitude in their hearts:

Mixtam[600] Incense was the name of the copal incense carried by Balam Quitze.

Caviztan Incense was the name of the copal incense carried by Balam Acab.

And Cabavil[601] Incense, as it is called, was carried by Mahucutah.

These three were the copal incenses that they burned, waving their censers toward the rising sun. They wept bitterly as they waved their censers, burning the sacred copal incense before they saw and witnessed the birth of the sun.

And when the sun came forth, all the small animals and great animals rejoiced. They came up from the rivers and from the canyons. They were there on the mountain peak. As one they turned their faces toward the coming forth of the sun. Then the pumas and the jaguars cried out. The first bird to sing was the parrot, as it is called. All the animals truly rejoiced. The eagles and the white vultures, all the small and great birds, spread their wings.

The bloodletters and sacrificers were kneeling. They greatly rejoiced along with the bloodletters and sacrificers of the Tamub and the Ilocab,

---

[598] lines 6044–6289

[599] Throughout Mesoamerica the first dawn of the sun is a symbol, not only for the birth of a new age, but for the divine sanction of power to a lineage or allied group (León-Portilla 1969, 30–31; Akkeren 2000, 164).

[600] Campbell (1981) derives *Mixtam* from the Nahua *mixtan* (Place of Clouds); Carmack and Mondloch (1983, 232 n. 187) cite Domingo de Vico, who wrote that *mictan ajaw* was a "demon," although this description was undoubtedly colored by Father Vico's Roman Catholic bias. Edmonson derived *mixtam* from *mictlan*, Nahua for the underworld.

[601] *K'ab'awil* (god, divine). Classes of copal incense called *K'ab'awil* and *Mixtam* are still sold in Chichicastenango (Schultze-Jena 1954, 91).

along with the Rabinals and the Cakchiquels, the Ah Tziquinahas and the Tuhalhas, the Uchabahas and the Quibahas, the Ah Batenas and the Yaqui Tepeus. However many nations there are today, innumerable people, they all had but one dawn.

Then also the face of the earth was dried by the sun. Like a person was the sun when he revealed himself. Hot was his face and thus he dried the surface of the earth. Before the sun had come forth the face of the earth was wet; it was soggy prior to the coming forth of the sun. But when the sun ascended upward, he was like a person. His heat could not be endured. This was but his self-revelation when he was born. What is left is but a mirror. What appears now is not the true sun, according to their account.

Then straightaway Tohil, Auilix, and Hacavitz became stone, along with the sacred images of the puma and the jaguar, the rattlesnake and the pit viper. Zaqui Coxol[602] took them and hid himself in the trees. When the sun,

Figure 63. "Like a person was the sun when he revealed himself." Sun deity, from a mural at Chichen Itza (drawing by Linda Schele).

[602] *Saqi K'oxol* (white/noisy/lively person). According to Basseta, this is the name given to any frightening spirit or phantasm, but specifically the *duende*, a dwarf-like denizen of the mountains and forests that the highland Maya believed to be the guardian of animals and messenger of the earth deity. Coto identifies him as a phantasm associated with mountains: "The *duende* who walks in the mountains they call: *ru vinakil che* [the person/personification/ manifestation of tree], or çaki qoxol" (Coto 1983, 355–356). In the *Annals of the Cakchiquels*, he appears as a spirit within the Volcano of Fuego:

> Afterwards they left there, they left Chiyol and Chiabak, and twice they traveled their road, passing between the volcanoes which stand abreast, those of *Fuego* [Fire] and *Hunahpu*. There they met face to face the spirit of the Volcano of Fire, he who is called *Zaquicoxol*. "Verily, the Zaquicoxol has killed many, and it is surely terrifying to see this thief," they said. There, in the center of the Volcano of Fuego was the guardian of the road by which they arrived and which had been made by Zaquicoxol (Recinos and Goetz 1953b, 61).

moon, and stars appeared, they all turned to stone. Perhaps we would not be alive today because of the vicious[603] animals—the puma and the jaguar, the rattlesnake and the pit viper, as well as Zaqui Coxol. It would not be our day if the sun had not come forth and turned the first animals to stone.[604]

Great was the joy in the hearts of Balam Quitze, Balam Acab, Mahucutah, and Iqui Balam when it dawned. There were not many people then. There were only a few on top of the mountain of Hacavitz. There they dawned and there they burned incense, waving their censers toward the coming forth of the sun. This was their mountain, their plain. There came they who are named Balam Quitze, Balam Acab, Mahucutah, and Iqui Balam. There they multiplied on the top of the mountain that was to become their citadel. There it was that the sun, moon, and stars truly appeared. Everything on the face of the earth and beneath the sky had its dawn and became clear.

Thus began their song called Our Burial.[605] Their hearts and bowels wept as they sang. And this is what they said in their song:

"Alas we were lost! At Tulan we split ourselves apart. We left behind our older brothers and our younger brothers. Where did they see the sun? Where were they when it dawned?"

This they sang concerning the bloodletters and sacrificers of the

---

Stories about *Saqi K'oxol* are common in highland Guatemala today as well, where he is described as a mountain spirit. At times he can be merely mischievous, playing tricks on people for his own entertainment. He can also be quite dangerous or deadly if proper respect is not shown to the wild things of the mountains or to the earth god himself (Tax 1947; Bode 1961, 213; Cook 2000, 201). In the popular dance drama, "The Dance of the Conquest," performed by the Maya throughout the highlands, one of the main characters is K'oxol, who successfully predicts the Spanish conquest through a divinatory ceremony. Following the Conquest, he refuses baptism and escapes into the forest where he gives birth miraculously to the son (portrayed as a small doll dressed in red) of Tecum, the great Quiché warrior who died fighting the Spaniards (Bode 1961; *Baile de la Conquista* 1991; B. Tedlock 1982, 149–150). In Momostenango, the *K'oxol* is the patron of *aj q'ij* priests, the source of the divination power that awakens their blood (B. Tedlock 1982, 147–148; B. Tedlock 1986, 135; Cook 2000, 201). As such he represents the ancient power of traditional Maya worship, a survival of the world prior to the Spanish conquest. It is interesting that even for the Precolumbian Quichés, *Saqi K'oxol* was a survivor from a previous age.

[603] Literally "biting."

[604] Barbara Tedlock notes that this tradition is still remembered in the community of Momostenango: "One diviner I know possesses the stone shoe of the original C'oxol or Tzitzimit; he found it in the mountains near Chinique and keeps it with his divining seeds and crystals. He explained that at the time the earth became hard, the Tzitzimit was hiding in a tree and dropped his shoe. Like the animals, it turned to stone. Momostecan diviners visit Minas, a foothill of the Cuchumatanes, where they find small stone concretions that are the animals who were turned to stone by the sun dring the creation of the world. These concretions are placed in the family shrine called the *mebil*" (B. Tedlock 1982, 148).

[605] *Muq* is "to be buried, covered, or hidden by earth, fog, cloud, etc."

Yaqui people. Tohil is the god of the Yaqui people, who they call Yolcuat Quitzalcuat.[606]

"We were separated there at Tulan Zuyva. We left them to come here. But we were complete[607] before we came here."

This they said among themselves when they remembered their older brothers and their younger brothers, the Yaqui people. These dawned there in Mexico, as it is called today. Thus surely a portion of them remained there in the East, they whose names are Tepeu[608] and Oliman.[609]

"We left them behind," they said.

Thus they were greatly troubled in their hearts there on top of Hacavitz.

The Tamub and the Ilocab felt the same. They whose name was Amac Tan were merely in the forest when the bloodletters and sacrificers of the Tamub dawned with their god.

Tohil is the sole name for the god of the three groups of Quiché people. This is also the name for the god of the Rabinals. Only a little bit different is his name: One Toh being the name of the god of the Rabinals. They say it this way because of their desire to make it one with the language of the Quichés.

There the language of the Cakchiquels was changed, for when they came from Tulan Zuyva, the name of their god was Chimalcan.[610] This was the god received by the Bat House[611] people. Along with their god, this lineage also received their titles: Ahpo Zotzil[612] and Ahpo Xahil[613] they are called.

[606] Yolcuat (Nahua: *yol*—heart, *coat*—serpent) Quitzalcoat (Nahua: *quetzal*—quetzal bird, quetzal feathers, *coat*—serpent). Quetzalcoatl, generally translated as "Feathered Serpent," was a prominent deity in the pantheon of the Central Mexican Toltecs and Aztecs. Here the authors of the *Popol Vuh* suggest that this god of the Yaquis (Mexicans) was equivalent to their own patron deity, Tohil.

[607] Literally "its completetion/wholeness/perfection our faces."

[608] *Tepeu*. This people's name is derived from Nahua, meaning "sovereign, power."

[609] *Oliman* (Rubber People/Ballplayers). This is likely a reference to the Olmeca-Xicalanca from the area of the southern Gulf Coast (see footnote 503).

[610] The authors of the text apparently assert here that the god of the Cakchiquels is the same as theirs, but that he was called by a different name when their language changed. In the Cakchiquel language, *chamalqan* is a serpent of great size that moves calmly/quietly (Varea).

[611] *Tzotz'i Ja* (Bat House) is the principal lineage of the Cakchiquels.

[612] *Ajpo Sotz'il* (Bat Lords). *Ajpo* is a contracted form of *aj pop* (he/she of the mat), the highest office in highland Maya hierarchies, and may be loosely translated as "lord." See footnote 33 on the significance of the mat. This was one of the principal Cakchiquel ruling lineages at the time of the Spanish conquest. They resided at Iximché.

[613] *Ahpo Xahil* (Dance Lords). The Xahil were the other principal lineage of the Cakchiquels. Their main center of occupation was at Sololá above the northern shores of Lake Atitlán. The Annals of the Cakchiquels was compiled under the direction of the Xahil (Recinos and Goetz 1953, 11).

This god changed their speech when he was received there at Tulan. It was a stone that was the cause of the change in their speech when they came from Tulan in the darkness. Yet all the nations were sown as one when the names of the gods were given to each of the groups.

We shall now tell of their residence, their sojourn there on the top of the mountain. They were as one, the four of them—Balam Quitze, Balam Acab, Mahucutah, and Iqui Balam. Their hearts cried out to Tohil, Auilix, and Hacavitz, who were amidst the bromelia flowers and the hanging moss.

OFFERINGS ARE MADE TO THE GODS[614]

THESE, then, are the burnings and the offerings placed beneath Tohil when they went before the faces of Tohil and Auilix. They went there to see them and to worship them. They gave thanks before them for the dawn. They knelt humbly with heads bowed low[615] before the stones there in the forest.

It was only the revelation of the god's spirit essence that spoke when the bloodletters and sacrificers arrived before the face of Tohil. What they carried was not great, nor were their burnt offerings. It was only pine resin, the remnants of pitch, along with pericón[616] flowers that they burned before the face of their god.

Then spoke Tohil. It was only his spirit essence that gave knowledge to the bloodletters and sacrificers. Then the gods spoke:[617]

Figure 64. "Set the skins of the deer aside and watch over them." Deer skins used in rituals conserved in a ceremonial house, Santiago Atitlán.

[614] lines 6290–6503

[615] *Wonowoj* is to humble oneself, bowing over so severely that the chin touches the knees (Basseta).

[616] *Iya'* (Spanish *pericón*) is a marigold-like plant with small yellow flowers (*Tagetes lucida*).

[617] From the end of this quotation, it is clear that all three deities—Tohil, Auilix, and Hacavitz—are speaking, not just Tohil.

"It is here that our mountain and our plain shall be. We have come to be yours. Great is our day. Great as well is our birth, because of all your people and all the nations. We shall surely be your companions then, your citadel. We shall give to you your knowledge. Do not reveal us before the nations when they come up to us. For truly they shall become many. Thus do not let them set traps for us. But give to us the children of the grasses and the fallen[618] grain. Bring to us a little of the blood of the female deer and

Figure 65. "When you are asked, 'Where is Tohil?' It will be this deerskin bundle that you shall show them." Deity holding torches hovers over a sacrificed deer, from the Dresden Codex, p. 45c (Villacorta and Villacorta, 1930).

the female bird. Take pity on us. Set the skins of the deer aside and watch over them. These shall be a means of concealing identity.[619] The deer will become the means by which you shall deceive them. These will surely be our substitutes before the faces of the nations. When you are asked, 'Where

---

[618] Grain that has "fallen from age or overripeness" (Basseta).

[619] Literally "buried/hidden/clouded face."

[620] Sacred bundles of this type were well known by the indigenous people of Mesoamerica prior to the Spanish conquest. Fr. Juan de Torquemada cited the existence of a sacred bundle in central Mexico called the *Haquimilolli* which consisted of clothing believed to have been worn by the god Xolotl when he offered himself as an auto-sacrifice to enable the sun to rise for the first time. The mantles worn by the god were wrapped in a bundle along with

is Tohil?' It will be this deerskin bundle[620] that you shall show them. But do not reveal yourselves. Do this now and your existence shall become great. You shall conquer all the nations. They must bring to you their blood. Their flowing blood shall be brought before our faces. Let them come to us and embrace us. They are ours now," said Tohil, Auilix, and Hacavitz.

The gods would appear as boys when they were seen, when offerings were burned before their faces. Thus they began to seek out the offspring of birds and deer which were taken and offered by the bloodletters and the sacrificers. They would find the birds and the young deer, and go to place their blood in the mouths of the stones. Tohil and Auilix drank this therefore. It was the bloody drink of the gods. Straightaway, then, the stones spoke when the bloodletters and sacrificers came to give their burnt offerings.

They did the same before the deerskin bundles. They would burn pine resin, pericón flowers, and stevia[621] flowers. There was a deer skin bundle for each of them on the tops of the mountains.

The dwellings and the homes of our ancestors were not in the sun. They walked only in the mountains. And this is what they would eat: Only hornet[622] larvae, only wasp larvae, only bee larvae[623] would they seek. At first

certain green stones representing the god's heart, as well as the skins of a serpent and a jaguar (Torquemada 1969, 6.xlii, 78). In Santiago Atitlán, deerskins are kept in a confraternity house dedicated to traditional Maya ceremonies. These skins, with the head and antlers still attached, are periodically worn in a dance honoring a powerful deity they call Martín, associated with animals, maize, and rebirth. Prior to the dance, a special priest dedicated to the veneration of Martín called the *nab'eysil* blesses the deerskins, addressing them as "King Martín, Lord of the Three Levels, Lord of Rain, Lord of Maize, and Lord of all the Mountains" (Christenson 2001, 160). Martín is referred to as "King Martín" because he is more ancient than any other god, and father to them all (Mendelson 1957, 462; 1958b, 5). The deer is his specific emblem, and a bundle kept in the confraternity house contains very old garments painted with designs associated with tufts of animal hair. The cult of Martín is likely associated with the ancient god Tohil and his deerskin bundle (Mendelson 1958a, 121, 124). The Great Dance of Tohil took place in the month of *Tz'ikin Q'ij*, just prior to the principal maize harvest in November, coinciding with the Dance of Martín on November 11 (Christenson 2001, 169–176). The Maya deity Martín is derived from St. Martin of Tours (November 11 is his day on the liturgical calendar), who is often depicted in Roman Catholic paintings and sculpture seated on a horse. The early Maya consistently confused horses with deer (Hill 1992, 151). Even today both animals bear the same name in most Maya languages.

[621] *Jolom Okox* (Head Mushroom). This is not a mushroom, but an herb called stevia (Spanish *pericón blanco*), whose small white flowers resemble the head of a mushroom. Duncan Earle noted that the *pericón* and stevia are still given as minor offerings in rituals by the Quichés (Earle 1983, 294, 297; D. Tedlock 1996, 308 n. 164).

[622] *Wonon*. For modern Quichés this is the honeybee of the stinging type introduced from Europe. Many Quiché communities, particularly in the region around Momostenango, cultivate these bees for their honey. The Precolumbian Maya kept bees and harvested their honey, but these were of a stingless variety. As will become apparent later in the text, these insects could sting. Coto lists *wonon* as a hornet, or the stinger of a wasp or hornet.

they did not have good food or water. The pathway leading to their homes was not clear. Nor was it clear where their wives dwelt.

The other nations were crowded together. All of them would unite, joining together with one another. They would raise a din[624] there on the roads. Their paths were clear.

But it was not clear where Balam Quitze, Balam Acab, Mahucutah, and Iqui Balam were. When they would see the nations passing by on the roads, they would cry out on the peaks of mountains. They would cry out with the call of the coyote and the call of the fox. They would make the call of the puma and the jaguar. And when the nations heard this there was great discussion about it:

"This is merely the cry of the coyote and of the fox," said the nations. "It is merely the puma and the jaguar," the nations said.

The nations did not realize that these were people.[625] It was merely a way of deceiving the nations that this was done. It was not the desire of their hearts to truly frighten them. Thus they would make the call of a puma or jaguar, and then when they would see one or two people out walking, it would be their desire to destroy them.

Each day they arrived at their homes with their wives bearing only hornet larvae, wasp larvae, and bee larvae. And each day also they went before Tohil, Auilix, and Hacavitz, saying in their hearts:

"We give merely the blood of deer and birds to Tohil, Auilix, and Hacavitz. We merely prick our ears and our elbows. We plead for our strength and our endurance to Tohil, Auilix, and Hacavitz. Who shall be responsible for the death of the nations? Shall we kill them only one at a time?" This they said to each other when they went before Tohil, Auilix, and Hacavitz.

Then they pierced their ears and their elbows before the faces of their gods. They scooped up their blood and rubbed it inside the mouths of the stones. Yet they had not truly become stones. Each of them appeared as young boys when they came. They rejoiced for the blood of the bloodletters and sacrificers.

Then came the sign of their deeds:

---

[623] *Aqal*. These are stingless, honey-producing bees that the Maya domesticated. Today the Quichés cultivate the stinging European type of bee for their honey, and *aqal* is now used to refer to a variety of wasps that live in nests. Nevertheless, many highland Maya languages retain memory of the honey produced by the older varieties of bee when referring to sticky, sweet substances such as honey or molasses, as *aqat* or *aqal*.

[624] *B'olow* is the sound of a crowd all speaking at once (Coto).

[625] Literally "not like people in their hearts."

"Conquer many lands. This is your authority.[626] It came from Tulan when you brought us here," they were told.

Then was given the breast[627] at the place called Pa Zilizib.[628] And behind[629] it came blood, a rain of their blood as an offering for Tohil, along with Auilix and Hacavitz.

[626] Literally "self-liberation," meaning the "authority, sanction, or right to act."

[627] *Tz'um* (woman's breast, skin). This continues the play on words whereby the nations were tricked into offering to *tu'nik* (give the breast, suckle, nurture), a metaphor for nurturing or giving sustenance. In reality, however, they were being tricked into offering their own breasts in the form of heart extraction sacrifice.

[628] *Pa Silisib'* (Place of Staggering/Shaking).

[629] This is an oddly-phrased sentence in the original because the authors are continuing with the play on words between breast as "suckling or nurturing," and the physical breast that is being offered in sacrifice. The authors are saying that "behind" the breast is the source of the blood, and the rain of blood. In other words, that is where the heart is located that will be sacrificially extracted.

THE SACRIFICIAL KILLINGS BEGIN[630]

THIS is the beginning of the abduction of people from the nations by Balam Quitze, Balam Acab, Mahucutah, and Iqui Balam.

THEN also was the killing of the nations. They were taken in this way:

Only one would go out walking, or two would go out walking. It was not clear how they were taken. Then they would be taken to be sacrificed before the faces of Tohil and Auilix. Afterward their blood and skulls[631] would be placed on the road. Thus the nations would say, "a jaguar ate them." This they would say because only the tracks of a jaguar were left behind. They would not reveal themselves. Many were abducted from the nations until, after a long time, the nations came to their senses:[632]

"Perhaps Tohil and Auilix have come after us. We shall merely seek out the bloodletters and the sacrificers. Let us follow their footprints[633] when they go to their homes," the nations all said when they planned[634] among themselves.

Thus they began to follow the footprints of the bloodletters and the sacrificers. But they were not clear. They were only deer tracks and jaguar tracks that they would see. Their footprints were not clear. Nowhere was it clear where the tracks began. Their footprints were just like the pawprints of animals.[635] It was merely confusion for them.

Neither was the pathway clear. None of the nations could see, because there would form clouds, there would form dark rain, there would form mud, and there would form drizzling rain. Thus they would weary their hearts searching. They would mourn, for great was the essence of Tohil, Auilix, and Hacavitz.

Thus this was done for a long time atop the mountain on the borders of the nations. They would kill them when the abductions began. These were murderous assaults when they would seize the people of the nations on

---

[630] lines 6504–6597

[631] *Jolom* is the word for both "head" and "skull." It is impossible to know which is meant here.

[632] Literally "felt themselves."

[633] *Raqan* (their feet/legs). The Quiché language does not distinguish between feet and legs; nor does it distinguish between feet and the tracks they make.

[634] Literally "gathered their thoughts."

[635] *Pich* are the feet (and the tracks they make) of animals, as well as infant humans who crawl on all fours.

the roads. They would then sacrifice them before the faces of Tohil, Auilix, and Hacavitz.

Thus the boys were preserved there on the top of the mountain. Tohil, Auilix, and Hacavitz had the appearance of three boys when they went out walking. These were the spirit essences of the stones.

There was a river where they would bathe along the banks as a way of revealing themselves. And this was what gave it its name: "Bath of Tohil" became the name of the river. Many times the nations would see them, but then suddenly they would vanish. When the people of the nations saw this, they would report where Balam Quitze, Balam Acab, Mahucutah, and Iqui Balam could be found. Thus the nations plotted how to kill them.

THE NATIONS PLOT
TO SEDUCE THE GODS[636]

ABOVE all else, the nations desired to plan for the defeat of Tohil, Auilix, and Hacavitz. All the bloodletters and sacrificers spoke before the nations. They assembled themselves together, summoning all of them. Not one group, nor two groups, were left behind. All of them gathered together, summoning one another. Then they gathered their thoughts. They spoke, asking one another:

"What would ensure the defeat of the Cavec Quiché people? For the children of our women, and the sons of our men are finished. It is not clear how they caused the loss of these people. But if these abductions continue we shall be finished. If Tohil, Auilix, and Hacavitz are to become great and glorious, then Tohil shall come to be our god. But we shall be preeminent. They will not succeed in defeating us. Are our people not many? And these, the Cavec, are there not but few of them?" This they asked when they all came together.

Then some of them spoke before the nations:

"Who, perhaps, are they that bathe by the banks of the river each day? If they are Tohil, Auilix, and Hacavitz, then we shall surely defeat them first. Thus shall begin the defeat of the bloodletters and the sacrificers," they said.

Then they inquired:

"How then will we defeat them?" they asked.

"This shall be our means of defeating them: Because the boys appear at the river, let two maidens go there that are truly chosen. They should be the fairest[637] of maidens. Thus may they be objects of desire for them," they said.

"Very well then. We shall search for two of the best maidens," they said.

And so they sought among their daughters for the truly fairest of maidens. Then they instructed these maidens:

"Go, our daughters, to wash clothes[638] at the river. If, then, you see the

---

[636] lines 6598–6699

[637] *Saqloq'oj.* The root of this word is *saq* (white, clear, bright, clean, pure, light), something like the English word "fair," which does not necessarily refer to skin complexion.

[638] *Kixb'ek ix qa mi'al ojich'aja' ri k'ul* (go our daughters to wash the clothes). In a literal sense, the daughters are told to physically wash clothes at the river. In Quiché, however, *ch'aj* (wash) is also used to describe menstruation (Ajpacaja et al. 1996, 61) and childbirth (Coto) indicating that these women are of child-bearing age and thus available for marriage.

three boys, undress yourselves before their faces. And if their hearts should desire you, then you shall offer yourselves[639] to them. When they shall say to you, 'we shall come unto you,' then you shall say, 'yes,' when you are petitioned. When they ask, 'Where do you come from? Whose daughters are you?' then you shall reply: 'We are the daughters of lords.' Then they will give something to you if they should desire you. And if so, then you shall surely give yourselves to them. If you do not give yourselves to them, then we will kill you. But our hearts will be content when you bring their sign here. This therefore will be a sign to our hearts that they have come unto you." Thus said the lords when they instructed the maidens.

These, then, were the names of the two: Lady Lust[640] and Lady Weeping.[641] There were two of them.[642] Lady Lust and Lady Weeping were their names. These were sent there to the river, to the Bath of Tohil, Auilix, and Hacavitz. This was the plan of all of these nations.

[639] *Chok* is "to invite, offer, entice."

[640] *Xtaj.* X- is the prefix indicating "female," or a diminutive such as "little." *Taj* is "sexual desire, lust, or promiscuity."

[641] *Xpuch'.* In Quiché, *Puch'* is "weeping from illness or pain rather than sadness." Tedlock suggests that this maiden is a Precolumbian precursor of the *Llorona* (Spanish: Weeper/ Wailer), tales of which are told throughout Mesoamerica (D. Tedlock 1996, 310–311). In most versions of this tradition, the *Llorona* is the spirit of a wronged woman who seeks vengeance by searching in the night for children to murder or steal away. Akkeren suggests, however that the name is more likely derived from Kekchi or Poqom, languages spoken by the ancient *Amaq'* (Nations) lords. In these languages, *puch* is "washing clothes," with the connotation of "menstruating," meaning the girl is marriageable (Akkeren 2000, 103–105). This reading is fully consistent with the episode described here in which the maidens go to the River of Tohil to wash clothes.

[642] The *Título Totonicapán* also includes this episode in its account of Quiché history, however, it lists three maidens corresponding to the three deities who were to be enticed (Chonay and Goetz 1953, 174–175; Carmack and Mondloch 1983, 87–95, 179–181). The name of the third maiden in that version is *K'ib'atz'un Ja.* The most likely derivation of this name is from the verb *b'atz'*, which is to "tie up, wind, make thread." It is also a euphemism, however, for a woman prostituting herself (Coto). Akkeren prefers to read this as a lineage name, *B'atz'* being the ruling lineage at Chichen, the principal center of the Alta Verapaz region during this period which was one of the centers of power for the *Amaq'* (Nations) lords (Akkeren 2000, 101–105).

THE SEDUCTION OF LADY LUST
AND LADY WAILING [643]

THEN they went. They were adorned in finery, and truly they appeared beautiful when they went there to the place where Tohil bathes. They carried their wash[644] on their heads as they went. Thus the lords rejoiced because of their two daughters that they had sent there.

Figure 66. "And when they arrived at the river, they began to wash." Quiché women washing clothes near Momostenango.

And when they arrived at the river, they began to wash. Each of them undressed herself and got down on her hands and knees before the stones.

Then Tohil, Auilix, and Hacavitz came together. They arrived there on the bank of the river. But they paid little attention[645] to the two maidens that were washing. Straightaway therefore the maidens were ashamed when Tohil arrived. Tohil did not desire the two maidens.[646] Then they inquired:

---

[643] lines 6700–6775

[644] Ch'ajo'n may have a double meaning here. In its literal sense, it means "wash, laundry." In a metaphoric sense it also refers to a young woman of child-bearing, and thus marriageable, age (Akkeren 2000, 134), as well as menstruation (Coto).

[645] Literally "only a little they passed by their faces."

[646] "Not therefore went their desire to the two maidens." The "they" of this passage makes

"Where do you come from?" they asked the two maidens. "What do you want by coming here to the bank of our river?" they were asked.

"We were sent here by the lords, therefore we came. 'Go to see the faces of Tohil and speak with them,' the lords said to us. 'Thus may you receive a sign that you truly saw their faces,' we were told."

This is what the two maidens said when they explained their mission. This, then, had been the desire of the nations—that the maidens be violated[647] by the spirit essence of Tohil. Thus said Tohil, Auilix, and Hacavitz when they spoke to Lady Lust and Lady Weeping (the names of the two maidens):

"It is good that you should take the sign of our word with you. You shall wait for it and give it to the lords," they were told.

Thus they counseled with the bloodletters and sacrificers. They spoke with Balam Quitze, Balam Acab, Mahucutah, and Iqui Balam:

"Paint[648] three robes,[649] writing upon them your essence.[650] They shall be

it clear that all three of the gods spurned the advances of the maidens, and not just Tohil. This is one of several instances in the text where the authors refer to Tohil, Auilix, and Hacavitz collectively as Tohil. Note that two paragraphs later the maidens state that their fathers told them to go to see "the faces" of Tohil. This may be of theological significance, in that the three gods are to be considered as one god. Or it may simply be a shorthand way of referring to all three. The latter interpretation is supported by the tendency of the authors in some cases to name only Balam Quitze (or Balam Quitze and Balam Acab) when referring to all four progenitors—Balam Quitze, Balam Acab, Mahucutah, and Iqui Balam (see pp. 213–214, 216, 251; lines 5461–5462, 5492–5493, 5624–5625, 7147–7148).

[647] *Jox* (to have sex, violate, disgrace). In both colonial dictionaries and contemporary Quiché usage, illicit sex is subject to strict social constraints. The most common way today of referring to sex is simply *-b'an mak* (to do sin), and the meaning is clear without further explanation. It is not known if this was also a characteristic of Precolumbian society, although the context of this episode would indicate that the daughters were being forced to do something beyond the bounds of propriety. In addition, the nations hoped that they could defeat the gods by enticing them into an act that would destroy their power in some way. In contemporary Aztec society, violations of sexual morality bore heavy penalties including death. The severity of such violations may be seen in this series of admonitions given to a young Aztec girl by her father:

> Look now at something else which I want to impress on you, communicate to you, my human creation, my little daughter. Do not permit the lords from whom you are born to be mocked. Do not throw dust or rubbish on them; do not cast any uncleanness on their history, on their black and red ink [writings], on their fame. Do not insult them in any way, such as wanting things of this earth, such as seeking to enjoy them out of season, those which are called sexual things. And if you do not withdraw from them, can you ever come near the gods? Better that you should perish immediately (León-Portilla 1969, 139).

[648] *Tz'ib'aj*. In ancient Quiché, this refers to both writing and painting. This is logical since both were generally done with a paintbrush. In addition, however, the act of writing a word (*tz'ib'*) also metaphorically brings the thing referred to into material existence. Thus a written word, in this case a painted hieroglyph, is not conceptually different from a visual

taken to the nations by means of the two maidens who are washing. Give these to them," Balam Quitze, Balam Acab, and Mahucutah were told.

image of the thing, or even the thing itself. This will become apparent when the painted images on the robes come to life and defeat the lords of the enemy nations. This is much the same as the actions of the gods who brought the earth into existence simply by expressing the word "earth" (p. 71; lines 219–228).

⁶⁴⁹ *K'ul* (covering). It is difficult to know precisely what type of clothing this might have been in Precolumbian times. Basseta refers to it as a *manta*, a shawl or a blanket worn wrapped around the body like a cloak or robe.

⁶⁵⁰ *K'oje'ik* (existence, nature, essence, being).

THE NATIONS ARE DEFEATED
BY THE PAINTED ROBES[651]

THUS the three[652] of them painted. First, Balam Quitze painted the image of what came to be a jaguar. He painted it on the face of the robe.

Next Balam Acab painted the image of an eagle.

Then Mahucutah painted hornets all over it. Everywhere he painted the images of wasps on the face of the robe.

Thus the three of them finished their paintings. Three forms they painted on the robes and gave them to Lady Lust and Lady Weeping, as they are called.

Then said Balam Quitze, Balam Acab, and Mahucutah:

"This is the sign of your word. You shall go before the faces of the lords and say: 'Truly Tohil spoke to us,' you shall say. 'This, then, is the sign we have brought,' you shall say to them. Then they will wear the robes that you will give to them." In this way were the maidens instructed.

So then they returned, carrying the painted robes. And when they arrived, straightaway the lords rejoiced when they saw their faces and that which was draped across their arms. Thus the maidens were entreated:

"Did you not see the face of Tohil?" they were asked.

"We did see him," replied Lady Lust and Lady Weeping.

"Very well then. Where is the sign that you have brought? Is it not true?" the lords asked.

For the lords felt it was the sign of their disgrace. Thus the maidens untied the painted robes. Everywhere there were jaguars, everywhere eagles, and everywhere hornets and wasps. The paintings inside the robes shone brightly. Thus they desired the faces of the robes and put them on about them.

The image of the jaguar did nothing at first around the lord. Then another lord put on the second painted robe with the image of the eagle. The lord felt good inside it. He turned about before them. He opened up his robe[653] before them all. Then another lord put on the third painted robe

---

[651] lines 6776–6919

[652] Only Balam Quitze, Balam Acab, and Mahucutah are involved in this episode. Iqui Balam does not participate, likely because he did not have a patron deity or a posterity that survived.

[653] Literally "he disrobes his covering before their faces all of them." This may mean that he took off his own clothes publicly to put on the new robe. More likely he wrapped the new

with the hornets and wasps inside. And when he put it around him he was stung by the hornets and wasps. He could not bear it; he could not endure the stinging insects. Thus he cried out because of the painted images of the insects within the robe. This was the painting of Mahucutah, the third of the paintings. And thus they were defeated.

Then the lords rebuked the maidens, they who were named Lady Lust and Lady Weeping:

"What are these robes that you have brought here? Where did you go to get them? You are deceivers." Thus the maidens were asked when they were rebuked.

Thus all of the nations were defeated by Tohil. They had desired that Tohil would get gratification from Lady Lust and Lady Weeping. But these, then, became seductresses.[654] They came to be temptations to the heart of the nations. Thus the nations did not achieve the defeat of the enchanted people—Balam Quitze, Balam Acab, and Mahucutah.

Then all the nations considered again:

"How can we do it? Truly great their natures have come to be," they said.

Then they gathered their thoughts:

"We shall merely pursue them and kill them. We shall arm[655] ourselves with arrows and with shields. Are we not many? There shall not be even one or two left of them," they said when they gathered their thoughts.

Thus all the nations armed themselves. They were crowded with killers when all the nations gathered. They were killers.

Now Balam Quitze, Balam Acab, Mahucutah, and Iqui Balam were on the top of the mountain Hacavitz. This was the name of the mountain where they were. Thus their sons were established on the top of the moun-

robe around him with the painted images inside, which he then opened up to display to the other lords present. If the third lord did the same, then the insects that came to life would be in close contact with his skin. Often times the Maya kept powerful tokens or images hidden in bundles or under clothing. The highland Maya today believe that inappropriate display of such objects is extremely dangerous. Thus in the town of Santiago Atitlán, a bundle of very old garments painted with designs reminiscent of animal pelts, which they call Martín, is kept hidden in a carved wooden chest except at rare times when it is taken out for display. The bundle itself is unwrapped only once a year, on November 11, by a special priest called the nab'eysil. The nab'eysil opens the bundle at midnight with all the electric lights turned off, and with the doors and windows closed and locked. He then wears the garments as he dances in a circular pattern around the inside of the darkened room by candlelight. He does this with his arms slightly apart to display the garment. Participants believe that if the bundle were opened with the windows or doors opened, wind would rush out and devastate the world (Mendelson 1965, 57; Christenson 2001, 162).

[654] *Joxol ch'ek* (scratchers knee). This is a play on words, a particularly prevalent Maya prac-

tain. They were not many then. They were certainly not as numerous at first as the people from the nations. They occupied only a small part of the mountain top.

Thus the nations plotted to kill them. They all gathered together. They arrived, all of them having been summoned.

tice when referring to sexual things as a way of speaking about it indirectly. *Jox* is "to have sex," and also "to hoe or to scratch." A woman "knee scratcher" is a fornicator, prostitute, or one who wishes to seduce someone to have sex. The more common expression today is "leg burner" which also means seductress.

    [655] Literally "adorn."

THE NATIONS ARE HUMILIATED[656]

THUS all the nations gathered together. They were all armed with arrows and shields. Their precious metal adornments were innumerable. All of the lords and warriors were beautiful in their appearance. But in fact they were mere boasters,[657] all of them. Truly they would all come to be enslaved.[658]

Figure 67. "They were all armed with arrows and shields. Their precious metal adornments were innumerable. All of the lords and warriors were beautiful in their appearance." Warriors preparing for battle, from a wall panel, Chichen Itza (drawing by Linda Schele).

"This Tohil, he is a god. We also shall worship him. But we shall capture[659] him," they said among themselves.

But Tohil learned of it, and so too did Balam Quitze, Balam Acab, and Mahucutah. They heard what was being planned. They did not sleep, nor did they rest.

Thus all the warriors had adorned themselves. They rose up in the night with confidence in their hearts.[660] But although they went out, they did not reach their destination. All the warriors merely slept in the road. Then was their defeat by Balam Quitze, Balam Acab, and Mahucutah. They merely slept in the road, completely senseless. All of them were exhausted with

[656] lines 6920–7075

[657] *B'anoj tzij* (making words). These are liars, boasters, people that are "just talk, not doers."

[658] *Alab'il.* This is literally "stepsons, godsons." It is also used to refer to war captives and slaves. In ancient Aztec warfare, once a captive had been taken in war, the victor seized his opponent by the hair and addressed him as "my beloved son," indicating that the captive was subject to him with the loyalty due a father.

[659] *Kanab'ij* is to capture, and also to make use of something.

[660] *Xkokib'ej chi ki k'ux* (they believed in their hearts).

sleep. Then they began to have their eyebrows plucked,[661] along with their whiskers.[662] The precious metal was untied from their clothing, as well as from their headdresses and their necklaces. The precious metal was taken from the necks of their staffs. This was a punishment upon their faces, and a plucking as well. This was done as a sign of the greatness of the Quiché people.

And when they arose, straightaway they reached for their headdresses and the necks of their staffs. But now there was no precious metal on the necks of their staffs, nor on their headdresses.

"Who has taken us?[663] By whom were we plucked? Where did they who stole our precious metal come from?" all the warriors asked. "Perhaps it was those deceivers[664] that abduct people. But they will not succeed in frightening us. Surely we shall invade their citadel. We shall see again the face of our precious metal and once more make it ours," said all the nations.

But this was merely boasting. Thus the hearts of the bloodletters and sacrificers were comforted on the top of the mountain. Balam Quitze, Balam Acab, Mahucutah, and Iqui Balam merely exercised their wisdom.

Then Balam Quitze, Balam Acab, Mahucutah, and Iqui Balam considered. They made a palisade around the edge of their citadel. They placed wooden planks and pointed stakes about their citadel. Then they made effigies that looked just like people. They arranged these on top of the palisade, arming them with shields and with arrows. They placed headdresses with precious metal on their heads. They adorned these effigies of mere carved wood with the precious metal of the nations that they had taken on the road. With these they encircled the citadel.

Then also they entreated Tohil with their thoughts:

"What if we should die? What if we are defeated?" they asked.

Thus their hearts wept before the face of Tohil.

"Do not mourn. I am. You shall use these against them. Do not fear." Thus he spoke to Balam Quitze, Balam Acab, Mahucutah, and Iqui Balam. And they were given the hornets and wasps. So they went out to gather

---

[661] *U mich'ik ki muquwach rumal* (its plucking their eyebrows by them). This phrase has a double meaning. On one level, "plucking" is a metaphor for tricking or deceiving someone. In a material sense, to pluck out facial hair is to show shame, contempt, disdain, or scorn.

[662] *Kismachi'* (their whiskers). The Quiché language has only one word for facial hair, and thus does not distinguish between beards and moustaches.

[663] This is a common Quiché expression, similar to the English "we've been taken" or "we've been had." This parallels the following phrase, "by whom were we plucked?" which is an expression for "who deceived us?"

[664] *K'axtok'* (demons, deceivers).

them, and they returned bearing them. And these they placed inside four great gourds, which they positioned in four places around the edge of the citadel. The hornets and wasps were closed up within the great gourds. They used these as weapons against the nations.

The citadel was being spied upon, watched in ambush, scrutinized as a target by the messengers of the nations.

"There are not so many," they said.

And then they saw the effigies of carved wood which were motionless, carrying their arrows and their shields. They appeared to be true people. Like killers they appeared to be when the nations saw them. All the nations rejoiced then, for they did not see many of them. But there were crowds of people from the nations. Their people had countless warriors, killers, and murderers that had come against Balam Quitze, Balam Acab, and Mahucutah, who were on top of the mountain named Hacavitz.

We shall now speak of this invasion.

Figure 68. "And they were given the hornets and wasps." A wasp, from the Madrid Codex, p. 105b (Villacorta and Villacorta, 1930).

THE NATIONS ARE DEFEATED[665]

THERE they were, Balam Quitze, Balam Acab, Mahucutah, and Iqui Balam, united on top of the mountain with their wives and their children.

Then came the warriors and the killers. There were not merely sixteen thousand or twenty-four thousand[666] from the nations that encircled the citadel. They yelled, armed with their arrows and shields. They would cry out, clamoring, hustling about, shouting their mockery, and whistling.

But the bloodletters and sacrificers went inside beneath their citadel, fearing nothing. They merely looked to the palisade at the edge of their citadel as they gathered together with their wives and their children. Thus they were reassured,[667] and the words of the nations were sweet to them.

Then the warriors ascended a little way up the face of the mountain. But it was only a little way, for they did not reach the entrance to the citadel. And then they opened the four gourds that were in the citadel, and out flew the hornets and the wasps. They were like clouds of smoke when they came out of each of the gourds. The warriors were thus finished off because of the insects. They landed on their eyes and on their noses; on their mouths, on their legs, and on their arms. Wherever they were, the hornets and wasps went to catch them. Wherever they were, these went to swarm around them. Everwhere there were hornets and wasps. They would swarm around them stinging their eyes. There were great numbers of insects around each of the people.

Thus they became disoriented[668] because of the hornets and the wasps. Neither could they now grasp their arrows or their shields. They hunched over with their faces to their knees on the surface of the ground. They were scattered. They fell senseless before the face of the mountain. Then they were struck with arrows and chopped with axes, although they were only pieces of dry wood that Balam Quitze and Balam Acab used on them.[669] Their wives also came upon them as killers.

[665] lines 7076–7206

[666] *Ka chuy, ox chuy* (two eight thousands, three eight thousands).

[667] *Ku'l ki k'ux* (seated their hearts). This is "to be reassured, confident, or have faith in something."

[668] *Q'ab'arik*. In current Quiché usage this is "to be drunk, enebriated." According to Basseta, however, it may also mean "to be disoriented, or to faint."

[669] The authors wish to emphasize that the victory was purely a matter of divine intervention, without need for conventional arms. Thus the pieces of wood acted as if they were arrows or axes.

Thus only a portion of them were able to return. Only a few people from the nations were able to escape. At first they tried to flee, but when they were caught they were finished off. They were killed. And it was not just a few of the people who died. And of those that did not die, the insects came upon them and tormented their hearts. They were no longer able to wage war. They did not take up their arrows or their shields again. Thus all the nations were humiliated and begged humbly before the faces of Balam Quitze, Balam Acab, and Mahucutah:

"Pity us. Do not kill us," they said.

"Very well then. Certainly you shall become obedient.[670] You shall be servants[671] as long as there is sun and light," they were told.

Thus was the defeat of all the nations because of our first mothers and our first fathers. It was done on the top of the mountain Hacavitz, as it is called today. This was the beginning. There they multiplied and became many. They had daughters and they had sons on top of Hacavitz. They rejoiced then, for they had defeated all the nations there on top of the mountain. Thus they had done this. They had surely defeated the nations, indeed all the nations.

Thus their hearts were reassured. They spoke to their sons as the time approached when they would die. For they truly desired to die.

Now we shall tell of this also, of the deaths of they who are called Balam Quitze, Balam Acab, Mahucutah, and Iqui Balam.

---

[670] *Kame'l* (humble, obedient). This is a play on words since *kamel* is "one who dies." Thus the captives are saying that rather than be *dead*, they are to be humble and obedient.

[671] *Aj patan* (he/she of the pack strap) is a servant, or more specifically a bearer. *Patan* is both the pack strap worn by men around the forehead to carry loads, as well as metaphorically any task or errand. In a larger sense, the term may be used to describe someone who is subsidiary such as a vassal or tribute payer.

THE DEATHS OF
THE FOUR PROGENITORS [672]

THEY sensed their impending death and disappearance.[673] Thus they gave instructions to their sons. They were not ill, nor did they groan from sickness, nor did they breathe with difficulty. Yet they left behind their word with their sons. These, then, are the names of the sons:

Balam Quitze had two sons. Co Caib[674] was the name of the firstborn, and Co Cavib[675] was the name of the secondborn. These were the sons of Balam Quitze, the grandfather and father of the Cavecs.

Balam Acab of the Nihaibs also had two sons. Co Acul was the name of his first son, and Co Acutec was the name of his second son.

Mahucutah had only one son, whose name was Co Ahau.[676]

These three had sons, but Iqui Balam had no sons.

These, then, were the names of their sons, who were true bloodletters and sacrificers.

The four of them were united as they sang of the pain in their hearts. Their hearts wept within their song. Our Burial was the name of the song that they sang. And these were the instructions that they gave to their sons:

"You, our sons, we shall go but we shall also return again. Words of light[677] and counsels of light[678] we give to you."

And then they spoke to their wives:

"You have come here from a far away mountain, you, our wives," they said.

---

[672] lines 7207–7360

[673] Literally "loss."

[674] *K'o Kaib'* (Lord Two). *K'o* is an irregular verb construction meaning "there is, or he/she/ it possesses." However when used as a title it suggests "nobility, lordship, or authority." Thus Coto lists *Qo ch'u vi* (there is on his head, or above) as "to be charged, or have jurisdiction/ authority"; *Qo r'a* (there is breath) as "to have authority"; or *Qo u ɛij* (there is his day) as "to have authority, great thing, famous or glorious." *Kaib'* is simply the number two. Thus this name would be something like "Lord or Sir Two." When used as a verb, *kaib'aj* is "to multiply or divide." The name may refer to the fact that he had a large posterity, or that his was a significant division of the lineage. Alternatively, the "Two" may simply mean that he represents the second generation of lords (Akkeren 2000, 53).

[675] *K'o Kawib'* (Lord Adornment).

[676] *K'o Ajaw* (Lord/Sir Lord).

[677] *Saqil tzij* (light word).

[678] *Saqil pixab'* (light instructions, counsel, law).

Then they were counseled:

"We go to our people.[679] Our Lord Deer is now established,[680] mirrored in the sky. We shall thus return, for our work is accomplished, and our day is now finished. Remember us.[681] Do not forget us.[682] Do not sweep us away. You shall surely see your homes and your mountains where you will settle. Thus let it be so. Go therefore, go to see the place from whence we came." This was the counsel they were given.

Then they left behind the sign of the existence of Balam Quitze:

"This is the token of my memory that I shall leave with you. This is your glory. These are my instructions, the result of what I have pondered," he said when he left behind the sign of his existence. Bundled Glory,[683] it

[679] *Qamaq'* (our people, tribe, nation).

[680] *Cholan* is to "be ordered, aligned, established, placed, or declared." Thus "Our Lord Deer," one of the titles for their patron god Tohil (see pp. 234–235; lines 6343–6352), had achieved a permanent, fixed position. From the following phrase, this appears to have been symbolized by some astronomical phenomenon. There appear to be deer constellation references in both the Dresden and Madrid codices. Gabrielle Vail associates the deer-trapping sections of the Madrid Codex as having astronomical associations, identifying the deer constellation as Virgo (Bricker and Vail 1997, 99–107).

[681] *Kojina'.* Literally "sense/feel us." This is stronger in the Quiché language than to merely have memories of someone. To an extent, traditionalist Maya do not consider powerful individuals of the past to be dead. Nicolás Chávez Sojuel, a sculptor in the community of Santiago Atitlán, carved an image of Diego Kihu, a powerful *nab'eysil* (priest) who died in the 1970s, on a panel of the central altarpiece in the church. In this panel, Kihu is walking at the head of his own funeral cortège. When I asked how this was possible, Nicolás said that he hadn't really died. He then related the following story: "Diego Kihu... could work many miracles. He had the face of a saint's image. He had power over water and rain. He could make it rain whenever he wished, and yet when he walked in the rain he never got wet.... He was very old when he died, about 128. But he didn't die of illness, he just decided to leave because he wanted to be with the other *nab'eysils* in *Paq'alib'al* [a cave located southwest of the community where the saints and deified ancestors live]. He told people that he would leave at 6:00 pm on a Wednesday and said goodbye to everyone and gave them his blessing. Everyone placed candles around his bed and he left right at 6:00, as he had said. That evening he visited many people in dreams and told them not to worry about him because he was in *Paq'alib'al.* When he was buried a great wind and earthquake passed through the cemetery to prove that he was not dead" (Christenson 2001, 211). The highland Maya frequently tell stories about visitations from ancestors who continue to work on behalf of their community whenever necessary. Recently I gave an old photograph, depicting a group of elders from Santiago Atitlán taken in the late nineteenth century, to a friend of mine who is the son of a prominent elder in that community. When I asked how he knew them, considering that they had died long before he was born, he replied: "We all know them. They still visit us in dreams and in person. We know their faces. They are still very powerful—the soul of the town. Their minds and their souls are white [*saq*: white, light, pure, clear, clean]. This is our heritage. These people are still alive because I live. I carry their blood. I remember. They are not forgotten."

[682] Literally "do not lose us."

[683] *Pisom Q'aq'al. Q'aq'al* is derived from the root, *q'aq'* (flame). In this form, it refers to "power, glory, splendor."

was called. Its contents were not clear for it was truly bundled. They did not unwrap it, nor was its stitching clear. No one had seen it when it was bundled.

This, then, was their counsel when they disappeared there atop the mountain Hacavitz. They were not buried by their wives, nor their children. Neither was their disappearance clear when they vanished. But their counsel was clear. Thus the Bundle came to be precious to them as a memorial to their father. Straightaway they burned offerings before it as a memorial to their father.

Thus the people were established by the lords following this beginning by Balam Quitze, the grandfather and father of the Cavecs. His sons, named Co Caib and Co Cavib, were not lost.

Thus were the deaths of our four grandfathers and fathers when they disappeared, when they left their sons there on top of the mountain Hacavitz. These sons tarried there.

But the day of all the nations had fallen, and they were humiliated and lacking in power.

The people had become numerous by then, and all of them gathered together each day to remember their father. The Bundle was precious[684] to them. They did not open it. It remained bundled. Bundled Glory they called it when it existed. They also named it their Wrapping. It had been left behind by their fathers as the true sign of their existence. Thus was the disappearance and end of Balam Quitze, Balam Acab, Mahucutah, and Iqui Balam, the first people who came from across the sea in the East. Anciently they came here. They died in their old age, they who were called bloodletters and sacrificers.

[684] Literally "great its day."

THE SONS OF THE PROGENITORS
JOURNEY TO TULAN[685]

THEN they remembered in their hearts the journey they were to make there to the East. They remembered the instructions given by their fathers who had died long ago. The nations had since given wives to them, thus becoming their fathers-in-law. Thus the three of them had married women.

And they said when they left:

"We go to the East from where our fathers came." Thus said the three sons when they began their journey.[686] Co Caib was the name of the first, the son of Balam Quitze of the Cavecs. Co Acutec was the name of the son of Balam Acab of the Nihaibs. Co Ahau was the name of the other, the son of Mahucutah of the Ahau Quichés. These, then, were the names of the three who went across the sea. They had wisdom and knowledge. They were more than ordinary people in their nature. They left behind their counsel to all their older brothers, and their younger brothers.

They rejoiced when they left:

"We will not die. We will return," they said when the three of them left.

Thus they passed over the sea, arriving there in the East. They went there to receive their lordship.

This, then, is the name of the lord, the lord of the East, when they arrived:

---

[685] lines 7361–7411
[686] Literally "took their road."

THE SONS RECEIVE
AUTHORITY TO RULE[687]

THEN they arrived before the face of the lord, whose name was Nacxit.[688] He was the only judge[689] over a great dominion.[690] He then gave to them the signs and symbols of their lordship. Thus they received the signs of office for the Ah Pop,[691] and the Ah Pop of the Reception House.[692] They received the signs of their glory and lordship that pertained to the offices of Ah Pop and Ah Pop of the Reception House. These, then, are the names of the tokens of their glory and lordship:

[687] lines 7412–7450

[688] Nacxit is derived from the Nahua words *nawi* (four) and *ikxit* (foot) (Campbell 1983, 84), perhaps referring to the extent of his power to the four cardinal directions of the earth. This is also one of the titles for the feathered serpent deity known as Kukulcan in the Maya lowlands and as Quetzalcoatl in Central Mexico (Recinos 1950, 207 n. 3; Roys 1967, 83; Edmonson 1982, 16 n. 220; Nicholson 2001, 228). It is likely that Nacxit was a ruler from some major political center in the general direction east from the Maya highlands. Nacxit was apparently one of the titles used by Maya rulers at both Chichen Itza and Mayapan, indicating their attempts to claim Central Mexican authority as an important component of their own right to rule (Nicholson 2001, 228–229).

[689] *Q'atol tzij*. Literally "guardian/cutter of the word."

[690] *Ajawarem* is "lordship or sovereignty" when referring to the power of the office, and "dominion or domain" when referring to the physical extent of a lord's territory and its people.

[691] *Aj Pop* (He of the Mat). This is the highest office within the ruling Nima Quiché lineage. The office belonged to the line founded by Co Caib, son of Balam Quitze of the Cavecs. The ancient lords of the Maya sat on mat thrones, and these became symbolic of lordship and authority itself. The mat represented the power not only of the ruler, but also of his subjects. In this sense, the interlaced reeds of the mat represented the members of the community, linked in a common purpose. Thus Ximénez translated *popol* as "community." This office might then be translated "he of the community" or "master of the community." Coto lists various offices, all of which held the title of *ah pop*: "constable, chief, counselor, dignitary, and lord." None of these European titles, however, is equivalent with the Maya concept of the office. "He of the Mat" is misleading without extensive elaboration of the meaning of "mat." I have chosen therefore to leave the title untranslated.

[692] *Aj Pop K'am Ja* (He of the Mat Reception House). This is the second highest office among the Nima Quichés, serving as an advisor and representative of the *Ah Pop*. The title was held by representatives of the secondary line founded by Co Nache, the illegitimate son of Co Caib's wife by Co Cavib (Carmack and Mondloch 1983, 181–182). The "reception house" may refer to a building or hall used for receiving petitioners, visiting dignitaries, or perhaps tribute. The latter possibility is supported by Colonial dictionaries that list *k'amajal* as "to send or pay tribute" (Varea). The importance of tribute collection as the focus of high office may be seen in Las Casas' description of Pre-Conquest Quiché administration: "That supreme king had certain principal men of counsel who had charge of justice and determined what should be done in all business affairs. It is said today by the Indians who saw it, that they were like the Oidores of Guatimala in the Royal Audience. They saw the

Canopy[693] and throne,
Bone flute[694] and drum,[695]
Shining Black Powder[696] and Yellow Stone,[697]
Puma Paws and Jaguar Paws,
Head and Hooves of the Deer,[698]
Arm Band[699] and Snailshell Rattle,
Tobacco Gourd[700] and Food Bowl,[701]
Macaw Feathers and Snowy Egret Feathers.[702]

Figure 69. "They received the signs of their glory and lordship that pertained to the offices of Ah Pop and Ah Pop of the Reception House." A Quiché lord adorned with the tokens of rulership, redrawn from a mural at the ancient Quiché capital, Cumarcah (Drawing by K. Kurbjuhn and Dwight T. Wallace, in Carmack 1981, 297).

tribute which was collected from the kingdom and they divided and sent to the king what was needed for the support of his person and for his estate" (Las Casas 1967, III.ccxxxiv.500. Translation by author). Alternatively, Akkeren reads the word as k'amaja (almost, close) in the sense that he holds a position just below the Ah Pop. The title would thus be something like "Vice Ah Pop" (Akkeren 2000, 213).

   [693] Muj is a "canopy, mantle, throne, or cushion of a throne or seat" (Coto). Muj is literally "shadow" and likely refers to the shadow cast by the canopy. Alonso de Zorita noted that prior to the Spanish conquest, the Quichés had "three lords" who were distinguished by the number of canopies they had: "The principal lord had three canopies or mantles adorned with fine featherwork over his seat, the second had two, and the third one" (Zorita 1963, 272).

   [694] Coto identifies this as a small bone flute used in dances.

   [695] The standard musical instruments used in ritual processions and ceremonies are the

All these they brought when they returned. They also brought the writings[703] of Tulan from the other side of the sea. These were the writings, as they were called, that contained the many things with which they had been invested.[704]

flute and large drum. Each is considered a living entity. Among the modern highland Maya, the drum often has a hole, or cluster of holes, in its side called its "mouth." Attendants periodically pour liquor into this hole to give the drum strength when it gets "thirsty."

[696] Basseta identifies *tatil* (a variant of *titil*), as a shining black powder or saltpetre used to dry ink when writing. Ximénez interprets *titil* as an "unguent with which they [Quichés] paint/smear" (Ximénez 1985, 536). In this context, it, along with the "yellow stone" that is paired with it, were likely pigments used as face or body paint connected with ceremonial performances.

[697] Coto identifies *ɛan abah* (yellow stone) as face paint.

[698] Deerskins were the symbol of Tohil, the patron deity of the Quichés. They are still kept in many highland Maya communities as tokens of deities and worn in dances (see footnote 620).

[699] *Makutax* from the Nahua *macuetlaxtli* (*mah*—hand, arm; *cuetlax*—leather) (Campbell 1983, 84; cf. Edmonson 1971, 218; D. Tedlock 1996, 316 n. 179). Because it is paired with a musical instrument, this perhaps has dangles that make sounds when danced.

[700] *K'us B'us* (Tobacco Gourd). This is likely derived from a combination of the lowland Maya word for tobacco (*k'utz*), and a small wild gourd used to hold ground tobacco (*b'ux*). Tobacco plays a major role in Maya ceremonies, both ancient and modern. Deities, rulers, and priests are often depicted wearing a tobacco pouch in Precolumbian art.

[701] Tedlock identifies *kaxkon* with the Nahua *caxcomulli* (bowl for eating) (D. Tedlock 1996, 316 n. 179).

[702] *Astapulul* is likely the great heron or snowy egret, a word derived from the Nahua *aztapololli* (*aztatl*—great heron or snowy egret; and *pol*—great, large) (Campbell 1983, 84; cf. Recinos 1950, 209 n. 5; D. Tedlock 1996, 316 n. 179).

[703] *Tz'ib'al* is both "writings and paintings." These were likely painted codices. Alonso de Zorita visited Utatlan soon after the Conquest and was shown certain "paintings that they had which recorded their history for more than eight hundred years back, and which were interpreted for me by very ancient Indians" (Zorita 1963, 272).

[704] These paintings and tokens of lordship gave the Quichés their sanction to rule, received from the hand of a "Toltec" lord who had the proper authority. The painted texts were likely a record of this sanction, prepared at the court of Nacxit to be used as proof of the lords' newly-acquired legitimacy as rulers.

THE MIGRATIONS OF THE QUICHÉS[705]

And when they arrived there atop their citadel called Hacavitz, they gathered all the Tamub and Ilocab together. All the nations rejoiced when Co Caib,[706] Co Acutec, and Co Ahau arrived. These alone received the lordship of the nations. The Rabinals, the Cakchiquels, and the Ah Tziquinahas rejoiced when the sign of the greatness of their lordship was revealed to them. Great then would become the essence of the nations. For their lordship was not truly complete when they were at Hacavitz. When they were on top of the mountain the only people there were those who had come from the East. But now there were many of them. By then the wives of Balam Quitze, Balam Acab, and Mahucutah had died.

Then they left, they abandoned their mountain and searched for another mountain to settle. They settled innumerable mountains, giving each of them honorific epithets and names. Our first mothers and fathers gathered together and became strong, according to what the ancient people say. Thus they abandoned their first citadel, called Hacavitz.

Thus they arrived, they founded a new citadel called Chi Quix.[707] Here they spent a great deal of time atop this unified citadel group. They had daughters and sons when they were there. Although they were on four mountains, there was only one name for the entire citadel.

They gave away their daughters in marriage to their sons. They gave away their daughters merely as an act of compassion, as gifts without payment in return. They did only that which was good.

---

[705] lines 7451–7550

[706] According to the *Título Totonicapán*, the Quiché lords sent both of the sons of Balam Quitze on this mission. Co Caib traveled East, and his brother Co Cavib went West. Co Caib was successful in bringing back the tokens of authority whereas Co Cavib returned without accomplishing his purpose (Carmack and Mondloch 1983, 181). Upon his return, Co Cavib fell into further disgrace: "Then (C'ok'awib) demonstrated his weakness and fornicated with his sister in law, the wife of C'ocaib. Balam C'ok'awib engendered a son and the child was still in the cradle when it was told to C'ocaib" (Ibid.). It is this same Co Nache who succeeded his father (see p. 262; line 7557) and founded the title of Ah Popol (see p. 293; line 8520). Perhaps because of his illegitimacy, the *Título Totonicapán* suggests that he should have held the secondary office of *Ah Pop K'amja* (Ah Pop of the Reception House)j, which is, indeed, the office held by his descendents beginning with Iztayul (Carmack and Mondloch 1983, 182). Co Caib's legitimate son Xmayquej apparently succeeded to the higher office of Ah Pop (Carmack 1981, 129–130).

[707] *Chi K'ix* (Thorny Place). Akkeren places this site at the confluence of the Chixoy River and the Calá River where it is known today as Chi Cruz (Akkeren 2000, 94, 107–108).

[708] *Chi Chak* (Wound/Thorn Place).

Then they passed through each division of the citadel. These were the names of the mountains of Chi Quix where they tarried: Chi Chac,[708] Humetaha,[709] Culba,[710] and Cavinal.[711]

Then they investigated the mountains near their citadel. They looked for a mountain on which to dwell, for they had become numerous. They who had received lordship in the East were now dead. They who had come to the peaks of each citadel had become aged grandfathers. But they were not content.[712] They passed through numerous afflictions and misfortunes until at last they discovered the citadel of the grandfathers and the fathers.

This therefore was the name of the citadel that they came to:

---

[709] *Jumeta Ja* (Bark House). According to the *Título Totonicapán*, the Quichés settled this area briefly after they had abandoned Hacavitz: "They arrived at the place they called *Chi-Humet*, because there was an abundance of limestone and because they built their dwellings of it. They found some plantains and little birds. Nevertheless, they suffered many hardships in those mountains" (Chonay and Goetz 1953, 182; Carmack 1973, 290–291).

[710] *K'ulb'a* (Landmark), based on *k'ulb'at* (Basseta). In the *Título Totonicapán*, this site is referred to as Culba-Cavinal, indicating that they are closely-related sites.

[711] *Kawinal* (Armory), based on *cawij*, "to arm, adorn, prepare, embellish" (Basseta). The Late Postclassic site of Kawinal is located on the *Ka'ala* (Calá) River two kilometers north of where it empties into the Chixoy River (Akkeren, personal communication). The mountain above this site is still called Cerro Cauinal (Fox 1978, 249). It is likely that Chi Quix, Chi Chac, Humetaha and Culuba were located nearby, although their precise location is unknown (Recinos 1950, 211 n. 9). The *Título Totonicapán* and the *Título C'oyoi* list Humeta and Culba-Cavinal as places of refuge for the Quichés following their abandonment of Hacavitz. (Chonay and Goetz 1953, 182–183; Carmack 1973, 289). The Quichés allied themselves to the local Aq'ab' inhabitants here, although it must have been an unequal relationship since they received tribute from them (Carmack 1973, 289–291).

[712] Literally "they did not receive their faces," which is "to settle down, be content, or become comfortable."

THE FOUNDATION OF CHI IZMACHI[713]

CHI IZMACHI,[714] then, was the name of the mountain on which they dwelt as their citadel. There they settled and tested their glory. They ground their lime plaster and their whitewash[715] in the fourth generation of lords. It is said that Co Nache[716] and Beleheb Queh[717] ruled then, along with the Lord Magistrate.[718]

It was there at Chi Izmachi that Lord Co Tuha[719] and Iztayul[720] ruled as Ah Pop and Ah Pop of the Reception House. Under them it came to be a very fine citadel.

---

[713] lines 7550–7707

[714] *Chi Ismachi'* (Place of Whiskers). The ruins of this settlement are located on a hill just across a small canyon southwest of the later Quiché capital of Cumarcah, occupied at the time of the Spanish conquest. According to the *Título Tamub (Historia Quiché de Don Juan de Torres)*, the founding of this citadel marked the beginning of the true *ajawarem* (lordship) of the Quichés (Recinos 1957, 43–45), likely reinforced by the presence there of the tokens of office brought from Tulan by Co Caib. All three major lineages of the Quichés (Nima Quichés, Tamub, and Ilocab) occupied Chi Izmachi. After the Nima Quichés moved on to their eventual capital at Cumarcah, the Tamub were left behind as the sole inhabitants of Chi Izmachi. The disgraced Ilocab occupied the site of Chisalin (also known as Mukwitz Pilocab), located across a small canyon northeast of Cumarcah (Carmack 1981, 234–239).

[715] This is the first settlement described as having plastered and whitewashed buildings, characteristic of important Precolumbian centers as opposed to smaller communities built from adobe and wood.

[716] *K'o Na Che'* (Lord House Tree), where *na* is the Lowland Maya form of the Quiché *ja* (house). The Maya often refer to trees as metaphors for lineages, the branches (posterity) growing out of the trunk (founder).

[717] *B'elejeb' Kej* (Nine Deer). This is the first occurence in the text of a historical figure whose name is derived from a day on the Highland Maya calendar, a common practice at the time of the Conquest and into the Spanish Colonial period. It is likely the day on which he was born.

[718] *Q'alel Ajaw*. This is another office within the Quiché hierarchy that has no English equivalent. It is the third highest position within the Nima Quiché line (after Ah Pop and Ah Pop of the Reception House). The title is specifically linked with the Nihaib lineage. Neither the Cavec, the Ajau Quichés, nor the Zaquics (the other three lineages within the Nima Quiché alliance) have a *Q'alel* title. Colonial dictionaries give a variety of descriptive meanings to it including "*cacique*" (Spanish for a native chief), "generous person, prince" (Coto), or simply an "important person" (Varea). Coto also lists *ah ɛalel* as a "constable." Basseta defines *calel achi* as a "captain of soldiers." In modern Quiché, the title is given to judges, and some early dictionaries suggest that this office may have included judicial functions as well. The title is likely something akin to "magistrate" with duties that include peacekeeping and military activity. *Ajaw* is "lord."

[719] *K'o Tuja* (Lord Sweatbath). According to other highland Maya documents, the rise of the Nima Quichés under the leadership of Co Tuha aroused the envy of the Ilocab at Chi Izmachi. At first they tried to create tension between Co Tuha and Iztayul, the Ah Pop of the Reception House. When this plan did not succeed, the Ilocab ambushed a group of Quiché lords and warriors as they bathed in a canyon. The Ilocab were eventually defeated

Figure 70. "Chi Izmachi, then, was the name of the mountain on which they dwelt as their citadel." View of the hill on which the ruins of Chi Izmachi are located.

Only three great houses[721] were built there at Chi Izmachi, not the twenty-four great houses of today. Yet there were three great houses:

Just one great house of the Cavecs;

Just one great house over the Nihaibs;

And just one of the Ahau Quichés.

There were only two swollen[722] great houses, one each for the two lineage divisions at Chi Izmachi. Their hearts were united. There were no bad feelings or anger, only steadfast[723] lordship. There was no contention or

and the survivors taken back to Chi Izmachi to be sacrificed, but Co Tuha subsequently disappears from the records and apparently died in the revolt. The records say that this was the beginning of regular human sacrifice at Chi Izmachi which caused all the people of the region to fear them greatly (Carmack and Mondloch 1983, 194). Soon after this incident the old alliance broke up and the Nima Quichés abandoned Chi Izmachi.

[720] Campbell suggests that this name is derived from the Nahua *ista*—white, and *yol*—heart, giving a reading of "White Heart" (Campbell 1983, 85–86).

[721] *Nim Ja* (Great House) may refer to both a large building or palace, as well as the lineage to which it was dedicated. In this case, the reference is to the lineage, since the three great houses were quartered in only two buildings. This is where administrative and judicial decisions were made for each of the major lineages. The *Popol Vuh* mentions that the negotiation of bride exchange in particular took place in the great houses. The great houses likely also served as the residences for the lineage heads as well as the repositories for the tokens of authority brought from Tulan.

[722] *Kumatzil.* This is "swollen, enlarged, inflated" (Basseta). It likely refers here both to the size of the structures, as well as to the fact that they were overcrowded.

[723] *Li'anik* is "steadfast, flat, tranquil, pacific."

disturbance. There was only purity and a tranquil sense of community in their hearts. There was no envy[724] or jealousy.[725]

Yet their glory was still meager. They had not pulled together,[726] nor had they become great. They attempted to strengthen their defenses[727] there at Chi Izmachi. This act was surely a sign of their sovereignty. It was surely a sign of their glory, as well as their greatness.

However this was seen by the Ilocab, who fomented war. They desired that Lord Co Tuha be murdered. They desired that there be but one lord over them. Thus the Ilocab wished to convince Lord Iztayul to murder him. But this plot against Lord Co Tuha did not succeed. Their envy merely fell on their own backs. This first attempt by the Ilocab to kill the lord failed. Yet it was the foundation of strife and the clamor for war.

Thus the Ilocab made a first attempt at invading the citadel, coming as killers. It was their desire that the Quichés be destroyed.[728] They wished to exercise lordship in their own hearts. But when they came to seize it they were captured and despoiled, and few of them were ever set free again.

Then began the sacrifices. The Ilocab were sacrificed before the face of the god as payment for their offenses against Lord Co Tuha. Thus many were taken into captivity and enslaved. They became servants. They merely gave themselves up in defeat as a result of their clamor for war against the lord as well as his canyon-citadel.[729] They had desired in their hearts to ruin and mock the lordship of the Quichés. But this was not accomplished. Thus they commenced to sacrifice these people before the face of the god.

Then they built their war defenses, and this was the beginning of the fortification of the citadel at Chi Izmachi. Thus they began to lay the foundation of their glory, because the sovereignty of the Quiché lord was surely

---

[724] *Moxwachinik* (left/crazy facing).

[725] *Q'aq'wachinik* (fire facing).

[726] The Quiché expression reads *kanuk'maijoq* (drawn/pulled together). It is an interesting coincidence that this metaphor is similar to our English expression "pull it together," meaning to get one's life or affairs in order.

[727] *Xkikowisaj pokob'* (they strengthened shield). *Kowisaj* is not only "to strengthen," but specifically "to plaster" (Coto). Thus the Quichés were fortifying their citadel with plastered walls.

[728] Literally "the loss of their faces."

[729] *Siwan tinamit* (canyon citadel). These two terms together refer to the fortified hilltop center as well as the surrounding population living in the canyons and valleys where crops were cultivated. Many contemporary Quiché towns are still referred to as *siwan-tinamit* when referring to the urban center plus its surrounding dependent communities. Bunzel notes that this phrase is always used to refer to the town of Chichicastenango in ritual contexts (Bunzel 1952, 2; Schultze-Jena 1954, 28).

great. Everywhere there were enchanted lords. None came to humiliate or mock them. They were but workers of greatness.

There they put down roots at Chi Izmachi, and there also their bloodletting god increased in greatness. And all the nations, the small and the great, became afraid. They witnessed the arrival of captive people to be sacrificed and killed by the glory and sovereignty of Lord Co Tuha and Lord Iztayul, in alliance with the Nihaib and Ahau Quichés. There were only three divisions of lineages there at the citadel named Chi Izmachi.

And yet again they began to feast and to drink to their daughters. They who were called the Three Great Houses gathered together to celebrate. They would drink their drinks and eat their food, and this alone was the bride price for their sisters and their daughters. There was only joy in their hearts when they feasted within their great houses:

"We give only our thanks and our gratitude as a sign of our agreement;[730] as a sign of our word regarding the boys and girls born of their mothers," they said.

They gave one another honorific titles, and gave names to their lineages, their seven nations, their fortified cities.

"We have intermarried, we the Cavecs, we the Nihaibs, and we the Ahau Quichés," they said.

These three lineages, and these three great houses, dwelt a long time there at Chi Izmachi. But then they looked for and found another citadel. And so they abandoned the peak of Chi Izmachi.

---

[730] *Tzijel* (word, news, agreement). In this context, *tzijel* refers to the covenant or agreement reached in marriage negotiations. It also has a double meaning, as *tzijel* may refer to "sons, descendents, posterity" (Coto).

THE FOUNDATION OF CUMARCAH[731]

THUS they rose up again and came to the citadel that the Quichés would call Cumarcah.[732] The lord Co Tuha, along with Cucumatz[733] and all the lords, came there. There had been five moves and five generations of people since the beginning of the light, the beginning of the nations, the beginning of life and creation. There they built many homes. They also built houses for the gods at the center, on the highest point of the citadel.

Thus they came and began to be great in their lordship. They were many now, crowded together. They planned their great houses. They gathered

Figure 71. "Thus they rose up again and came to the citadel that the Quichés would call Cumarcah." View of the ruins of Cumarcah. The ruins of the Temple of Tohil may be seen on the far left.

---

[731] lines 7708–7787

[732] *Q'umarkaj* (Ancient/Rotten Canes/Reeds). The name of this citadel has generally been translated "Place of Rotten Canes" (Recinos 1950, 215, D. Tedlock 1996, 183). *Q'umarik,* however, also refers to something ancient, while *aj* can be used for a wide variety of reeds. The more likely translation of the citadel is thus "Place of Ancient Reeds." This ties the city figuratively with the ancient place of their origin at Tulan (Place of Reeds). Following the Spanish conquest, Cumarcah was renamed *Utatlan* by the Tlaxcalan allies of the invaders. In the Tlaxcalan dialect of Nahuatl, this name means "among the reeds," a close translation of the Quiché name (Carmack 1981, 143). Cumarcah was the capital of the Nima Quichés at the time of the Spanish conquest. The ruins of the citadel are located approximately two kilometers west of the modern city of Santa Cruz del Quiché. Little remains of its buildings,

together. And yet they were also divided because there began to be contention. They began to envy each other regarding the bride price for their sisters and their daughters. For it was no longer merely food and drink that they demanded. This, then, was the root of their division. They turned on each other, desecrating[734] the bones and the skulls of the dead. They became infuriated with one another and split apart. Thus there came to be nine lineage divisions because of this contention over the sisters and the daughters. Therefore, when lordship was conceived, twenty-four great houses came to be.

When they arrived in ancient times at the top of their citadel, they completed twenty-four great houses there in the citadel of Cumarcah. This citadel was blessed by the lord bishop[735] after it was left abandoned.

partly because it was burned by Pedro de Alvarado during his conquest of the Maya highlands in 1524, and partly because of extensive looting of its stones for buildings elsewhere since that time. Cumarcah was constructed atop a small plateau with nearly vertical cliffs on all of its sides. Anciently, the citadel was accessible only by a narrow causeway and bridge from the southeast, and by a steep stairway on the west side (Fox 1978, 22–24), making it easily defended from attack. The move to Cumarcah was apparently necessitated by conflict among the major Quiché lineages. As a result, the Nima Quichés founded Cumarcah as their capital in ca. 1400, while the Tamub remained at nearby Chi Izmachi, and the Ilocab founded a new settlement at Mukwitz Chilocab (Burial Mountain of the Ilocab), now called Chisalin, also located in the vicinity (Recinos 1957, 43–44; Fox 1978, 36). Archaeologically, Mukwitz was by far the smallest of the three, indicating the decline in power suffered by the Ilocab (Carmack 1981, 167). The first occupation in the Cumarcah region actually dates to ca. 1250, thus it is likely that the "move" as described here is less a literal migration than the establishment of the citadel as a center of power as the Cavec lineage becomes more prominent (Akkeren, personal communication).

[733] Q'ukumatz (Quetzal Serpent) was likely the son of Co Tuha, who acceded upon the death of his father at the hands of the Ilocab. The manuscript always spells the name of this lord as Cucumatz, whereas the creator deity with the same, or similar, name is spelled Qucumatz. The variant spellings may be the result of multiple scribes working on the manuscript, each with his/her own creative ways of spelling. Alternatively, it may simply be a means of distinguishing between the deity and this lord. With Cucumatz, who reigned ca. 1400–1425, we are entering into a period of Quiché history in which historical details are better known. Under the direction of Cucumatz the power of the Quichés expanded northward to the area of present-day Sacapulas in a series of campaigns aided by allied Cakchiquel warriors (Recinos 1957, 133–139).

[734] Literally "turning over." The ancient Maya kept and revered the bones of their ancestors as the foundation of their power and legitimacy. To disturb these bones would be far more serious than to insult the living members of the lineage. It is likely that the bones of the ancestral founders were kept in the great houses. Thus López-Medel wrote that great rulers were buried in the great houses beneath the place where they had exercised rule in life (Carmack 1981, 193).

[735] The authors of the Popol Vuh are identifying the citadel of Cumarcah as the capital city of the Quichés at the time of the Spanish conquest. The ruins of its destroyed temples and palaces were blessed by the Roman Catholic bishop Francisco Marroquín in 1539: "The very illustrious and reverend Señor Don Francisco Marroquín... was in that court, and blessed the place, and there he fixed and raised the standard of faith, the sign of our Redemption; it

They were advanced in rank,[736] differentiated by their benches and their cushions. They were set apart, each according to their glory. Each of the lords of the nine lineages was distinguished by rank:

Nine lords of the Cavecs;

Nine lords of the Nihaibs;

Four lords of the Ahau Quichés;

And two of the Ahau Zaquics.

Thus they came to be numerous. Many there were behind each of the lords. From the beginning they were the heads of numerous vassals and servants.[737] Each of the lineages of lords became crowded.

We shall now give the titles of each of the lords and of each of their great houses:

was in the same place where for so many years the Prince of Darkness, that idol Tojil, had reigned; thus it was a sign of triumph and conquest" (Ximénez 1929–31, I.xxxix.115). Thus the site of Cumarcah remained a center of occupation for survivors of the conquest for at least a few decades following the conquest. Dominicans administered this settlement, which they called Santa Cruz Utatlán. A new city was built nearby in 1555 named Santa Cruz el Quiché (Spanish "Holy Cross of the Quiché). Today Santa Cruz is the capital city of the State (*Departamento*) of El Quiché, Guatemala.

[736] *Xeq'aq'ar* (they were glorified, advanced in rank). The verb form is derived from *q'aq'al* (glory, power).

[737] The political organization of the citadel is based on kinship terms, although no true familial relationship need exist. Here the terms are *al, k'ajol* (child of woman, son of man) which are metaphors for vassals and servants.

THE TITLES OF THE CAVEC LORDS[738]

THESE, then, are the titles of the lords over the Cavecs.[739] The first lords are:

Ah Pop[740] and
Ah Pop of the Reception House;[741]
Ah Tohil and
Ah Cucumatz;[742]
Great Steward of the Cavecs[743] and
Councilor of the Stacks;[744]
Emissary of the Deer House,[745]
Councilor in the Ballcourt of Punishment,[746] and
Mother of the Reception House.[747]

---

[738] lines 7788–7802
[739] Literally "lords before the faces of the Cavecs."
[740] *Aj Pop* (He of the Mat), the highest office in the Quiché hierarchy.
[741] *Aj Pop K'am Ja* (He of the Mat Reception House). This is the second highest office. Coto lists this office as a "messenger, errand boy." Considering the importance of this position, a more likely translation would be "emissary, legate, or vice-*ah pop.*" "Reception House" likely refers to a reception hall for meeting with visiting dignitaries or for receiving tribute.
[742] *Aj Tojil, Aj Q'ukumatz* (He of Tojil, He of Cucumatz). These are likely priests of the two major patron deities. *Q'ukumatz* (Quetzal Serpent) was one of the creator deities (see pp. 61, 68–72, 80–82; lines 25, 140–154)
[743] *Nim Ch'okoj Kaweq* (Great Seating Cavec). *Ch'okoj* is "to seat," but when used as a title it refers to one who calls people to service, or to a banquet (Varea). Thus Ximénez glosses *chocoh* as being associated with a "wedding or banquet" (Ximénez 1985, 200). The *ch'okoj* is also charged with providing the food and drinks for state functions, as well as making pronouncements and public discourses. The nearest English terms for such an office would be a "steward or master of ceremonies," although these are comparatively minor functions in most modern societies. It is not a minor role in Maya communities. In Santiago Atitlán, it is the *cabecera* (Spanish: "head person"), the head of the entire confraternity system, that is charged with overseeing the preparation of food and drink, as well as leading the procession of such dishes for large public events. Until the secularization of Guatemalan communities after World War II, the *cabecera* was the principal political and ecclesiastical authority in traditional Maya communities. Within each individual confraternity, it is the wife of the confraternity head that is charged with preparing the food for communal meals, and it is the confraternity head himself who pays for it, distributes it, and gives a brief discourse welcoming those in attendance and, where appropriate, explaining the meaning of the event. Bunzel suggests that at Chichicastenango, the ceremonies of the confraternity are "little more than a series of sacramental meals in which the sacred character of food, especially maize and cacao, holds the center of interest, even to the exclusion of the saint in whose honor the ceremony presumably is held." In conjunction with such meals, "there are long speeches of blessing and a special type of music" (Bunzel 1952, 45–46). The concluding remarks of the *Popol Vuh* text suggest that the authors were, indeed, the *Nim Ch'okoj* of the three major Quiché lineages. In that passage the three *Nim Ch'okoj* are referred to as the

THESE, then, are the lords over the Cavecs.

There are nine lords for each of the great houses and these shall now be shown:

"givers of birth, the mothers and fathers of the word," presumably referring to the text of the *Popol Vuh* itself (see p. 305; lines 8702–8703).

[744] *Popol Winaq Chi T'uy* (Councilor of the Stacks). *Popol Winaq* (Mat Person) is the head of a ruling or deliberative council, the unity of the council being symbolized by the interlaced reeds in a woven mat. *T'uy* is a "stack, pile." This latter term is likely a reference to tribute. It is common in scenes depicting throne rooms on ancient Maya ceramic vessels to see stacks of tribute in the form of textiles, bark paper, exotic feathers and skins, cacao beans, etc.

[745] *Lolmet Kej Nay* (Emissary of the Deer House). *Lolmet* (or *Lolmay*) is an "emissary or ambassador." *Kej* is deer. *Na[y]* is the Lowland Maya version of the Quichéan *Ja[y]* (house).

[746] *Popol Winaq pa Jom Tzalatz* (Councilor in the Ballcourt of Punishment). *Jom* is "ballcourt." *Tzal* is "war, battle, conflict," while *tzalatz* means "punishment, or penalty" (Coto).

[747] *U Chuch K'am Ja* (Mother of the Reception House). This is likely the overseer of the hall where dignitaries are received, or the building where tribute is stored.

THE TITLES OF THE NIHAIB LORDS[748]

THESE, then, are the lords over the Nihaibs. The first lords are:
Lord Magistrate[749] and
Lord Herald;[750]
Magistrate of the Reception House[751] and
Great Reception House;[752]
Mother of the Reception House[753] and
Great Steward of the Nihaibs;[754]
Auilix,[755]
Yacolatam (Corner of the Reed Mat) Zaclatol,[756] and
Great Emissary of the Sprout Giver.[757]
Nine, then, were the lords of the Nihaibs.

[748] lines 7803–7814
[749] *Ajaw Q'alel* (Lord Magistrate).
[750] *Ajaw Aj Tzik' Winaq* (Lord Herald Person). *Aj Tzik'* is a "crier, proclaimer, speaker, herald, announcer."
[751] *Q'alel K'am Ja* (Magistrate Reception House).
[752] *Nima K'am Ja* (Great Reception House).
[753] *U Chuch K'am Ja* (Its Mother Reception House).
[754] *Nim Ch'okoj Nijaib'ab'* (Great Steward Nijaibs).
[755] *Awilix.* This is the patron god of the Nijaibs. Likely this is the title for the god's priest.
[756] *Yakolatam, U Tza'm Pop Zaklatol.* This is a singular instance in the *Popol Vuh* text where a Nahua language title is supplied with a Quiché translation by the authors. *Yakolatam* is derived from the Nahua *yacatl* (point, edge) and *tam* (leaves). This is followed by a comma in the manuscript, a fairly rare grammatical mark which in this case may indicate a pause for the authors to give a translation of the preceding word into Quiché. *U tza'm pop* (Quiché: its nose/point/edge/border reed mat) is a rough translation of *yakolatam*. *Zaklatol* is a combination of the Nahua *zacatl* (grass) and *tollin* (reed), a translation of the preceding *pop* (reed mat).
[757] *Nima Lolmet Ye'ol T'ux* (Great Emissary Giver of Sprouts). *T'ux* is a "sprout, or budding blossom."

THE TITLES OF THE
AHAU QUICHÉ LORDS[758]

THESE, then, are the titles of the lords of the Ahau Quichés:
Herald Person[759] and
Lord Emissary;[760]
Great Lord Steward of the Ahau [Quichés][761] and
Lord Hacavitz.[762]
These are the four lords over the Ahau Quichés. These are the great houses.

---

[758] lines 7815–7822
[759] *Aj Tzik' Winaq* (Herald Person).
[760] *Ajaw Lolmet* (Lord Emissary).
[761] *Ajaw Nim Ch'okoj Ajaw [K' iche']* (Lord Great Steward Ahau [Quiché]). The authors did not include the full name of the Ahau [Quiché] lineage, although this is implied.
[762] *Ajaw Jakawitz* (Lord Hacavitz). This is likely the priest of the god Hacavitz, the patron deity of the Ahau Quichés.

THE TITLES OF THE ZAQUIC LORDS[763]

THERE are also two lineages of Zaquic lords:
Maize Flower House[764] and
Magistrate of the Zaquics.[765]
There is only one house for the two lords.

---

[763] lines 7823–7828
[764] *Tz'utuju Ja* (Maize Flower House).
[765] *Q'alel Saqik* (Magistrate Zaquic).

THE GLORY OF
THE LORDS OF CUMARCAH[766]

THUS were established the twenty-four lords as well as the twenty-four great houses.

Then their glory and their sovereignty were increased in Quiché. The grandeur and importance[767] of the Quichés was glorified and made sovereign. Then as well the canyon-citadel[768] was whitewashed and plastered. The nations came there, the small and the great. Thus the lord who made Quiché great has his name.

Figure 72. "Then as well the canyon-citadel was whitewashed and plastered." Model of the site of Iximche, a well-preserved highland Maya site contemporary with Cumarcah.

Then were created their glory and their sovereignty. Then they created the homes of their gods, as well as the homes of the lords. But they themselves did not do it, nor did they work to build their homes or the homes of their gods. Instead it was their vassals and their servants, who had become numerous. They did not need to lure them, or abduct them, or

---

[766] lines 7829–7943

[767] *Alal nimal* (greatness weightiness/importance). When paired, the combination means "power" (Basseta).

[768] Thus not only were the buildings of the fortified hilltop citadel plastered and whitewashed, but the dependent communities in the valleys and canyons below were similarly well built.

carry them off by force, for they truly belonged to each one of the lords. This place also came to be crowded with the lords' older brothers and younger brothers.[769] The lords were ever-solicitous,[770] each of them receiving numerous petitions. They were truly beloved. Great was the authority[771] of the lords. The birthdays of the lords were honored and respected by their vassals and servants.

Figure 73. "In another transformation he would make himself into an eagle." Lord transformed into an eagle, redrawn from a gold disk discovered at Chichen Itza (Lothrop 1952, fig. 41. Copyright by the President and Fellows of Harvard College).

Thus they multiplied there in the canyon-citadel. Yet they were still not as many as those who fell under submission from among the nations. Even when war came upon their canyon and their citadel, they were glorified because of the spirit essence of their lords, Lord Cucumatz and Lord Co Tuha.

Cucumatz became a truly enchanted lord. In one transformation[772] he would rise up into the sky, and in another transformation he would go down to Xibalba. In another transformation he would be a serpent, truly becoming a serpent. In another transformation he would make himself into an eagle; and in another transformation into a jaguar. Truly his appearance would be that of an eagle and of a jaguar. In another transformation he would become a pool of blood. Mere pooled blood he would become. Truly he was an enchanted lord in his essence.

---

[769] *Atz, chaq'* (older brother of a male, younger brother of a male). These likely refer to allies or affiliated lineage heads rather than fraternal brothers.

[770] Literally "accumulated their existence." This is to be "assiduous, solicitous, vigilant, preoccupied."

[771] In modern Quiché usage, *q'ale'm* is both "authority," as well as "responsibility for the well-being of someone."

[772] *Wuq'.* I base this reading on *wuq'e* which is "to embody, convince" (Coto). It may also be "to wrap one's self, envelop, or bundle," perhaps a reference to the clothing and accoutrements worn in transformational dances.

Thus all the lords were frightened before his face. Tales about him were quickly spread abroad[773] and all the lords of the nations heard of the nature of this enchanted lord.

This, then, was the beginning of the increase of the Quichés. Lord Cucumatz founded the grandeur of his descendents. The faces of his grandchildren and his sons were not lost in his heart. He did not do this so that he would be the sole lord. But his nature was enchanted and thus he toppled all the lords of the nations. This he did merely to reveal himself. Yet because of it, he became the head of the nations. The enchanted lord named Cucumatz was of the fourth generation of lords. He alone was both Ah Pop and Ah Pop of the Reception House. He left behind his heritage for his descendents. For they became glorious, and sovereigns as well.

And then they begat sons, even their own sons, making them numerous. Thus were begotten Tepepul and Iztayul. These exercised true lordship. They were the fifth generation of lords that came to be. They begat sons as well, each a generation of lords.

---

[773] Literally "broke open/shattered its hearing." This implies an instantaneous and widely disseminated spread of the tale, something like the English expression, "breaking news."

THE VICTORIES OF LORD QUICAB[774]

THESE, then, are the names of the sixth generation of lords. There were two great and glorious lords: Quicab[775] was the name of the first lord, and Cauizimah[776] was the name of the other. These accomplished a great many

---

[774] lines 7944–8032

[775] *K'iq'ab'* (many hands), the son of Cucumatz, reigned as the Ah Pop of the Nima Quichés from ca. 1425–1475 (Carmack 1981, 122). The name of this lord suggests his power to accomplish what would be impossible for someone with only two hands. It may also suggest the number of vassals and servants he possessed. Quicab's father, Lord Cucumatz, died in battle in an attempt to avenge the death of his daughter at the hands of his son-in-law, Tecum Sicom, a rival lord at Coha, located somewhere near the modern town of Sacapulas (Recinos 1957, 138–141; Carmack 1981, 134–135), or alternatively Quetzaltenango (Akkeren 2000, 23, 212–213). More recently places Coha in the Quetzaltenango area, although it was allied with the Sacapulas region in opposing the rising power of the Quichés (Akkeren 2000, 23, 212–213). Two years later, his son Quicab along with his Cakchiquel allies invaded the town, seized a large cache of jade and precious metal, and burned the town of Coha to the ground. The surviving lords of Coha were taken back to Cumarcah to be sacrificed (Recinos 1957, 140–147). Quicab also brought the bones of his father back to Cumarcah where they were kept in a bundle. This campaign resulted in the conquest of the northern border regions of the Quiché's territory. This included the lands of the Cumatz and Tuhal around Sacapulas as well as that of the Mam of Zaculeu. Quicab subsequently expanded his empire by subduing the rival Sajcabaja, Caukeb and Cubulco (Ikomaquib) in the east and extending his influence as far as the upper Usumacinta and Motagua River Valleys. In the west his forces reached the Ocós River near the Isthmus of Tehuantepec in Chiapas, Mexico. Further conquests extended from the Alta Verapaz in the north to the Pacific Ocean near Escuintla in the south, an area of approximately 26,000 square miles (Fox 1978, 3–4). At the height of his power, Quicab fell victim to an internal revolt ca. 1470 (Carmack 1981, 136–137; Carmack and Mondloch 1983, 195–196). As recorded in the *Título Totonicapán*, all the major lineages, including the Tamub, Ilocab, Rabinals, Cakchiquels, Ah Tziquinahas, and the inhabitants of Sacapulas and Aguateca, gathered at Cumarcah to observe the "Great Dance of Tohil," the patron deity of the Cavec Quichés. In the presence of all the lords, rebel nobles, apparently related to the same faction that had rebelled against Co Tuha, danced with the deities of the various groups present dressed in skins and hunting attire. At the climax of the dance, the son of a Quiché ah pop began to give sacrificial offerings to Tohil. This act was a cue for rebels to initiate an attack against Quicab and his supporters (Carmack 1981, 136; Carmack and Mondloch 1983, 196; Akkeren 2000, 325–335). Although Quicab survived the revolt, his power and authority were severely diminished. He was forced to "humble himself" before the rebel warriors, who "seized the government and the power" (Recinos and Goetz 1953b). One by one the former vassal states within Quicab's empire broke away. His old allies, the Cakchiquels, remained loyal but were soon beset by attacks and insults from the new lords of Cumarcah. As a result, according to the *Annals of the Cakchiquels*, Quicab counseled them to leave the city as well as their old settlement at Chiavar, and establish their own capital independent of the Quichés:

"The die is cast. Tomorrow you will cease to exercise here the command and power which we have shared with you. Abandon the city to these *k'unum* (penises) and *k'achaq* (dung). Let them not hear your words again, my sons" (Recinos and Goetz 1953, 97).

Figure 74. View of the valley of Chuvi Miquina, present-day Totonicapán.

deeds. They made the Quichés great, for their essence was truly enchanted. They broke apart and shattered the canyons and the citadels of the small nations and the great nations. Anciently these citadels were close together:

The mountain of the Cakchiquels was where Chuvila[777] is today.

The mountain of the Rabinals was Pa Maca.[778]

The mountain of the Caocs[779] was Zaccabaha.[780]

The citadels, then, of the Zaculeus[781] were Chuvi Miquina,[782] Xelahu,[783] Chuva Tzac,[784] and Tzoloh Che.[785]

These all paid homage[786] to Quicab. They had made war, but they were broken apart. The canyons and citadels of the Rabinals, the Cakchiquels, and the Zaculeus were shattered. All the nations collapsed and were split apart. Yet for a great while Quicab's warriors persisted. There were not then even one or two groups among the nations that did not bring their trib-

Soon thereafter, in ca. 1470, the Cakchiquels under their lords Huntoh and Vucubatz (who had fought alongside Quicab as his allies) founded the citadel of Iximche', an act that initiated a series of disastrous wars between the Quichés and Cakchiquels that persisted until the coming of the Spaniards in 1524. The Ah Tziquinahas were already independent for most, if not all, of the time of their occupation around Lake Atitlán, leaving the Quichés isolated and surrounded by their enemies.

[776] *Ka Wi' Simaj* (Two Heads/Tips Sharp). If this lord's name has significance beyond being a proper name, it may have a double meaning. The "sharpness" may refer to the points of the weapons under his command, but it may also refer to the "sharpness" of his mind (a common expression among the Quichés just as it is in English). The latter is all the more impressive because he has "two heads" with which to be clever. Together, these two rulers combine the benefits of "many deeds" and "many thoughts."

[777] *Chuwi' La* (Above the Stinging Nettle). This is the site of the modern town of Chichicastenango, which at the time of the Spanish conquest was a Quiché community (as

ute. Their citadels fell, and they brought tribute before Quicab and Cauizimah.

These lords invaded the lineages, who were bled and shot while bound to wooden posts.[787] Their day came to nothing, nor did they ever have descendents. It was merely arrows that were the means of shattering the citadels. Straightaway the mouth of the earth would be split open and thunder

Figure 75. View of the hills above Chuva Tzac, present-day Momostenango.

it still is today). The original Quiché version of the *Popol Vuh* manuscript was discovered here by Francisco Ximénez.

[778] *Pa Mak'a'* (Place of Water Droplets). Alternatively this may be *Pa Mak'a* (Place of Dawn), a contracted form of *mak'ahan* (morning, dawn). Akkeren (personal communication) suggests that this may be an abbreviated form of *Pa Amaq' A'* (Place of the Water of the Nations), the ancient name for the River Motagua which is located some 10 km. away (Hill 1996, 357; Akkeren 2000, 136–137). This is the present-day town of Zacualpa (Fox 1978, 236–237; Carmack 1981, 185).

[779] *Ka'okeb'* (Caocs). The name is likely derived from *kawoq*, one of the twenty named day-signs of the traditional highland Maya calendar. In the late Postclassic, many of the Caocs moved to the area of Sacatepequez where they were subjugated by the Cakchiquels (Akkeren 2000, 217–218). These are likely the ancestors of the people who settled two communities west of present-day Guatemala City named Santiago Cauque (Sacatepequez) and Santa Maria Cauque (Sacatepequez) (Recinos 1950, 221 n. 4; D. Tedlock 1996, 324 n. 187).

[780] *Saqkab'a Ja* (Plastered House). This is the present-day town of San Andrés Sajcabaja.

[781] *Saq Ulewab'* (White Earths). These are the Mam speakers. Their ancient capital, Zaculeu, is located four kilometers west of present-day Huehuetenango. The Mam region was conquered soon after the campaigns of Quicab against the Sacapulas Valley sites. The Mam remained subject to the Quichés and fought with them against the Spaniards (Fox 1978, 147).

[782] *Chuwi' Miq'ina'* (Above Hot Water). This is likely the site known locally as Chuitinamit, located 700 meters above a series of hot water springs near present-day Totonicapán (Recinos 1950, 221; Fox 1978, 161). This and the next three settlements in the list were all heavily populated Quiché communities at the time of the Spanish conquest, attesting the effectiveness of Quicab's military campaigns. They continue to be occupied by Quiché speakers today.

would shatter the stones. Thus the nations would suddenly become frightened and make offerings before the Pine Resin Tree. This has become a sign for the citadels, for today there is a mountain of stones, only a few of which were not cut cleanly as if cut by an axe. It is there in the plain called Petatayub[788] where it may be clearly seen by all the people who pass by it. This is the sign of the war prowess of Quicab. He was not killed, nor was he defeated. He was truly a warrior, and he received tribute from all the nations.

Then all of the lords planned, sending blockaders around the canyons and around the citadels, all the fallen citadels of the nations.

---

[783] *Xe' Laju* (Below Ten). This is a contracted form of the full name of this site, *Xe' Laju[j No'j]* (Below Ten No'j—a day on the traditional highland Maya calendar). According to native chronicles, this was the principle settlement in the southern Quetzaltenango basin, although its precise location is unknown. Modern Quetzaltenango is the second largest city in Guatemala.

[784] *Chuwa Tz'aq* (Before Wall/Altar). This is present-day Momostenango (Nahua "Place of the Altars). This community is still known as *Chuwa Tz'aq* by its Quiché inhabitants. The ruins of the ancient citadel are now called Pueblo Viejo (Spanish "Old Town), located some six kilometers northwest of town.

[785] *Tz'oloj Che'* (Willow Tree). This is in the area of Santa María Chiquimula, likely the nearby ruins known as Pugertinamit located southwest of town (Fox 1978, 129; Carmack 1981, 186). The region became subject to the Nima Quichés in the mid-fifteenth century (Carmack 1973, 291; Recinos 1957).

[786] *Xrixowaj.* This reading is based on *xowaj,* "to respect, obey, revere, pay homage" (Basseta).

[787] This refers to an early form of highland Maya ritual sacrifice or execution. The following is a description from the *Annals of the Cakchiquels*:

> Then began the execution of Tolgom. He dressed and covered himself with his ornaments. Then they tied him with his arms extended to a poplar tree to shoot him with arrows. Afterwards all the warriors began to dance. The music to which they danced is called the song of Tolgom. Following this they began to shoot the arrows, but no one of them hit the cords [with which he was tied], but instead they fell beyond the gourd tree, in the place of Qakbatzulú where all the arrows fell. At last our ancestor Gagavitz shot the arrow which flew directly to the spot called *Cheetzulú* and pierced Tolgom. After which all of the warriors killed him. Some of the arrows entered [his body] and others fell farther away. And when that man died, his blood was shed in abundance behind the poplar. Then they came and completed the division [of pieces of him] among all the warriors of the seven tribes that took part in the offering and the sacrifice, and his death was commemorated thereafter in the month of Uchum. Every year they gathered for their festivals and orgies and shot at the children, but instead [of arrows] they shot at them with alder branches as though they were Tolgom. Thus our grandfathers related of old, oh, our sons! (Recinos and Goetz 1953, 74–75; for a discussion of this sacrificial ritual see Akkeren 2000, 335–341).

[788] Campbell suggests that this location is the area today known as Ayutla, near Tapachula, Mexico (located just across the border from Guatemala). The name is likely derived from the Nahua *petlatl*—reed mat (Campbell 1983, 84).

THE QUICHÉS GARRISON THE
CONQUERED REGIONS[789]

THUS the sentinels went forth as lookouts against enemy warriors. They became the lineage of watchmen, guardians of the mountains:

"If the nations come again, these will be the guardians," it was said.

Then all the lords gathered their thoughts and sent out their orders:

"They shall be as our stockade, as the representatives of our lineage, as our fortress. They shall become our palisade, the expression of our anger, our prowess in war," said all the lords.

Then the orders were sent out to each of the lineages who were to oppose the enemy warriors. They instructed all of them who were to be sent as guardians of their mountain nations:

"Go, for these are our mountains now. Do not fear. If there are still warriors that attack you or kill you, come at once to notify us and we shall go and kill them." Thus spoke Quicab, along with the Magistrate and the Herald by way of instruction.

And so they went to "put the notch of the arrow to the center of the bowstring,"[790] as it is said.

Thus the grandfathers and fathers came to be separated. All the Quiché people were placed, each of them, on a mountain as guardians. They were guardians of arrows and bowstrings. They went as guardians against war. Thus they did not have a single dawn, nor did they have a single god. They went out to blockade all the citadels:

Ah Uuila[791] and Ah Chulimal,[792]

Zaqui Ya[793] and Xahbaquieh,[794]

Chi Temah[795] and Vahxalahuh,[796]

---

[789] lines 8033–8180

[790] Literally "set the mouth (notch) of the arrow on the mouth (the center point) of the bowstring." The expression refers to being ready for battle.

[791] *Aj U Wi' La* (They of Its Top Stinging Nettles). This is a contracted form of *Aj Chuwi' La* (They of Above Stinging Nettles), which is Chichicastenango. The inhabitants of Chichicastenango are referred to by this name in the *Título de la Casa Ixcuin Nihaib* (Recinos 1957, 71; see also footnote 777).

[792] *Aj Chulimal*. This is perhaps a transcription error for *Aj Ch'umilal* (They of the Stars), one of the lineages mentioned earlier in the text (see footnote 518).

[793] *Saqi Ya'* (White River). Akkeren identifies this as a site west of Chichicastenango (2000, 171).

[794] *Xajb'a Kiej* (Dancing Place/Costume Deer).

Along with Ah Cabracan,[797] Chabi Cac,[798] and Chi Hunahpu,[799]
With Ah Maca[800] and Ah Xay Abah,[801]
Ah Zaccabaha[802] and Ah Ziyaha,[803]
Ah Miquina[804] and Ah Xelahuh.[805]

These went forth as war sentinels to the plains and to the mountains.
They were guardians of the earth. They were sent out by Quicab and
Cauizimah, the Ah Pop and the Ah Pop of the Reception House, as well as
by the Magistrate and the Herald. Four lords sent them out to act as sentinels against the warriors.

Quicab and Cauizimah were the names of the two lords over the
Cavecs;

Quema[806] was the name of the lord over the Nihaibs;

Achac Iboy,[807] then, was the name of the lord over the Ahau Quichés.

These, then, were the names of the lords that sent out messengers and
envoys. They left their vassals and their servants on the mountains, on each
one of the mountains.

And soon after they left, they began to bring back female captives[808]
and male captives, who were presented before Quicab, Cauizimah, the

[795] *Chi Temaj* (At the Tilt/Slope). Akkeren identifies this, as well as Vahxalahuh as sites near
Chichicastenango (2000, 171).

[796] *Wajxalajuj* (Eighteen).

[797] *Aj Kab'raqan* (They of Earthquake). This is perhaps related to a small community that
still carries a similar name, Chicabracan (Place of Earthquakes), nine kilometers east of
Utatlan, where there is a group of Precolumbian ruins including a small masonry temple
(Fox 1978, 42).

[798] *Ch'ab'i Q'aq'* (Arrow Fire). This is a comet (Coto), or a meteor. Perhaps the same as the
settlement of the Uchabahas (see footnote 517).

[799] *Chi Junajpu* (Hunahpu Place).

[800] *Aj Mak'a'* (They of Water Droplets, or alternatively, They of Dawn). Likely the inhabitants of *Pa Mak'a'*, which is today Zacualpa (see footnote 778).

[801] *Aj Xay Ab'aj* (They of Combed Mountain). Akkeren (personal communication) suggests
that this should be Ah Xoy Abah (Polishing Stone/Jasper). The Xoy lineage lived along the
Chixoy River, centered at the place where the road from the Verapaz region crosses it on its
way to Sacapulas. A branch of this lineage settled the modern area of Joyabaj. According to
Ximénez, Joyabaj marked the border between the Central Quiché to the west and the Rabinal
to the east (Ximénez 1929–31, I.lxxiv.484).

[802] *Saqkab'a Ja* (Whitewashed House). Mentioned as the place of the Caocs. This is the
present-day town of Sajcabaja (see footnote 780).

[803] This is likely a transcription error for *Aj Sija'* (They of Flowering Tree Water). This is
the present-day community of Santa Catarina Ixtahuacán.

[804] *Aj Miq'ina'* (They of Hot Water). The same as *Chuwi' Miq'ina'* (Above Hot Water), which
is Totonicapán (see footnote 782).

[805] *Aj Xe' Lajuj* (They of Below Ten). This is Quetzaltenango (see footnote 783).

[806] *Kema* (Weaving). This may be based either on the verb (to weave) or the noun (textile).
I have chosen "Weaving" as it may be understood as either.

Magistrate, and the Herald. They made war with the notch of the arrow and the center of the bowstring, taking female captives and male captives. These envoys came to be warlike then.

Thus they were given gifts. They were increased. The lords provided for[809] them when they came to deliver all of their female captives and male captives.

Thus the lords Ah Pop, Ah Pop of the Reception House, Magistrate, and Herald gathered their thoughts. Then they made a proclamation:

"We shall ennoble[810] they who are truly first among these lineages who have carried the burden of being watchmen."

"I am the Ah Pop."

"I am the Ah Pop of the Reception House."

"The emblems of office of the Ah Pop shall now become yours. You shall be adorned as Lord Magistrates and as Magistrates," said all the lords when they gathered their thoughts.

The Tamub and the Ilocab did the same. The three groups of the Quichés were united.[811]

Thus they ennobled them, giving them their titles. This, then, was their consensus. But it was not there that they ennobled them. There was a designated mountain on which the first vassals and servants were ennobled. Thus all of them were summoned from each of their mountains. They gathered together as one.

THE names of the mountain where they were ennobled were Xe Balax[812] and Xe Camac.[813] This was the edict that was given. There at Chulimal[814] it was done.

---

[807] Achaq Ib'oy (Droppings/Backside/Buttocks Armadillo).

[808] Anab' (sister of a man). In this context these are female captives.

[809] Literally "heartened." In Quiché terminology, this is "to tend to, look after, provide for needs."

[810] Literally "to take, grasp, seize," apparently referring to some ceremonial action when raising a person to the rank of nobility.

[811] "Same face."

[812] Xe' B'alax (Under Twisted Cord).

[813] Xe' K'a'amaq' (Under String).

[814] This mountain was mentioned earlier as one of those conquered by Quicab.

THE TITLES GIVEN TO
THOSE WHO WERE ENNOBLED[815]

THESE, then, were their titles, their nobility, and the tokens of their office:

Twenty magistrates and twenty ah pops, who were raised to nobility by the Ah Pop and the Ah Pop of the Reception House, as well as by the Magistrate and the Herald. Thus all of the magistrates and ah pops received their offices.[816]

Eleven Great Stewards, Magistrates of the Lords, Magistrates of the Zaquics, Military Magistrates,[817] Military Ah Pops, Military Palisade Masters, and Military Border Masters.

These were the titles of the men who were elevated in rank.

They were also named to their seats and to their cushions.[818] These were the first among the vassals and servants of the Quiché people. They were their watchers and their listeners, the notch of the arrow and the center of the bowstring. They encircled the Quichés as their stockade, their enclosure, their fortress, and their palisade.

The Tamub and the Ilocab did likewise. They also ennobled and gave titles to the first among their vassals and their servants on each of the mountains. This therefore was the foundation for the magistrates and ah pops who are assigned to each of the mountains today. This is also the order in which they go out behind the Ah Pop and Ah Pop of the Reception House, and behind the Magistrate and Herald.[819]

---

[815] lines 8181–8231

[816] *Eqalem* (burden, office, stewardship).

[817] *Q'alel Achij* (Magistrate Warriors). *Achij* is "man" but may also refer to "warriors," as in this case. Basseta lists this title as "captain." This office and those that follow are likely military ranks.

[818] In Maya custom, dignitaries are seated on their thrones or benches according to rank.

[819] This likely refers to the order such officers take when walking in procession, or going out to war. Processions are common in traditional Maya communities, and the order of sequence as to who walks behind who is rather rigid.

THE NAMES OF THE GODS' HOUSES[820]

We shall now tell the names of the houses of the gods. These houses were simply named after the gods themselves:

Great Temple of Tohil[821] was the name of the temple that served as the house of Tohil of the Cavecs.

Auilix was the name of the temple that served as the house of Auilix of the Nihaibs.[822]

Figure 76. Temple of Tohil at Cumarcah. Drawing from Rivera y Maestre, *Atlas Guatemalteco*, ca. 1834.

[820] lines 8232–8325

[821] These three temples, dedicated to the patron deities of the Quichés, were the tallest buildings at the site and were arranged on three sides of the central plaza at Cumarcah, although the structure identified as the Hacavitz temple faces away from the plaza (Fernández-Valbuena 1996, 78–80; Cook 2000, 204). The tallest of these was the Temple of Tohil (Carmack 1981, 225–226). Unfortunately, all the stone that once faced the temple has been looted, leaving only its rubble core. It is still possible, however, to determine that the main entrance to the sanctuary faced east, toward the rising sun. According to Ximénez, who visited the site when it was in much better condition, the temple of Tohil had stairways on all four sides, oriented to the cardinal directions (Ximénez 1929–31, I.xxvii.74–75). This is confirmed by a drawing of the temple made by Rivera y Maestra in 1834 which clearly shows stairways on each of its visible sides. The Temple of Tohil was thus similar to other radial stairway temples constructed by the Maya since at least the Late Preclassic Period (Ca. 200 BC-AD 250). Examples include Structure E-VII-sub at Uaxactun, the Lost World Pyramid at

Figure 77. Ruins of the Temple of Auilix at Cumarcah.

And Hacavitz was the name of the temple that served as the house of the god of the Ahau Quichés.[823]

Maize Flower House may surely be seen; Sacrifice House is its other name.

These were great temples wherein were the stone gods. There all the lords of the Quichés worshiped. All the nations worshiped there as well. The nations would enter therein to burn offerings before Tohil first. Then they would worship the Ah Pop and Ah Pop of the Reception House. They would come to give their quetzal feathers and their tribute before the lords—each in turn they would give provisions and sustenance to the

Tikal, Structure 4 at Copan, Structure A-3 at Seibal, El Castillo at Chichen Itza, the Temple of the Seven Dolls at Dzibilchaltun, and the principal temple at Chutixtiox (not far from Cumarcah near Sacapulas). Schele and Mathews associate such radial temples with the first mountain to emerge from the primordial sea at the time of creation (Schele and Mathews 1998, 40–42, 179–182, 368 n. 31). Karl Taube further identifies radial stairway structures as loci for New Fire-making rituals connected with the primordial hearth of creation (Taube 1998, 441–442). Tohil was primarily a fire god, who provided "new fire" for his people by means of a twist-drill (see p. 214; line 5499). John Lloyd Stephens described the appearance of the Temple of Tohil, which he called the *Sacrificatorio* (Spanish: Place of Sacrifice) in the late 1830s:

> It is a quadrangular stone structure, sixty-six feet on each side at the base, and rising in a pyramidal form to the height, in its present condition, of thirty-three feet. On three sides there is a range of steps in the middle, each step seventeen inches high, and but eight inches on the upper surface, which makes the range so steep that in

Figure 78. Ruins of the Temple of Hacavitz at Cumarcah.

Ah Pop and the Ah Pop of the Reception House, the great lords who had brought down their citadels.

Cucumatz and Co Tuha were enchanted people and enchanted lords. Quicab and Cauizimah were also enchanted lords. They knew if there would be war. It was clear before their faces. They saw if there would be death, if there would be hunger. They surely knew if there would be strife. There was an instrument of sight—there was a book. Popol Vuh was their name for it.

But it was not only because of this that they were lords. They were great in their essence. Great as well were their fasts. In order to venerate their

descending some caution is necessary. At the corners are four buttresses of cut stone, diminishing in size from the line of the square, and apparently intended to support the structure. On the side facing the west there are no steps, but the surface is smooth and covered with stucco, gray from long exposure. By breaking a little at the corners we saw that there were different layers of stucco, doubtless put on at different times, and all had been ornamented with painted figures. In one place we made out part of the body of a leopard, well drawn and coloured. The top of the Sacrificatorio is broken and ruined, but there is no doubt that it once supported an altar for those sacrifices of human victims which struck even the Spaniards with horror. It was barely large enough for the altar and officiating priests, and the idol to whom the sacrifice was offered (Stephens 1969, II, 183–184).

Stephens' mention of a jaguar (he incorrectly called it a leopard) mural on the temple of Tohil is significant. Tohil was the principal deity of Balam Quitze whose *nawal*, or animal counterpart, was the jaguar (see p. 245; lines 6766–6779).

temples and venerate their sovereignty, they fasted for long periods of time, and sacrificed[824] before the faces of their gods.

And this was their method of fasting: For nine score days[825] they would fast, and for nine they would sacrifice and burn offerings. Then for thirteen score days they would observe a fast and for thirteen[826] they would sacrifice and burn offerings before the face of Tohil, as well as before the faces of the other gods. They would eat only zapotes, matasanos, and jocotes.[827] They would not eat food made from maize. If they were to sacrifice for seventeen score days, then they would fast for seventeen. Nor did they eat maize. Truly great was the performance of their sacred obligations.[828] This was the sign of their essence.

Neither would they sleep with their women. They would merely provide for each other, fasting in the houses of the gods. Each day they would merely worship, merely burn offerings, and merely offer sacrifices. They were there in the darkness and at dawn, weeping in their hearts and in their bowels, pleading for the light and the lives of their vassals and servants. They would lift up their faces to the sky for their lordship.

This, then, is their pleading before the faces of their gods. This is the crying out of their hearts:

[822] The Auilix Temple is located just east of the Temple of Tohil across a small plaza. It consists of two terraces with a small sanctuary atop the second terrace. A single wide stairway on the west side gives access to the first terrace (Carmack 1981, 272–274). Thus the principal facades of these two temples face one another.

[823] The Temple of Hacavitz is likely the large mound situated on the south side of the main plaza at Cumarcah. Like the other two temples, all the surface stone has been removed and its ancient appearance is thus difficult to determine. Rivera y Maestre (1834) included it in his plan of the city as a pyramidal structure labeled *sacrificatorio* (Spanish: "place of sacrifice"). According to this aerial view plan, the temple faced south onto its own court and complex of great house structures (Carmack 1981, 277–281).

[824] *K'ajb'ik*. This is specific to the sacrifice of human beings (Coto).

[825] *B'elej winaq* (nine people/scores). As a number this is 9 x 20, or 180. It is evident from the context of this passage that the authors are referring to periods of time, although they do not specify what period it is. For purposes of clarity of meaning I have chosen "days," which is the likely implied meaning here.

[826] The authors are indulging in a bit of shorthand here. My understanding of the text is that the "score" here is implied. Thus for each period of thirteen score days they fast, they would sacrifice for thirteen scores of days more.

[827] These are all tropical fruits (see footnotes 463–469).

[828] *Awasinik* (sacred ritual; divinely sanctioned obligations). These fasts are therefore ritually sanctioned abstinences.

THE PRAYER OF THE LORDS TO THEIR GODS[829]

"YEA, pleasing[830] is the day, you, Huracan, and you, Heart of Sky and Earth, you who give abundance[831] and new life,[832] and you who give daughters and sons. Be at peace, scatter your abundance and new life. May life and creation be given. May my daughters and my sons be multiplied and created, that they may provide for you, sustain you, and call upon you on the roads, on the cleared pathways, along the courses of the rivers, in the canyons, beneath the trees and the bushes. Give, then, their daughters and their sons.

May there be no fault, confinement, shame, or misfortune. May no deceiver come behind them or before them. May they not fall[833] or be wounded. May they not be dishonored[834] or condemned. May they not fall below the road or above the road. May they not be stricken[835] or have impedi-

---

[829] lines 8326–8490

[830] *Atob'* is "desirable, pleasing" (Basseta).

[831] *Q'anal,* "yellowness" (richness, abundance, ripeness). This is specifically the abundance of ripe yellow maize, however it is used by the Quichés to refer to abundance or wealth of any kind (B. Tedlock 1982, 114). According to Ruth Bunzel, it may also refer to rebirth and regeneration: "*Qanil (milpa,* cornfield). Symbolic of the regeneration of the earth, of rebirth after, death, as exemplified in the growth of corn. '*Qanil* is the day of the milpa, a good day. It is a day to give thanks for one's *siembres* [plantings], for harvest and planting. After the harvest one waits for the day *qanil,* either 2 or 3 *qanil,* to give thanks. And likewise after planting. This is optional. But it is obligatory for all people to give thanks for their food and their land on the day 8 *qanil.* And each year one does this, until one dies'" (Bunzel 1952, 282).

[832] *Räxal,* "green/blueness" (vitality, newness, freshness, fertility). The combination of green and yellow is still used ceremonially to refer to the concept of "abundance." Thus in the prayers of Quiché *aj q'ij* priests, the litany of deities they invoke include the "green shoulder, yellow shoulder of the world," described as "the procreative powers of the earth" (Bunzel 1952, 266).

[833] *Mepajik* (may they not fall). This is to fall physically as well as morally (into scandal or shame). A common expression today when saying goodbye, or when passing someone on the road, is *matzaq pa b'e* (don't fall on the road).

[834] *Mejoxowik* (may they not be dishonored, seduced, disgraced). This may refer to any type of disgrace, but it applies most particularly to violations of sexual prohibitions.

[835] *Pak'* (strike, blow). This may be physical but it also refers to calumny or slander. The highland Maya are somewhat obsessed by slander and envy, because such things may lead to the ancestors or gods punishing them with illness or death if such words are believed. For this reason they are constantly asking what people are saying about them. When a person falls ill, people discuss at great length whether this is due to some fault on the part of that person, or whether it is the result of groundless slanders. The following is a ceremonial prayer to the Earth deity given by a priest as protection from envy on the day 8 *Aq'b'al,*designated as the

ments[836] placed behind them or before them. May you place them on green roads and on green pathways. May they not be blamed or confined. Do not hide yourselves from them nor curse them. May their existence be favored, so that they may be providers and sustainers to you, to your mouths and to your faces, you, Heart of Sky and you, Heart of Earth, you, Bundled Glory,[837] and you as well Tohil, Auilix, and Hacavitz, Womb of Sky and Womb of Earth, the Four Sides and the Four Corners. May there be only light, only security within your mouths and before your faces, O gods."

Thus it was that the lords fasted during the nine score days, the thirteen score days, and the seventeen score days as well. They fasted often, crying out in their hearts on behalf of their vassals and servants, as well as on behalf of all their women and children. Thus each of the lords carried out his obligations. This was their way of showing veneration for their lordship. This was the lordship of the Ah Pop, the Ah Pop of the Reception House, the Magistrate, and the Herald. They would go in, two by two in succession,[838] to bear responsibility for the nations and all the Quiché people. In unity went forth the foundation[839] of their word, and the foundation of their provision and sustenance. The root of the word went forth as well from the Tamub and the Ilocab, along with that of the Rabinals and the Cakchiquels,

---

day when ceremonies are to be performed as protection from slander: "Hail, World Tsokomá, come hither; reveal your face and aspect. Thou my seat, thou, my shrine, thou seest me, thou hearest me before this World and the white light of day. It is I who kneel and bow me down before the world of Heaven. Perhaps it is my mission, perhaps it is my sacred office that makes it necessary that I go about before the face and person of the world. Perhaps I pray for wealth from my business and from my land; out of my house and out of my corn and out of my wheat and out of my food and drink. It seems I am in this world. It is not my fault, and also there is no fault in my wealth. Divine World, come hither! If we do well, somewhere people feel pain because of it; and also if we are poor, people mistreat us. Always there are slanders and calumnies, fires and flames of envy in the world. But for my part, Divine World, I know that God sees us in the cold wind, at dawn, at midday and at sunset. The Lord of the Clear Light sees us.... And also my beloved wife, may she not fall into error; and may there be no slanders or calumnies concerning her. And perhaps we, too, have slandered and maligned in our folly. Do we not judge and speak before great people and small people? But we do not wish this. We wish only good words before God. And also that good fortune be granted us, to go about as did the people of past time" (Bunzel 1952, 346; cf. Schultze-Jena 1954, 43–44). Watanabe suggests that this conspicuous uneasiness characteristic of highland Maya societies with regard to what the neighbors are thinking and saying "creates the reserve found in Chimalteco interpersonal relations" (Watanabe 1992, 100–101).

[836] *Toxk'om* (impediment, stumbling block) is a physical impediment or obstruction, but also implies stumbling from faults, disputes, or life's difficulties.

[837] *Pisom Q'aq'al* (Bundled Glory/Flame). This is the sacred bundle left by the four progenitors before their deaths (pp. 254–255; lines 7276–7300).

[838] *Kejalow kib'* (to succeed or replace in office).

[839] *Xe'* (root) refers to the "source, foundation, beginning."

the Ah Tziquinahas, the Tuhalahas, and the Uchabahas. In unity they would go forth to bear the burden of the Quichés. For this was done for all.

They did not merely exercise their lordship. They did not merely receive gifts, nor were they merely provided for or sustained; nor did they merely receive food and drink. All this was not without purpose. They did not achieve their lordship, their glory, or their sovereignty by deception or theft. They did not merely crush the canyons and the citadels of the small nations and the great nations. Great was the price that the nations gave in return. They sent jade and precious metal, the size of four fingers across and even the size of a fist across with the thumb extended. They sent precious gems and glittering stones. They sent as well cotinga feathers,[840] oriole feathers,[841] and the feathers of red birds.[842] The tribute of all the nations thus came before the faces of the enchanted lords Cucumatz and Co Tuha; and also before the faces of Quicab and Cauizimah, the Ah Pop and Ah Pop of the Reception House, Magistrate and Herald. It was no small thing that they did. Nor was it merely a few of the nations that were brought down. Many groups of nations came with their tribute for the Quichés.

The lords had suffered affliction, but they overcame. Their glory did not come quickly, for it was not until Cucumatz that the greatness of their lordship began.

We shall now give, then, the sequence of the lords' generations, along with the names of all the lords.

[840] *Raxon* (*Cotinga amabilis*) is a dovelike tropical bird with turquoise-blue plumage and a purple breast and throat. According to the *Annals of the Cakchiquels*, the highly prized feathers of the cotinga were given as tribute by the Cakchiquel clans to the lords of Tulan in the East (Recinos and Goetz 1953, 48). In the *Popol Vuh*, the cotinga is often paired with the larger quetzal (see p. 68; lines 145–146), and perhaps that bird's iridescent blue/green feathers are also implied here.

[841] *K'ub'ul*. This is the lowland Maya word for the oriole, as well as other related birds with predominantly yellow feathers.

[842] *Ch'aktik*. According to Basseta, this is "a colorful bird." In Yucatec, *ch'ak* is the color red. Likely these three birds were chosen as representative of all the exotic feathers the Quichés received in tribute because they comprise the principal colors of green/blue (the same word in the Quiché language), yellow/orange (also the same word in the Quiché language), and red.

THE GENERATIONS
OF QUICHÉ LORDS[843]

THESE are the generations and the house divisions of lordship, of all who had their dawn:

Balam Quitze, Balam Acab, Mahucutah, and Iqui Balam were the first of our grandfathers and fathers when the sun appeared, along with the moon and stars.

These, then, are the generations and the house divisions of lordship. We shall truly begin here at the roots. The lords acceded in pairs, each generation of lords succeeding their grandfathers and the lords of the citadel, even each and every one of the lords.

Here, then, shall appear the face[844] of each of the lords, even each and every one of the lords of the Quichés:

---

[843] lines 8491–8515

[844] This passage may refer to an illustration of the heads or faces of each lord. Similar illustrations appear in the lowland Maya *Books of Chilam Balam* (Craine and Reindorp 1979; Edmonson 1982, 1986).

THE DYNASTY OF CAVEC
QUICHÉ LORDS[845]

BALAM Quitze was the founder[846] of the Cavecs.

Co Caib was the second generation after Balam Quitze.

Balam Co Nache, who initiated[847] the office of Ah Popol, was the third generation.

Co Tuha and Iztayub were the fourth generation.

Cucumatz and Co Tuha were the foundation[848] for the enchanted lords. They were the fifth generation.

Tepepul[849] and Iztayul were, then, the sixth house division.

Quicab and Cauizimah were the seventh succession of lords, who attained the pinnacle of enchantment.

Tepepul[850] and Iztayub were the eighth generation.

Tecum[851] and Tepepul were the ninth generation.

---

[845] lines 8516–8555

[846] *Xe'nab'al* (root-beginning).

[847] *Xtikib'an* (he planted).

[848] *U xe'* (its root).

[849] *Tepepul*. This name is likely derived from the Nahua *tepeuh* (conqueror, majesty) and *pul/pol* (great), giving the reading "Great Conqueror." The Quiché word *tepewal* is "glory, majesty, sovereignty." Alternatively, the name may be derived from the Nahua *tepe* (mountain) with an augmentative suffix *pul/pol* (great, large) yielding "Great Mountain" (Campbell 1983, 85).

[850] During the reign of this Tepepul (acceded ca. 1475), a severe frost caused a famine at the Cakchiquel capital of Iximche. A spy informed the Quichés of the resultant weakness in the Cakchiquels' defenses and for a year they prepared their warriors for a decisive invasion. At last Tepepul and Iztayul, accompanied by their patron god Tohil, marched on Iximche. The Cakchiquels, however, had been informed of the attack and were ready for them:

> When the sun rose on the horizon and shed its light over the mountain, the war cries broke out and the banners were unfurled; the great flutes, the drums, and the shells resounded. It was truly terrible when the Quichés arrived. They advanced rapidly, and their ranks could be seen at once descending to the foot of the mountain.... Then came the encounter. The clash was truly terrible. The shouts rang out, the war cries, the sound of flutes, the beating of drums and the shells, while the warriors performed their feats of magic (Recinos and Goetz 1953, 103).

The resulting defeat of the Quichés was a devastating blow from which they never fully recovered. The *Annals of the Cakchiquels* claims that more than 16,000 Quiché warriors died in the battle (Recinos and Goetz 1953, 103). Tepepul and Iztayul were taken prisoner, as was the image of the god Tohil. The Quichés never again attempted to strike the citadel of Iximche again, although border conflicts and court intrigues continued for decades.

[851] *Tekum*. This is likely "enthroned" based on the Nahua *tecalli* (throne, seat). Tedlock cites a Quiché dictionary compiled by Fermín Joseph Tirado in 1787 which lists tekum as a "large, black butterfly that flies with great speed" (D. Tedlock 1996, 333 n. 195).

Vahxaqui Cam[852] and Quicab were the tenth generation of lords.

Vucub Noh[853] and Cauatepech[854] were the eleventh house division of lords.

[852] *Wajxaqi K'a'am* (Eight Cord). Recinos (1950, 230 n. 9) suggests that this is likely a Quiché translation of a Nahua language date on the Mexican Calendar, *Chicuey Malinalli* (Eight Grass).

[853] *Wuqub' No'j* (Seven Thoughts) reigned ca. 1500–1523. This is a day on the traditional 260 day calendar, and is likely the day on which this lord was born. His reign was marked by continued war with the Cakchiquels. In the year 1514, two wars were fought, the first at the river Sotzil and the second at Mukche. The Quiché Magistrate of War (*Q'alel Achi*) died in the latter conflict and many prisoners were taken. Carmack identifies this lord with Ahpop Tuh, the father of Yaxonkik who was soundly defeated in battle with the Cakchiquels in 1517 (Carmack 1981, 138). The *Annals of the Cakchiquels* claims that "during this year our fathers and grandfathers destroyed the Quichés once again; they exterminated them as if by lightning" (Recinos and Goetz 1953, 114). In his day, the Quichés also came into closer contact with the Aztecs of Central Mexico. In 1501, the Aztec king Ahuitzotl sent "merchants and officials" to the court of Cumarcah, likely to demand tribute and/or vassalage. The Quichés ordered them out of their territory (Fuentes y Guzmán 1932–33, 6, 47). Apparently Vucub Noh did not feel as comfortable in his position by 1510, for in that year the Quichés began to pay tribute to the Aztec lord Moctezuma in the form of quetzal feathers, gold, precious stones, cacao, and cloth. These payments continued until the fall of the Aztec empire to the Spaniards (Recinos 1957, 84; Carmack and Mondloch 1983, 142). These ties were strengthened by marriage alliances. According to the *Buenabaj Pictorials*, recently discovered by Carmack in the Momostenango area, "the lord Quiché... wed two of the daughters of Mendectzum [Moctezuma] called Malintzin" (Carmack 1973, 371). In 1512, Moctezuma sent an emissary named Witzitzil to warn the Quichés of the arrival of the Spaniards along the Mexican Gulf Coast. He warned them to prepare to defend themselves (Recinos 1957, 84–85). In 1519, a plague broke out at Iximche: "First they became ill of a cough, they suffered from nosebleeds and illness of the bladder. It was truly terrible, the number of dead there were in that period.... Little by little, heavy shadows and black night enveloped our fathers and grandfathers and us also, oh, my sons! when the plague raged" (Recinos and Goetz 1953, 115). The plague lasted at least until 1521 and, although Quiché records do not mention it, it is likely that it spread throughout the Guatemalan highlands. Edmonson suggests that this may have been an epidemic of smallpox, a disease brought by the early Spanish explorers (Edmonson 1965, 5). A similar plague struck Yucatán in 1516: "A pestilence seized them, characterized by great pustules, which rotted their bodies with a great stench, so that the limbs fell to pieces in four or five days" (Landa 1941, 42). Perhaps in order to present a united front against the Spanish threat, Vucub Noh negotiated peace with the Cakchiquel lord Belehe Qat in 1522, ending the protracted war that had raged between the two nations since the time of Lord Quicab (Recinos and Goetz 1953, 118). This cessation of hostilities did not, however, prevent the Cakchiquels from allying themselves with the invading Spaniards against the Quichés.

[854] *Kawatepech*. Tedlock suggests that this name is derived from the Nahua *cauani* (to leave a memory behind) and *tepechtli* (base, foundation), yielding a compound that may be read as "founder" (1996, 333 n. 195).

[855] *Oxib' Kiej* (Three Deer). A day on the traditional 260 day calendar. Shortly before the Spanish invasion of Guatemala in 1524, lord Vucub Noh died leaving Oxib Quiej to face the

Oxib Quieh[855] and Beleheb Tzi[856] were the twelfth generation of lords. These exercised lordship when Donadiu[857] arrived. They were hung[858] by the Castilian[859] people.

foreign threat (Fuentes y Guzmán 1932–33,7.390).

[856] *B'elejeb' Tz'i'* (Nine Dog). A day on the traditional 260 day calendar.

[857] *Donadiu* (or *Tonatiu*) was the name given to Don Pedro de Alvarado, the Spanish captain of Hernán Cortés who conquered the highland Maya region of what is today Guatemala. This is the Quiché Maya version of Tonatiuh (Nahua for "sun, heat"), the name by which Alvarado was known to the Aztecs and his Tlaxcalan mercenaries. He likely received this nickname because of his blonde hair, a physical trait unknown in the Precolumbian New World (other than albinos, which are still called "children of the sun" in many Quiché communities). The name may have had further significance for the Quichés, however. Earlier in the *Popol Vuh* text, the appearance of a new sun represented the death of the old world and the establishment of new, divinely-sanctioned political power. Alvarado as the new "sun" destroys the old world and its gods inaugurating a new age. For this reason, Jesus Christ as the newly-established patron deity is equated with the sun throughout the Maya world (La Farge and Byers 1931, 113–114; La Farge 1947, 104; Mace 1970, 24; Thompson 1970, 234; Vogt 1970, 4; Morley et al. 1983, 465; Cook 1986, 140, 148; Tarn and Prechtel 1986, 174, 180–181; Freidel et al. 1993, 292; Cook 2000, 215–219). At Jacaltenango, there is a myth for the foundation of the town in which Christ's birth is associated with the first rise of the sun, whose rays kill his enemies who had tried to hide in caves and under water. This allows Jacaltenango to be founded in the center of the world. La Farge and Byers suggest that this myth is a syncretized version of the account of the dawn in the *Popol Vuh*, which also ended the previous age and turned its inhabitants to stone (La Farge and Byers 1931, 113–114). At Santiago Atitlán, Maya sculptors carved a vessel bearing a sun on the left and right sides of the community's colonial era church altarpiece. In his explanation of the sun vessels, one of the sculptors, Diego Chávez Petzey, said that the sun on the left represents a tortilla, because maize is the Maya "sun." The sun on the right is the Christian eucharistic Host. He went on to say that life cannot exist without sacrifice. Maize must be crushed on a grinding stone before it can be made into tortillas. The wheat in the sacramental Host must also be ground and baked. The sun can only rise in the east after it has been buried in the west: "Tortillas, the Host, Jesus Christ, and the sun give life because they are first killed. Tortillas and bread result from the death of maize and wheat so that they can give us life. They are therefore gods." Nicolás Chávez Sojuel, who also worked on the altarpiece carvings, told me that when the Spaniards came the earth died along with the ancient gods and kings. When I asked him how the world could die, he replied: "The earth has died many times. Each time the world and its gods are reborn to new life and they regain their former power and new gods are added.... The saints today have Spanish names because the old earth died in the days of the Spanish conquerors. When the spirit keepers of the world appeared again they were the saints, but they do the same work that the old gods did anciently" (Christenson 2001, 135).

[858] Following a brief and disasterous defensive campaign led by the ruler's grandson, Tecum (who was killed at the decisive battle at Quetzaltenango), the Quiché lords Oxib Quieh and Beleheb Tzi invited Pedro de Alvarado and his conquering army to enter their capital city of Cumarcah without resistance on March 7, 1524. Once inside the city, Alvarado suspected treachery and ordered the arrest, torture, and execution of the lords. The following is taken from his report to Hernán Cortés: "And I saw that by occupying their land and burning it I could bring them into the service of His Majesty. Thus I decided to burn the lords who, at the time I desired to burn them, as would appear in their confessions, admitted that they were the ones who had ordered and carried on the war.... Therefore since I knew them to have such ill will toward the service of His Majesty, and for the good and tranquility of the land,

Tecum[860] and Tepepul[861] paid tribute before the faces of the Castilian people. These had been begotten as the thirteenth generation of lords.

I burned them, and I commanded to be burned the town of Utatlan [the Nahuatl language
version of Cumarcah as named by Alvarado's Tlaxcalan mercenaries] to its foundations, for
it was dangerous and strong.... All they that were taken prisoners of war were branded and
made slaves" (Alvarado 1946 [1524], 457–459, translation by author). The Cakchiquel version
of this incident, as recorded in the *Annals of the Cakchiquels*, confirms that the Quiché lords
were burned: "Then [the Spaniards] went forth to the city of Gumarcaah, where they were
received by the kings, the Ahpop and the Ahpop Qamahay, and the Quichés paid them
tribute. Soon the kings were tortured by Tunatiuh. On the day 4 Qat [March 7, 1524] the kings
Ahpop and Ahpop Qamahay were burned by Tunatiuh. The heart of Tunatiuh was without
compassion for the people during the war" (Recinos and Goetz 1953b, 120). It is unclear
whether Alvarado's suspicion of treachery was well-founded, however, Fray Bartolomé de las
Casas believed that the Quiché lords were executed for failing to satisfy Alvarado's demand
for gold, which is rare in Guatemala: "Guiltless of other fault and without trial or sentence,
he immediately ordered them to be burned alive. They killed all the others with lances and
knives; they threw them to savage dogs, that tore them to pieces and ate them; and when
they came across some lord, they accorded him the honour of burning in live flames. This
butchery lasted about seven years from 1524 to 1531. From this may be judged what numbers
of people they destroyed" (MacNutt 1909, 352–353). This version of events is supported
by the sixteenth century account of the trip to Spain by don Juan Cortés in 1557, in which
Alvarado is accused of burning the grandfather of don Juan because he "did not give him
gold" (Carrasco 1967, 253).

The "hanging" mentioned in this passage of the *Popol Vuh* likely refers not to the
execution of the lords, which was by flame, but rather to the torture and elicitation of
confessions mentioned by both Alvarado and the Cakchiquel document. Tedlock notes that
the method for obtaining such confessions, according to the Spanish methods of the time,
was to hang a prisoner by the wrists while inflicting various types of torture (D. Tedlock
1996, 334 n. 195). Undoubtedly this must have been done in a very public way to have
impressed the authors of the text writing decades after the event.

[859] Castilian. Technically the inhabitants of the Castile region of Spain, however, the term
was used in the sixteenth century to refer to Spaniards in general.

[860] These were the sons of the Ah Pop and Ah Pop of the Reception House executed by
the Spaniards during the Conquest. They served as lords of Santa Cruz Utatán, built over
the ruins of the old capital Cumarcah. Although at first they paid tribute to the Spaniards,
there is some evidence that they eventually rebelled. Carmack identifies Tecum as a certain
Chignauiucelut (Nahua for 9 Jaguar), the leader of a revolt mentioned by Fuentes y Guzmán
who was "put in possession of the government at Utatlan by Don Pedro de Alvarado on the
death of his father" (Fuentes y Guzmán 1932–33, 8.48; Carmack 1981, 308). His rebellion
was likely tied to the revolt that involved the communities of Aguacatan, Sacapulas, and
Utatlan and which was described in the *actas de cabildo* dated at the end of 1534: "The devil
appeared before them and told them that soon all the Christians of this city [Santiago] would
die and that they should kill those other Spaniards found in towns outside of the city. Thus
it was that in some of these towns more than ten Spaniards were murdered and sacrificed,
along with a great number of their Indian slaves and servants" (Kramer 1994, 122). The
rebellion was quickly put down by Pedro de Alvarado's brother Jorge who punished the
rebels by "killing them, throwing them to the dogs, hanging them, and throwing them
into pits" (Ibid., 122). Lord Tecum was likely one of those hung after he was captured in
Chiquimula in 1534 or 1535.

[861] Tepepul is identified by the Nahua version of his calendric name Chicuey Quiaguit
(Nahua: "8 Rain") in the early Colonial document, *Don Juan Cortés, cacique de Santa Cruz*

Don Juan de Rojas[862] and Don Juan Cortes[863] were the fourteenth generation of lords, begotten sons of Tecum and Tepepul.

Quiché (Carrasco 1967, 253). According to the *Annals of the Cakchiquels*, the Quiché lord
Quivawit Caok (8 Rain), was hung by Alvarado on May 26, 1540 along with the Cakchiquel
lord Ahpozotzil Cahi Ymox. They were both in prison at the time for rebellion (Recinos
and Goetz 1953, 132). Colonial records list a Quiché ruler named Sequechul (likely a poor
transcription for Tepepul) who was imprisoned for participating in an insurrection and
eventually hung in 1540 (Recinos 1950, 232 n. 12). Soon after this incident, Alvarado left
Guatemala in search of a western sea-route from Mexico to the Spice Islands (Philippines).
He never returned, dying in Michoacan a year later in 1541 (Akkeren 2003).

[862] Juan de Rojas, son of Tecum (9 Jaguar), was eventuallly recognized by the Spaniards
as the Ah Pop of the Cavec lineage. At some point following the Spanish conquest, the
surviving lords of the highland Maya lineages were baptized as Christians and adopted
Spanish names. Ximénez doubted that this took place when Alvarado invaded highland
Maya territory, and suggested that the baptisms began several years later when the first
missionaries arrived in Guatemala (Ximénez 1929–31, I.xli.128). Roman Catholicism was
not formally established in Guatemala until 1534, when Bishop Francisco Marroquín arrived
in the capital city of Santiago de los Caballeros (Pueblo Viejo, a town not far from the present-
day city of Antigua), recently founded by Jorge de Alvarado, the brother of the conqueror
Pedro de Alvarado. Over the next few years, Bishop Marroquín sent a few missionary friars
with portable altars to the various Indian towns and villages to baptize the inhabitants and
destroy any remnants of "idolatry" and "paganism" that may have survived the purges of the
conquest itself. There were instances of serious resistance to the labors of the missionaries.
The following is an account given by Ximénez:

> It happened in this kingdom soon after being conquered that, hearing of the lives
> of Christ and of Our Lady, John the Baptist, and Saint Peter and others which the
> priests had taught them, there arose a Mexican Indian, a pseudo-prophet. He taught
> them that Huhapu [Hunahpu] was God, and that Hununapu [One Hunahpu] was the
> son of God; Xuchinquezal, which is Mexican, or Aquiexquic [Xkik', or Lady Blood]
> was Saint Mary; Vaxaquicab was Saint John the Baptist, and Huntihax was Saint Paul.
> This caused so much commotion among the Indians that the kingdom was nearly lost
> because of it, for they came to imagine that our Holy Gospel told them nothing new
> and that they already knew of it (Ximénez 1929–31, I.xxiii.57).

Early evangelization efforts focused on survivors of the old highland Maya nobility in
the hope that they would set an example for the rest of the people. Baptism was also a
necessary step for any Maya of noble birth who aspired to a place in the new political order,
since without it the Spanish authorities would not recognize their legitimacy or territorial
claims. That this is the case here is evident by the title "Don." This was given to those Maya
noblemen who professed faith in Christ as well as those who could prove their legitimacy
in court. Many of the documents composed by the Maya in the sixteenth century were
"titles" written for the purpose of establishing the legal legitimacy of former ruling lords
and their descendents in an effort to recover hereditary honors. As noblemen recognized
by the Spanish Crown, they were allowed to receive some tribute from their subjects, to be
exempt from compulsory labor, and to ride horses. In addition, baptism afforded a measure
of protection from the excesses of Spanish rule. Without it, unconverted Maya were subject
to enslavement until the reforms of Governor Alonso López de Cerrato abolished the practice
after 1548.

Don Juan de Rojas was likely named after the Spanish captain Diego de Rojas who came
to Guatemala at the orders of Hernán Cortés in the latter half of 1524 with fifty Spanish
soldiers (Akkeren 2003). Thus, Juan de Rojas must have been born sometime between this
year and ca. 1530 when Diego de Rojas departed for Peru. When his father was hung in ca.

1535, Juan de Rojas would have been too young to rule, leaving the Quichés without effective leadership for some time. He had begun to exercise some measure of power by at least 1550, when he became involved in a land dispute and demanded that certain merchants from the Utatlan area pay tribute to him (Lutz 1994, 25–26 n. 28). In his mature years as a native *cacique*, Juan de Rojas collected tribute, carried out censuses, provided labor, enforced church attendance and instruction, and acted as the principal judge in local disputes (Carmack 1981, 313). According to Ximénez, Juan de Rojas was given a special hall at the Royal Palace of Guatemala next to that of the president. Here he administered the affairs of the Maya as the vassal lord of the Spaniards (Ximénez 1929–31, I.xxviii.79).

[863] Juan Cortés, son of Tepepul, was recognized by the Spaniards as the Ah Pop of the Reception House. Juan Cortés petitioned the Spanish crown to restore the rights and privileges of lordship that the ancient Quiché lords had enjoyed prior to the Conquest. Accompanied by a Dominican priest, he sailed to Spain in 1557 to press his claim before King Philip II (Carrasco 1967). Unfortunately his ship was attacked by French pirates who seized his documents, which may have included Precolumbian painted codices. He was nevertheless granted audiences before high officials in Spain. Ultimately, Franciscans who opposed the efforts of the Dominicans in favor of the Quiché lords succeeded in opposing these claims on the grounds that it would foster further revolts by the Indians. Spanish authorities in Guatemala also urged caution in granting too much authority to the old Quiché nobility. In a letter to the Spanish crown written in 1552 by Alonso López Cerrato, Governor of Guatemala, the ancient Quiché lords wielded tremendous religious as well as political power over their subjects and could prove dangerous if they were to rebel, "because anciently they revered [them] as gods, and if this persists, the lords could raise the land easily" (Carmack 1973, 379).

THE GREAT HOUSES
OF THE CAVEC LORDS[864]

THESE are the generations, the house divisions of lordship, for the Ah Pop and Ah Pop of the Reception House over the Cavec Quichés. We shall now name the great houses of each of the lords of the lineages after the Ah Pop and Ah Pop of the Reception House.

These are the nine great houses of the nine lineages of the Cavecs, along with the titles for each of the lords of the great houses:

Lord Ah Pop has one great house; Guarded House[865] is the name of this great house.[866]

Lord Ah Pop of the Reception House; Bird House[867] is the name of this great house.

Great Steward of the Cavecs has one great house.

Lord Ah Tohil has one great house.

Lord Ah Cucumatz has one great house.

Councilor of the Stacks has one great house.

Emissary of the Deer House has one great house.

---

[864] lines 8556–8595

[865] *K'u Ja* (Guarded House). *K'u* is "guarded, hidden, covered." Coto lists *Qu hay* as a "granary," indicating that such guarded houses may have been used to hold food stores or tribute payments.

[866] John Lloyd Stephens, who visited the site of Cumarcah in the late 1830s, gave the following description of the principal palace (or great house) there:

> In part, however, the floor remains entire, with fragments of the partition walls, so that the plan of the apartments can be distinctly made out. This floor is of a hard cement, which, though year after year washed by the floods of the rainy season, is hard and durable as stone. The inner walls were covered with plaster of a finer description, and in corners where there had been less exposure were the remains of colours; no doubt the whole interior had been ornamented with paintings (Stephens 1969, II, 183).

This was likely the principal great house of the site belonging to the Ah Pop of the Cavecs located in the southwest corner of Cumarcah. Wauchope began excavation of this palace complex in 1970 and uncovered a small fragment of a mural in the northern section depicting "a blue lake with yellow shells, covered by an ornamented canopy, with a much-plumed green snake winding above it" (Wauchope 1965, 67). This was painted on the walls of a small room with white-plaster floors and clay walls. Wallace continued work at the site and uncovered further traces of these murals. The principal scene depicts a warrior painted in Mixteca-Puebla style covered with jade beads and feathers and carrying a shield in one hand and a rattle in the other (Carmack 1981, 291). Another mural discovered by Wallace depicts the lower portion of a dancing monkey, perhaps a reference to the twin sons Hun Batz and Hun Chouen who were transformed into monkeys and became the patron deities of scribes and artists.

[867] *Tz'ikina Ja* (Bird House).

Figure 79. The ruins of a complex of "great houses," or palaces, at Cumarcah.

Councilor in the Ballcourt of Punishment guards his great house.

Tepeu Yaqui[868] has one great house.

THESE, then, are the nine lineages of the Cavecs. Numerous are the vassals and servants that pertain to the nine great houses.

[868] *Tepew Yaki* (Sovereign Yaqui/Mexican). This office does not appear in the previous list of Cavec titles. This office appears in place of the "Mother of the Reception House." There is a people with a similar name (see p. 229).

THE DYNASTY OF NIHAIB LORDS[869]

THESE, then, are the nine highest of the great houses of the Nihaib. We shall first give the dynasty[870] of lords:

They had but one root, planted before the root of the sun and the light of the people. Balam Acab was their first grandfather and father.

Co Acul and Co Acutec were the second generation.

Co Chahuh[871] and Co Tzibaha[872] were the third generation.

Beleheb Queh[873] was the fourth generation.

Co Tuha[874] was the fifth generation.

Batza[875] was the sixth generation.

Iztayul was the seventh generation.

Co Tuha headed the eighth house division of lordship.

Beleheb Queh was the ninth house division.

Quema,[876] as he is called now, was the tenth generation.

Lord Co Tuha was the eleventh generation.

Don Christoval, as he is called, exercised lordship under the Castilian people.

Don Pedro de Robles is the Lord Magistrate today.

---

[869] lines 8596–8631

[870] *Le'ab'al rib' ajawarem* (self-generation lordship). This is a dynastic list or genealogy.

[871] *K'o Chajuj* (Lord Guardian).

[872] *K'o Tz'ib'a Ja* (Lord Writing/Painting House).

[873] *B'elejeb' Kej* (Nine Deer). A day on the traditional 260 day calendar.

[874] *K'o Tuja* (Lord Sweatbath).

[875] *B'atz'a* (Thread/Howler Monkey).

[876] *Kema* (Loom).

THE GREAT HOUSES
OF THE NIHAIB LORDS[877]

THESE, then, are all the lords who follow behind the Lord Magistrate. We shall list now the lords of each of the great houses:

Lord Magistrate is the first lord over the Nihaibs. He has one great house.

Lord Herald has one great house.

Lord Magistrate of the Reception House has one great house.

Great Reception House has one great house.

Mother of the Reception House has one great house.

Great Reception House has one great house.

Great Steward of the Nijaibs has one great house.

Lord Auilix has one great house.

Yacolatam (Corner of the Reed Mat) has one great house.

THESE, then, are the names of the great houses over the Nijaibs, of the nine lineages of the Nijaibs, as they are called. There are many lineages among them, each exercising lordship. We have listed the first among these.

[877] lines 8632–8663

THE DYNASTY OF
AHAU QUICHÉ LORDS[878]

THESE, then, are they of the Ahau Quichés:
Mahucutah was their grandfather and father. He was the first person.
Co Ahau was the name of the second generation lord.
Caq Lacan,[879]
Co Cozom,[880]
Co Mahcun,[881]
Vucub Ah,[882]
Co Camel,[883]
Co Yaba Coh,[884]
Vinac,[885]
Bam.[886]

---

[878] lines 8664–8679
[879] *Kaq' Lakan* (Red/Fire Banner).
[880] The manuscript reads *qo cozom*. This is most likely *K'o Q'osom* (Lord Thicket/Bramble/Chaff) The precise meaning of this name is unclear, however, because of the limitations of the Latin alphabet used. *Cozom* may also be read as *Kosom* (Fatigued/Perplexed); *K'osom* (Reclined); or *Qosom* (Turkey Ruffling His Wings).
[881] *Maj Kun. Aj Kun* is a "healer/doctor." The *m-* prefix is a negative marker, which would make the name read something like "Not a Healer." As a verb, *maj* is "to seize, steal, grasp." Thus an alternative might be "Seizes Medicine."
[882] *Wuqub' Aj* (Seven Reed/Cane). A day in the traditional 260 day calendar.
[883] *K'o Kame'l* (Lord Humble).
[884] *K'o Yab'a Koj* (Lord Sick Puma).
[885] *Winaq* (Person).
[886] *B'am* (Counselor/Doer).

THE GREAT HOUSES OF
THE AHAU QUICHÉ LORDS[887]

These, then, are the lords over the Ahau Quichés. These are their generations and house divisions as well. These are the titles of the lords within each of the great houses. There are only four great houses:

Herald Lord is the name of the first lord. He has one great house.
Emissary Lord is the second lord. He has one great house.
Great Steward Lord is the third lord. He has one great house.
Hacavitz, then, is the fourth lord. He has one great house.
Thus there are four great houses over the Ahau Quichés.

---

[887] lines 8680–8695

[888] lines 8696–8716

[889] The *Nim Ch'okoj* (Great Stewards) of the three principal Quiché lineages identify themselves here as the authors of the "word," likely the *Popol Vuh* manuscript itself.

[890] *Ilb'al* (means of seeing, instrument of sight). This is the term used exclusively in the manuscript to describe the original Precolumbian codex version of the *Popol Vuh* (see pp. 64, 287; lines 50–57, 8276).

[891] *Sachinaq* (lost, vanished).

[892] Bishop Francisco Marroquín blessed the ruins of Cumarcah in 1539, renaming it Santa Cruz (Spanish: "Holy Cross"). In about 1555, the Spaniards founded a new administrative center three miles to the east, which they also named Santa Cruz del Quiché (Spanish: Holy Cross of the Quiché). This was likely carried out under the direction of Alonso de Zorita who administered affairs in various Guatemalan provinces beginning in March 1555, including the area of Utatlan. Akkeren suggests that this compilation of the *Popol Vuh* was carried out

THE THREE GREAT STEWARDS AS
MOTHERS OF THE WORD[888]

THESE, then, are the three Great Stewards. They are like the fathers of all the Quiché lords. As one the three stewards gathered together as the givers of birth, the mothers of the word, and the fathers of the word.[889] Great, in a small way, is the essence of these three stewards.

THESE are: The Great Steward before the Cavecs; before the Nijaibs is the second Great Steward; and before the Ahau Quichés is the third Great Steward. Thus there are three stewards, one before each of the lineages.

But this is the essence of the Quichés, because there is no longer a way of seeing[890] it. It was with the lords at first, but it is now lost.[891]

There is only this. All is now completed concerning Quiché, called Santa Cruz.[892]

Figure 80. Flower market on the steps of the church at Chichicastenango, where the Popol Vuh manuscript came to light at the dawn of the eighteenth century.

in conjunction with the abandonment of the old capital (Akkeren 2003). The resettlement process, which the Spaniards called *congregación* (congregation), followed a uniform pattern throughout Guatemala (García Peláez 1943, 161–166; Betancor and Arboleda 1964). First, a church was erected at the center of the proposed site fronted by an open plaza, or *atrio*, for large assemblies to gather for public ceremonies and indoctrination. The rest of the town was organized into squares divided by streets laid out to the cardinal directions. While the new settlement was under construction, families planted their maize on plots the Spaniards assigned to them in the nearby countryside. When the crops were ready to harvest, the older Precolumbian structures were destroyed to prevent reoccupation, and the people moved into their new homes. Christian missionaries staged elaborate dances and festivals to celebrate the event "so that they would forget their ancient dwellings" (García Peláez 1943, 163).

BIBLIOGRAPHY

Acuña, René.
1969   "Título de los Señores de Sacapulas." In *Folklore Américas,* Vol 28. Los
        Angeles.
1982   *Relaciones geográficas del Siglo XVI: Guatemala.* México: Universidad
        Nacional Autónoma de México.
1998   *Temas del Popol Vuh,* Instituto de Investigaciones Filológicas, Ediciones
        especiales 10. México: Universidad Nacional Autónoma de México.
Ajpacaja Tum, Pedro F., Manuel I. Chox Tum, Francisco L. Tepaz Raxuleu, and Diego
A. Guarchaj Ajtzalam.
1996   *Diccionario K'iche'.* Guatemala: Proyecto Lingüístico Francisco Marroquín.
Akkeren, Ruud W. van.
2000   *Place of the Lord's Daughter.* Leiden: Research School CNWS, Leiden
        University.
2003   "Authors of the Popol Wuj." *Ancient Mesoamerica,* Spring 2003 (In Press).
Alarçon, Baltasar de.
c. 1575 *Sermones en lengua cakchiquel, escritos por varios padres de la Orden de San
        Francisco.* Manuscript in the Bibliothèque Nationale, Paris.
Alvarado López, Miguel.
1975   *Léxico médico quiché-español.* Guatemala: Instituto Indigenista Nacional.
Alvarado, Pedro de.
1979   *Muerte de Pedro de Alvarado: Cartas de Relación de Alvarado a Hernán
        Cortés.* Biblioteca de Cultura Popular, vol. 4. Guatemala: Editorial "José de
        Pineda Ibarra."
Angel, Fray.
c. 1775 *Arte de la lengua cakchiquel.* Manuscript in Bibliothèque Nationale, Paris.
c. 1775 *Vocabulario de la lengua cakchiquel.* Manuscript in Bibliothèque Nationale,
        Paris.
Anleo, Bartolomé de.
c. 1660 *Arte de lengua kiche.* Manuscript in Princeton University Library.
Arzápalo Marín, Ramón.
1987   *El Ritual de los Bacabes.* Edición Facsimilar con Transcripción Rítmica y
        Traducción. Universidad Nacional Autónoma de México, México.
Aulie, H. Wilbur, and Evelyn W. Aulie.
1978   *Diccionario ch'ol-español, español-ch'ol.* México: Instituto Lingüístico de
        Verano.
Baile de la Conquista.
1991   Texto del Municipio de Cantel Quetzaltenango, Guatemala. Guatemala:
        Editorial Piedra Santa.
Barrera Vásquez, Alfredo.
1995   *Diccionario Maya.* México: Editorial Porrua.
Basseta, Fr. Domingo de.
1921 [1698] *Vocabulario en lengua quiché.* Typescript by William Gates of the
        original in the Bibliothèque Nationale, Paris. In the W.E. Gates Collection,
        Special Collections and Manuscript Archives, Harold B. Lee Library,
        Brigham Young University.

Bassie-Sweet, Karen.
  1991   *From the Mouth of the Dark Cave: Commemorative Sculpture of the Late
           Classic Maya.* Norman: University of Oklahoma Press.
  1996   *At the Edge of the World: Caves and Late Classic Maya World View.* Norman:
           University of Oklahoma Press.
Betancor, Alsonso Paez, and Fray Pedro de Arboleda.
  1964   "Relación de Santiago Atitlán, año de 1585." *Anales de la Sociedad de
           Geografía e Historia de Guatemala* 37: 87–106.
Bode, Barbara.
  1961   "The Dance of the Conquest of Guatemala." In *The Native Theatre in
           Middle America.* Middle American Research Institute, Publication 27, pp.
           205–92. New Orleans: Tulane University Press.
Brasseur de Bourbourg, Charles Étienne.
  1857–9 *Histoire des Nations Civilisées des Mexique et de l'Amerique Centrale.* 4
           Volumes. Paris: Arthus Bertrand.
  1860   *Vocabulario quiché y cakchiquel.* Manuscript in Bibliothèque Nationale,
           Paris.
  1861   *Popol Vuh: Le livre sacré et les mythes de l'antiquité americaine.* Paris: A.
           Bertrand.
  1862   *Rabinal-Achi ou le drame-ballet du tun.* Paris: A. Bertrand.
  1961   *Gramática de la lengua Quiché.* Guatemala: Editorial del Ministerio de
           Educación Pública.
Bricker, Victoria R.
  1981   *The Indian Christ, the Indian King.* Austin: University of Texas Press.
Bricker, Victoria R. and Gabrielle Vail.
  1997   *Papers on the Madrid Codex.* Middle American Research Institute
           Publication 64. New Orleans: Tulane University.
Brinton, Daniel G.
  1881   *The Names of the Gods in the Kiché Myths, Central America.* Philadelphia:
           McCalla and Stavely.
  1885   *Annals of the Cakchiquels.* Philadelphia: Library of Aboriginal American
           Literature.
  1894   "Nagualism: A Study in Native American Folklore and History." In
           Proceedings of the American Philosophical Society 33:11–103.
Bunzel, Ruth.
  1952   *Chichicastenango: A Guatemalan Village.* American Ethnological Society
           Publication no. 22. Locust Valley, N.Y.: J. J. Augustin.
Burgess, Dora M. de, and Patricio Xec.
  1955   *Popol Wuj.* Quetzaltenango: El Noticiero Evangélico.
Campbell, Lyle R.
  1970   "Nahua Loan Words in Quichean Languages." *Chicago Linguistics Society*
           6:3–11.
  1983   "Préstamos lingüísticos en el Popol Vuh." In *Nuevas perspectivas sobre el
           Popol Vuh.* Ed. Robert M. Carmack and Francisco Morales Santos, pp.
           81–86. Guatemala: Piedra Santa.
Carlsen, Robert S.
  1997   *The War for the Heart and Soul of a Highland Maya Town.* Austin:
           University of Texas Press.

Carlsen, Robert S., and Martin Prechtel.
1991   "The Flowering of the Dead: An Interpretation of Highland Maya
         Culture." *Man* 26:23–42.
1994   "Walking on Two Legs: Shamanism in Santiago Atitlán, Guatemala."
         In *Ancient Traditions: Culture and Shamanism in Central Asia and the
         Americas.* Ed. Gary Seaman and Jane Day, pp. 77–111. Niwot: University
         Press of Colorado.
Carmack, Robert M.
1968   "Toltec Influence on the Postclassic Culture History of Highland
         Guatemala." In *Archaeological Studies of Middle America.* Middle American
         Research Institute, Publication no. 26, 49–92. New Orleans: Tulane
         University.
1973   *Quichean Civilization.* Berkeley: University of California Press.
1981   *The Quiché Mayas of Utatlán: The Evolution of a Highland Guatemala
         Kingdom.* Norman: University of Oklahoma Press.
1995   *Rebels of Highland Guatemala: The Quiché-Mayas of Momostenango.*
         Norman: University of Oklahoma Press.
Carmack, Robert M., John W. Fox, and Russell E. Stewart.
1975   *La formación del reino quiche.* Instituto de Antropología e Historia de
         Guatemala Special Publication no. 7. Guatemala.
Carmack, Robert M. and James L. Mondloch.
1983   *El Título de Totonicapán.* México, D.F.: Universidad Nacional Autónoma de
         México.
1989   *El Título de Yax y otros documentos quichés de Totonicapán, Guatemala.*
         México: Universidad Nacional Autónoma de México.
Carmack, Robert M., and Francisco Morales Santos.
1983   *Nuevas perspectivas sobre el Popol Vuh.* Guatemala: Editorial Piedra Santa.
Carrasco, Pedro.
1967   "Don Juan Cortés, cacique de Santa Cruz Quiché." *Estudios de cultura
         Maya* 6:251–66.
Cervantes, Fernando.
1994   *The Devil in the New World: The Impact of Diabolism in New Spain.* New
         Haven: Yale University Press.
Chávez, Adrián I.
n.d.   *Ki-Chè Tzib, escritura Ki-chè, y otros temas.* Guatemala: Libreria Evangélica.
1979   *Pop Wuj: Libro de acontecimientos.* México: Ediciones de la Casa Chata.
1997   *Pop-Wuj: Poema Mito-histórico Ki-ché.* Quetzaltenango, Guatemala: Centro
         de Estudios Maya TIMACH.
Christenson, Allen J.
1988   "The Use of Chiasmus by the Ancient Maya-Quiché." *Latin American
         Indian Literatures Journal* 4 (Fall): 125–50.
2001   *Art and Society in a Highland Maya Community.* Austin: University of
         Texas Press.
Chonay, Dionisio José, and Delia Goetz.
1953   *Title of the Lords of Totonicapán.* In *The Annals of the Cakchiquels and Title of
         the Lords of Totonicapán,* 161–196. Norman: University of Oklahoma Press.
Ciudad Real, Antonio de.
1929   *Diccionario de Motul: Maya Español.* Ed. Juan Martínez Hernández.
         Mérida: Talleres de la Compañia tipográfica Yucateca.

Codex Borbonicus.

1974 *Codex Borbonicus, Bibliothéque de l'Assemblée Nationale, Paris (Y120).* Karl
A. Nowotny y Jacqueline de Durand-Forest, eds. Graz: Akademische Druck
und Verlagsanstalt.

Coe, Michael D.

1973 *The Maya Scribe and His World.* New York: The Grolier Club.

1980 *The Maya.* London: Thames and Hudson.

1982 *Old Gods and Young Heroes: The Pearlman Collection of Maya Ceramics.*
Jerusalem: The Israel Museum.

Cogolludo, Diego López de.

1957 [1688] *Historia de Yucatán.* 2 vols. Introduction and notes by J. Ignacio Rubio
Mañe. Colección de Grandes Crónicas Mexicanas, no. 3. México, D.F.:
Editorial Academia Literaria.

Colop, Sam.

1999 *Popol Wuj: Versión Poética K'iche'.* Guatemala: Cholsamaj.

Cook, Garrett W.

1986 "Quichean Folk Theology and Southern Maya Supernaturalism."
In *Symbol and Meaning Beyond the Closed Community: Essays in
Mesoamerican Ideas.* Ed. Gary H. Gossen, pp. 139–153. Albany: Institute for
Mesoamerican Studies, University at Albany, SUNY.

2000 *Renewing the Maya World: Expressive Culture in a Highland Town.* Austin:
University of Texas Press.

Cortés, Hernán.

1986 *Letters from Mexico.* Tr. Anthony Pagden. New Haven: Yale University
Press.

Cortés y Larraz, Pedro.

1958 *Descripción geográfico-moral de la diócesis de Goathemala.* 2 vols. Sociedad
de Geografía e Historia de Guatemala Publication no. 20. Guatemala:
Biblioteca "Goathemala."

Coto, Thomás de.

1983 [1656] *Thesaurus Verborum—Vocabulario de la lengua cakchiquel o guatemalteca:
nuevamente hecho y recopilado con summo estudio, trabajo y erudición.* Ed.
René Acuna. Mexico, D.F.: Universidad Nacional Autónoma de México.

Craine, Eugene R., and Reginald C. Reindorp.

1979 *The Codex Pérez and the Book of Chilam Balam of Maní.* Norman:
University of Oklahoma Press.

Delgado, Damián.

1725 *Compendio del arte quiché.* Manuscript in Princeton University Library.

Earle, Duncan M.

1983 "La etnoecología quiché en el Popol Vuh." In *Nuevas perspectivas sobre el
Popol Vuh.* Ed. Robert M. Carmack and Francisco Morales Santos, pp.
293–303. Guatemala: Piedra Santa.

Edmonson, Munro S.

1965 *Quiché-English Dictionary.* Pub. 30 of Middle American Research Institute.
New Orleans: Tulane University.

1967 "Narrative Folklore." In *Social Anthropology.* Ed. Manning Nash. Vol. 6 of
Handbook of Middle American Indians. Ed. Robert Wauchope. Austin:
University of Texas Press.

1971 *The Book of Counsel: The Popol Vuh of the Quiché Maya of Guatemala.*

Pub. 35 of Middle American Research Institute. New Orleans: Tulane University.

1982   *The Ancient Future of the Itza: The Book of Chilam Balam of Tizimin.* Austin: University of Texas Press.

1986   *Heaven Born Mérida and its Destiny: The Book of Chilam Balam of Chumayel.* Austin: University of Texas Press.

Estrada Monroy, Agustín.

1979   *El mundo K'ekchi' de la Vera-Paz.* Guatemala: Editorial del Ejército.

1993   *Vida esotérica Maya-K'ekchi.* Guatemala: Serviprensa Centroamericana.

Fernández Valbuena, José A.

1996   *Mirroring the Sky: A Postclassic K'iche-Maya Cosmology.* Lancaster, CA: Labyrinthos.

Fox, John W.

1975   Centralism and Regionalism: Quiché Acculturation Processes in Settlement Patterning. Ph.D. Dissertation, SUNY, Albany.

1978   *Quiché Conquest: Centralism and Regionalism in Highland Guatemalan State Development.* Albuquerque: University of New Mexico Press.

Freidel, David, Linda Schele, and Joy Parker.

1993   *Maya Cosmos.* New York: W. Morrow.

Fuentes y Guzmán, Francisco de.

1932–33 *Recordación Florida.* Vols. 6–8. Guatemala City: Biblioteca Goathemala.

1967 [1699] *Recordación Florida.* Biblioteca de Cultura Popular, vol. 9. Guatemala: Editorial "Jose de Piñeda Ibarra."

Gage, Thomas.

1958 [1648] *Travels in the New World.* Ed. J. Eric S. Thompson. Westport: Greenwood Press.

García Elgueta, Manuel.

1892   *Etimologías kiche.* Manuscript in Harold B. Lee Library Manuscript Archives, Brigham Young University.

c. 1900 *Borrador para la formación del vocabulario de lengua kiché.* Manuscript in Harold B. Lee Library Manuscript Archives, Brigham Young University.

c. 1910 *Sumario de las materias; ensayos gramaticales, vocabularios kiché español con su parte de literatura indígena, y un pequeño paralelo entre los idiomas kiché, kakchekel, tzutuhil y mam.* Manuscript in Harold B. Lee Library Mauscript Archives, Brigham Young University.

García Hernández, Abraham, and Santiago Yac Sam.

1980   *Diccionario Quiche-Español.* Ed. David Henne Pontious. Guatemala: Instituto Lingüístico de Verano.

García Peláez, Francisco de Paula.

1943   *Memorias para la historia del antiguo reino de Guatemala.* Guatemala: Biblioteca "Payo de Rivera."

Girard, Rafael.

1948   *Esoterismo del Popol-Vuh.* México: Editores Mexicanos Unidos.

Gossen, Gary H.

1974   *Chamulas in the World of the Sun: Time and Space in a Maya Oral Tradition.* Cambridge: Harvard University Press.

1986   *Symbol and Meaning Beyond the Closed Community: Essays in Mesoamerican Ideas.* Albany: Institute for Mesoamerican Studies, SUNY.

1999   *Telling Maya Tales.* New York and London: Routledge.

Guiteras-Holmes, Calixta.
1961   *Perils of the Soul: The World View of a Tzotzil Indian.* New York: The Free Press of Glencoe.
Guzmán, Pantaleón de.
1984 [1704] *Compendio de Nombres en la Lengva Cakchiqvel.* Ed. René Acuña. México: Universidad Nacional Autónoma de México.
Harrington, John P.
1922.   *Popol Vuh.* Manuscript transcription of a phonetic rendition of the Quiché text by Cipriano Alvarado. Gates Collection, Special Collections and Manuscripts, Harold B. Lee Library, Brigham Young University, Provo, Utah.
Hatch, Marion Popenoe.
1997   *Kaminaljuyu/San Jorge: Evidencia arqueológica de la actividad económica en el Valle de Guatemala, 300 a.C. a 300 d.C.* Guatemala: Universidad del Valle de Guatemala.
Hellmuth, Nicholas M.
1975   *The Escuintla Hoards: Teotihuacan Art in Guatemala.* Guatemala City: Foundation for Latin American Anthropological Research.
1987   *Human Sacrifice in Ballgame Scenes on Early Classic Cylindrical Tripods from the Tiquisate Region, Guatemala.* Culver City: Foundation for Latin American Anthropological Research.
Herrera, Francisco.
1745   *Vocabulario de la lengua castellana y quiché.* Manuscript in Bibliothèque Nationale, Paris.
Heyden, Doris.
1975   "An Interpretation of the Cave Underneath the Pyramid of the Sun in Teotihuacan, Mexico." *American Antiquity* 40:131–147.
1981   "Caves, Gods, and Myths: World-View and Planning in Teotihuacan." In *Mesoamerican Sites and World Views,* edited by Elizabeth Benson. Washington: Dumbarton Oaks Research Library and Collections, pp. 1–35.
Hill, Robert M. II.
1992   *Colonial Cakchiquels: Highland Maya Adaptation to Spanish Rule 1600–1700.* New York: Holt, Rinehart and Winston.
1996   "Eastern Chajoma (Cakchiquel) Political Geography. Ethnohistorical and Archaeological Contributions to the Study of a Late Postclassic Highland Maya Polity." *Ancient Mesoamerica* 7. Cambridge: Cambridge University Press.
Hill, Robert M. II, and John Monaghan.
1987   *Continuities in Highland Maya Social Organization: Ethnohistory in Sacapulas, Guatemala.* Philadelphia: University of Pennsylvania Press.
Himelblau, Jack J.
1989   *Quiché Worlds in Creation.* Culver City, CA: Labyrinthos.
Hunt, Eva.
1977   *The Transformation of the Hummingbird.* Ithaca: Cornell University Press.
Instituto Indigenista Nacional de Guatemala.
1988   *Lenguas Mayas de Guatemala.* Guatemala: Ministerio de Cultura y Deportes.
Isagoge histórica apologética de las indias Occidentales.
1935   Biblioteca "Goathemala" de la Sociedad de Geografía e Historia de Guatemala, Vol. 8. Guatemala: Tipografía Nacional.

Ixtlilxochitl, Fernando de Alva.
   1952   Obras históricas. Vol. 1. México, D.F.: Editora Nacional.
Jones, Oakah L., Jr.
   1994   Guatemala in the Spanish Colonial Period. Norman: University of
            Oklahoma Press.
Kidder, Alfred V., Jesse D. Jennings, and Edwin M. Shook.
   1946   Excavations at Kaminaljuyu, Guatemala. Carnegie Institution Publication
            561. Washington: Carnegie Institution.
Kramer, Wendy.
   1994   Encomienda Politics in Early Colonial Guatemala, 1524–1544: Dividing the
            Spoils. Dellplain Latin American Studies, no. 31. Boulder: Westview Press.
La Farge, Oliver.
   1947   Santa Eulalia: The Religion of a Cuchumatán Indian Town. Chicago:
            University of Chicago Press.
La Farge, Oliver, and Douglas Byers.
   1931   The Year Bearer's People. Middle American Research Series Publication
            no. 3. New Orleans: Department of Middle American Research, Tulane
            University of Louisiana.
Landa, Fr. Diego de.
   1941 [1566] Relación de las cosas de Yucatán. Trans. A. M. Tozzer. Papers of the
            Peabody Museum, Vol. 18. Cambridge, Mass.: Peabody Museum of
            American Archaeology and Ethnology.
Las Casas, Fr. Bartolomé de.
   1958 [ca. 1550] Apologética historia de las Indias. Vol 13. Madrid: Biblioteca de
            Autores Españoles.
   1967   Apologética historia de las Indias. 2 Volumes. México: Universidad Nacional
            Autónoma de México.
   1974   The Devastation of the Indies. Tr. Herma Briffault. Baltimore: The Johns
            Hopkins University Press.
   1992   In Defense of the Indians. Tr. Stafford Poole. DeKalb: Northern Illinois
            University Press.
Laughlin, Robert M.
   1975   The Great Tzotzil Dictionary of San Lorenzo Zinacantán. Smithsonian
            Contributions to Anthropology 19. Washington, D.C.: Smithsonian
            Institution Press.
Lee, Thomas A., Jr.
   1985   Los Codices Mayas. Tuxtla Gutierrez: Universidad Autónoma de Chiapas.
León, Juan de.
   1954   Diccionario quiché-español. Guatemala: Landivar.
León-Portilla, Miguel.
   1961   Los antiguos Mexicanos a través de sus crónicas y cantares. México, D.F.:
            Fondo de Cultura Económica.
   1963   Aztec Thought and Culture. Norman: University of Oklahoma Press.
   1969   Pre-Columbian Literatures of Mexico. Trans. Grace Lobanov and Miguel
            León-Portilla. Norman: University of Oklahoma Press.
   1980   Native Mesoamerican Spirituality. Ed. Miguel Léon-Portilla. New York:
            Paulist Press.

Lienzo de Tlaxcala.

1892   *Homenaje a Cristóbal Colón: Antiguedades mexicanas publicadas por la Junta Colombina de México en el cuarto centenario del descubrimiento de América.* México: Oficina Tipográfica de la Secretaria de Fomento.

López Ixcoy, Candelaria Dominga.

1997   *Ri Ukemiik ri K'ichee' Chii': Gramática K'ichee'.* Guatemala: Editorial Cholsamaj.

Lothrop, Samuel Kirkland.

1952   *Metals from the Cenote of Sacrifice, Chichen Itza, Yucatan.* Memoirs of the Peabody Museum of Archaeology and Ethnology, Harvard University, Vol. 10, No. 2. Cambridge: Peabody Museum.

Lucie-Smith, Edward.

1972   *Symbolist Art.* London: Thames and Hudson.

Lutz, Christopher H.

1994   *Santiago de Guatemala, 1541–1773:* City, Caste, and the Colonial Experience. Norman: University of Oklahoma Press.

MacNutt, Francis Augustus.

1909   *Bartholomew de Las Casas: His Life, His Apostolate, and His Writings.* New York: G. P. Putnam's Sons, Knickerbocker Press.

Mace, Carroll Edward.

1970   *Two Spanish-Quiché Dance Dramas of Rabinal.* New Orleans: Tulane University.

Marroquín, Francisco.

1905   *Doctrina cristiana en lengua guatemalteca.* Santiago de Chile: Imprenta Elzeviriana.

Martínez, Marcos.

c. 1575   *Arte de la lengua utlateca o kiché, vulgarmente llamado el arte de Totonicapan.* Manuscript in Bibliothèque Nationale, Paris.

McAnany, Patricia A.

1995   *Living with the Ancestors: Kinship and Kingship in Ancient Maya Society.* Austin: University of Texas Press.

Mendelson, E. Michael.

1957   *Religion and World-View in a Guatemalan Village.* Microfilm Collection of Manuscripts on Middle American Cultural Anthropology, no. 52. Chicago: University of Chicago Library.

1958a   "A Guatemalan Sacred Bundle." *Man,* Vol. 58 (August 1958): 121–126.

1958b   "The King, the Traitor, and the Cross: An Interpretation of a Highland Maya Religious Conflict." *Diogenes* 21 (Spring): 1–10.

1959   "Maximon: An Iconographical Introduction." *Man* 59 (April): 57–60.

1965   *Los escándalos de Maximón: Un estudio sobre la religión y la visión del mundo en Santiago Atitlán.* Seminario de Integracion Social Guatemalteca Publication no. 19. Guatemala: Tipografía Nacional.

Michels, Joseph W.

1979   *The Kaminaljuyu Chiefdom.* University Park: Pennsylvania State University Press.

Miller, Mary E., and Karl Taube.

1993   *The Gods and Symbols of Ancient Mexico and the Maya.* London: Thames and Hudson.

Millon, René.
    1993   "The Place Where Time Began." In *Teotihuacan: Art from the City of the
            Gods*. Kathleen Berrin and Esther Pasztory, eds. New York: Thames and
            Hudson.
Molina, Alonso de.
    1944 [1571]. *Vocabulario en lengua castellana y mexicana*. México, D.F.: Editorial
            Porrúa.
Mondloch, James L., and Eugene P. Hruska.
    1975   *Basic Quiché Grammar*. Guatemala: Centro Indígena.
Morley, Sylvanus G., George W. Brainerd, and Robert J. Sharer.
    1983   *The Ancient Maya*. Stanford: Stanford University Press.
Morris, Earl Halstead.
    1931   *The Temple of the Warriors at Chichen Itza, Yucatan*. Washington: Carnegie
            Institution of Washington.
Motul Dictionary.
    1929 [16th C] *Diccionario de Motul, maya-español, atribuido a Fray Antonio de Ciudad
            Real y Arte de la lengua maya por Fray Juan Coronel*. Ed. Juan Martínez
            Hernández. Mérida, Yucatán, México: Compañíia Tipográfica Yucateca.
Nicholson, Henry B.
    2001   *Topiltzin Quetzalcoatl*. Boulder: University Press of Colorado.
Oakes, Maud.
    1951   *The Two Crosses of Todos Santos*. Bollingen Series, 27. Princeton: Princeton
            University Press.
Orellana, Sandra L.
    1984   *The Tzutujil Mayas: Continuity and Change, 1250–1630*. Norman: University
            of Oklahoma Press.
Par Sapón, María Beatriz, and Telma Angelina Can Pixabaj.
    2000   *Ujunamaxiik ri K'ichee' Ch'ab'al: Variación Dialectal en K'ichee'*. Guatemala:
            Proyecto Cholsamaj.
Pérez Mendoza, Francisco, and Miguel Hernández Mendoza.
    1996   *Diccionario Tz'utujil*. Antigua, Guatemala: Proyecto Linguistico Francisco
            Marroquín.
Peterson, Jeanette Favrot.
    1993   *The Paradise Garden Murals of Malinalco*. Austin: University of Texas Press.
Preuss, Mary H.
    1988.   *Gods of the Popol Vuh: Xmukané, K'ucumatz, Tojil, and Jurakan*. Culver City,
            Calif.: Labyrinthos.
Raynaud, Georges.
    1964   *Popol Vuh: El Libro del Consejo*. Tr. Georges Reynaud, J. Manuel González
            de Mendoza, and Miguel Ángel Asturias. México: Universidad Nacional
            Autónoma.
Recinos, Adrián.
    1950   *Popol Vuh*. Trans. Delia Goetz and Sylvanus G. Morley. Norman:
            University of Oklahoma Press.
    1953   *Popol Vuh: Las antiguas historias del Quiché*. México, D.F.: Fondo de
            Cultura Económica.
    1957   *Crónicas indígenas de Guatemala*. Guatemala: Editorial Universitaria.
Recinos, Adrián, and Delia Goetz.
    1953   *The Annals of the Cakchiquels*. Norman: University of Oklahoma Press.

Reents-Budet, Dorie.
1994   Painting the Maya Universe: Royal Ceramics of the Classic Period. Durham,
         N.C.: Duke University Press.
Remesal, Antonio de.
1964   Historia general de las Indias Occidentales, y particular de la gobernación de
         Chiapa y Guatemala. Madrid: Ediciones Atlas.
Rivera y Maestre, M.
1834   Atlas guatemalteco en ocho cartas formadas y grabadas en Guatemala.
         Guatemala.
Roys, Ralph L.
1967   The Book of Chilam Balam of Chumayel. Civilization of the American
         Indian, vol. 87. Norman: University of Oklahoma Press.
Sáenz de Santa María, Carmelo.
1940   Diccionario Cakchiquel-Español. Sociedad de Geografía e Historia de
         Guatemala Publication no. 281. Guatemala: Tipografía Nacional.
Sahagún, Bernardino de.
1938   Historia general de las cosas de Nueva España. 3 vols. México: Editorial Pedro
         Robredo.
1959–63 Florentine Codex: General History of the Things of New Spain. Trans.
         Charles E. Dibble and Arthur J. O. Anderson. Monographs of the School
         of American Research and the Museum of New Mexico. 13 vols. Salt Lake
         City: University of Utah and School of American Research.
Saler, Benson.
1969   Nagual, brujo, y hechicero en un pueblo quiché. Cuadernos del Seminario
         de Integración Social Guatemalteca Publication no. 20. Guatemala:
         Ministerio de Educación.
Sanders, William T.
1977   Teotihuacan and Kaminaljuyu: a Study in Prehistoric Culture Contact.
         University Park: Pennsylvania State University Press.
Santamaría, Francisco J.
1959   Diccionario de Mejicanismos. México, D.F.: Editorial Porrúa.
Santo Domingo, Tomás de.
c. 1690 Vocabulario en la lengua cakchiquel [y española]. Manuscript in Bibliothèque
         Nationale, Paris.
Saravia E., Albertina and Rodrigo Guarchaj.
1996   Popol Vuh: K'ichee'-Español. Guatemala: Editorial Piedra Santa.
Scarborough, Vernon L., and David R. Wilcox, eds.
1991   The Mesoamerican Ballgame. Tucson: University of Arizona Press.
Schele, Linda, and Mary Ellen Miller.
1986   The Blood of Kings. Fort Worth: Kimball Art Museum.
Schele, Linda, and David Freidel.
1990   A Forest of Kings: The Untold Story of the Ancient Maya. New York: William
         Morrow.
Schele, Linda, and Peter Mathews.
1998   The Code of Kings: The Language of Seven Sacred Maya Temples and Tombs.
         New York: Scribner.
Scherzer, Karl von.
1856   Mitteilungen über die Handschriftlichen Werke des Padre Francisco Ximénez in
         der Universitäts-Bibliothek zu Guatemala. Vienna.

Schultze-Jena, Leonhard.
   1944   *Popol Vuh: Das heilige Buch der Quiché Indianer von Guatemala.* Stuttgart.
   1954   *La vida y las creencias de los indígenas Quichés de Guatemala.* Guatemala:
            Ministerio de Educación Pública.
Sexton, James D.
   1992   *Mayan Folktales: Folklore from Lake Atitlán, Guatemala.* New York: Anchor.
Sexton, James D., and Ignacio Bizarro Ujpán.
   1999   *Heart of Heaven, Heart of Earth, and Other Mayan Folktales.* Washington:
            Smithsonian Institution Press.
Shaw, Mary.
   1971   *According to our Ancestors: Folk Texts from Guatemala and Honduras.*
            Guatemala: Instituto Lingüístico de Verano en Centro America.
Siméon, Rémi.
   1977   *Diccionario de la lengua nahuatl o mexicana.* México: Siglo Veintiuno.
Smith, Carol A.
   1990   *Guatemalan Indians and the State: 1540 to 1988.* Austin: University of Texas
            Press.
Stephens, John Lloyd.
   1969 (1841) *Incidents of Travel in Central America, Chiapas and Yucatan.* 2 Volumes.
            New York: Dover.
Stone, Andrea J.
   1995   *Images from the Underworld: Naj Tunich and the Tradition of Maya Cave
            Painting.* Austin: University of Texas Press.
Stross, Brian.
   1983   "The Language of Zuyua." *American Ethnologist* 10:150–64.
Sutton, George Miksch.
   1951   *Mexican Birds.* Norman: University of Oklahoma Press.
Tarn, Nathaniel, and Martin Prechtel.
   1986   "Constant Inconstancy: The Feminine Principle in Atiteco Mythology." In
            *Symbol and Meaning Beyond the Closed Community: Essays in Mesoamerican
            Ideas.* Ed. Gary H. Gossen. Albany: Institute for Mesoamerican Studies,
            University at Albany, SUNY, pp. 173-184.
   1990   "Comiéndose la fruta; Metáforos sexuales e iniciaciones en Santiago
            Atitlán." *Mesoamérica,* 19:73–82.
   1997   *Scandals in the House of Birds: Shamans and Priests on Lake Atitlán.* New
            York: Marsilio Publishers.
Taube, Karl.
   1986   "The Teotihuacan Cave of Origin." *Res* 12:51–82.
   1992   *The Major Gods of Ancient Yucatan.* Studies in Pre-Columbian Art and
            Archaeology 32. Washington, D.C.: Dumbarton Oaks.
   1994   "The Birth Vase: Natal Imagery in Ancient Maya Myth and Ritual." *The
            Maya Vase Book, Vol. 4.* Justin Kerr, ed. New York: Kerr and Associates.
   1998   "The Jade Hearth: Centrality, Rulership, and the Classic Maya Temple."
            In *Function and Meaning in Classic Maya Architecture.* Ed. Stephen D.
            Houston. Washington, D.C.: Dumbarton Oaks, pp. 427–478.
Tax, Sol.
   1947   *Notes on Santo Tomás Chichicastenango.* Microfilm Collection of
            Manuscripts in Middle American Cultural Anthropology, no. 16. Chicago:
            University of Chicago Library.

Tedlock, Barbara.
    1982   *Time and the Highland Maya.* Albuquerque: University of New Mexico
            Press.
    1986   "On a Mountain Road in the Dark: Encounters with the Quiche Maya
            Culture Hero." In Gary H. Gossen, ed. *Symbol and Meaning Beyond the
            Closed Community: Essays in Mesoamerican Ideas.* Albany: Institute for
            Mesoamerican Studies, The University of Albany, pp. 125–138.
Tedlock, Dennis.
    1983a   "Las formas del verso quiché." In *Nuevas perspectivas sobre el Popol Vuh.* Ed.
            Robert Carmack and Francisco Morales Santos. Guatemala: Piedra Santa,
            pp. 123–32.
    1983b   *The Spoken Word and the Work of Interpretation.* Philadelphia: University of
            Pennsylvania Press.
    1985   *Popol Vuh.* New York: Simon and Schuster.
    1992   "The Popol Vuh as a Hieroglyphic Book." In *New Theories on the Ancient
            Maya.* Ed. Elin C. Danien and Robert J. Sharer. University Museum
            Monograph 77. Philadelphia: University Museum, pp. 229–40.
    1993   *Breath on the Mirror.* San Francisco: Harper.
    1996   *Popol Vuh.* New York: Simon and Schuster.
Thompson, J. Eric S.
    1970   *Maya History and Religion.* Norman: University of Oklahoma Press.
    1971   *Maya Hieroglyphic Writing: An Introduction.* Norman: University of
            Oklahoma Press.
    1972   *A Commentary on the Dresden Codex.* Philadelphia: American Philosophical
            Society.
Torquemada, Fr. Juan de.
    1943   *Monarquia Indiana.* 3d ed. México, D.F.: Salvador Citavez Hayhoe.
Townsend, Richard F.
    2000   *The Aztecs.* New York: Thames and Hudson.
Vare[l]a, Francisco de.
    1929 [1699] *Calepino en lengua cakchiquel.* Typescript by William Gates. Gates
            Collection, Manuscript Archives, Harold B. Lee Library, Brigham Young
            University.
Vázquez de Espinosa, Fr. Antonio.
    1969   *Compendio y descripción de las Indias Occidentales.* Biblioteca de Autores
            Españoles, 231. Madrid: Real Academia Española.
Vásquez, Francisco.
    1937   *Crónica de la provincia del santisimo nombre de Jesús de Guatemala.* Sociedad
            de Geografia e Historia de Guatemala Publication no. 14. Guatemala:
            Biblioteca "Goathemala."
Velázquez, Primo Feliciano.
    1945   *Códice Chimalpopoca: Anales de Cuauhtitlan y Leyenda de los Soles.* México:
            Universidad Nacional Autónoma de México.
Vico, Domingo de.
    c. 1550 *Theologia indorum en lengua quiché.* Manuscript in Princeton University
            Library.
    c. 1555 *Vocabulario de la lengua cakchiquel y quiché.* Manuscript copy of original in
            the Bibliothèque Nationale, Paris. Newberry Library, Chicago.

Villacañas, Benito de.
    1692   *Arte y vocabulario en lengua cakchiquel*. Manuscript in University Museum
            Library, University of Pennsylvania.
Villacorta C., J. Antonio, and Carlos A. Villacorta.
    1930   *Códices Mayas*. Guatemala: Tipografía Nacional.
Vogt, Evon Z.
    1969   *Zinacantan*. Cambridge: Harvard University Press.
    1970   *The Zinacantecos of Mexico*. New York: Holt, Rinehart and Wilson.
    1976   *Tortillas for the Gods: A Symbolic Analysis of Zinacanteco Rituals*. Norman:
            University of Oklahoma Press.
Wagley, Charles.
    1941   *Economics of a Guatemalan Village*. Memoirs of the American
            Anthropological Association, no. 58. Menasha: American Anthropological
            Association.
    1949   *The Social and Religious Life of a Guatemalan Village*. Memoirs of the
            American Anthropological Association, no. 71. Menasha: American
            Anthropological Association.
    1957   *Santiago Chimaltenango: Estudio antropológico-social de una comunidad
            indígena de Huehuetenango*. Seminario de Integración Social Guatemalteca,
            no. 4. Guatemala City: Tipografía Nacional.
Watanabe, John M.
    1992   *Maya Saints and Souls in a Changing World*. Austin: University of Texas
            Press.
Wauchope, Robert.
    1949   "Las edades de Utatlan e Iximche." *Antropología e Historia de Guatemala*
            1:10–22.
    1965   *They Found the Buried Cities*. Chicago: University of Chicago Press.
Welch, John W.
    1981   *Chiasmus in antiquity: structures, analyses, exegesis*. Hildesheim:
            Gerstenberg Verlag.
Ximénez, Francisco.
    c. 1701–4 *Popol Vuh*. Manuscript, Ayer Collection, Newberry Library, Chicago.
    c. 1701–4 *Arte de las tres lenguas q'aq'chiquel, quiche, y tz'utuhil*. Manuscript, Ayer
            Collection, Newberry Library, Chicago.
    1929–31 [1722] *Historia de la provincia de San Vicente de Chiapa y Guatemala*.
            Biblioteca "Goathemala" de la Sociedad de Georgrafía e Historia de
            Guatemala Publication 1. 3 Volumes. Guatemala Tipografía Nacional.
    1967   *Historia natural del reino de Guatemala*. Guatemala: Editorial "José de
            Piñeda Ibarra."
    1985   *Primera parte del tesoro de las lenguas cakchiquel, quiche y zutuhil, en que las
            dichas lenguas se traducen a la nuestra lengua*. Edición crítica por Carmelo
            Sáenz de Santa María. Academia de Geografía e Historia de Guatemala.
            Publicación especial No. 30. Guatemala.
Zorita, Alonso de.
    1963   *The Brief and Summary Relation of the Lords of New Spain*. Tr. Benjamin
            Keen. New Brunswick, N.J.: Rutgers University Press.

INDEX

MAPS

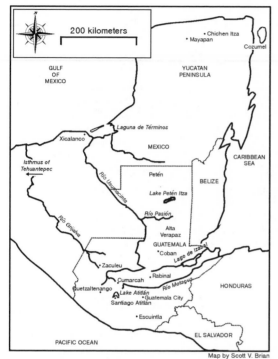

Map 1. The Maya region.

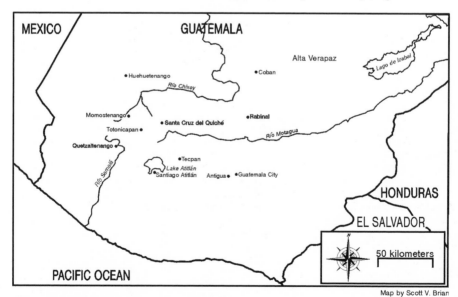

Map 2. Southern Guatemalan highlands.

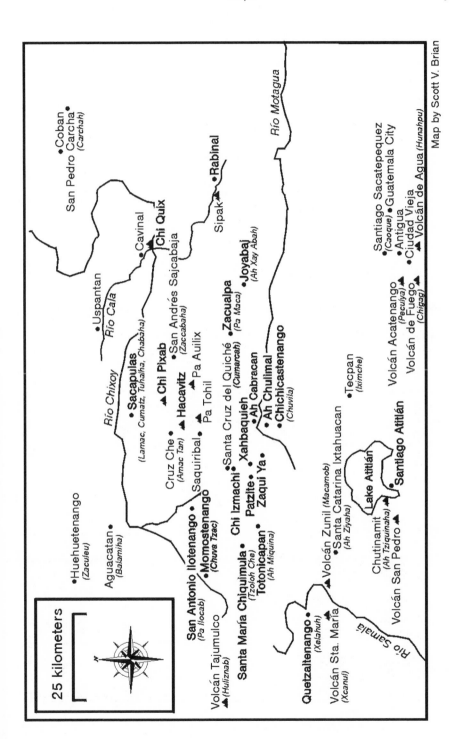

Map by Scott V. Brian

Map 3. The Quiché region.

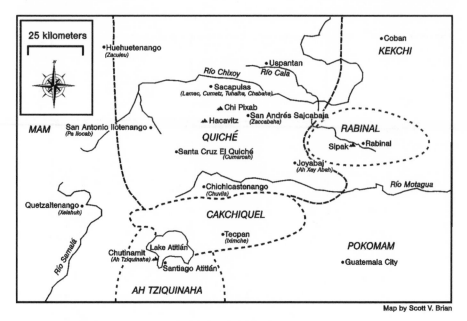

Map 4. Quichean lineages and their spheres of influence.

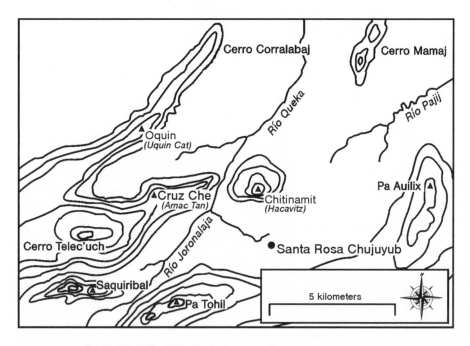

Map 5. Early Quiché settlements (adapted from Fox 1975).

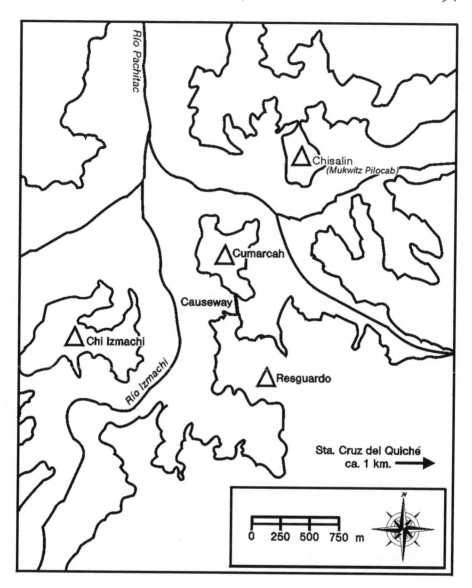

Map 6. Cumarcah region at the time of the Spanish Conquest (adapted from Fox 1975).